WAREHOUSE SAFETY

A Practical Guide to Preventing Warehouse Incidents and Injuries

George Swartz, CSP

Government Institutes
An imprint of
The Scarecrow Press, Inc.
Lanham, Maryland • Toronto • Oxford

Published in the United States of America
by Government Institutes, an imprint of The Scarecrow Press, Inc.
A wholly owned subsidiary of
The Rowman & Littlefield Publishing Group, Inc.
4501 Forbes Boulevard, Suite 200
Lanham, Maryland 20706
http://govinst.scarecrowpress.com

PO Box 317
Oxford
OX2 9RU, UK

British Library Cataloguing in Publication Information Available

Library of Congress Cataloging-in-Publication Data

Swartz, George.
    Warehouse safety / by George Swartz.
        p.   cm.
    Includes bibliographical references and index.
    ISBN: 0-86587-647-9
    1. Warehouses—Safety measures.   I. Title.
TS 189.6.S83   1998
658.7'85'0289—DC21   98-44134

Table of Contents

List of Figures and Tables

Foreword

Warehouse Safety: This is a complete practical guide to warehouse safety written by a safety professional. A side benefit to following guidelines set out in this book are reduced injuries, less equipment damage, higher employee morale, higher production rates, and enthusiastic management support.

As a practicing safety professional, this book will be useful to me as insightful reference material for making future decisions regarding the safe operation of warehouses under my control. *Warehouse Safety* was written to meet the daily needs of those who make decisions, inspect warehouses, and plan future safety programs aimed at eliminating property and casualty losses. Among those who will find the book useful are warehouse managers, safety committee representatives, human resource managers, and union leaders. Because of its breath of subjects, *Warehouse Safety* would serve as an excellent textbook in the educational environment.

The purpose of the book is to give useful suggestions regarding warehouse safety from soup to nuts. The book includes all aspects of safety programming not normally considered (e.g., conveyors, chemical safety, and ergonomics). The book closes the loop by providing management a tool to gauge program success; auditing.

This book is not intended to give any legal advice—this comes from codes, standards, and regulations. The broad generalized guidelines and suggestions presented will enable the reader to tailor their warehouse program to meet the individual needs of their warehouse.

While each chapter is filled with useful information, *Warehouse Safety* is strengthened by the addition of a section for self-assessment. The checklist is located in Chapter 2. Chapters 3, 17, and 18 address preventing a loss through employee training and Job Hazard Analysis. Chapter 16 addresses the nature, causes, and results of injuries while at the same time it walks one through accident reporting and injury investigation.

What can one expect from this book? Real life experiences from a 28-year veteran of safety, and knowledge transfer from a student of safety. Safety to the outside profession is often said to be *Common Sense*. Protecting people, property, and the environment is the task of highly educated and experienced safety professionals. Mr. Swartz, in his book, has shared much of the *Common Sense* gained throughout his years of applying technical and proven warehouse safety techniques.

As the past president of the American Society of Safety Engineers, and Vice President of Technical Service for Aon Worldwide Resources, I recommend this book to everyone who wants to improve their workers compensation experience, advance employee morale, meet customers orders on schedule, and gain management support.

This book is packed with useful and technical information and will round out your library regarding safety in warehouses.

Jerry Ray, CSP

Aon Worldwide Resources

Preface

Up to now there has not been much material developed on the subject of warehouse safety. Periodic articles discuss safe procedures for lift trucks, lifting, pallet safety, fire safety, and racking. However, on the whole, warehouse safety has not been a major focus of any publication or organization. Moreover, seminars on warehouse operations frequently omit the subject of safety. Even at safety conferences, seminars and specialty sessions rarely address the topic of overall warehouse safety.

This book has been developed to fill the void that exists between what is practiced and written about warehouse safety and what it should be. The awareness level on this subject must be raised so that the workplace becomes safer. For example, much can be done to reduce injuries and deaths caused by powered industrial trucks. Over 100 deaths occur each year in the workplace as a result of powered industrial truck incidents, many of which occur in warehouses. Some 97,000 serious and less than serious injuries take place from a variety of factors associated with lift trucks. Some of these injuries involve the loss of limbs, paralysis, and total disability. Periodically, a serious lift truck incident makes the local headlines.

Additional focus must be placed on improved workplace ergonomics, which can reduce back injuries and allow warehouses to become more efficient. This will not happen unless management makes a commitment to think of the economic bottom line in terms of reduced injuries and greater efficiencies. Some of the most costly workers' compensation claims are back injuries and injuries associated with repetitive motion and soft-tissue pain; surely these types of claims are worth reducing or eliminating.

Chapter Five addresses fire safety in warehouse operations, including information on some very serious warehouse fire losses. The reports from the National Fire Protection Association (NFPA) point out that each of the fires was preventable. One fire, in particular, resulted in a $280 million loss. Paying attention to housekeeping practices, maintenance of fire systems, and safe storing and handling of product will lower the risk associated with fires. Trained engineers can offer guidance on complete fire safety.

A July 28, 1997, article from the *Chicago Sun Times* cited a recently published report from the *Archives of Internal Medicine*. The researchers culled the data from government and other sources and produced what they believed to be the first national estimates of job-related injuries and illnesses for an entire year.

They reported that in each workday 18 deaths and 36,000 injuries occur in the workplace. This data exceeds the government's estimates of 17 deaths and 9,000 injuries. In addition, the researchers stated that occupational illnesses—such as lung disease and lead poisoning—caused 60,300 deaths and 862,000 illnesses in 1992.

The costs associated with these numbers are staggering—almost $178 million each day. Indirect costs, such as lost wages, time spent on investigations, overtime needed for the missing worker, product damage, etc., add many more billions of dollars to these totals. Workplace injuries and illnesses are costing the United States more than monies spent on AIDS, Alzheimer's disease, cancer, cardiovascular and cerebrovascular disease combined.

Gerry Scannell, current president of the National Safety Council and former head of OSHA during the Bush administration, stated that the cost of workplace injuries and illnesses is greater than the combined 1996 profits of the twenty largest corporations in the United States. A statement such as that should be an eye-opener for any business.

The unfortunate truth is that most of the injuries and illnesses are preventable. The unsafe workplace will not be corrected if management does not step forward with leadership. Workers must be properly trained because safety is a learned characteristic– not an inborn one.

Safety professionals agree that any safety effort is better than no effort. However, if an employer seeks to become a world-class organization, improve workplace efficiencies, and maintain a better bottom line, a comprehensive safety program is needed. Some employers may feel that they have a safe workplace and a sound safety program because they have issued hard hats and glasses and have warned employees "to be safe." What does a safe workplace entail? Is the warehouse free of risk? How is the compliance performance at the site compared to the requirements of OSHA? To some, being safe means no one has been seriously hurt lately.

The sense of "being safe," one that is held by many employers, is a sense of false security because it allows for significant dollar losses through damaged product, damaged property, missed shipping dates, grievances, higher insurance premiums, and higher workers' compensation losses. Safety must be looked upon as a future investment that will return much more to the corporation than that which was originally invested. It's a falsehood to state that safety costs money without adding any value to the product—injuries and illnesses require more money to produce the product.

For those desiring to excel at safety, this book provides a wealth of information. Chapters include information on safety programs, materials storage, materials handling, fire safety, lockout/tagout, guarding, powered industrial trucks, dock safety, job hazard analysis, housekeeping, PPE, inspections, chemicals, ergonomics, new employee orientation, emergency programs, batteries, and a comprehensive "miscellaneous" chapter.

The material is presented as a practical "guidebook" and includes information on the requirements of OSHA regulations. A variety of forms are included to assist the safety programs of readers. There are many visual aids to complement the material in each chapter.

There are a few topics that the book does not address. Environmental compliance is briefly touched on, but it does not receive significant discussion. Warehouse security is not addressed. Department of Transportation regulations are also absent since regulations regarding highway and shipping apply, for the most part, outside the building. This book is a safety book and could not go beyond the typical industrial setting. Those needing information about EPA, and DOT regulations, and facility security, should seek professional guidance.

The need for improved workplace safety is vital in today's business climate. Corporations must control costs to be competitive. Monies lost on injuries, illnesses, and incidents is money that is lost forever. *Warehouse Safety* can help readers achieve a safer workplace. Many states are now requiring safety and health programs. California, for example, maintains strong safety and health legislation. OSHA is moving toward more formal safety programs, and has passed several new safety standards.

Throughout the book, there has been a de-emphasis on the word *accident*. The use of the words *injury* and *incident* are the most commonly used terms to describe a loss-producing event. The word *accident* has come under fire recently as to its true meaning, and the manner in which we use it throughout industry. The word *accident* implies an unforeseen event. If a worker fails to wear protective goggles and is splashed in the eye with battery acid, is this an accident? The hazard was very apparent, as was the lack of protective eyewear. This is an injury; not an accident.

The National Safety Council has embarked on a program to eliminate, as far as possible, the word *accident* from their vocabulary. Their annual publication *Accident Facts*, will now be titled, *Injury Facts*. If management places a focus on the root causes of an injury in the workplace, the word *accident* should not be used. This way of thinking may take years to modify, but the effort may well be beneficial to all of industry—both management and labor.

Readers are urged to use this book to improve their safety programs and reduce injuries in their warehouses. By being proactive in program development, and allowing employee participation in the safety process, management can achieve a safer, more profitable workplace.

George Swartz, CSP

April, 1999

About the Author

George Swartz has been involved in the safety profession for twenty-eight years. His experience includes manufacturing, warehousing and distribution, auto repair shops, and heavy construction. He has been a safety officer with Pittsburgh Bridge and Iron Works and Buell Division of Envirotech Corporation, and is currently with Midas International Corporation. He also has particular expertise in the area of safety auditing. In 1997, Mr. Swartz authored *Forklift Safety*, published by Government Institutes. A frequent lecturer, speaker, author, and trainer, Mr. Swartz has given presentations throughout the United States, Canada, and Central America. He has traveled extensively throughout the U.S., Canada, and Europe in his profession.

Mr. Swartz currently serves on the boards of directors for the National Safety Council and Project Safe Illinois. He is vice president for business and industry for the National Safety Council, outgoing chairman of the editorial board for *Professional Safety* magazine, and a member of the safety and health advisory committees at the University of Illinois - Chicago and Northern Illinois University. He is also a lecturer for safety courses at Northern Illinois University. He testified before OSHA in Washington, D.C., during hearings regarding the dangers of asbestos exposure for brake mechanics.

Mr. Swartz has been awarded the honor of Fellow by the American Society of Safety Engineers (ASSE), the Distinguished Service to Safety Award by the National Safety Council, the Outstanding Service Award by the Environmental Resources Institute, the Charles V. Culbertson Outstanding Volunteer Service by the ASSE, and the Safety Professional of the Year by the ASSE Management Division.

Mr. Swartz holds a B.A. from the University of Pittsburgh, an M.S. in Safety from Northern Illinois University, a C.A.S. in Safety from Northern Illinois University, and an M.S. in Managerial Communications from Northwestern University. Mr. Swartz has been a Certified Safety Professional since 1980.

Acknowledgements

The author wishes to thank the following organizations for their contribution of materials and information for this publication: Clark Material Handling Company; Rite-Hite Corporation; The National Safety Council; *Material Handling Engineering* magazine; The Hyster Company; *Modern Materials Handling* magazine; The Industrial Truck Manufacturers Association; The American Society of Safety Engineers (ANSI); Advance Technology, Inc.; and the Occupational Safety and Health Administration.

In addition, without the able assistance of Phyllis Luzader and Laura Swartz, the preparation of this entire manuscript would not have been possible.

The author would also like to thank the following individuals for their assistance and technial review of the manuscript: Karl Benson; Larry Oldendorf; Ron Koziol, of the National Safety Council; and Rita M. Mosley, Industrial Safety Consultant/Supervisor for the Department of Illinois Commerce and Community Affairs.

Disclaimer

The reader should not rely on this publication for identification of specific equipment operations and maintenance repairs, or specific points that apply to a particular manufacturer's equipment or authorized substitution. The author and publisher make no representation or warranty, express or implied, as to the completeness, correctness, or utility of the information in this publication. In addition, the author and publisher assume no liability of any kind whatsoever resulting from the use of or reliance upon the contents of this book.

Follow manufacturers' standards for the use, maintenance, and repair of equipment. Refer to manufacturers' operating, training, and maintenance manuals for guidance on repairs and replacement parts. Call manufacturers for technical assistance on operating or maintenance procedures not provided for in the manufacturers' manuals. The Occupational Safety and Health Administration (OSHA) can also provide information on proper operating methods.

1

Introduction to Warehouse Safety

Data indicate that the warehouse and distribution center activity continues to grow. Warehouse expenditures for services in North America in 1997 totaled $69 billion. That number includes estimated expenditures for private warehouses as well as for public or contract facilities. Warehouses and distribution centers spent $150 billion, excluding land, for corporate equipment and new plants in 1997. The average size of a new facility will be 350,000 square feet.

Customers as well as corporations continue to put on pressure to reduce warehouse costs. Every time a facility handles a piece of material, it takes human work effort to complete it. The likelihood of error, which could result in injuries, grows as a result of increased demands for speed, accuracy, productivity, and value-added services. On-time deliveries at over 99 percent are expected by customers.

However, the industry as well as site management must not forget to include the safety of the workers in their business plans.

There is a need for a greater safety focus in warehousing and distribution centers. The potential hazards in a warehouse are many, as is evidenced by national statistics. On the other hand, many organizations have recognized the benefits of maintaining excellent safety performance and are now experiencing fewer injuries. The bottom line of the organization receives a substantial economic benefit from reducing injuries. Additional benefits include improved morale, reduced insurance premiums, fewer grievances, and fewer OSHA citations.

A NATIONAL CONCERN FOR SAFETY IN THE WORKPLACE

The warehousing sector as a whole has not placed enough focus on safety performance. Statistically, public warehousing's rate of injuries per 100 workers is 6.51, while on a national basis, the average for all industries is 1.64.

How dangerous are warehouses? Note the numbers in Table 1-1. The data identifies the five main events that have caused fatalities in warehouses from 1992–1995. This report was published by the National Safety Council and provides data that should be of concern to the warehousing industry.

1

Table 1-1. Fatal Occupational Injury by Event or Exposure

Event/Exposure	1992	1993	1994	1995
Contact with objects/equipment	1,004	1,045	1,017	915
Struck by object	557	556	590	546
Caught in or compressed by object	316	309	280	256
Caught in running equipment or machinery	159	151	147	131
Caught in or crushed in collapsing materials	110	138	132	99

In addition to the safety statistics which are generated from warehouses, a much larger problem with all workplace injuries has been recently recognized. The American Medical Association published a detailed study on workplace injuries in July 1997. The report stated that workplace injuries and illnesses cost an estimated $171 billion each year and result in approximately 6,500 workplace deaths and over 60,000 deaths from disease.

The study reported that "to our knowledge, no prior study uses national data to generate estimates of the burden and costs of occupational injuries and illnesses in the U.S." The report studied fourteen primary sources and 200 secondary sources of data, and went on to identify larger numbers than previously reported in national studies. Between 66,000 and 111,000 new cases of cancer are caused by occupational factors each year, while an estimated 36,000 to 73,000 new or recurrent cases of coronary heart disease are associated with workplace factors.

According to this very detailed study, the figures usually sited underestimate the true burden and costs of occupational illness in the United States. The costs associated with occupational injuries and illnesses are large compared with other diseases.

A comparison of the costs of on-the-job illnesses to the costs of illnesses in the general public, is quite revealing. The cost of acquired immuno-deficiency syndrome (AIDS) was estimated at $30 billion. Alzheimer's disease was estimated to cost $66 billion. Cardiovascular and cerebrovascular disease is estimated at $164 billion. In 1992 the costs of cancer were estimated at $170 billion.

The National Safety Council, in another statistics-related article, stated that the total cost of injuries and illnesses is staggering. "The total cost is equal to the combined 1996 profits of the 20 largest corporations in America," stated Gerry Scannell, NSC president. Mr. Scannell, former head of OSHA during President George Bush's administration, stated that "companies need to make safety a value in their workplace; not only do effective safety programs save lives, they're also good business."

Every day, an average of 17 workers die and about 18,000 injuries are reported. Some 6.6 million workplace injuries and illnesses occur each year. Most workplace injuries, illnesses, and fatalities can be prevented by using sound safety programs. Chapter Two identifies many of the various program elements that can be used to achieve a safer warehouse.

The cost of one work-related fatality averages about $790,000 according to the National Safety Council. The council also reported that the cost of a serious disabling workplace injury averages about $26,000. OSHA feels that the agency needs the partnership of business, labor, and other advocates to help reduce the workplace toll of injuries and illnesses.

WAREHOUSE SAFETY STUDY

A comprehensive study was conducted by OSHA in the early 1980s to determine the injury rates, causes of injuries, scope of existing safety programs, and other factors involving injuries in warehouse operations. The study identified 2,700 warehouse workers who were injured in September 1984. Twenty-six states participated in this one-month study program. Some of the key details summarized in the study were:

- 47 percent of the injured workers were employed in wholesale trade.

- 21 percent of the injured workers were employed in retail trade.

- 15 percent of the injured workers were employed in manufacturing.

- 8 percent of the injured workers were employed in transportation and public utilities.

- 4 percent of the injured workers were employed in service trades.

- 5 percent were employed in other services.

- Almost 30 percent of all injuries occurred while unloading a vehicle.

- More than 13 percent of the injured workers were hurt while operating powered equipment.

- Nearly 65 percent of all the injured workers were manually lifting, carrying, or handling materials at the time of their injuries.

- One out of five workers reported that they felt the operating space was not adequate for use of the equipment they were working with.

- Almost 50 percent of the workers were injured while in the storage area of the warehouse.

- 29 percent of injuries occurred at the dock; approximately half of those were in a truck.

- Overall, 38 percent of the workers were injured by overexertion while lifting or handling materials.

- Twenty-six percent of the workers were struck by falling, flying, or swinging objects.

- Falls from elevations represented 6 percent of the total.

- The most common objects causing the injuries included:

  - Barrels, boxes, or containers (29 percent)

  - Structural metal, pipes, fittings, or fasteners (11 percent)

- Working surfaces (11 percent).

■ Some 55 percent of the injured workers experienced muscle sprains, strains, torn ligaments, or pulled muscles.

■ Lost work days were experienced by 77 percent of the workers as a result of their injuries, for an average of 16 days for each claim.

■ Almost one-half of the injured workers stated that working conditions in the warehouse contributed to their injures.

■ Three out of four workers felt that their type of injury could have been prevented.

■ When asked if their employers had taken action after their injury to correct conditions:

- 43 percent said that they did not know of any actions taken.

- 41 percent said no actions were taken.

- 16 percent noted that preventive action had been taken.

■ Forty-two percent of the workers had five or more years of experience in warehousing.

■ Regarding the wearing of personal protective equipment by the warehouse workers:

- 5 percent used hard hats.

- 23 percent used gloves.

- 22 percent wore steel toe boots or shoes.

- 5 percent used glasses or goggles.

- 1 percent used a safety belt and lanyard.

- 65 percent were not wearing their equipment at the time of the injury.

■ Forklift training was provided to only 23 percent of the workers.

■ Housekeeping and safe-job-procedures training was given to 24 percent of the workers.

■ Safe lifting techniques were taught to 28 percent of the workers.

■ Some 48 percent of the workers never received safety training for the assigned job.

■ Only 20 percent of the workers attended safety meetings.

Although this study was published in 1984, the data can be just as useful in evaluating today's workplace. It appears that employee training was lacking, as well as management involvement and corrective actions regarding workplace hazards. Many of the 2,700 injuries occurring during the month of the study were indeed preventable.

THE NEED FOR WAREHOUSE SAFETY

The warehouse industry is not always quick to enact change. In the case of industrial safety and injury prevention, more change is needed. Statistics bear this out. One of the largest areas that requires improved performance is that of powered industrial trucks. OSHA statistics indicate that approximately 100 employees are killed each year as a result of incidents from powered industrial trucks. In addition, some 33,800 serious injuries and 61,800 nonserious injuries occur. Considering that there are more than 980,000 pieces of power equipment in industry, many of which are in warehouses, the need for injury prevention in relation to powered industrial trucks has never been greater.

The cost of goods stored in warehouses continues to increase and the product must be protected from damage. Costly damage could easily take place from lift truck impact, fire, or from water discharged from damaged sprinklers or pipes. Every day many thousands of incidents take place in warehouses. Management has to focus on the near miss, product damage, and property damage in order to reduce injuries.

There is increasing evidence that organizations can reduce the risk of injuries and illnesses and produce cost savings as well. To accomplish this, they must look at safety as an investment in the company's profitability.

Many companies are beginning to recognize that they cannot just add safety and health to their programs, but that they have to integrate these programs into their business strategy. This process involves the assistance of facility engineers, safety and health professionals, insurance carriers, and equipment manufacturers. If worker safety is to be improved, processes must be improved.

At the dock, there has been an increase in the number of dock doors in warehouses. Parking lots and aprons must now accommodate 53-foot trailers. Although larger warehouses now have replaced numerous smaller facilities, it is estimated that there will be an increase in warehouse locations over the next few years. The reductions in the workforce caused by corporate downsizing can result in product being moved out the doors of the warehouse by fewer employees. Greater demands on the workforce can easily result in an increase in injuries.

SAFETY NEEDS FOR WAREHOUSES

The nature of a warehouse is to receive, store, and distribute product. Warehousing is a fast-paced industry that relies on the movement of selected goods to maintain its position in free commerce. Though not as dangerous as a factory, a warehouse operation holds many risks and hazards that must be controlled by management to protect the worker.

The hazards are many. As mentioned earlier, the operation of powered industrial trucks is probably the one element that causes the most injuries and incidents. Additional hazards can be found in the use of conveyors, stored or handled chemicals, movement of material at docks, trailers moving in and out of dock wells, and pedestrians in the aisles. Highly automated warehouses or distribution centers may utilize robotics, and the hazards associated with this technology would have to be recognized and controlled. The exposure to noise, fire, the manual handling of bulky product, and ergonomics factors pose hazards to all employees and, at times, to visitors.

Every warehouse should have an in-depth safety program that includes controls for all of the following:

- Materials storage

- Fire safety

- Materials handling

- Personal protective equipment

- Safe handling of chemicals

- Powered industrial trucks

- Dock safety

- Machine guarding/guarding of hazards

- Ergonomics

- Manual handling of product

- A comprehensive safety program

- Facility emergency plans.

It is evident that to have a safe warehouse, management must incorporate and include many elements of safety and health planning. Injuries and illnesses will not be reduced unless an effective program is implemented. This book provides program guidelines for the above list as well as controls for many other hazards.

Briefly, the control factors of the key elements identified above are:

Materials storage. Product must be stored safely so that it will not fall onto employees or visitors. Safe storage also helps to reduce product damage. For appearance, storage that is straight and correct improves housekeeping. Also, the storage of product involves the safe use of powered industrial trucks as well as secure and safe racking to support the loads deposited there.

Fire safety. To protect the assets of the building and workers as well, fire safety must be a top priority in any warehouse. Storage of certain products can result in a greater risk of fire. Flammable liquids can easily ignite and raze a warehouse to the ground. Sprinklers, fire extinguishers, and an emergency plan will help safeguard people and property. Some of the largest fire losses in industry have occurred in warehouses.

Materials handling. The lifeblood of a warehouse involves the movement of product, equipment, and or materials. This must be accomplished in a safe manner as well as with a concern for the protection of the product being handled. Injuries can unfortunately be associated with this process and management must ensure that every precaution is taken to protect workers while materials are being moved.

Personal protective equipment. There are times that hazards cannot be eliminated or guarded. To protect against injury, there may be a need to wear hard hats, steel toe shoes, gloves, hearing protection, and other gear to safeguard the employee. Many warehouses fail to enforce the wearing of protective equipment.

Safe handling of chemicals. Chemicals are very common in a warehouse. If not handled or stored safely, some chemicals can cause harm to employees. Chemicals may arrive at a dock in containers or on a pallet. Other chemicals may be a part of the standard work environment in the building. Also, problems can be caused by chemicals such as carbon monoxide that is produced from internal combustion engines on powered equipment or trailer trucks.

Powered industrial trucks. To move product in the building, a forklift, or other piece of power equipment, is essential. Forklifts are involved in many deaths and injuries each year throughout industry. Operators must be properly trained. Safety rules must be enforced. Maintenance of the equipment must be ongoing.

Dock safety. Docks are busy by nature and also hazardous. Many injuries occur when lift trucks go off a dock, when product falls on an employee or visitor, or when someone is struck by a piece of equipment. Fires are not uncommon at a dock. Chemical spills also occur for which extensive cleanup plans are required.

Machine guarding/guarding of hazards. Though not as common as in other industries, hazards that need safeguarding are present in warehouses. Hazards can be eliminated or minimized through design, barrier guarding, signage, or color coding. When injuries occur as a result of exposed gears, pulley belts, or pinching motions of machine parts, the injuries tend to be very serious. For that reason, lockout/tagout controls are another critical consideration in any warehouse.

Ergonomics. Safe design of the workplace is essential to productivity and loss control. Through improved ergonomics, warehouses can move pieces of product more safely as well as more efficiently. The workers' compensation costs associated with back injuries and repetitive motion injuries are staggering. Ergonomics can help to reduce the costs of claims.

Manual handling of product. Despite the fact that most of the product in warehouses is transported by powered industrial trucks, employees can still be injured. Product can easily fall on the feet of employees, hands can be pinched between boxes while handling them, and most back injuries occur when product is being moved in some manner. Manual handling of product is an everyday part of many warehouse operations.

Comprehensive safety programs. Such programs are an essential part of each successful warehouse operation. Safety programming is needed if injuries are to be reduced, if the insurance carrier deems it necessary, and as a means to satisfy state, Canadian provincial, or federal OSHA regulations. Comprehensive programs should also be a part of global business applications. There are many recommendations in Chapter Two regarding those elements that should be placed in a safety program. The selections are broad and offer many components to reduce injuries and benefit the bottom line.

Facility emergency plans. These should include plans for handling medical, chemical, weather, and fire-related emergencies in the warehouse. Annual fire drills should take place along with training employees and supervisors in first aid and CPR.

OSHA CONSIDERATIONS

Company management must not forget that federal and state safety laws must be adhered to. In addition to the legal requirements, which are part of safety in each warehouse, the economic impact of noncompliance must be considered. Identified in Table 1-2 are the top ten subparts cited by OSHA, all of which are a part of a warehouse environment.

Table 1-2. Top 10 Citations by Subpart for General Industry, Fiscal 1997

(29 CFR Part 1910)

Rank	Subpart	Item/Description	Total Citations
1	Z	Toxic and Hazardous Substances	8,572
2	O	Machinery and Machine Guarding	7,657
3	S	Electrical	5,656
4	J	General Environment Controls	4,554
5	I	Personal Protective Equipment	3,960
6	H	Hazardous Materials	3,895
7	D	Walking Working Surfaces	2,924
8	E	Means of Egress	2,248
9	N	Material Handling and Storage	2,069
10	L	Fire Protection	1,558

(Note: 66 percent of the citations issued under Subpart Z were for the Hazard Communication Standard - 1910.1200; if these were excluded, it would drop Subpart Z to seventh place)

Management must be reminded that citations can be very costly. In 1991, OSHA modified the penalty structure and increased the maximum cost sevenfold. The maximum penalty for a willful or repeat OSHA violation is now $70,000. The maximum penalty for a serious violation is now $7,000. It is not unusual for OSHA to issue citations totaling $50,000, $100,000, or even $1 million in penalties.

It should be pointed out that many organizations have been very slow in coming into compliance with OSHA regulations. Some employers reason that there are only so many OSHA inspectors to inspect some 6.2 million workplaces. The probability of an inspection can be remote, depending on the state in which one resides. The real economic impact of workplace safety will be reflected in workers' compensation costs, not necessarily in OSHA citations.

Employers who fail to develop safety and health programs, enforce safety rules, train employees, and guard workplace hazards will feel the economic impact of workers' compensation costs long before the OSHA compliance officer pays a visit. A fast-growing part of workplace budgets is the cost of workers' compensation. Medical costs have increased nationally on an average of approximately 10 percent each year. A poor workers' compensation insurance rating based on injury experience could financially hurt an organization. On the other hand, those organizations that have improved their safety performances have actually added additional dollars to the bottom line. Safety protects the bottom line as well as the worker.

SUMMARY

Safety and health protection in warehouses and distribution centers is a must. Statistics show that warehouses can be hazardous locations, especially as a result of the movement of powered industrial trucks. Other hazards that could harm employees include: lack of personal protective equipment, hazardous chemical exposure, poor ergonomic controls, unguarded machines, lack of a lockout/tagout program, and poor product storage and product handling. Protecting the bottom line and the health and safety of the warehouse workers is vital to any location. The chapters that follow will outline the various program elements that can assist management in achieving a safer work site.

REFERENCES

BNA Reporter. "Statistics - Workplace Injuries, Illnesses Cost $171 Billion, Cause 65,000 deaths Annually." Washington, D.C.: Bureau of National Affairs, Inc., July 30, 1997, pp. 260–61.

BNA Reporter. "Statistics - Work Related Fatalities, Injuries, Cost Nation $121 Billion, Council Says." Washington, D.C.: Bureau of National Affairs, Inc., August 13, 1997, p. 412.

Chicago Sun Times Business. "Cost of Job Injuries, Illnesses Tallied." July 28, 1997.

Cooke, James Aaron. "Warehousing: Great Expectation." *Logistics Management*. July 1998, pp. 52–53.

Harrington, Lisa. "The New Warehousing." *Industry Week*. July 20, 1998, pp. 52–58.

Hulihan, Maile. "Workplace Safety: More than a Quick Fix." *Treasury and Risk Management*. September 1997, p.4.

Lear-Olimpi, Michael. "The Way It Is in Warehousing." *Warehousing Management*. July 1998, pp. 12–18.

Lipp, Paula. "Survival of the Fittest." *Warehousing Management*. July/August 1997, pp. 6–14.

Modern Materials Handling. "Workplace Safety." September 1994, p. 17.

"OSHA: Top 10 Citations by Subpart for General Industry." *Compliance Magazine*. November/December 1997, p. 14.

Schultz, George. "Warehouses Are a Key Part of the Enterprise." *Management Automation*. December 1997, pp. 19–27.

U. S. Department of Labor, OSHA. "Injuries to Warehouse Workers." Bureau of Labor Statistics. April 1986, Bulletin 2257, p. 24.

U. S. Department of Labor, OSHA. Proposed Powered Industrial Truck Operator Training, *Federal Register* 60:13782–13831, March 14, 1995.

Verespej, Michael. "There's Money in Safety." *Industry Week*. July 6, 1992, pp. 28–31.

WERC Sheet. "High-Tech Safety Measures." July/August 1997, pp. 1–4.

2

Effective Warehouse Safety Programming

Safety professionals agree that an effective safety program is one of the most important areas of emphasis an organization can provide to the employees. If a well-managed organization or facility intends to reduce costs, be competitive, and be a vital part of the economy, it must implement comprehensive safety and health programs. Many organizations find themselves competing economically with similar business in other countries that can offer products at lower prices. Workers' compensation costs can be a stumbling block to being competitive if workplace injuries are reducing profits. To reduce injuries, management must consider worker safety as important as quality, parts produced per hour, and earnings per share of stock.

This chapter will focus on a variety of methods and programs to reduce injuries, increase profitability, reduce OSHA citations, improve worker morale, and maintain a cleaner, more organized workplace. Many organizations do not venture out to improve their safety efforts out of fear that safety costs too much. Workers' compensation costs and increased insurance premiums can many times exceed any costs an organization could channel toward improved safety. It is the injuries and illnesses that cost, not safety.

DUPONT CORPORATION AS A LEADER

The DuPont Corporation has been the leader in workplace safety for many years. This prestigious position was not reached overnight, but took years of modeling and improving. As a result, the safety efforts and achievements of DuPont should be emulated if an organization is sincere in reducing injuries. DuPont has achieved the reputation of the world's safest chemical company by applying the following principles:

- All injuries and occupational illnesses can be prevented.

- Management, from the CEO or president to the first line supervisor, is directly responsible for preventing injuries and illnesses. Each management level is accountable to the one above and responsible for the one below.

- Safety is a condition of employment. Each employee must assume responsibility for working safely. It is as important as production, quality, and cost control.

- Training is essential. Working safely does not come naturally; it is a learned behavior. To eliminate injuries, management must teach, motivate, and sustain employee safety knowledge. This involves establishing procedures and safety performance standards for each job function.

11

■ Safety audits, internal and external, must be conducted to assess the effectiveness of facilities and programs, and to detect areas for improvement.

■ All deficiencies must be corrected promptly, either through modifying facilities, changing procedures, improving employee training, or disciplining constructively and consistently. Follow-up audits will verify effectiveness.

■ It is essential to investigate all unsafe practices, incidents with injury potential, and injuries.

■ Safety off the job is as important as safety on the job.

■ It is good business to prevent illness and injury, because they involve tremendous direct and indirect costs.

■ People are the most critical element in the success of a health and safety program. Management responsibility must be complemented by employees' suggestions and their active involvement in keeping workplaces safe.

DuPont's ten principles can be applied to a warehouse environment. As pointed out in Chapter One, injuries in warehouses are double that of all private industry. Injuries can be prevented through effective programming and enforcement. DuPont continues to strive for lower and lower injury rates. In 1994 DuPont had a lost time injury rate of 0.1 and a 0.89 loss rate for recordable injuries. By 1997 these same numbers fell to 0.02 for lost time injuries and 0.38 for recordable injuries. Only 16 disabling injuries occurred in 1997 among the 97,000 employees in all of their facilities. DuPont's belief is that safety is good business. Management, labor, and safety professionals agree that the following elements are common contributors to workplace injuries.

UNSAFE CONDITIONS

Many believe that hazardous conditions are the primary cause of workplace injuries. Without a doubt, unsafe conditions can and do contribute to many injuries. If a machine is unguarded, if the brakes are defective on a forklift, or if a handrailing is missing from an elevated work area, workers can be injured. The Occupational Safety and Health Administration concentrates on unsafe physical conditions of the workplace and does not usually consider behavioral issues. Most of the OSHA standards focus on identifying "things" in the workplace as opposed to not focusing on how workers behave. However, many times an unsafe condition is a direct result of the failure of management or employees to take corrective action.

If a machine is properly guarded and an employee fails to replace the guard after maintenance or setup, an injury can now be related to two causes: the conditions and the worker's behavior. If management fails to inspect the workplace and enforce the machine-guard rule, an additional cause can be traced to an injury. If the employee was not properly trained to understand the need for machine guards, the efforts of management must once again come into question.

The same logic would apply to defective brakes on a forklift, or a missing handrail. Conditions, yes; but what preceded the conditions? Forklifts must be thoroughly inspected prior to each shift. Use a checklist so that all targeted items are evaluated. If such a program does not exist, defective brakes, steering, or any other problem can arise. Perhaps the employee has failed to use the checklist provided, or half-heartedly inspected the equipment and never told management of the condition. Perhaps the defective brakes have been repeatedly reported to management and they failed to take action.

The missing handrail on a mezzanine is a very dangerous condition. Falls kill many workers each year, some from heights of less than 6 feet. Perhaps the handrail had to be removed to make room for a pallet full of product being lifted from the floor. Perhaps the pallet was not empty and this prevented the employee from returning the handrail to the proper closed position. Perhaps management frequently walks by this elevated work area, yet fails to notice the missing rail or regards its absence as commonplace. There are devices that can be used to safeguard handrails on mezzanines.

As one can see from the above discussion, there can be many causes of unsafe conditions, but, usually unsafe conditions are not the sole cause of an injury. It is believed by many that unsafe behavior accounts for 80 to 90 percent of all injuries. Some contend that OSHA's focus on "things," such as machine guards, handrails, and protective equipment, will prevent only 20 percent of all injuries. However, safe behavior is mostly management's responsibility, not OSHA's. Therefore, management must focus more on a comprehensive safety program; just abiding by OSHA regulations is not the answer.

COMBINATION OF FACTORS

Injuries are caused by a combination of factors. When investigating an injury or incident, those involved must look at conditions existing at the time of the injury, what behavior the employee was exhibiting, and what procedures management required and enforced. Dan Petersen, a highly respected safety professional who has studied safety behavior for many years, insists that it is not the elements of a safety program that get results, but rather the culture and the climate in which those elements exist.

Petersen suggests that line managers and safety directors look to world-class companies to discover what they are doing for safety. Even though the organizations may differ, they all have essential criteria in place. When evaluating a warehouse safety program, management should ask the following questions:

- Does the safety system force supervisory performance by establishing accountability?

- Does the safety program involve middle management; are they active participants?

- Does upper management visibly demonstrate what the safety priorities are for the organization?

- Does the safety program allow for and receive active employee participation?

- Do employees perceive the safety program as positive; is it well received and respected?

- Is it possible to change and reorganize the safety program?

SAFETY ROLES FOR EVERYONE

To be successful, safety and health programs require participation at all levels.

Management

Must commit to providing a safe and healthy place of work for each employee. There must be a cooperative effort between the employer, managers, supervisors, and workers. The common goal is to reduce and eliminate injuries.

Responsibilities must be shared by all. The employer has to provide visible and financial support for the overall program. Policies and procedures must be developed. All employees must share the safety goals and objectives of the organization. Accountability must be assigned for the implementation of safety policies, work procedures, and company goals. To ensure that the safety message is known and adhered to, all members of management must abide by all safety rules and practices. Supervisors should be able to identify workplace hazards and make corrections on an ongoing basis. New employees must be properly briefed before working. Supervisors are responsible for communicating safety and health information to employees and ensuring that they are properly trained.

Supervisors are accountable for investigations of incidents and injuries, ongoing maintenance of machines, and surveys in each department of the warehouse.

Workers

Should commit to participate in the safety and health program. Employees must wear all prescribed safety and health equipment as required. Following the required safety rules is a necessity since employees may work unsupervised at times. All injuries and incidents should be reported and investigated to ensure that corrective action has been taken to prevent recurrence.

Workers are also responsible for knowing and understanding those workplace rules that apply to them. Workers should never say they understand the rules if they do not know them. Ongoing inspection of equipment, such as a daily forklift inspection, is the responsibility of the worker assigned to the equipment. Teams or committees should be involved in production and safety functions, etc.

RATING SUPERVISORS' PERFORMANCE IN SAFETY

In many organizations, the supervisor continues to be the link between management and labor. Thus, the enforcement of safe work practices is in the hands of the supervisor. He/she must have knowledge of safety rules and participate in training programs to become better educated in departmental safety.

Establishing and implementing a safety program can be difficult because work habits may have to change. New procedures have to be discussed with employees, then monitored and enforced. There is no doubt that the supervisor has a difficult task, coping with production issues, personnel problems, and regulatory concerns. Safety is somewhere in that list of responsibilities and it's up to the organization to spell out the expectations regarding safety performance and programming.

Many organizations use injury totals as a means of measuring the safety performance of supervisors. If the department's injury totals decrease, the supervisor most likely has met the objectives and is rewarded. If the injury count goes up, the supervisor may not receive any additional compensation during the annual review. The problem with this one-dimensional system is that a supervisor could contribute next to nothing toward the safety program and be rewarded for having fewer injuries. If those program elements that contribute to injury reduction are infrequently adhered to, unsafe conditions or unsafe work practices and the resulting injuries will eventually catch up with the department.

A good method of establishing annual safety objectives is by establishing safety tasks for the supervisor. The organization must ask: What are those elements in the safety program that give us the biggest benefit, yet are within the grasp of the supervisor to accomplish? The following items have been used as basic components of a safety program and provide a way to measure safety compliance by a supervisor:

- Are the supervisors attending safety meetings? Do they conduct safety meetings? Are they participating in training programs such as CPR, first aid, forklift, hazcom, etc.? Are new employees provided with training during orientation?

- Is the supervisor inspecting the department on a regular basis? Are deficiencies being corrected? Are work orders being processed to correct unsafe conditions and maintenance deficiencies?

- Is the supervisor completing a job hazard analysis every X months? (The facility manager can determine the quota.) Are employees involved in JHA?

- When there is an injury, does the supervisor thoroughly investigate it? Are the proper forms filled out?

- For those noninjury incidents that occur in the department, is the supervisor investigating, correcting, and documenting them properly? Are incident reports frequently being completed?

- What is the supervisor's overall attitude toward safety?

USE OF THE RATING FORM

The six items above have been selected for use because of their simplicity and because they are common to every safety program. Any of them can be substituted, if the organization wants other program elements used instead. Only six elements are being used here because the process must be effective, yet simple in design.

Once the activities for the supervisor have been determined and agreed upon, each supervisor performing the same duties should be measured on the same criteria. If, for some reason, departmental duties are significantly different, certain line items can be modified.

For annual merit reviews or bonus programs, there are usually minimum and maximum ranges for increases. Many times, the increase involves several measurements to arrive at a total percentage. There may be additional objectives, such as parts picked per hour, tonnage shipped, control of employee turnover, shipping schedules met, and injury reduction.

For improved safety performance, a form should be developed, listing the six items previously noted with a rating scale for the supervisor on each of those tasks. The portion of the merit increase determined by safety performance should be in the range of 10 to 20 percent. Arriving at a fair and honest evaluation of the supervisor can be made easier by using the form in Figure 2-1.

Figure 2-1. Supervisors Review Rating Sheet for Safety Performance
(Circle Appropriate Evaluation Points for Performance)

Rating Items: 0 None or N/A; 1 Adequate; 2 Average; 3 Excellent; 4 Distinguished   PERFORMANCE RATINGS

1. SAFETY MEETING/SAFETY TRAINING

Does the supervisor conduct a safety meeting each month for his/her department?	0	1	2	3	4
Does the supervisor attend a department or plant safety meeting each month?	0	1	2	3	4
Does the supervisor attend training programs such as first aid, CPR, forklift, etc?	0	1	2	3	4
Does the supervisor give new or transferred employees a safety orientation?	0	1	2	3	4

2. SAFETY AND HEALTH INSPECTIONS

Is the supervisor conducting monthly safety/health inspections?	0	1	2	3	4
Is the proper inspection form being used?	0	1	2	3	4
Are unsafe actions or conditions being corrected as soon as possible?	0	1	2	3	4
Are work orders for corrective action being submitted?	0	1	2	3	4

3. JOB HAZARD ANALYSIS (JHA)

Is one JHA completed each quarter?	0	1	2	3	4
Are employees participating in each JHA?	0	1	2	3	4
Is quality of JHA meeting company standards?	0	1	2	3	4

4. INJURY INVESTIGATION

Are the forms completed and submitted within 24/48 hours?	0	1	2	3	4
Are the forms completely filled out on company form?	0	1	2	3	4
Have recommendations for corrective action been completed?	0	1	2	3	4
For zero injuries, has a simulated report been completed?	0	1	2	3	4

5. INCIDENT/NONINJURY REPORTS

Are significant incidents being investigated?	0	1	2	3	4
Is the completed incident form being submitted with a photo?	0	1	2	3	4
Is corrective action taken on each incident?	0	1	2	3	4

6. SUPERVISOR'S SAFETY ATTITUDE

Does the supervisor demonstrate a sincere interest in his/her employee's safety?	0	1	2	3	4

DATE: _____ Total Scoring: _____

Scoring Key

Name of Supervisor: _____   30-48 Points = Adequate @ 5% of Review

Signature of Manager: _____   49-55 Points = Average @ 10% of Review

Facility: _____   56-63 Points = Excellent @ 15% of Review

Overall Point/Performance Total: _____   64-72 Points = Distinguished @ 20% of Review

The form lists the safety-related activities in the left column. The scale of rating runs from none to distinguished (0 to 4 points). Note the definitions of the rating scale.

- *None or Not Acceptable:* The supervisor did not complete anything on this (item or it is not applicable). (0 points)

- *Adequate:* Just passing, the lowest rating possible to secure a point rating. (1 point)

- *Average:* Meeting minimal expectations, average performance. (2 points)

- *Excellent:* Well above average performance; significant accomplishments in the program. (3 points)

- *Distinguished:* Highest rating possible; fully satisfies all categories. (4 points)

Management must merely ask the questions listed on the rating sheet and the supervisor should be able to produce the required reports. There may be cases where the forms could be collected in advance and rated before any formal discussion takes place with the supervisor.

Once the discussions are complete, simply add up the circled numbers in each column on the form and arrive at a point total. In the example used on the form in Figure 2-1, the following percentages would be paid out for the safety portion of the supervisor's annual merit increase:

- 64–72 points needed to earn the maximum 20 percent (portion devoted to safety) of the total merit increase possible

- 56–63 points needed to earn 15 percent

- 49–55 points needed to earn 10 percent

- 30–48 points needed to earn 5 percent.

So if a supervisor held a safety meeting each month, attended training, regularly inspected the department, processed work orders for maintenance deficiencies, completed two JHAs, investigated injuries, investigated incidents, and had a positive outlook on safety, fully 20 percent of the bonus could come from safety.

A few additional comments regarding the evaluation process:

- Once management has developed a rating sheet and decided on a bonus percentage for safety, each supervisor should be trained in what the form is, why it has been developed, what results are expected, and what merit increases can be expected as a result of the program.

- Each supervisor should be given a copy of the form and told what to expect at the next review. If it is nearly time for the annual review, the warehouse manager may wish to make adjustments on the form, grading activity month by month rather than on an annual basis.

- If the long-range plans of the corporation change, the specific elements on the rating sheet may also change. Any new changes must also be communicated to supervisors.

- Completed forms must always be kept on file following a formal salary review.

■ Considerations for supervisory promotion or upgrading should include safety performance and the results of the numerical ratings.

Programs such as this help to move supervisors toward being more professional. If management fails to establish goals that are realistic and germane to the facility, progress will not be made. Programs that measure involvement must be implemented to achieve these goals in order to achieve a safe workplace.

Targets must be attainable and realistic, but not so easily attained that they carry no meaning or significance. It would be of no value to assign tasks or projects to supervisors who lack the training and knowledge to achieve those tasks. Job hazard analysis is an example of a program that requires specific training; management should not assign JHA as a task if supervisors have not been trained.

ELEMENTS OF SUCCESSFUL SAFETY PROGRAMS

The National Safety Council has continually conducted research into what makes effective safety programming. In 1967 and again in 1992, the council asked safety professionals for their opinions on this subject. Their efforts and assistance helped contribute to the NSC's document. Various safety and health practices can be successful in one organization and yet fail in others. As successful safety programs evolve and compliance increases, the costs of maintaining those programs are reduced along with expenses for injuries, lost productivity, and product damage. The workplace and workforce are changing. Global economics are shaping business. To effectively compete, safety and health programming are vital to the bottom line.

The following is a listing of the fourteen elements identified in the council publication. Only the key points have been highlighted here from this 221-page manual.

Element 1. HAZARD RECOGNITION AND CONTROL

■ Hazard Recognition and Evaluation
  • Job safety analysis
  • Safety inspections
  • Injury/illness/incident investigation
  • Industrial hygiene exposure assessments
  • Systems safety reviews
■ Hazard Control
  • Engineering controls and redesign
  • Preventive maintenance
  • Personal protective equipment

Element 2. WORKPLACE DESIGN AND ENGINEERING

■ Design and Start-up Review
■ Ergonomic Factors
■ Codes and Standards
■ Machine Safeguarding
■ Material Handling
■ Life, Safety, and Fire Protection

Element 3. SAFETY PERFORMANCE MANAGEMENT

- Roles and Responsibilities in Safety Performance
- Performance Objectives
  - Conformance to standards
  - Accountability
- Performance Reviews and Appraisals
  - Communicating the results
- Safety Performance Management Review

Element 4. REGULATORY COMPLIANCE MANAGEMENT

- Identifying Applicable Standards
  - OSHA and the Environmental Protection Agency (EPA)
  - The Mine Safety and Health Act (MSHA)
  - State and local programs
- International Regulations and Standards
  - Canada
  - Mexico
  - Staying informed
- Assessing Compliance

Element 5. OCCUPATIONAL HEALTH

- Occupational Health Professionals
  - Occupational physicians
  - Occupational health nurses
  - Industrial hygienists
  - Health physicists
- Employee Health Services
- First Aid
- Medical Records
- Employees with Disabilities
- Worksite Monitoring
- Periodic Medical Examinations and Medical Surveillance
- Worksite Health Promotion Programs

Element 6. INFORMATION COLLECTION

- Cost Analysis
- Information Management
- Reports on Workplace Conditions
- Data Analysis
- Injury and Illness Case Analysis
- OSHA Forms
- Off-the-Job Injury Data

Element 7. EMPLOYEE INVOLVEMENT

- Team Concepts
  - Options: Self-directed work teams, team circles, task forces
- Organizational Roles
- Tenure of Team Members
  - Training the team
  - Selecting problems and measuring results
- Joint Safety and Health Committees
  - Organization
  - Scope and focus
  - Meetings
  - Communication
  - Union participation
- Individual Efforts
  - Responsibility and accountability
  - Soliciting individual opinions, suggestions, and input
  - Employee recognition

Element 8. MOTIVATION, BEHAVIOR, AND ATTITUDES

- Definition of Motivation
  - Specification of safety objectives or goals
  - Reinforcement of desired behaviors
  - Attainment of commitment and involvement
- Description of Motivation Models
- Description of Selected Motivational Techniques
  - Communication
  - Awards, incentives, and recognition
  - Employee surveys

Element 9. TRAINING AND ORIENTATION

- Training Standards
  - Regulatory training standards
  - U.S. training standards
  - European training standards
  - ISO 9000 international quality assurance
  - Training standards of other countries
  - Company training standards and controls
- Types of Training
  - Safety management training
  - Orientation training
  - Safety technique training
  - Task training
- Post Training Events
  - Periodic observation and contacts

Element 10. ORGANIZATIONAL COMMUNICATIONS

- Defining Communication
  - Types of communication
- Communication Filters
- Regulations, Safety Procedures, Goals, and Results
- Public Relations and Media Management
- Senior Management Policies

Element 11. MANAGEMENT AND CONTROL OF EXTERNAL EXPOSURES

- Contractor Control Programs
  - Assuring contractor safety
  - Verifying contractor insurance and appropriate training
- Vendors
  - Assuring liability exposure
  - Addressing exposure and ensuring protection
- Product Safety Control
  - Assessing exposure
  - Ensuring protection
- Public Liability Exposures
  - Potential exposure
  - Assessing liability potential
- Disaster Preparedness
  - Assessing potential exposure

Element 12. ENVIRONMENTAL MANAGEMENT

- The Environmental/Safety and Health Connection
  - Compliance - the driving force
- Beyond Compliance - Managing Environmental Risk
  - Recordkeeping and documentation
  - Planning for emergencies
  - Adequate technical support
  - Communication
  - Employee involvement
  - Training

Element 13. WORK FORCE PLANNING AND STAFFING

- Hiring and Job Placement
  - Safety orientation
  - Age and gender
- Safety and Health Work Rules
  - Characteristics of effective rules
  - Keys to success
- Employee Assistance Programs
- Americans with Disabilities Act (ADA)
  - Preparation

- Job placement
- Accommodations
- Accessibility
- Emergency preparedness

Element 14. ASSESSMENTS, AUDITS, AND EVALUATIONS

- Meeting the Assessment Needs of the Organization
  - Management effectiveness: qualitative assessments
  - Safe job performance: observations and samplings
  - Attitudes and acceptance: perception surveys
- Self-Assessments
  - Maintaining objectivity
  - Training employees to conduct self-assessments
  - Advantages of self-assessment: continuity, control, involvement
- Third-Party Assessments
  - Selecting a third-party auditor
  - Advantages of third-party assessments: objectivity, depth, and credibility
- Reporting and Follow-up
  - Assessment reports
  - Follow-up
- Voluntary Regulatory Assessments
- Voluntary Protection Programs

DELIVERING THE PROGRAM TO EMPLOYEES

It is one thing to develop a comprehensive safety and health program, but to fully communicate it to all levels of management is another. In an article on communicating with and changing frontline employees, authors T.J. and Sandar Larkin advise a change in communication methods. Their research indicates that the Wyatt Company investigated 531 United States organizations that were undergoing change and restructuring. When CEOs were asked what they would do differently about the change in the process, they said, "the way I communicated with my employees."

Their research indicates that when change is needed, the most effective process is for supervisors to communicate face-to-face with employees. Supervisors must be the group driving the changes. For a reinvention of a safety program, this same method of change should be employed. Management must recognize, as a result of injuries, costs, and noncompliance, that a change in the safety program is needed and then relate the program changes to the supervisors. The supervisors should then proceed to discuss with all of the employees the need for program changes and the methods through which change will take place.

Simple, yet direct, communication appears to be needed to invoke change. Old habits are hard to break. To turn the elements of the program into work rules and guidelines, a plain-English approach is needed. However, there is a word of caution here— nearly 32 million people in the United States speak languages other than English. More than 20 percent of adults read at or below a fifth grade level. With this in mind, preplanning of the safety program is essential. A simple, yet effective, means of communicating with employees is a bulletin board such as the one shown in Figure 2-2.

For those organizations that operate multiple warehouses, monthly safety performance can be tracked from a central location. Figure 2-3 presents a form for each warehouse to log their monthly activity on a calendar year basis. A copy of this form can be forwarded to the head office for the purpose of tracking compliance activities associated with the established safety program.

Figure 2-2. The topics for the current and future safety meetings are displayed on this bulletin board.

MANAGEMENT RESPONSIBILITY

World-class organizations have developed individual safety programming elements and most subscribe to the following six elements:

1. The safety responsibilities of first-line supervisors should be made clear to them by management. Although the ultimate goal of a safety program is zero injuries, using that measurement for supervisory responsibility is not very effective. Rather, management should charge supervisors with tasks resulting in a modification of the safety culture in the workplace environment. These tasks should include elements such as job safety analysis, conducting safety meetings, department inspections, and safety training. Accountability for these activities should be part of each supervisor's annual performance review and/or bonus program.

2. Middle management must be actively involved in the safety program. Petersen feels that the middle manager has a three-fold role—to ensure subordinate supervisory performance, to ensure the quality of the performance, and to do some things himself that demonstrate active participation in the safety program by all levels of management.

3. Top management must do more than sign off on a policy statement. Senior management should be contacted and asked what the CEO or COO would like to do to support the safety effort.

4. Employee involvement is the trend of the 90s. Allowing safety committees or safety steering committees to shape the programs is very beneficial. Much can be learned from those individuals that operate the machines, handle the product, and move the business along. Allow employees to be a part of decision making.

5. The safety program must be flexible to accommodate ongoing program choices for supervisors and program revisions as required by changes in workers' compensation codes, new OSHA standards, and special focus programs.

6. Do employees perceive the safety program to be a positive one? A NIOSH study in 1978 found that the three most important characteristics of an effective safety system are:

Figure 2-3. Monthly Safety Activity

FACILITY: _____

Activity / Date	JAN	FEB	MAR	APR	MAY	JUN	JULY	AUG	SEPT	OCT	NOV	DEC
Safety Meetings												
Safety Committee Meetings												
Incident Reports												
Safety Inspection												
Title of Film Shown												
Sprinkler Testing												
Forklift Training												
New Employee Orientation												
Fire Drill												
LOTO Meeting												
First Aid Training												
Audit (Memo) Response												
JHA Review												
Others												

(Note that some items on this list are completed only once per year but are listed to serve as a reminder.)

- A very high, vividly expressed management commitment

- A very humanistic approach to safety that concentrates on one-to-one contacts between supervisor and worker

- A focus on finding employees doing things right and then providing them positive reinforcement

Observations of employees on a daily basis is highly recommended as a means of complimenting them for safe behavior. The supervisor should also correct any unsafe behavior observed and ask employees if they have any safety issues to discuss. Daily observations also provide the opportunity to evaluate the work area for any safety conditions that may need correction.

VOLUNTARY PROTECTION PROGRAMS

For those employers wishing to attain recognition for their successful safety programs, OSHA offers a means of recognition. In the early 1980s, OSHA developed the Voluntary Protection Program (VPP).

OSHA has long recognized the fact that they have limited resources and that the agency cannot perform a regular inspection of all worksites. At OSHA's beginning in 1971, safety professionals commented that OSHA would have been better off had they enacted regulations that required establishments to develop and implement basic safety management programs. OSHA inspections are important to the workplace, but comprehensive safety management programs are far more important for the reduction of injuries and illnesses. Inspection alone will not accomplish the goal of a safer workplace.

Only a few states require safety and health programs. At the time of this writing, OSHA has not been able to enact legislation requiring comprehensive safety and health programs.

The VPP program goes beyond OSHA compliance. VPP sites have embraced comprehensive safety and health programs and have enlisted the aid of facility workers. VPP sites are examples of organizations that take safety and health seriously. Many times these organizations are ahead of the curve when it comes to legislation. If a new standard is on the horizon, VPP sites usually adopt it before the standard becomes mandatory.

Currently there are nearly 500 VPP sites nationwide, and many organizations have multiple sites.

Benefits of VPP

Why should an employer choose to become a VPP site? What are the benefits in this program? The following list of program benefits has been provided by the VPPPA and other VPP members:

- VPP is an excellent business management tool. It contains elements of total quality management and recognizes excellence.

- VPP establishes a cooperative relationship with OSHA. OSHA, business, and labor work together to achieve STAR quality, the highest rating OSHA bestows on a facility. The site(s) serve as industry models. OSHA and other businesses consult with the site to gather information about best practices.

■ VPP status removes the site from the OSHA random inspection process for three years. Because of OSHA's limited resources, the VPP program allows OSHA to focus on employers whose sites are most likely not in compliance.

■ VPP helps to build employee ownership, which helps to ensure continuity with the program.

■ Site liability is reduced. Lower workers' compensation costs and fewer third- party lawsuits are a large part of the site's progress. The site also becomes a valued member of the community.

■ Fewer injuries occur at VPP sites. Nationally, VPP sites experience from 40 to 60 percent fewer injuries than like industries, when measured against Bureau of Labor Statistics (BLS) figures.

■ Contractor performance is much improved at a VPP site. One of the specific details requiring admission to VPP status is to have a program that evaluates any non- employee group on the worksite. Safety for all employees is required.

■ The annual VPP site evaluation helps to quantify progress of the program. Goals and recommendations of the work site are tracked. The site's annual plans for the future are forwarded to OSHA, helping to maintain program continuity and progress.

Other benefits and key performance indicators include:

■ Fewer grievances

■ Improved housekeeping

■ Improved product quality

■ Fewer incidents and damage to product and structures

■ Improved reliability

■ Reduced overall costs of claims

■ Increased productivity

■ Less absenteeism

■ Increased employee pride

■ The ability to mentor with other organizations

■ Enhanced cost savings

■ A greater competitive advantage

■ VPP sites make good community neighbors.

Many VPP sites have shown significant drops in injuries and lost days associated with injuries, as well as reductions in workers' compensation costs and insurance premium costs. As this information indicates, there are many reasons for an organization to strive for VPP status. If all of the benefits could be summed up into one key message for business, it would be that VPP brings an improved bottom line. After all, this is what senior executives and CEOs look for: What will this effort or program contribute to our bottom line? Without a doubt, VPP adds to a healthy bottom line.

OSHA's Awards for Excellence in Safety and Health

The VPP program offers three distinct levels of site participation. The separate programs have graded requirement elements to allow sites to enter and , over a period of time, work to achieve a higher level of recognition. The three levels of awards and recognition are:

Star. This award recognizes employers who provide effective, comprehensive worker safety and health protection. STAR is the most selective of the awards in the VPP. OSHA expects that STAR participants will be on the leading edge of hazard prevention methods and technology. If a site is recognized as STAR, a reevaluation from OSHA will not take place for at least three years. An annual self-evaluation of the entire safety program must be forwarded to OSHA by the employer.

Merit. Being recognized as a MERIT site indicates that the employer is willing to provide good protection and is committed to reach STAR status. OSHA provides MERIT sites with a set of program elements designed to help them reach an optimal safety and health program. MERIT sites are usually given one to one and one-half years to firm up their program before a revisit from OSHA.

Demonstration. Employers who want to show that they can provide "STAR quality" protection by following the required program criteria can be recognized as a DEMONSTRATION site. These sites may be in industries lacking VPP experience, where OSHA needs to develop more information about what is effective. A check with the local VPP coordinator should determine if the site falls under the DEMONSTRATION guidelines.

Figure 2-4 shows a VPP STAR award ceremony at a Midas International warehouse in Perrysburg, Ohio. Region V OSHA made the formal presentation.

Figure 2-5 illustrates a sign identifying an accident-free workplace.

The Application Process

OSHA has specific requirements for the VPP application. It is recommended that prospective VPP sites make contact with their

Figure 2-4. VPP ceremonies provide a means of celebrating success; every employee is honored for this achievement at the Midas International site in Perryburg, Ohio.

Figure 2-5. This sign shows the number of days without an accident—a great track record.

local OSHA office and discuss the application process with the local VPP coordinator. For example, many regions ask that two copies of the application be forwarded to the regional VPP representative. A few regions ask that the prospective applicant bring the application into the regional OSHA office for discussion and review.

Once OSHA has received the applications, they will be reviewed for content. If any elements required in the application process are missing, the site will be contacted by OSHA for the deficient program materials. OSHA may also ask for more details about specific safety programs within the application. Until the VPP coordinator finds the application complete, the clock has stopped for the application process.

Not only should the application contain all of those elements that OSHA requires, but also the quality of the documents should be high. Copies of specific documents, such as a job hazard analysis, a facility audit, a safety committee report, injury and incident investigation forms, the facility emergency program, the employee hazard notification program, and a contractor's safety program should be included. The site can determine what to include in the application by contacting local VPP sites, the regional VPP coordinator for OSHA, or attending VPP regional or national meetings.

The application may be in any format convenient for the site. Each item identified below must be discussed in the application. The numbers identified in front of each element should be used in the process of preparing the application. When OSHA reviews the application, referencing those specific numbers will help speed the application process. None of the information from the VPP application will be used for enforcement purposes.

Any applicant wishing to withdraw the application may do so at any time.

Application Guidelines

I. General Information

    1. Company Name:

        Site Address:

        Company Address (if different than site):

        Site CEO:

        Title:

        Site VPP Representative:

        Address (if different than site):

        Phone Number:

    2. Corporate Name (if different than company name):

        Corporate VPP Representative (if applicable):

Title:

Address:

Phone Number:

3. Collective Bargaining Agent(s):

Address(es):

Phone number(s):

4. Number of Employees:

Number of Contract Workers (if used routinely):

5. Type of Work Performed and Products Produced:

6. Industry SIC code (3–4 digit number):

7. Injury Incidence Rate:

(Give yearly rates for last 3 complete calendar years, plus average of all 3 years combined)

Injury incident rates are calculated (N/EH) X 200,000 where:

N = number of recordable injuries in one year

EH = total number of hours worked by all employees in one year

200,000 = equivalent of 100 full-time employees working 40 hour weeks 50 weeks per year.

8. Lost Workday Injury Case Rate:

(Give yearly rates for last 3 complete calendar years, plus average of all 3 years combined.) Injury lost workday case rates are calculated with the same equation as above where:

N= number of injuries resulting in lost workdays or restricted work activity.

II. Management Commitment and Planning

(Section VIII contains a sample statement regarding management commitment to safety and health and to participation in a Voluntary Protection Program, which is required for the application.)

1. *Commitment*. Attach a copy of your site's established occupational safety and health policy.

2. *Organization*. Describe how the site safety and health function fits into your overall management organization. (An organizational chart is preferred but is not required.)

3. *Responsibility*. Describe how your company assigns line and staff safety and health responsibility. This is an item for which VPP participants are required to have written procedures and/or documentation as part of their health and safety management systems.

4. *Accountability*. Describe the accountability system you use for line managers and supervisors. Appropriate examples may include job performance evaluations, MBOs, etc. Explain how the system is documented.

5. *Resources*. Describe personnel and other resources devoted to the safety and health program.

6. *Planning*. Indicate how safety and health practices are integrated into comprehensive management planning.

7. *Contract Workers*. Describe the method you use to assure safe and healthful working conditions for all employees even where more than one employer has employees at the same site. This includes general industry sites if contract employees intermingle with regular employees.

8. *Employee Notification*. Describe how you will notify employees about participation in the VPP, their right to register a complaint with OSHA, their right to obtain self-inspection and accident investigation results upon request, etc. (Various methods may include one or more of the following: new employee orientation, bulletin boards, tool box meetings or work group meetings.)

9. *Site Plan*. Attach a site map or general plant layout.

III. Worksite Analysis

1. *Pre-Use Analysis*. Explain how new equipment, materials, and processes are analyzed for potential hazards prior to use.

2. *Comprehensive Surveys*. Indicate how you spot potential safety and health hazards at the site. Examples are industrial hygiene surveys, comprehensive safety reviews, and/or project safety reviews at the time of design.

3. *Self-Inspections*. Describe your worksite safety and health inspection procedures. Include information about inspection schedules and industrial hygiene sampling and monitoring. Indicate who performs inspections and how any necessary corrections are tracked. (You may attach sample forms and internal time frames for correction.) Where applicable to health hazards, summarize the testing and analysis procedures used and qualifications of personnel who conduct them.

4. *Job Hazard Analysis*. Relate how you review jobs, processes, and/or interaction of activities to determine safe work procedures. (Not to be confused with self-inspections.) Include procedures or guidance techniques used in conducting job hazard analysis. In construction, relate phase-planning, and describe how results are used in training employees to do their jobs safely. Also, how are results used in planning and implementation of your hazard correction and control program?

5. *Employee Notification of Hazards*. Describe how employees notify management of potential health or safety hazards. What is management's procedure for follow-up and tracking corrections? (An option providing for written notification must be a part of the system.)

6. *Accident Investigations*. Explain your company's accident investigation procedures. What training/guidance is given to investigators? How do you determine which accidents warrant investigation? What about near-miss incidents?

7. *Medical Program*. Describe both your onsite and offsite medical service or physician availability. Indicate the coverage provided by employees trained in first-aid, CPR, and other paramedical training, and indicate which training they have received. Give a detailed description of how you address specific programs such as hearing conservation, etc.

IV. Hazard Prevention and Control

1. *Professional Expertise*. Provide details concerning your use of the services of certified professionals. What industrial hygiene services and broad-based safety expertise are available to you?

2. *Safety and Health Rules*. List your company's rules, and describe the disciplinary system you use for enforcing them.

3. *Personal Protective Equipment*. Describe your company's personal protective equipment requirements. If respirators are used, attach a copy of the written respirator program.

4. *Emergency Preparedness*. Describe your company's emergency planning preparedness program. Include information on emergency or evacuation drills.

5. *Preventive Maintenance*. Provide a summary and description of your procedures for preventive maintenance of your equipment.

V. Safety and Health Training

1. *Safety and Health Training*. Describe formal and informal safety and health training programs for your employees. Include supervisors' training schedules and information on: hazard communication, personal protective equipment, and handling of emergency situations. (Sample attendance lists and tracking methods, if any, may also be attached if desired.)

VI. Employee Involvement

1. List the ways employees are involved in your safety and health program. Provide specific information about decision processes that employees impact, such as hazard assessment, work analysis, safety and health training, or evaluation of the safety and health program.

2. If you have a safety and health committee, complete the following information where applicable

    a. Date of committee inception

    b. Method of selecting employee members

    c. Name, job, and length of service of each member

    d. Average length of service of employee members

    e. Description of committee meeting requirements

        frequency

        quorum rules

        minutes (You may attach samples.)

    f. Description of committee role

        frequency and scope of committee inspections

        procedures for inspecting entire work site

        role in accident investigation

        role in employee hazard notification

        other

    g. Describe your hazard recognition training procedures. If previously covered under Safety Health and Training, indicate "See Training."

    h. List safety and health information accessible to and used by committee.

VII. Program Evaluation

1. *Safety and Health Program Self-Evaluation*. Provide a copy of last year's comprehensive review and evaluation of your entire safety and health program. Assessments of the effectiveness of the areas listed in these applications' guidelines should be included.

2. *Rate Reduction*. If your injury rates are above industry average, specify your short and long term goals for reducing them to or below industry average. Include specific methods you will use to address this problem.

3. Include any other information you may consider crucial to the application.

VIII. Statement of Commitment

1. *Union Statement*. If your site is unionized, the authorized collective bargaining agent(s) must sign a statement to the effect that they either support the VPP application or that they have no objection to the site's participation in VPP. The statement must be on file before OSHA comes on site.

OSHA's Onsite Visit

Prospective applicants usually have many questions regarding the onsite visit by the OSHA team. The following details may help to remove the fear of this process.

The local OSHA VPP coordinator will make contact with the facility to arrange for a mutually convenient time for the visit. The onsite team should include at least three OSHA representatives. Their job is to verify that the site's safety and health program, as detailed in the VPP application, is fully operational and addresses all potential hazards at the site. It must be noted that none of the team members will be enforcement personnel from the local OSHA office.

The OSHA team will stay for at least two days. If the site is large, the team can spend additional time as needed. The team will have an initial introductory meeting with management and workers who have been selected to serve as VPP representatives. The OSHA team leader will describe the process and what the team expects to accomplish. A room where the VPP team can meet and evaluate forms should be made available.

The review team will conduct an initial walk-through of the site. Employees may be contacted during the tour and key questions may be asked. During the course of the team's visit, several walk-throughs by different team members may take place. If a team member recommends that an item be corrected during a facility walk-through, if possible, management should correct it as soon as feasible. If a part or item must be ordered to correct the issue at hand, notify the OSHA team member that it has been corrected or the part has been ordered.

Site Document Review

OSHA will examine records for the past three years to verify implementation of the safety and health program. The site should have all of these documents available for the team. Reports on safety meetings, training, inspections, etc., should be placed in chronological order so that the forms are easier to review.

Typically, these are the documents that are requested during a review:

- OSHA #200 logs and corresponding worker compensation records.

- Industrial hygiene monitoring of the facility. The site must ensure that a certified industrial hygienist (CIH) has recently conducted a comprehensive site survey.

- A recently completed safety survey of the site conducted by a certified safety professional (CSP) must also be available.

- Documents identifying employee and supervisory training must be available.

- Attendance at these meetings must be documented.

- Site self-inspection reports along with corrective action are necessary. If a checklist is used for site surveys, a narrative section on each form must also be completed.

- First aid logs.

- Facility safety and health rules. Have employees been given copies of the rules?

- Safety manuals, handbooks, and safety policies.

- Job hazard analysis and employee involvement in this process.

- Personal protective equipment (PPE) programs and the written PPE programs.

- The bloodborne pathogens program.

- Listings of employees trained in first aid and CPR.

- Injury investigation reports, along with the guidelines for investigation.

- Incident reports and accompanying corrective action notes and photos.

- Hazard communication program, chemical listing, and material safety data sheets (MSDS).

- Lockout/tagout programs with accompanying inventory of items that require zero energy action and the methods to achieve that action.

- Listing of crane, forklift, power presses, and other pieces of equipment that need inspection and ongoing maintenance. Daily checklists are important in this section.

- Audits and surveys performed by outside professionals: fire inspections, facility audits, and workers compensation data are all a part of the document survey.

- Employee hazard notification programs and accompanying documents.

- Minutes from employee meetings, safety committee meetings, steering committee minutes, and VPP employee team minutes (if applicable).

- Facility emergency plan for fire, chemical, medical, and weather-related emergencies.

- Ergonomic improvements and any written ergonomic guidelines or programs.

- A confined space program.

Any additional information that shows the quality and depth of the safety and health program of the facility will also be requested. Various levels of management may be questioned regarding documents and written programs. OSHA will also calculate the incident rates and lost workday case rates for the facility.

SUMMARY

Managing safety can be a difficult task, but the efforts are beneficial to the employees and to the organization's bottom line. The economic benefits of fewer injuries begin with a reduction in workers' compensation insurance losses and continue with lower indirect costs associated with those losses. Safer warehouses tend to be well run and more productive. Often a facility will experience an improvement in both safety and business at the same time.

Safety programs require commitment, planning, cooperation, and resources. Management must commit to improving safety performance. The time to improve and move forward is not after a serious injury or a high OSHA penalty, but before any catastrophic or serious incident occurs.

Organizations such as the National Safety Council and the American Society of Safety Engineers can be of assistance in providing materials and training. Once a facility has the safety program in place and the statistics are as low as possible, pursuing STAR or MERIT status in the Voluntary Protection Program would bring national recognition for the facility's progress.

REFERENCES

Birkner, Lawrence R. and Ruth K. The Plant Tour: A Tool for Improving Performance. *Occupational Hazards*. September. 1997, pp. 55–56.

Bureau of Business Practice. "DuPont Tackles the Safety Plateau." *Safety Management*. Number 423, June 1998.

Connors, Mary. "The Battle For Industrial Safety." *Fortune*. August 4, 1997, pp. 116(c)–116

Krikorian, Michael. "Elements of a Plant Safety Program." *Plant Engineering*. December 24, 1986, pp. 42–45.

Larkin, T. J., and Sandar, Larkin. "Reaching and Changing Frontline Employees." *Harvard Business Review*. May–June 1996, pp. 95–104.

"Management Must Set the Goals - and Example - for Plant Safety." *Engineers Digest*. March 1987, p.18.

Markiewicz, Dan. "Put It to People Plainly." *Industrial Safety and Hygiene News*. September 1997, p. 14.

National Safety Council. *14 Elements of a Successful Safety and Health Program*. Itasca, IL, 1994, 222 pp.

Personick, Martin E. "Injury and Illness Risks to Warehouse Workers." *Compensation and Working Conditions*. September 1993, pp. 1–2.

Richardson, Margaret. *Managing Worker Safety and Health for Excellence*. New York, NY: Van Nostrand Reinhold. 1997.

Sheridan, Peter J. "The Essential Elements of Safety." *Occupational Hazards*. February 1991, pp. 33–36.

Swartz, George. "Safety in Supervisors Salary Review - A Formal Approach." *Professional Safety*. May 1991, pp. 21–24.

Toft, Doug. "How to Run a Successful Safety-Incentive Program." *Safety and Health*. January 1997, pp. 62–65.

Topf, Michael D. "10 Lessons for Safety Trainers." *Occupational Hazards*. August 1997, pp. 37–40.

Yeager, Doyle L. "Integrating Safety Incentives into Your Mix of Strategies." *Industrial Safety and Hygiene News*. September 1997, p. 30.

Zeimet, Denis. "A Comprehensive Safety and Health Program for the Small Employer." *Occupational Health and Safety*. October 1997, pp. 127–33.

3

New Employee Orientation

The proper orientation of new employees is often one of the most neglected elements in a safety and health program. What better time to demonstrate the values and direction of an organization and warehouse than during the first day on the job? The turnover of many new employees occurs within the first few weeks. Some of this turnover is attributable to a lack of real interest in the new employee by the employer.

New employee orientation can set the tone for an employee's career with a company. In employee orientation, as in any relationship, first impressions count. This is the opportunity for the employer to introduce the organization to the individual in terms of its culture, values, goals, and safety practices.

The new employee's immediate supervisor should be actively involved in the orientation process that identifies activities in the warehouse. In addition, the personnel or human resources department usually plays a key role in the orientation process. There are obviously many administrative details that are important to the organization, and the new employee must know what they are.

In order to save time and effort, organizations have been known to postpone orientations until a suitable number of new employees are at hand. However, orientation is needed from the very first day. When it comes to safety issues, any delay in instructing the employee can be serious because of the potential for injury. Too often a new employee is taken to a department or specific job and told, "Watch Joe over there—he has been with us for awhile; he will tell you how to do the job." The unfortunate thing is that "Joe" may not be a safe employee. Joe might be the world's worst conveyor of safety information. Although it is admirable that Joe has been with the organization for some time and is a good worker, management must ensure that the orientation is given by an employee who places great importance on the safety of each individual.

Figure 3-1. Safety Posters can help identify the emphasis on safety. (Courtesy of the National Safety Council).

In those warehouses where there is a sound working relationship between workers and management, new employees are often given orientations by fellow employees. Facility tours are provided by safety team leaders or safety committee members. Any new employee forms opinions about the new employer. Something as basic as observing the condition of the parking lot,

35

front office, and rest rooms easily conveys management's concern for safety and housekeeping. When fellow employees become involved in safety orientation, the new employee usually walks away with a stronger feeling about warehouse safety. Figure 3-1 identifies the emphasis on safety in poster form.

SUGGESTED DISCUSSION AND TOUR TOPICS

What should a new employee be shown during a facility tour? What should be discussed with the employee? How long should the orientation last? What is considered important for the new employee to know will vary from employer to employer. Larger corporations usually have more sophisticated programs because of tradition, broad-based company programs, and their safety culture. Smaller organizations may lack the economic resources to devote a significant amount of time and effort to orientations. If there is high turnover with new employees, the employer may be reluctant to devote scarce resources to a program with a suspected poor return on investment.

In any new employee orientation, there will be of course, a discussion of wages, benefits, insurance, vacations, and work assignments for particular machines or departments. This chapter, however, will focus only on the safety orientation.

A golden opportunity exists at the time of hire to indoctrinate the new worker with safety beliefs of the organization. The following items should be considered in any new employee safety orientation:

- The organization has a history of safe workplace performance and the new employee is expected to work safely at all times.

- There is no job that is so important that it is worth risking personal injury. If in doubt, ask management or a fellow worker about safe work procedures. Employees have the right to refuse to work at an unsafe task or in an unsafe environment.

- Personal protective equipment (PPE) is required on many jobs. The worker is expected to wear prescribed PPE.

- Report any injury, no matter how slight it may appear, to the supervisor.

- Movement of powered equipment has inherent dangers. Always be on the alert for equipment.

- Obey signs, alarms, signals, and written instructions.

- Housekeeping is to be maintained at superior levels at all times. The employee is expected to keep the work area clean and assist in housekeeping in other areas or departments.

- Disciplinary action can be taken if personal safety or the safety of fellow workers is jeopardized.

- Knowing how to handle emergencies is very important. Discussion should include the guidelines for the following site emergency situations:

  - Medical care, treatment of injuries
  - What to do in event of a fire
  - What to do in event of a chemical spill
  - What to do in event of weather-related emergencies.

ADDITIONAL PROGRAM ELEMENTS

New employees should be provided with a tour of the work site before starting the job. Some employers insist that new employees be introduced to the work area as well as the job they may be performing prior to being hired. This may appear to be a waste of time, but it does have an effect on those employees that "don't know what they are getting into." There can be a cost-saving by using this prehire "tour the building first" method. It is less expensive to have an employee decide not to accept a particular job before being hired, rather than quitting after a week or two. An investment in the new employee has already taken place once he/she is hired.

Just as important is the manner in which the initial safety message is conveyed to the new employees. The tone, attitude, and sincerity (or lack of it) will be felt by the new workers. If new employees are a part of a warehouse walk-through, they will notice how fellow workers are conducting themselves. If a hard-hat rule exists and the employee has been told to wear a hard hat, it is expected that fellow workers, supervisors, and visitors will also be wearing hard hats. If there are requirements for safe forklift operations and professional driving skills, the new worker should be able to observe this. If management states one thing and allows the opposite to take place, the new worker will see this disparity of work practices.

It is an accepted part of safety programming that new workers abide by facility safety rules based on what they see and hear. If a new worker observes that fellow workers habitually break safety rules, the new worker can easily join this parade. If a supervisor talks with the new employee and never inquires about the worker's failure to wear required PPE, a big message about management commitment is being sent. On the other hand, if a new worker is reluctant to wear PPE, workers in those operations that maintain excellent safety programs will remind the new worker that the equipment is required and that he runs the risk of injury or discipline for noncompliance.

During the orientation process, management will often ask the new employee, "Do you understand?" "Are there any questions?" Surprisingly, the employee's immediate need for employment sometimes gets in the way of safety education. If the new employee has any questions, he may be too timid or embarrassed to ask them. New employees frequently seek out answers from their peers. As a result, if their peers are not safety conscious, new employees could easily fall into a pattern of unsafe practices. The employer should be wary of employees who just nod their heads in agreement every time they are asked if they understand.

There are some employers who give new employees written questionnaires to ensure that most of the orientation message has been received and retained. Questions can be general and developed in other languages if needed. If new employees, usually eager to please the employer, are told up front that they will be asked questions about safety at the completion of their orientations, they will more likely pay greater attention to detail.

An employer may wish to pose some general or specific questions to new employees during an orientation. The following list of suggestions can be modified to fit a particular program or emphasis in the warehouse:

- Who is responsible for safety in your department?

- What are the hazards that may be present in your department?

- Can you properly react if there is an emergency? (Explain)

- Are you familiar with the personal protective equipment required for your job? (Explain)

- How would you report a hazardous situation in your department?

- Explain the safety recognition program.

Some employers hire groups of workers at one time rather than individually. An orientation for a group may start with an introduction to safety and a tour of the site, followed by assembling the workers for a question and answer period. The employer may wish to pose questions to the group, requesting a show of hands in answering. To draw in reluctant participants, individuals can be asked to verify what has just been said or asked if they agree with particular statements. A worker should never be embarrassed or challenged by a question. The intent is for the employer to be assured that each member of the group has grasped many (if not all) of the safety requirements of the job. It is reasonable to assume that no employee can retain all that has been seen and heard in a safety orientation. Much of the material may be new and it may take time to learn more about the processes.

Visual aids are a key part of employee training and should be considered as an addition to safety orientation. It is unlikely that any employee would remember all of the details of one safety film, let alone information in a series of films. One general safety orientation film can go a long way in assisting new employees. The length of the film should be between ten and fifteen minutes. Many employers make the mistake of showing each new employee a series of films on such subjects as lockout/tagout, fork lift safety, PPE, bloodborne pathogens, hazard communication, and safe lifting practices. This is a mistake on management's part if the final measure of viewing the films is in the learning. There is no way that any person could absorb all of the those subjects and go into the workplace with a good grasp of all of the safety information used in the visual aids.

A word of caution regarding safety films or slide presentations that focus on gory types of injuries. An employer can be making a tactical error in using safety messages full of blood and mangled body parts. Employees may easily become frightened about the warehouse in which they will work. This is not a good way to convey information on possible warehouse hazards. Films that appeal to the logic of injury avoidance and the benefits of safe behavior for the workers and their families will provide greater dividends.

WAREHOUSE SAFETY RULES

It would be difficult to maintain any workplace without the existence of general work rules. The same holds true for safety. If safety is to be enforced as well as directed, safe-working rules are important. During the new employee process, warehouse safety rules should be discussed. At union sites, collective bargaining agreements will also help to highlight the required safety rules.

What is the best way to convey the safety rules? First, the rules should be in writing. Often, safety committees help to develop site-specific safety rules as a result of injuries or close-calls. It is recommended that a list of all of the safety rules be provided to new employees. A spoken overview of the rules can take place, but employees may begin to yawn and lose attention during this type of presentation.

An employee safety handbook that can conveniently fit into a pocket is an excellent way to make all of the safety rules available at one time. A perforated tear-out sheet at the back of the handbook is intended to be signed, dated, and provided to management by the new employee. The tear-out sheet verifies that he/she has received the facility safety rules.

A handbook may contain safety rules for many of the workplace departments or activities. It is not expected that employees will recite and memorize all of the many dozens of rules and guidelines in the booklet; the intent is to provide a convenient reference guide to assist the employee. Chapters may consist of such topics as materials handling, crane safety rules, PPE, materials storage, housekeeping, powered equipment, machine guarding, ladders, stairs and walking surfaces, medical care guidelines, safe handling of chemicals, ergonomics, lockout/tagout, and fire safety. If an employee needs to change departments or perform another job, a check of the general safety guidelines for a particular subject can be beneficial. The handbooks can also be used for departmental safety meetings.

The following general safety rules and guidelines are useful in any warehouse and should be considered for employee safeguarding. If a specific set of safety rules is needed, it can easily be pulled from the following list.

- Wear required personal protective equipment at all times. The equipment is intended for the protection of the worker.

- Observe workplace signs, labels, alarms and written workplace and manufacturers instructions.

- Safely store and stack materials. Always place larger, heavier materials on the bottom and smaller, lighter materials on the top.

- Be alert for the movement of overhead cranes, hoists, and powered industrial trucks. Stand clear of movement of any powered equipment.

- Observe no-smoking rules where posted.

- Read, understand, and abide by chemical labels on containers and material safety data sheets. If you cannot read or understand the label, contact your supervisor.

- Never tie down or make any safety device inoperative.

- Keep machine guards in place. If a guard is missing or defective, do not operate the machine—report this condition to your supervisor.

- Seek assistance if you are unsure of any operation.

- Housekeeping is to be maintained at an excellent level at all times. This includes the work area, lunchroom, rest rooms, locker rooms, and grounds around the warehouse.

- Know the location of emergency exits, fire extinguishers, first aid kits, chemical spill cleanup kits, and emergency evacuation maps.

- Sirens, loudspeakers, or alarms may be part of the warehouse emergency plan; know what these signals are and what to do when you hear them.

- When lifting from a lower level, use your arms and legs to assist in the lifting. Do not bend over at the waist to lift. If possible, use mechanical means to assist in the lifting.

- Use ladders for gaining access to product on racking or shelving; never climb on racks or shelving.

■ Observe ergonomic guidelines which are ways to arrange your work area to be safe and efficient. For example, use rubber floor mats for standing by a fixed operation; adjust the table or working surfaces for your particular height and abilities.

■ Remove personal jewelry such as rings, necklaces, and earrings while on the job. Keep long hair tied back or tuck the hair inside a hard hat for personal safety.

■ Do not operate any equipment or machine unless authorized to do so.

■ Report unsafe conditions to your supervisor. If you can safely correct the condition yourself, we encourage you to do so.

■ Use lockout/tagout procedures to achieve a zero-energy state on the equipment. Devices such as locks, tags, chains, or other hardware are to be used for personal safeguarding.

■ If handling a load being suspended by a hoist or crane, never pull a load toward yourself and never walk under a suspended load.

■ Properly secure material and powered equipment against unintended or unexpected movement.

■ Keep railings, gates, and barriers in place to prevent falls or employee injury.

■ Before operating any piece of equipment, hand tool, power tool, or machine, ensure you have been properly trained and authorized to do so.

■ Do not climb over or under conveyors; use the proper stairs, walkways, or gate openings for access.

■ Do not stack empty wooden pallets more than 6 feet high. Fire regulations restrict the height of wood pallet storage because the high stacks of pallets create a chimney effect, and a fire would be more difficult to control.

■ Use caution when walking through the warehouse. Be alert for grease, oil, nails, boards, or other hazards that may be on the floor.

■ Keep your work clothing in good repair. Never wear loose clothing near any moving machinery or equipment.

■ Never enter a trailer unless the trailer has been secured with wheel chocks or trailer restraint devices.

■ When operating powered equipment, ensure that loads being transported are secure and stable, and that you can see over the load.

■ Report each injury to the supervisor, no matter how insignificant it may seem to be.

NEW EMPLOYEE ORIENTATION CHECKLIST

It is recommended that the supervisor or safety committee member use a checklist for the new employee orientation. The purpose of a checklist is to ensure that all of the key elements in the safety orientation are provided to the employee. Figure 3-2 illustrates a typical safety orientation checklist.

Figure 3-2. New Employee Safety Orientation

Employee Name: _____

Start Date: _____   Clock Number: _____

Department or Facility: _____

Safety orientation of new employees is important to our operation. Your supervisor has been instructed to give you a brief introduction of safety that will affect your job and work area. Each item on this list must be discussed with you and your supervisor during your first day of work. Your signature at the bottom of this page will indicate that you have been given a safety orientation.

Circle "Yes" once the safety item has been covered.

Safety Item	Yes, Covered	No, Not Covered
Discussion of Facility Safety Rules	Yes	No
Reporting of All Injuries No Matter How Slight	Yes	No
Reporting of Unsafe Conditions	Yes	No
Use of Hand Tools Required for Job	Yes	No
Demonstration of Safe Way to Do Assigned Job	Yes	No
Use of Personal Protective Equipment	Yes	No
Locations and Use of Fire Extinguisher	Yes	No
Housekeeping Practices	Yes	No
Safe Method of Manual Lifting	Yes	No
Caution to be Observed on Activities Involving Power Equipment	Yes	No
Safe Handling of Flammable Liquids, Batteries, etc	Yes	No
Safety Awards and Incentives	Yes	No
Video to be Shown on Haz-Com (Right to Know) and MSDS	Yes	No
Location of Right to Know Program, MSDS	Yes	No
Lockout/Tagout Program Discussion	Yes	No
Bloodborne Pathogens Discussion	Yes	No
Emergency Evacuation Procedures	Yes	No
Emergency and First Aid Care	Yes	No
Other: _____	Yes	No
Other: _____	Yes	No

Signature of Supervisor: _____   Date: _____

Signature of Employee: _____   Date: _____

RETURN THIS FORM TO THE SAFETY DEPARTMENT OR PERSONNEL DEPARTMENT FOR FILING

This form, when properly completed, can be a useful tool to demonstrate management's focus on new employee safety during an OSHA inspection. Many times OSHA will inquire about the safety orientation; completion of the form provides documentation. In addition, any warehouse interested in the Voluntary Protection Program (VPP), which is highlighted in Chapter Two, will need a comprehensive new employee orientation program as a part of the VPP application process.

The following are guidelines for the supervisor, safety committee representative, or an other individual that may conduct the new employee orientation:

Discussion of Warehouse Safety Rules. Briefly discuss the need for warehouse safety rules. It may not be practical to cover the rules line by line, but the overall intent of many of the more important rules should be discussed. A copy of these rules should be made available to each worker. Remind the employees that safety rules are important to any organization and that OSHA requires employers to maintain safe workplaces. Posting the safety rules on a bulletin board is also helpful. If the warehouse has developed a complete listing of safety rules in a handbook, a copy of the handbook should be given to each worker. Discuss the intent of the handbook to provide safety guidelines for many of the activities in the warehouse. When the employee has a need to learn more about a specific topic, the safety handbook should be used. It is not expected that the booklet be memorized, but the employee should be familiar with the rules. Have him/her sign the tear-out sheet and give it back to management.

Reporting of Injuries. The warehouse may strive to maintain zero injuries, but it is inevitable that first-aid-type injuries will occur. Where should the employee go for treatment? Is there a nurse on staff? Should the worker go directly to the supervisor? Assure the employee that great effort is put into injury prevention and that all will be done to keep injuries from occurring.

Reporting of Unsafe Conditions. If employees are required to recognize and report unsafe conditions, then management must train the workers to recognize what is safe and what is unsafe. During this phase of the orientation, specific examples may be cited or visual aids used. An in-house slide show could be very effective in illustrating known hazards and how to control them. A video of various warehouse departments could be of great benefit for highlighting hazards.

Proper Use of Hand Tools. How to use a tool and how to safely use a tool are one in the same. Employees may be required to use nail guns, hammers, and other hand-held tools. Safe use of hand tools must be included in the orientation process. Following the manufacturers guidelines is highly recommended.

Demonstration of Safe Way To Do Assigned Job. If a new employee is experienced in warehouse operations, many of the tasks assigned will be familiar to him/her. An employee who has never worked in a warehouse will need to have "show and tell" on all of the operations. Be sure to safely demonstrate all of the requirements of the job before allowing the new or experienced worker to work on his own. Allow the employee an opportunity to show the supervisor how he will perform the task after he has been briefed. Ensure that PPE requirements are stressed as well as ergonomics, material handling, and lifting procedures. Periodically return to the new worker to check on progress.

Wearing of Personal Protective Equipment (*PPE*). Some tasks require the use of PPE. Hard hats, steel toe shoes, gloves, goggles, safety glasses, face shields, and hearing protection are typical pieces of PPE for warehouses. If an organization requires additional PPE, this is a golden opportunity to discuss this specific equipment. The reasons for wearing the equipment must be discussed so that new employees understand why this rule is being enforced. This is also a good time to hand out the gloves, hard hats, safety glasses, or any other required equipment. Many times, safety shoes are purchased prior to work (or the work shift), but a shoe-mobile or in-house shoe service center can also provide safety footwear. Chapter 15 identifies the PPE issue in-depth. This includes the OSHA requirements for workplace evaluations.

Locations and Use of Fire Extinguishers. The first line of defense in fire fighting is fire prevention. If a fire does start, employees should know how to locate and use the proper fire extinguisher. This can be demonstrated without actually having a fire to practice on. Point out where the extinguishers are, lift one off the bracket, and demonstrate how it must be used. Allow the employee to do the same thing. If the employee cannot perform this task, instruct him/her on the need for evacuation and how to call for assistance.

Housekeeping Practices. Good housekeeping has a positive effect on safety, productivity, efficiency, and worker morale. Convey to the new employee the ongoing need for high standards in housekeeping.

Safe Method of Manual Lifting. Back injuries are very common in warehouses and distribution centers, but they can be prevented through effective workplace design. Storage of product can be modified to make manual lifting safer. The need to bend over and lift product is a daily task at any location. It must be stressed to the workers that lower back injuries can be prevented by proper bending of the knees and using the legs and arms to lift. A visual demonstration may be necessary.

Proper Use of Powered Equipment. Only authorized and trained employees may operate powered industrial trucks or other powered equipment. This must be stated and understood during the orientation process. This is not the time to discuss the training program for operators. Powered equipment can be very dangerous; this point must be properly conveyed to the workers.

In addition to powered industrial trucks, there are other devices designed to move product. Overhead cranes, hoists, conveyors, and magnetic lifting devices require special training. For some employees, this may be the first time they have seen this type of equipment in operation. Special safety precautions must be discussed with employees prior to working near these jobs. Follow manufacturer guidelines.

The function of warehousing is to accept product, store it, and ship it. The movement of product is the biggest part of warehouse operations. In the process of moving and handling product, hazards can develop. Some of the material handling is inherently dangerous. This subject must be further developed during orientation.

Safe Handling of Flammables and Batteries. The warehouse may have flammables being stored or handled by powered equipment. Workers should be taught the hazards involved with flammables. A brief discussion about safe storage, no-smoking procedures, proper handling, flash point, emergency procedures, and spill cleanup is essential. If flammables are being used as part of the job, the same safety information is needed. For battery safety involving forklifts, discussion is needed on PPE, fire fighting, spill cleanup, no smoking, safe handling, and charging.

Employee Recognition Programs. What safety awards are available for the employees? Plaques, trophies, and awards should be discussed at this time. Individual recognition for safe worker performance, lunches and safety apparel are a part of many safety programs for employees.

Video on MSDS and HAZCOM (Right to Know). Since OSHA's Hazard Communication standard is the regulation cited most often, employers have to ensure it is being taught to all employees. A discussion of

HazCom, along with a video to illustrate the scope of the law, is necessary in training employees. The written program for HazCom should be discussed along with a description of material safety data sheets (MSDS). When the training is completed, employees must be shown the location of the written program and the MSDS.

Use of Lockout/Tagout Procedures. Most employees do not perform lockout/tagout duties. Maintenance personnel usually handle this process. However, all employees must be familiar with lockout/tagout so they can identify the process when they see it and know when it is required. Remind employees that this is an OSHA requirement.

Bloodborne Pathogens. A brief discussion of the OSHA requirements by for bloodborne pathogens is essential. Show employees a copy of the written program, PPE requirements, cleanup procedures, proper disposal methods, and the requirements of this particular regulation. If a nurse is available, he/she could perform these training duties.

Warehouse Emergency Procedures for Fire, Chemical Spill, Medical, and Weather. A good emergency plan covers all of the possible events that could occur in a warehouse. It is very important that new employees understand the basic procedures to follow if a fire of any size breaks out, if a chemical spill occurs in a work area, if a medical emergency arises, and if a tornado, earthquake, or any other serious weather-related emergency arises.

Other. There may be additional items to discuss with the new employee that the organization can incorporate into the orientation program, for example, safety committees and safety teams. New employees should understand the function of the safety committee, how many employees serve on the committee, how one gets selected for this task, and the relationship between a committee member and the new employee. For instance, as mentioned earlier, often new employees are escorted through the warehouse by safety committee or safety team members. Figure 3-1 can be modified to fit the needs of any warehouse, with items added or deleted to accommodate the time, effort, and peculiarities of the warehouse.

SUMMARY

The ideal time to make an impression on new employees regarding safety is when they are being hired. The orientation process should be as comprehensive as possible to allow for maximum benefit. The intent of the orientation is to have the new employee recognize the scope of the safety program. The importance and value that management places on safety in the warehouse can be easily demonstrated.

Injuries are costly, and so is the turnover of employees, incidents, and damage to product. It behooves management to make the investment in the orientation process to reduce costs. First impressions are important, and the safety message must be strong enough during the orientation process to help protect employees.

REFERENCES

Business and Legal Reports, Inc. "New Employee Orientation." March. 1992, pp. 100-1 – 100-8.

National Safety Council. *Accident Prevention Manual*. Itasca, IL, 1997.

Tyler, Kathryn. "Take New Employee Orientation Off the Back Burner." *Human Resources Magazine*. May. 1998, pp. 49–57.

4

Safe Materials Storage

Safe storage of product in warehouse operations is very important. When product is handled properly and placed securely on sturdy and safe racks, bins, or shelves, the benefits are many. The danger of product or other objects falling onto employees is minimized or eliminated through safe storage. Housekeeping becomes more effective and the overall appearance of the warehouse improves. A decrease in the number of injuries helps to lower workers' compensation costs. Potential OSHA citations for unsafe storage are minimized. Also, damage to the building, racking, and product is reduced. All of these elements combined can result in a more efficient and profitable operation.

In basic terms, it is important to safely store product the *first* time it is handled. When done properly, there is no need to rehandle product or return to reinforce overloaded shelves or racks. Time is money and time can be saved by doing it right—the first time.

This chapter will focus on pallet safety, storage, rack safety, and mezzanine safety. Manufacturers of pallets, racks, and storage containers can offer much expertise in this area and should be contacted for assistance. All design and construction specifications are to be handled by a qualified engineer.

PALLET SAFETY

In a typical warehouse or distribution center, some 75 percent or more of available space is devoted to storage. Many of the loads are palletized. Various pieces of product, such as sacks, drums, metal rods, pipes, and boxes, are stacked onto pallets. Pallets are then placed on racks or shelving for storage until needed at a later time.

The load characteristics for pallet storage have two separate components:

Size. A typical pallet storage system can accommodate many different pallet sizes. The width of the pallet as well as the depth, along with load height, can differ significantly from one location to another.

Stackability. This is expressed by the number of pallets that can be safely stacked on top of each other without damaging product. Stackability depends on the size and shape of product on a pallet. For small warehouses without racking, placing single pallets on the floor without stacking may function well. When

45

product on the pallets is uniform and sturdy, pallets may be safely stacked on top of each other. Metal or plastic banding or shrink wrap help provide the extra margin of safety in securing product when handling or stacking pallets. Full pallets stacked two high may be safe, but when stacked three high or greater, the entire stack can easily topple over.

In addition, the friction surface between the type of pallet being stored and the racking surface must be evaluated for safety. As an example, wooden pallets appear to provide a better surface for traction than compressed wood pallets. This should be considered when purchasing specific pallets.

For any warehouse operation, the maintenance of pallet quality is essential. After all, most product cannot be moved unless it is on a pallet. To assist the reader in determining safety and quality issues, Figure 4-1 is a ten-point checklist for pallet quality established by the U. S. Postal Service.

The items on the checklist in Figure 4-1 were designed to help field inspectors determine whether a pallet needs to be repaired or discarded. If any of these conditions are present, the pallet is taken out of service. The checklist items apply to plastic or pressed wood pallets. Figure 4-2 identifies a defective pallet in storage.

Figure 4-1. U. S. Postal Service Ten Point Visual Checklist for Pallets

Plastic or Pressed Wood Pallets	Yes	No
Is any corner leg of a pallet broken in such a way that the leg cannot rest on a level surface?	☐	☐
Is any corner leg missing?	☐	☐
Is any center leg broken so that leg cannot rest on a level surface.	☐	☐
Are any two support legs broken so that the legs cannot rest on a level surface?	☐	☐
Are any two support legs missing?	☐	☐
Is over 25 percent of the pallet deck deformed such that this deformation is greater than one-half inch below the normal surface of the pallet?	☐	☐
Is any crack in the pallet 10 inches or longer that extends through the center of the pallet? (Note: this applies to structural foam plastic and twin-sheet thermoform pallets only.)	☐	☐
Is any crack 6 inches or longer that extends through the center of the pallet? (Note: this applies to presswood fiber pallets only.)	☐	☐
Is any hole in the pallet deck greater than the surface area of the opening in the pallet deck for a leg?	☐	☐
Is there any pallet deck deformation that includes cracks and holes along pallet edges of 3 inches or more into a leg assembly on pallet surface?	☐	☐

Figure 4-2. Departmental inspections should focus on the condition of pallets in addition to the regular items found in a warehouse. This damaged pallet must be removed.

The risk of fire must be a major consideration in product storage. Idle pallet storage introduces a severe fire condition that is incidental to most storage practices. Wooden pallets and certain solid plastic pallets should be stored no higher than six feet while indoors. Check the local fire regulations or ask for assistance from the insurance carrier to determine pallet storage requirements both inside and outside the warehouse.

ENVIRONMENTAL CONSIDERATIONS FOR PALLETS

An article in the *Wall Street Journal* stated that there are 1.5 billion pallets in the U.S., six for every resident. About 40 percent of domestic hardwood lumber goes into pallets. Production of pallets has climbed to 400 million per year. As a result of space problems, about one-third of all landfills will not accept pallets and other organizations charge fees for recycling pallets. It is estimated that more than 1 million forest acres are cleared every year for pallets. It should be noted that pallets are recyclable and, if kept in good repair, a pallet can serve as a long-term investment for product storage and handling.

RACKING

With regard to racking for materials storage, the safe working loads, widths, heights, equipment clearances, and equipment used should be determined by the designers and manufacturers of the systems. Since 75–80 percent of all warehouse space is devoted to storage, it is apparent that racking will occupy most of the floor space.

Figure 4-3 illustrates a safety checklist that can be used to inspect warehouse racking.

Figure 4-3. Safety Checklist - Warehouse Racking

SAFETY ISSUE	Yes	No
Has the racking been installed according to manufacturer specifications, guidelines, and instructions?	☐	☐
Has the racking been erected on sound, level floors?	☐	☐
Is the concrete/slab thick enough for anticipated loads?	☐	☐
If the racking is attached to the building, has an engineer approved the calculations?	☐	☐
Is the racking secured to the floor?	☐	☐
Have protective barriers been installed to prevent rack damage?	☐	☐
Are all protective barriers or posts securely mounted?	☐	☐
Has the proper material handling equipment been selected for the racking design?	☐	☐
Is there any physical damage to the racking?	☐	☐
Are there any missing pieces of racking?	☐	☐
Are the correct type of pallets being used?	☐	☐
Are the correct capacity/load limit signs in place?	☐	☐
Are the aisles wide enough to accommodate powered equipment?	☐	☐
Are double-sided runs connected and spaced using appropriate run spacers?	☐	☐
Are the connector locks securely fixed at both ends of the beam?	☐	☐
Is the height-to-depth ratio of the racking known?	☐	☐
Are any welds cracked or rusty?	☐	☐
Have powered equipment operators been trained on how to prevent racking damage?	☐	☐
Do personnel removing and replacing damaged racking know the safe method for this project?	☐	☐
Has the manufacturer been contacted regarding modifications, changes, or load requirements?	☐	☐
Are tunnels of the proper size to accommodate powered equipment?	☐	☐
Are cross members at tunnels or low clearance identified with black and yellow stripes?	☐	☐
Is heavy-duty mesh or double palleting used at tunnels?	☐	☐
Is metal or plastic strapping/banding being used to secure pallets in tunnels?	☐	☐
Do the base legs of posts show any sign of deterioration?	☐	☐

There are some very important items to be considered regarding product storage and racking:

■ Before moving beam levels, always consult with the manufacturer; correspondence should be in writing.

■ First-level cross beams should be low enough so that a stand-up (narrow-aisle) lift truck cannot drive under the racking.

■ Racking must be stable, especially where high racking is required.

■ Follow manufacturer guidelines for installation, repair, replacement, use, and capacity.

■ Ensure that the floor itself is thick enough to carry the loads being placed there. An engineer knowledgeable in this subject must be consulted.

■ Any damaged component reduces safety. The degree of risk depends on the damaged component and the extent of the damage.

■ If aisles are too narrow or if the incorrect powered equipment is being used, severe damage to the racking can easily occur.

■ Allow for spacing between back-to-back racks. If the racks are too close, a pallet being deposited in place could easily push a pallet into an aisle from the other side. This falling pallet and load could cause serious injury.

■ Tunnels in the racking should be wide enough and high enough for powered trucks. To help avoid rack damage from powered equipment and loads, the bars at the top of the tunnel should be striped with yellow and black tape. Place an additional pallet under existing pallets or add heavy-duty mesh to protect workers from falling objects while in a tunnel.

■ Keep racking clear of sprinklers and heaters. Product stored on racks should never interfere with sprinkler heights, (allow 3 feet of clearance), or heaters. Spontaneous combustion could take place and develop into a fire if product is too close to a heater.

■ Install protective posts or barriers at the ends of aisles and tunnel entrances to protect racking, as illustrated in Figure 4-4. Properly anchor the barriers to the floor. Highway-style barriers can be placed in strategic locations to protect racking, product storage, and the building.

Figure 4-4. Protective corner posts help protect racking and product.

- Do not overload bins so that the loads sag or bulge during storage.

- Horizontal air spaces created by the storage pallets significantly increase the spread of fire within a stacked pile, because they are out of reach of water from sprinklers. Prevention of fires is essential in warehouse operations.

- In earthquake-prone areas, racking must be provided with extra security to prevent it from toppling. Building columns provide for stability. Check with an engineer for guidance on how and where to anchor to the building.

- For the additional cost, which is minimal in most cases when projecting the long-term benefits, heavier racking should be purchased. Over-protecting can be advantageous in many ways; the racking is less likely to be damaged and safer storage is achieved. Heavier racking can provide long-term easier care and greater stability. The extra cost is a wise investment.

- Prohibit overloading of any pallet positions and of the overall racking system.

- Repair or replace defective racking immediately. Safely unload product and empty the damaged racking until repairs can be made. This will help prevent any collapse or stop product from falling. Consult a professional before repairing racking. Ensure employees and property are protected during repairs and replacement.

- It is important to maintain pallets in good, serviceable condition; this helps in preventing rack damage.

- Professionals can evaluate current racking systems and provide upgrades and improvements to allow for increased and safer storage.

- A job hazard analysis should be prepared by management and employees on the subjects of racking installation, racking repair, and racking disassembly.

- Add wire mesh, nylon webbing, or solid wall barriers, such as plywood, at the ends of racking to prevent small parts from falling to a lower level and striking someone.

- Operating aisles must be wide enough to accommodate the load and power equipment. When establishing aisles in warehouses, always allow enough space for the movement of powered equipment. If racking-to-wall clearances are too tight, the racking will always be vulnerable to damage from lift trucks. It is also advisable to select your powered equipment based on capacity as well as vehicle size.

- Most of the damage to racking is at the lower levels. As a result, the probability of collapse is increased. Any damage to racking components will reduce its load-carrying capacity. Damage will progressively weaken the structure and it may eventually collapse. Inspect racking on a regular basis and replace defective components.

Additional information on racking

Lift truck operators and supervisors may presume that a large safety factor has been built into racking by the manufacturer to allow for abuse. The manufacturers *do* provide a safety factor, but this assumes that all components are free from damage. In addition, this safety factor can be reduced when the installation has been altered from its original design. It is important to prevent racking damage and to correct defective racking as soon as possible. Powered equipment operators and supervisors should be thoroughly briefed on the need for safe racking.

There may be racking components in the facility that were damaged months or years ago. But, no one is sure when the racking will sag, break or collapse. Photos 4-5 and 4-6 identify racking damage caused by forklifts.

Figure 4-5. This leg of a racking section was damaged by the forks of a lift truck. The entire piece will have to be replaced.

Figure 4-6. When an operator fails to lower the mast on the forklift, damage like this can occur.

Safety locks on racking beams are intended to hold the beam above a pallet load to keep it from being lifted vertically and dislodged by the load below. Pallets can easily fall from racking if the safety locks are not fitted. It is highly likely that two or three pallets will fall as a result of this oversight.

Powered-equipment-operator training must include information on:

- How to operate power equipment in close clearance areas.

- What is needed to allow for safe clearance to avoid rack and product damage.

- The consequences of damaged racking

- Reporting damaged or unsafe racking

- The associated costs accompanying damage.

Slides, videotape, or photos of racking damage provide for improved operator training awareness. In some cases, the individuals responsible for damage to racking are the same ones that have to remove, replace, and correct the problem. This extra work also provides an opportunity for increased injuries to those involved.

When pallets, loads, ladders, roll cages, and other powered equipment are located in aisleways, it is not unusual for rack damage to occur. This damage is the result of improper clearance between the equipment, racking, and the object. These collisions can also cause racking collapse or lead to future collapse.

Housekeeping practices are also essential to racking safety. Notice the excellent housekeeping and neat storage in Figure 4-7. As a contrast, an incident was reported in which improper housekeeping was responsible for serious racking damage. A wire-guided forklift truck was sent off course because some shrink wrap was left lying in the trucking aisle. The plastic wrap was covering the .wire contact in the floor. When the lift truck went over this area, the operator lost control and the lift truck careened into the racking. No one was reported injured in this costly incident.

Figure 4-7. These materials are stored neatly and safety.

MEZZANINE SAFETY

Many warehouses are equipped with single- or multi-storied mezzanines. Small parts or highly valued product is usually stored on a mezzanine. There are some basic safeguards to follow for mezzanine safety and the handling of the product stored there:

- The design and construction of the mezzanine must be checked by an engineer to ensure safety from collapse and fire. Floor and load capacity limits are to be displayed through proper signage.

- Access to mezzanine levels should utilize stairways designed to OSHA specifications. Stairs should be nonskid and properly anchored. Handrails and tread nosings should be nonskid and highlighted with yellow paint.

Figure 4-8. Where electric lifts move product to and from a mezzanine, be sure the device is inspected on a regular basis and that all safeguards are in place.

- If a mechanical vertical lift is used, it must be properly inspected and certified according to local codes. A no-riders rule must exist for this device. Proper security railings, alarms, power disconnects, warning signs such as that in Figure 4-8, and the ability to lockout the lift are necessary.

Figure 4-9. This mezzanine gate is powered by a motor from a garage door opener. The openers for the gate are mounted on the lift truck.

- Railings on the mezzanine levels must be designed so that a worker cannot fall to a lower level. It is very common to move or open a handrail for a pallet being deposited by a lift truck. When the pallet is unloaded, the protective railing may not be closed. Automatic closing of handrails can be devised for employee safety. Figure 4-9 shows a moveable gate on a mezzanine.

- Place fire extinguishers at certain specific access points on the mezzanine. Identify the locations with the correct signage.

■ The wearing of personal protective equipment should be required as needed while working on a mezzanine.

■ Ensure that proper lighting is available. Emergency lighting may also be needed at stairways and other key areas.

■ Properly identify exits and install proper signage to identify workplace hazards.

■ Never use any powered equipment on a mezzanine unless an engineer authorizes this practice. Floor capacity is a serious consideration on mezzanines.

■ Place plastic sleeves or mesh covers over low-hanging fluorescent lights. If the bulbs are not protected against impact, they could easily shatter if struck.

■ Include life safety in all the planning; mezzanines are to be listed on emergency maps and evacuation procedures.

■ Mezzanines should be a no-smoking zone, along with all other departments in the warehouse.

■ If chemicals are stored on the mezzanine, keep emergency cleanup materials and first aid supplies available.

■ Place the proper National Fire Protection Association (NFPA) or Hazardous Materials Identification System (HMIS) label on any stored chemicals.

■ Keep materials away from sprinkler heads. Allow for 3 feet of clearance.

■ For safe lifting, keep heavier materials stored at knee-to-shoulder heights. Portable rolling ladders should be used if access to shelving is needed.

■ Cover sharp edges of corner posts with plastic caps or barriers to help prevent injury.

■ Housekeeping practices are to be maintained at an excellent level.

Figure 4-10 illustrates a striped crossbar placed in front of this lower mezzanine entrance. The bar is a warning to lift truck drivers to stay away from under the mezzanine.

SUMMARY

The safe storage of materials in warehouses and distribution centers involves numerous elements of control. Operators of powered equipment must be trained to respect product and places of storage. Damage to containers, shelving, and racking must be prevented. Product and structural damage exposes workers to hazards associated with racking collapse. The need for fire prevention is essential in materials storage.

Safe racking starts with the manufacturer's product. Layout of warehouse racking as well as proper capacity, height of racking, and style should be determined by the experts. It is highly recommended that racking be purchased for maximum-rated capacities. The extra money spent up front for heavy-duty racking will pay dividends in the future.

Figure 4-10. This additional racking bar with striped tape on it helps to prevent powered equipment from driving into the lower mezzanine area.

REFERENCES

Auguston, Karen. "What You Can Do to Improve Pallet Quality." *Modern Materials Handling*. August. 1996, pp. 34–37.

Beck, Larry. "How to Design Containers for Safety." *Modern Materials Handling*. December. 1985, pp. 70–71.

Beck, Larry. "Reducing Personal Injuries in Storage Operations." *Modern Materials Handling*. January 1988, pp. 76–78.

Bhardwaj, S.M. *The Pallet Storage System Selection Process*. Oak Brook, IL: Warehousing Education and Research Council. 1990.

Brown, Martin M. "General Indoor Storage." National Fire Protection Association. *Fire Protection Handbook*. Seventeenth Edition, pp. 8-33 – 8-51.

Guiher, William T. "Designing Rack Systems." *Plant Engineering*. September 1997, pp. 120–124.

Hunt, Keith. "Rack and Opinion." *Occupational Safety and Health*. Vol. 23, No. 6, pp. 20–26.

Hunt, Keith. "Racked Against the Odds." *WRAP*. August 1993, pp. 9–10.

"Keeping Well? Dexcons Rules for Safe Storage Systems." *Occupational Safety and Health*. Vol. 26, N012, pp. 13–18, 20–21.

Machalaba, Daniel. "As Old Pallets Pile Up, Critics Hammer Them As a New Eco-Menace." *The Wall Street Journal*. April 1, 1998, p. 1.

Material Handling Engineering. "Metal-Wood Shelving Gets Its Own Standard." August 1997, pp. 59–61.

National Safety Council. "Storage of Specific Materials." Itasca, IL: *Eleventh Edition Accident Prevention Manual*. 1977, pp. 389–396.

Pinel, Phillip. "Is Your Racking Safe?" *The Safety and Health Practitioner*. September 1996, pp. 28–31.

Racking Up Support. Oak Brook, IL: Warehousing Education and Research Council. September 1997, p. 13.

5

Fire Safety

Of primary importance in any warehouse is the subject of fire safety. Fire can be destructive not only to human life, but to the building, contents, and surrounding structures. Every safety program needs a plan to prevent fires as well as a program to fight fires. This chapter will focus on fire statistics, fire losses in warehouses, understanding fire and fire extinguishers, sprinkler systems, flammable liquids, the hazards of aerosol storage, and fires in racking storage.

FIRE STATISTICS

The data below provide strong evidence that fires are destructive and costly.

■ In 1996 approximately 1,975,000 fires in the United States caused an estimated $9.4 billion in property loss.

■ 87,150 firefighters were injured in the line of duty in 1996. An estimated 4,200 had to be hospitalized for their injuries. A breakdown of these major injuries included:

- Sprains, strains, and muscle pain   38.2%

- Cuts, bleeding wounds, and bruises   19.2%

- Smoke or gas inhalation   10.2%

- Burns   9.5%

■ Firefighters were also injured in 14,200 incidents, responding to or returning from fires.

■ The National Fire Protection Association (NFPA) estimates that in 1996 some 19,600 fire fighters were exposed to infectious diseases.

■ The costliest fire in 1996 occurred at a warehouse in Louisiana. The property loss in direct dollars was $280 million..

■ The Bureau of Labor Statistics (BLS) indicates that more than 700 lives are lost each year in the workplace from fire, explosions, and chemical spills or releases.

- The National Safety Council has estimated that emergencies and incidents cost some $121 billion annually.

According to a ten-year study by Factory Mutual, fires occurring during building construction and maintenance were caused by the following:

- Electrical causes   23%

- Smoking   18%

- Friction   10%

- Overheated materials   8%

- Hot surfaces   7%

- Burner flames   7%

- Combustion sparks   5%

- Spontaneous ignition   4%

- Cutting and welding   4%

WAREHOUSE FIRES

Fires in warehouses are not uncommon. Many of these fires are very serious, some resulting in loss of life and millions of dollars property and product damage. The following summaries of significant warehouse fires reinforce the importance of taking safety and fire prevention seriously. Summaries of significant warehouse fires are presented below:

- On March 10, 1997, in South Brunswick, New Jersey, a small fire in a warehouse belonging to the nation's largest records storage company was quickly controlled. A week later, this same organization had a much more serious fire in another company warehouse only a few hundred feet from the initial building. In this fire, over 250,000 boxes of records were destroyed or damaged. Two days later the first warehouse erupted again, with the fire destroying more than 800,000 boxes of records.

- A 72-foot-high warehouse, covering some 1,134,770 square feet, which was used for general storage, was destroyed in Louisiana. Two fires in nine hours took place. After the first fire, the sprinkler system was shut down. When the second fire began, the employees tried to turn the sprinklers back on, but the sprinklers could not control the tremendous blaze. Factors contributing to this $280 million loss were reported to be excessive clearance between ceiling sprinklers and the top of storage racks, the lack of in-rack sprinklers in the area where the fire originated, and no fire separation walls in the warehouse. Shutting down the sprinkler systems as well as restoring electrical power without evaluating the damage to the electrical systems also added to the loss.

- On Chicago's southwest side, more than 200 firefighters battled a blaze in an eight-story warehouse that covered one square city block. An adjacent warehouse full of flammable liquids was prevented from being ignited by this same fire. Additional businesses and nearby homes were sprayed with thousands of gallons of water per minute to keep the fire from spreading. The destroyed warehouse had contained dry goods, packing materials, and cardboard. All of this material burned very quickly. Workers in the building reported that a propane tank on the fourth floor blew up. The ruins of the building smoldered for days.

- Mattresses in a 30-foot-high warehouse in Kansas became the cause of a fire because they were stored too close to a mercury vapor light. When the mattresses ignited, the fire activated the heat-detection system and wet-pipe sprinkler system. Firefighters used two 1 ¾-inch fire hoses to combat the fire, which was brought under control after one hour. Damage to the structure and contents totaled $605,000.

- An 85,000-square-foot, 26-foot-high building supply store and warehouse in Georgia experienced a $9 million fire loss on April 16, 1996. A fire of undetermined causes began in the pool-chemical aisle and grew rapidly. Handheld fire extinguishers were used but could not control the blaze. It was found that oxidizers on racks were stacked higher and deeper than retail storage limits allow. There were no in-rack sprinklers in the area where the oxidizers were stored. The sprinklers were designed to discharge densities of water per areas of operation below that of current NFPA recommendations for oxidizer storage. There were no solid noncombustible vertical barriers between oxidizers and incompatible materials to help stop the fire.

- A one-story general-storage warehouse in New Jersey had a $84.5 million fire loss on January 10, 1996. The sprinkler system had been damaged two days earlier when the roof collapsed under the weight of snow. The roof on this 225,000-square-foot building was being repaired at the time. A cinder-block wall, which subdivided the building, had collapsed during the fire, contributing to the loss.

- At a 200,000-square-foot warehouse in Nebraska, radiant heat from a gas-fueled heater ignited wooden crates that were covered with cardboard. The building did not contain an automatic detection or suppression system. Total dollar loss was $10 million. One firefighter was injured fighting the fire.

- A fire in the third floor of a paper-storage warehouse in Illinois resulted in a $50 million loss. The building did not contain an automatic detection system, but it did have an automatic sprinkler system. Two firefighters were injured fighting the fire.

- A two-story general-storage warehouse for a mail-order company in Indiana experienced a $10 million fire on October 8, 1996. The fire started in a second-story supply room. The detection system on the second floor had been disconnected several years earlier. Sprinklers on the first level and in an adjacent structure activated but could not control the fire.

- In California, a waterfront warehouse was destroyed as a result of a fuel leak from a nearby car being repaired. The mechanic had jacked up the car to repair the leak and loosened two bands that held the fuel tank. While 20 feet away from the car, he noticed that the underside of the car was on fire. The broken bulb of his trouble light had ignited the gasoline. He alerted individuals in the warehouse who were evacuated. Total loss to the building and contents was $2,550,000.

UNDERSTANDING FIRE AND FIRE EXTINGUISHERS

In order to fully grasp the principles of fire safety, it is worthwhile to review fire basics. In fact, materials from this chapter can be directly inserted into a warehouse employee safety training program.

Fires are alike in many ways, yet different enough to require different fire-fighting techniques. Fire is one of the most destructive forces in nature and can level a building in a very short time. For those who have unfortunately been burned by a fire, the agony caused by burns can be the most painful of human experiences.

Fire needs four essential elements to start: oxygen, fuel, spark/ignition source, and a chemical chain reaction. The oxygen is available in the air we breathe, but oxygen can sustain a fire in concentrations as low as 15 percent (oxygen to air), lower than the typical 19.5 to 21 percent in air. A 10 percent concentration of oxygen would be necessary to suppress a fire. Also, heavy concentrations of oxygen can accelerate a fire.

The ignition source of a fire can be an open flame, sparks, excessive heat, or friction. Smoking, for example, is one of the main contributors of fires at work and at home. For industrial fires, this source of ignition accounts for 18 percent of all causes.

Sources of fuel for a fire are many. Warehouses are full of various products and chemicals that can easily provide a fire source. In fact, if not properly segregated and safeguarded, products that have caught fire may actually combine to make successful fire fighting more difficult. As an example, a sprinkler-equipped warehouse in the northeast experienced a devastating fire that was caused by a forklift striking and dropping cans of aerosols. The vapors from the leaking cans were ignited by the forklift. The fire was spread to adjacent areas by the burning aerosol cans being hurtled through the air. The intensity of the fire buckled the sprinkler system, causing it to be ineffective. Additional cans of flammables and butane lighters stored in other parts of the racking began to ignite—a great concern to everyone. The losses from the fire exceeded $100 million.

An estimated 1.8 million gallons of water were pumped onto the fire during the first day. The fire department was at the scene for seven days, putting out spot fires.

An analysis of the warehouse inventory records revealed that, at the time of the fire, the warehouse contained massive amounts of high-hazard materials including:

- 580,000 cans of petroleum-based aerosols

- 480,000 cans of alcohol-based aerosols

- 47,000 gallons of other flammable liquids in nonpressurized containers

- 101,700 gallons of combustible liquids in nonpressurized containers

- 19,000 cans of butane lighter fluid

- 109,000 disposable butane lighters

- 42,000 propane cylinders

- thousands of rubber tires.

It's obvious that sprinkler systems must be designed to match the hazards they are expected to protect. Ordinary warehouses pose a severe enough challenge for sprinklers without the added challenge of high-hazard commodities such as flammable aerosols.

Fire Extinguishers

Extinguishing a fire in a warehouse can be accomplished by fixed sprinkler systems, fire suppressant systems, or fire extinguishers. The chart in Table 5-1 identifies the fire classifications as well as means of extinguishing.

Table 5-1. Types of Fires and Means of Extinguishing

Class of Fire	Extinguisher to Use	Nature of Fire	Extinguisher Contents
A	Class A fires are in wood, paper, cloth, rags, plastics or rubber. Class A fires have hot embers and must be cooled by water to absorb the heat. The fire must be stirred around after extinguishing to ensure all the embers have been extinguished.	Class A fire extinguishers have a numerical rating such as 1-A, 2-A, etc. The higher the number, the larger the fire which can be extinguished. As an example, a 2-1 Unit can handle a fire twice as large as a 1-A unit. This unit must never be used on a flammable liquid or electrical fire.	These units may contain water, water-base foam, loaded stream, or can be a multi-purpose dry chemical. Travel distances to the extinguisher must not exceed 75 feet.
B	Class B fires are associated with flammable liquids such as oil, gasoline, solvents, and alcohols. In addition, flammable gases, greases, and some rubber and plastics are also in this classification.	Class B fire extinguisher ratings identify how many square feet the extinguisher can handle. As an example a 5-BC rated unit should be able to handle a five square-foot area.	Class B units can contain carbon dioxide gas, Halon 1211, Halon 1301, or dry chemicals such as sodium bicarbonate. Travel distances to these units must be no more than 50 feet.
C	Class C fires are predominately in live electrical systems.	Class C extinguishers use the same pattern for rating fire fighting as those for A or B types of fires.	Class C extinguishers may be carbon dioxide units, Halon 1211 or 1301 units, or dry chemicals such as sodium bicarbonate.
D	These fires involve combustible metals such as lithium, titanium, magnesium, sodium, zirconium, and potassium.	Class D firefighting equipment is not classified by a numerical system, and is intended for special hazard protection only.	Because combustible metal powders, flakes, or shavings can ignite, shovels full of the firefighting agents must be dumped onto the smoldering fire. Water must never be used. These firefighting agents should be as close to the source of combustion as possible.

Extinguishers marked ABC can be used on any A, B, or C class of fire.

A typical fire extinguisher has a duration of discharge for only ten to eighteen seconds. Figure 5-1 serves as a reminder that knowing where an extinguisher is and how to use it are important.

A National Association of Fire Equipment Distributors survey completed in 1996 found that portable fire extinguishers put out 95.3 percent of the fires as reported on the survey.

Tips to follow for fire extinguisher safety in warehouses include the following:

Figure 5-1. Know where extinguishers are and how to use them. (Courtesy of the National Safety Council)

■ OSHA requires that all fire extinguishers must be accepted, certified, labeled, or listed by a nationally recognized testing laboratory.

■ Employers must select fire extinguishers that are appropriate for their workplace hazards.

■ Place fire extinguishers in locations that provide for easy accessibility.

■ Be sure extinguishers are visible and identified with the appropriate sign.

■ Keep fire-fighting materials free from pallets, stock, powered equipment, and structures. Mount units on a bracket at doorway entrances and in areas where they will not be damaged.

■ Place appropriate classes of extinguishers on mezzanines and other raised structures or floors for use in an emergency.

■ Place an ABC or BC unit on powered industrial trucks that travel away from the building or into areas where fixed extinguishers are not readily available.

■ During each daily inspection, check extinguishers mounted on powered equipment. Each fire extinguisher should be inspected on a monthly basis. Figure 5-2 has been provided for this purpose.

■ Wipe off extinguishers during daily, weekly, or monthly warehouse inspections. In addition, check that the seal, pin, and gauge are in place, and properly mark the inspection date and initial on the tag.

■ When units need recharging, a substitute extinguisher must be placed on the bracket.

■ Remove any extinguisher from use that has been damaged or is not full.

■ Extinguishers must be periodically tested hydrostatically by professionals to ensure that the shell is intact. OSHA requires that the following testing intervals be adhered to:

Figure 5-2. Monthly Extinguisher Inspection Record

Location: _____

Date: _____   Inspector: _____

Fire Ext. No.	Location	Type	Full	Sealed	Comments

Fire Extinguisher Type Test Interval

Stored pressure water and/or antifreeze	5 years
Foam	5 years
Aqueous film forming foam (AFFF)	5 years
Carbon dioxide	5 years
Dry chemical with stainless steel shells	5 years
Dry chemical—stored pressure	12 years
Dry chemical—cartridge (Ansul type)	12 years
Halon 1211	12 years
Halon 1301	12 years

■ Water extinguishers must be hung in areas where they will not freeze.

■ Employees expected or anticipated to use fire extinguishers must be instructed on the hazards of fire fighting. They must also know how to properly discharge a fire extinguisher. In addition, procedures on what to do in event of an emergency must be known by all employees.

■ Be sure fire fighting and extinguisher use are a part of the total warehouse emergency plan. Hands-on training with extinguishers is an important part of safety training. This training should involve all of the employees in a facility, including office staff and supervisors.

■ When employees are being instructed on fire-extinguisher safety, a few simple rules will help them to remember the appropriate extinguisher to use.

  • Class A extinguishers are identified with the letter "A" inside a green triangle.

  • Class B extinguishers are identified with the letter "B" inside a red square.

  • Class C extinguishers are identified with the letter "C" inside a blue circle.

  • Class D extinguishers are identified with the letter "D" inside a yellow star.

■ When contractors are on warehouse property, it is important to maintain fire safety. Portable fire extinguishers should be taken onto the roof or to any other areas where work is being performed. Everyone within the building should know that contractors are in the building and prepare for any unusual circumstances.

■ During inspection, be sure that the correct class of extinguisher is properly located next to the hazard it is intended to control. Figure 5-3 represents a fire inspection checklist.

■ When fire extinguishers are not handled or moved for a period of time, the contents may settle, cake, and become solid. As a result, when the extinguisher is discharged, all of the powder may not be used. Professionals should properly loosen powder in extinguishers during servicing.

Figure 5-3. Fire Prevention Inspection Checklist

Warehouse: _____ Inspector: _____ Date: _____

SPRINKLERS	Yes	No	N/A
Are any sprinkler heads disconnected?	☐	☐	☐
Are any new sprinkler heads needed?	☐	☐	☐
Are sprinkler heads clear or stored product?	☐	☐	☐
Do sprinkler heads have at least 18"of clearance?	☐	☐	☐
Water pressure in pounds at the riser	☐	☐	☐
Any problems with potential freezing of sprinkler pipes?	☐	☐	☐
Have sprinkler alarms been tested?	☐	☐	☐
Are extra sprinkler heads available?	☐	☐	☐
WATER SUPPLY			
Was the fire pump activated to check serviceability?	☐	☐	☐
Is the water pump in good condition?	☐	☐	☐
Was the fire pump tested for churn ☐ rated ☐ overload ☐			
Was the automatic control tested?	☐	☐	☐
If applicable, was the fuel tank full?	☐	☐	☐
Is the pump room properly heated?	☐	☐	☐
Is there a water tank or reservoir?	☐	☐	☐
Is the tank/reservoir full?	☐	☐	☐
Is the heating system in service?	☐	☐	☐
Is the temperature on the cold water return 42° minimum?	☐	☐	☐
Is circulation adequate?	☐	☐	☐
EXTINGUISHERS AND HOSES			
Are extinguishers fully charged?	☐	☐	☐
Are any extinguishers missing?	☐	☐	☐
Are all extinguishers accessible?	☐	☐	☐
Are pins, seals, and tags in place?	☐	☐	☐
Are inside hoses in good condition?	☐	☐	☐
Are hoses accessible?	☐	☐	☐
Overall condition of yard hydrants?	☐	☐	☐

OCCUPANCY CONDITIONS	Yes	No	N/A
Are approved safety cans used for handling flammables?	☐	☐	☐
Are no-smoking regulations being observed?	☐	☐	☐
Are flammables safely stored and controlled?	☐	☐	☐
Is overall housekeeping in good or excellent condition?	☐	☐	☐
Are electrical panel boxes clear of product?	☐	☐	☐
Are waste receptacles emptied on a regular basis?	☐	☐	☐
Are any fire doors nonfunctional?	☐	☐	☐
Are any fire doors obstructed?	☐	☐	☐
Are empty wooden pallets stacked at 6' heights or less?	☐	☐	☐
Are combustible waste materials removed on a regular basis?	☐	☐	☐
Is overall neatness (housekeeping) in order?	☐	☐	☐
Is there any evidence of exposed wiring or electrical hazards?	☐	☐	☐
Are combustibles clear of heat lamps, lighting, or other hot surfaces?	☐	☐	☐
Does any welding or cutting take place in the warehouse?	☐	☐	☐
Are proper precautions taken as welding or cutting is used?	☐	☐	☐
Is there any roof overloading as a result of snow or ice?	☐	☐	☐
Is the roof in need of repair?	☐	☐	☐
Are aisleways clear?	☐	☐	☐
Are exits properly identified?	☐	☐	☐
Are emergency lights functional?	☐	☐	☐

COMMENTS:

_____

_____

_____

_____

_____

SPRINKLER SYSTEMS

Automatic sprinklers have been proven to be the most reliable form of fixed fire protection since their inception 100 years ago. This favorable record allows employers the opportunity to purchase fire insurance at reduced rates if they install sprinklers. Automatic sprinklers are needed anywhere there is a combustible occupancy and where combustible building materials are used.

The effectiveness of warehouse sprinklers was demonstrated during a February 1998 fire in Lilburn, Georgia. The original warehouse was constructed of brick in 1960 and was fully protected by a sprinkler system. At a later date, a second section was added to the building and was constructed of brick and concrete block. The new section of the warehouse, some 45,000 feet, was not sprinkler equipped.

A fire started in the new section of the warehouse, apparently by a forklift battery charger. The product stored in the building were rolls of plastic material used to stripe streets and parking lots. The fire devastated the building, warping structural steel and collapsing brick and concrete walls, until it reached the sprinklered portion.

When the concrete-block fire wall between the two building sections collapsed, the sprinkler system, now nearly forty years old, was triggered. Fifteen sprinkler heads created a water curtain that protected the structure until firefighters arrived. The loss to the unprotected part of the warehouse totaled $1.2 million.

The advantages of sprinkler systems include the following:

- Sprinklers are automatic and begin operating in the early stages of a fire. Small fires are much easier to extinguish than larger fires.

- Because they are automatic, sprinkler systems activate at anytime during the day or night. The fire alarm system can trigger an immediate electronic notification of the fire department or a central monitoring station. Thus a fire in a facility equipped in this way, even when unattended, can be reported to authorities more quickly than by waiting for someone to report the fire by telephone.

- Sprinklers use less water than that from firefighters' hoses.

- Economic loss due to product and building damage in a sprinkler-equipped building is usually limited when a fire occurs.

- Water from sprinkler heads is applied directly onto a fire.

- Sprinklers can be designed for use with almost any stored product or hazard.

- Sprinklers ideally eliminate the risk to firefighters when they have to enter a highly hazardous area.

A sprinkler system can be one of the most important fire-fighting items in any facility. If a fire starts, the sprinkler system must work effectively. The fire must be detected early and the system must deliver the proper amount of water to properly extinguish the fire. To be effective, sprinkler controls must be protected from lift truck damage. The most common cause of automatic sprinkler failure is that the water valve was turned off. The control valves in Figure 5-4 illustrates the protection provided by racking.

Sprinkler systems consist of integrated underground and overhead piping systems designed in accordance with fire protection engineering standards. The following are part of the water supply that would feed water through a system to a fire:

■ A connection to a main city water by underground piping

■ A fire pump

■ A gravity tank

■ A reservoir and/or a pressure tank.

Trained fire protection engineers must determine the type of system to install in a warehouse and must also design and supervise the correct installation of the system. The four basic sprinkler systems listed below can be installed individually or in combination with each other:

Figure 5-4. Sprinkler valves are protected by this barrier made of racking. The extinguisher should be mounted inside the barrier.

The wet pipe system. This is the most prevalent type of sprinkler system used; it holds water in the piping at all times. When a fire occurs, the hot air created by the fire rises to activate the sprinkler head(s). The sprinkler head is held together by a link made of solder. The solder melts and the head is activated. Water flows out of the opening created by the ejected parts that covered the sprinkler head opening. A deflector helps direct the flow of water into a fine spray, which falls onto the fire below.

The dry pipe system. When sprinklers are mounted in areas with a potential for water freezing, a dry pipe system can be installed. The sprinkler pipes are filled with compressed air, rather than the water used in the wet pipe system. When a fire occurs, the sprinkler head is activated and compressed air is released from the pipes. The function of the compressed air is to hold the dry pipe valve shut, preventing water from the other side from entering the system. When sufficient compressed air is released, the pressure in the system drops to a level where it can no longer hold the dry pipe valve closed against the water pressure. Water now enters the system, flowing through the piping and the sprinkler heads.

There are several disadvantages to dry pipe systems that should be noted:

■ There is a time delay in sprinkler head activation because of the time needed for the water to replace the compressed air in the piping.

■ Dry pipe systems are subject to alternating wet and dry exposure, resulting in possible corrosion of the piping. The system becomes wet while being tested and then back to dry when in service.

■ Proper placement of piping is necessary to prevent low spots that can hold water. If the pipes freeze, costly damage to the pipes can occur.

The deluge system. This system releases a water spray from the sprinkler heads. A deluge valve is activated by heat detectors mounted above the sprinkler heads. There is nothing within the system to hold back the water. This system could be used in a warehouse that stores drums of flammable liquids.

Like the dry sprinkler system, the deluge system has several disadvantages:

■ Significant volumes of water are required to flow through piping and spray out of each head at the same time

■ Installation costs of these systems can be prohibitive.

The preaction system. In libraries, museums, or other locations where special contents may be housed, the preaction sprinkler system must be used. Any operation of the sprinkler system in the absence of fire would be devastating to the building contents. Most fire safety professionals identify two events that must take place in order to activate the system. First, the heat of a fire will melt the fusible link in the sealed sprinkler heads. Second, a detector must open the deluge valve to admit the water. In the absence of either of these two events, the sprinkler system will not function. The biggest disadvantage of this system is the cost. However, when contents of great value must be protected, the expense of a preaction system may not be restrictive.

Select the correct sprinkler system to protect the building from a fire for the commodities stored there. Commodities are classified according to how fast they burn and how much heat they release. Table 5-2 identifies the classification of stored commodities. As an example, plastics burn quickly and produce twice the heat of burning wood.

Commodities are divided into five classes that have increasing requirements for sprinkler protection:

Products stored in a warehouse may vary from time to time, so a system should be chosen that will provide adequate protection for many years. The following changes may affect the level of protection needed.

Table 5-2. Classification of Stored Commodities*

CLASS	DESCRIPTION	EXAMPLES
I	Essentially noncombustible. Might be in light cartons. Might be on wooden pallets.	Glass, minerals, metals, ceramics.
II	Class I products with more and/or heavier combustible packaging and containers.	Class I products in multiwall cartons, boxes, or barrels.
III	Combustible products in combustible wrapping and/or containers on wooden pallets. Might have limited amount of plastic.	Products of wood, paper, leather, and some foods.
IV	Class I, II, or III with considerable plastic content in product, packaging, or pallets.	Typewriters and cameras with metal and plastic parts.
Plastics	Commodities containing a significant amount of plastic or Class I, II, III, or IV commodities with a significant amount of plastic packaging.	Computers, plastic dishware, rubber boots, compact discs.

■ Product packaging may be changed to plastic and/or polystyrene may be added to packaging, increasing combustibility. If a product is completely encased in plastic, it will burn as a plastic.

■ Changing from storage in cardboard boxes on wooden pallets to plastic boxes on plastic pallets increases the fire hazard. Greater protection is needed for product storage areas as well as areas where empty boxes and pallets are kept. Pallet storage must be in compliance with the NFPA code. Six feet is the established height for fire safety purposes in pallet storage. Figures 5-5 and 5-6 illustrate proper and improper pallet storage.

Figure 5-5. This is the correct storage method for pallets.

■ When the packaging of flammable liquids is changed from metal to plastic, a greater hazard exists. Plastic containers will melt in a fire and release the contents, creating a flammable-liquid spill fire.

■ If another level of storage is added by stacking higher or adding racks, more protection may be needed. More combustible material has been added to the space. Three feet of clearance is needed between the top of storage and sprinkler heads for effective spray distribution.

■ Adding racks to areas that previously had solid piled storage may increase the need for protection at the roof and may require in-rack sprinklers.

Where multiple-sprinkler head valves function for a large building, it is important to be able to react in an emergency. Pipes that run throughout the building can be color-coded to match a specific valve. If a head is leaking and needs to be replaced the color-coded line can be traced to

Figure 5-6. The NFPA limits the storage of pallets to six feet high for fire safety purposes. The painted line on the column shows the height limitation which is obviously being ignored.

the controls and the correct valve turned off. Figure 5-7 illustrates multiple valves.

Inspections of sprinkler control valves are necessary to ensure water pressure is correct in the system. Figure 5-8 can assist this purpose.

FLAMMABLE AND COMBUSTIBLE LIQUIDS

Within a warehouse or distribution center, flammable or combustible liquids may be present. The hazards associated with these liquids can be

Figure 5-7. Each one of these control valves and pipes are color-coded. The color is also on the piping throughout the warehouse. If a particular sprinkler head is open or leaking, the proper valve can be shut off easily.

rated as high. If the liquids are involved in a fire, the fire systems may not be able to handle it. To improve the safety in a warehouse, there are basic considerations for handling flammables safely.

- Flash point is the lowest temperature at which a flammable liquid gives off enough vapors to form a flammable mixture. This mixture takes place in the air directly above the surface of the liquids. When vapors are given off rapidly enough, they support continuous combustion.

- There are three classifications of flammable liquids based on flash point:

  - Class I are liquids with a flash point at or below 20° F.

  - Class II are liquids with a flash point above 20° F. and below 70° F.

  - Class III are liquids with a flash point above 70° F. but below 200° F.

- For combustible liquids, there are three classifications:

  - Class II are liquids that have a flash point at or above 100° F. and below 140° F.

  - Class IIIA are liquids that have a flash point at or above 140° F. and below 200° F.

  - Class IIIB liquids have a flash point at or above 200° F.

Energy is required for the ignition of flammable vapors. Flames must be present and within the flammable range to ignite the liquid. Flammable limits are divided into LFL or lower flammable limits and UFL, upper flammable limits. An LFL is a minimum concentration of vapor-to-air mixture in which propagation will not occur. UFL is a maximum concentration of vapor-to-air mixture in which propagation of a flame will not occur. The concentration of vapors must be between the UFL and LFL along with sufficient oxygen and flame/spark to ignite. Hot surfaces must be large enough and hot enough to ignite vapors. Static sparks,

Figure 5-8. Sprinkler Control Valve Inspections

Inspect locked or supervised valves at least monthly. Inspect all unlocked valves at least weekly. This form allows a listing of all inside and outside valves controlling sprinklers or water supplies. Gate valves, including nonindicating and indicator post gate valves must be physically "tried." A valve should not be reported as open unless the inspector has physically tried it. A visual check is needed for post-indicator valve assemblies (PIVAs), indicating butterfly valves (IBVs) and standard outside screw and yoke valves.

Valve Location	Area Controlled	Open	Shut	Locked	Sealed	Dry Pipe Valve	
						Air Press	Heat

	Yes	No
Were any valves operated since last inspection?	☐	☐
Were "valves shut" tags used?	☐	☐
Was the alarm signal to the security company tested?	☐	☐
Has the valve reopened fully and was a full flow 2-inch drain test made before the valve was relocked or resealed?	☐	☐

Warehouse: _____ Inspected By: _____ Date: _____

Comments: _____

(The "valve shut" tag method is used to guard against delayed reopening of valves. "Valve shut" tags should be used every time a sprinkler control valve is closed. When the valve is reopened the 2-inch drain should be flowed wide open to be sure there is no obstruction in the piping. The valve should then be resealed or relocked.)

friction sparks, and electrical sparks must have enough energy to ignite flammables. Energy from sparks or electrical sources must be of a certain intensity and duration for ignition. Flammables can also be ignited by heat generated from rapid compression.

All flammable liquids are volatile and evaporate rapidly. As they are evaporating they continuously give off vapors. It is the invisible vapors that present the fire threat. When the combustible vapors are mixed with air in certain proportions and combined, they are potentially explosive.

Flammable vapors are usually heavier than air so they naturally seek out and settle at the lowest possible level. This makes the detection of vapors more difficult. Vapors will move toward low points in the building. It's possible that a dock well could hold flammable vapors as a result of a spilled or punctured container of flammable liquids.

As an example, a drum of flammable solvent arriving at a warehouse dock is potentially a powerful bomb that careless handling or storage could detonate. Pound for pound, flammable liquids can explode with more force than dynamite. A 1-gallon can of gasoline has enough combustion energy to be comparable to 14 sticks of dynamite or 45 pounds of TNT. A 5-gallon can of gasoline is estimated to explode with a force equal to 415 pound of dynamite. Flammable or combustible liquid vapors ignite first in over 20 percent of all fires in industrial plants.

If a small amount of a flammable substance is used within the warehouse, specific regulations must be adhered to. As an example, if a gasoline-fueled lawn mower is being used, an FM/UL (Underwriters Laboratory) rating must accompany the portable gas can. The portable can must be equipped with a flame arrestor in the dispensing opening, a self-closing lid with a spring handle, and a leak-tight, corrosion-resistant body construction.

In a maintenance department, safe storage of flammable liquids is essential. OSHA permits up to 60 gallons of Class I or Class II liquids and up to 120 gallons of Class III liquids to be stored in safety cabinets close to work stations. An inplant storage cabinet will provide a fire and heat resistant enclosure for containers of flammable liquids. The cabinets should be made of double-walled 18-gauge steel with 1 ½ inches of insulating air space, and they should include self-closing doors.

If flammable liquids are being stored in the warehouse, be sure to contact a fire specialist/engineer to seek assistance in compliance with safety codes established by the National Fire Protection Association (NFPA), Factory Mutual (FM) and OSHA. Specific requirements for handling and storage are contained in the codes.

WAREHOUSE STORAGE

Many factors must be considered when designing a warehouse storage system. If the wrong choice is made in laying out storage racking, this error can be corrected before operations begin. If the sprinkler system is in error, it may take a fire to reveal the problem. At this point it is too late to correct the error and a serious fire loss may occur.

Both the product and its packaging affect the combustibility of the material and the rate at which the fire will burn. The storage arrangement, racking, palletized or solid-piled storage, and height of the stacks influence the burning rate and fire size. The distance between the sprinkler system and the top of the product storage is also a key factor. Three feet is an optimum distance for effective spray distribution.

The storage and classification of the commodity in the warehouse is also important. Commodities are classified according to how fast they burn and how much heat they release. Plastics, as an example, burn rapidly and release twice the heat of burning wood. A plastics fire can be hot enough to render some sprinkler systems inoperative: As fast as the water would flow from a sprinkler head, the water would vaporize. As a result of this problem, sprinkler systems must be designed to accommodate the storage of plastics.

Aerosols

Flammable liquids in small pressurized spray cans, such as paints, hair sprays, or engine cleaners, have the ability to explode from internal pressure when heated in a fire. The exploding cans create fireballs and are rocketing projectiles that leave a trail of burning liquid. Even a small quantity involved in a warehouse fire can have the potential to spread a fire and overtax the sprinkler system. Figure 5-9 illustrates a poster identifying the dangers of aerosols.

Figure 5-9. Aerosol cans will explode if heated. (Courtesy of the National Safety Council)

Sprinkler design and the consideration of the commodity being stored received significant attention during a fire several years ago. A big problem with sprinkler systems is that they are not designed for the material stored in the building. The fire apparently started in a warehouse when a box of flammable aerosol carburetor cleaner fell from a stack, broke open, and was ignited by a forklift. Employees attempted to fight the fire but were unsuccessful. The roof collapsed quickly, breaking the sprinkler piping. This rendered the sprinkler system inoperative.

NFPA 30B, Aerosol Products, classifies aerosol products into three hazard categories:

- Level 1 aerosol products are those with base products containing up to 25 percent by weight of materials with flash points of 500° F. (260° C.) or less.

- Level 2 aerosol products are those with base products containing more than 25 percent by weight of water-miscible materials with flash points of 500° F. or less, or with base products containing more than 25 percent but not more than 55 percent by weight of water-immiscible materials with flash points of 500° F. or less.

- Level 3 aerosol products are those with base products containing more than 55 percent by weight of water-immiscible materials with flash points of 500° F. or less, or with flammable propellant equal to or exceeding 80 percent of the net weight of the container contents.

Sprinkler systems involving aerosols should be specifically designed by a fire protection engineer. In-rack sprinklers may be necessary, along with isolation of the product, fire doors, chain link fences, and special storage cabinets to protect the warehouse from these hazards.

Fire Considerations in High-Rack Storage

Racking materials are common throughout warehouse storage areas. When the buildings that contain the racking are too high, fire fighting may be very difficult. If firefighters use the same tactics to fight a high-rack storage fire that they use to fight an ordinary dwelling or mercantile fire, the consequences could be serious.

Baled materials such as scrap paper or paper pulp can be deadly. Six firefighters died when piles of tissues that had soaked up sprinkler water collapsed. Some stored materials are packed with combustible strapping so that the bundles will collapse in a fire and aid in extinguishing the fire by smothering. Additional contents of high-racking storage could include flammables, flammable plastics, aerosols, and toxic chemicals. These elements pose obvious hazards.

When designing a high-rack storage area for a warehouse, employ professional engineers in the design and construction process. In-rack sprinklers may be needed and should be a part of the initial design as an economic factor. The commodity stored within the warehouse may change at a later date. Anticipating the volume of water from the sprinkler heads may require preplanning problem solving in the event of a fire.

Ensure that fire hoses are not blocked in the warehouse. Figure 5-10 illustrates accessibility to this hose.

SUMMARY

Fire protection in warehouses is a necessity. Data show that there are many warehouse fires each year that cost many millions of dollars. These losses do not have to occur if fire safety is taken seriously by management.

Figure 5-10. Fire hose and extinguisher locations have a red square with white trim painted on them for easy identification.

Fire systems have to be properly designed by professionals, installation of fire systems must be completed according to NFPA codes, and storage and handling of flammables and combustibles must be given the proper attention. Emergency planning, facility inspection, and an adherence to OSHA codes and practices will help to protect the property.

Fire safety is just one element in a comprehensive safety and health program. Ongoing attention must be given to sprinkler heads, alarms, valves, and controls to ensure they are functional. Keeping fire equipment and exit doors clear of obstructions is a necessity. Annual fire drills coupled with emergency team meetings will ensure worker safety during an emergency. In the event of a fire, an investigation should take place to prevent future fires from occurring. A form for investigating and reporting a fire is included in this chapter. Figure 5-11 can be used by supervisors for fire investigations.

Figure 5-11. Supervisor's Report of Fire

Exact location of fire:	
Cause of fire:	
Type of fire (Rubbish, wood, electrical):	
Date of fire:	Was the extinguisher accessible Yes ☐ No ☐
Action taken at time of fire:	
Could the fire have been prevented?	Yes ☐ No ☐
How?	
Persons extinguishing the fire (names):	
Any personal injuries?	Yes ☐ No ☐
If yes, give details:	
Was a spare extinguisher placed in the empty bracket?	Yes ☐ No ☐
Was the empty extinguisher returned for refilling?	Yes ☐ No ☐
Additional Comments:	
	Signed:
	Dated:
	Location:

REFERENCES

Badger, Steven. "Large-Loss Fires and Explosions." *NFPA Journal*. November/December. 1997, pp. 46–60.

Brannigan, Francis L. "High Rack Storage." *Fire Engineering*. May 1986, Vol. 139, No. 5, pp. 32–36.

BLR Pocket Guide—Fire Safety. Madison, CT: Business and Legal Reports, Inc. 1996, 46 pp.

Dannon, Walter A. "Guidelines for Inspecting and Maintaining Automatic Sprinkler Systems." *Plant Engineering*. March 8, 1984, pp. 171–175.

Davis, Larry, and Jeffrey Moore. "Warehouse Pre-Fire Planning and Fire Fighting Operations." *NFPA Fire Protection Handbook*. Quincy, MA, 1991, pp. 8–26/27.

Hankins, Joseph. "Firelight Will Reveal Bad Sprinkler Setup." *Industrial Fire Chief*. May/June 1995, pp. 22–24.

"Hazard Information Letter." *Fire Prevention*. Vol. Two, Issue Three, Sierra Vista, AZ: June 1997, 12 pp.

Karter, Michael J., and Paul R. Le Blanc. "U. S. Firefighter Injuries—1996." *NFPA Journal*. November/December 1997, pp. 66–77.

Long, Ken, and Robert Pick. "Responding to Incipient Fires." *Compliance Magazine*. September 1997, pp. 14–16.

McDonald, James M. "Flammable Liquids: Safe Handling in Production and Maintenance." *National Safety and Health News*. August 1985, pp. 47–52.

McQueen, Gregg. "Are You Really Ready?" *Industrial Maintenance and Plant Operation*. February 1998, pp. 23–24.

Moore, Jeffrey. "Why Sprinkler Systems Fail." *Fire Engineering*. April 1989, pp. 36–40.

Scuotequazza, Henry C. "Aerosol + Charging Operations." *National Fire Protection Handbook*: NFPA, 1991. Quincy, MA: pp. 2-217 – 2-223.

Seaton, Michelle. "For the Record." *NFPA Journal*. March/April 1998, pp. 68–73.

Sinclair, Lani. "Do You Take Your Fire Extinguishers for Granted?" *Safety and Health*. September 1997, pp. 62–66.

Sprinkler Age. "Same Time, Same Place — Totally Different Results." April 1998, pp. 10–11.

Stevens, Arthur M. "Handling Flammable Liquids Safely." *Plant Engineering*. June 28, 1984.

U.S. Department of Labor, OSHA. *Workplace Fire Safety*. Fact Sheet No. OSHA 1991-41.

Wilcox, William E. "Preventing Warehouse Fires — How Not to Get Burned." *Engineers Digest*. November 1996, pp. 32–38.

6

Safeguarding of Hazards

This chapter will focus on those warehouse hazards that need physical guarding or identification in some way. The proper design and construction of many physical safeguards requires that they be not only secure and substantial, but that they also meet OSHA guidelines. Something as basic as a physical pinch point exposure that requires a barrier guard should be of concern to each employee. Employees that work and travel through various parts of the warehouse could easily be exposed to many additional physical risks.

It would be unusual to find power presses, press brakes, table saws, joiners, drill presses, rollers, shears, and other machines such as these in a typical warehouse. These machines which are inherently dangerous, are usually found in heavy manufacturing and obviously require special guarding. What is forgotten many times, however, is that there are many other physical hazards in a warehouse that require safeguarding. Where possible, the hazard must be eliminated during the design stage or physically modified to protect workers. These hazards could easily be overlooked by those that feel warehouses are free of risk.

The following are typical safeguards that should be a part of every warehouse safety program:

- Handrail on mezzanines

- Wheel chocks/restraints

- Physical guarding of sprockets, pulley belts, and other exposures

- Crane hook latches

- Access ladders to docks and roofs

- Trash compactors

- Skylights

- Barriers for the protection of offices, racking

- Powered hand tools

- Guarding by color.

MEZZANINE SAFETY

Many warehouses utilize a second or third floor for storage, usually reserved for small parts or slow-moving items. The material must get from the floor of the warehouse to the appropriate floor level of the mezzanine. Many times this movement of product takes place by using a forklift truck. The problem lies in the fact that the pallet or load must be placed on the mezzanine floor; this may involve moving a handrail to do so.

Handrailing that is 42 inches high and contains a midrail and toeboard is an OSHA requirement. Employees expose themselves to a fall from the height of the mezzanine floor levels by allowing a section of guardrail to be removed or left open. Falls are the second leading cause of death in the workplace. Anytime a safeguard can be used to prevent a fall, the corrective process is well worth the effort.

Handrail sections that slide directly to the side are many times safer than a handrail that opens outward or inward. An outward-opening handrail means that a worker must reach out, unprotected many times, to draw the railing inward so it can be latched. Handrailing that opens inward can only be closed when the pallet load is empty and removed, thus creating a fall hazard until the work area is clear. Someone could fall while in the process of moving the handrailing.

A clever method to protect workers is to install an electric motor on the handrail. The lift truck operator could easily push a garage-door opener mounted on the lift truck to activate the sliding gate. From the floor level the operator pushes the button to open the gate. A light and audible alarm begins flashing and sounding to indicate the gate is opening. The operator then lifts the load and places it on the mezzanine floor— in far enough to allow the gate to be closed. The load is respotted; the lift truck backs up and then lowers the forks. Once again a button is pushed by the lift truck operator to close the gate, which then safeguards the worker on the mezzanine.

Appropriate signs are needed on the sliding gate to warn of its movement as well as fall hazards. The garage door opener controls are usually only on lift trucks that feed product onto a particular mezzanine.

This is a much safer method of safeguarding than others. It is not uncommon to walk through a warehouse and observe missing railing on upper elevations. Even during an installation or retrofit stage of construction, handrailing is many times installed last or even days later after the project has been completed.

In addition to safeguarding with proper handrail and toeboards, any holes in the mezzanine floor must be guarded. Nylon mesh or solid barriers should be placed on outside perimeter walls where product could fall to a lower level.

WHEEL CHOCKS/ TRAILER RESTRAINTS

Many employees are seriously injured or killed each year as a result of a lift truck falling off a dock to a lower level. Operators of powered equipment have the responsibility of ensuring the trailer is properly secured at the dock. The trailer must be restrained to prevent movement.

There are many hundreds of close calls each day in industry. A trailer moves and the lift truck falls in the gap between the trailer and dock. The operator isn't injured but is shaken up. When the trailer moves far enough from the dock, the forklift can easily fall to the dock floor. The operator can elect to stay with the forklift or attempt to jump clear. This is an example where using a seat belt can be a lifesaver.

Operators must be trained not to jump from a falling forklift, as this can be life-threatening. When a lift truck goes off the dock, the operator could be killed, suffer serious injuries, suffer less serious injuries, or be shaken up but not injured. By not securing the trailer properly , any one of these scenarios is possible.

Drivers of trailers are responsible for safely backing a trailer into the dock well. The trailer must be aligned properly so that it is spotted properly. At this point the operator may elect to leave the cab attached to the trailer or lower the landing wheels and spot the trailer on an approved pad. The tractor operator should properly place the wheel chocks in front of the trailer wheels to prevent any movement of the trailer. Each time a forklift enters and exits a trailer that has been spotted at a dock, the impact from this movement can easily cause the trailer to move forward. As often happens, the trailer could prematurely pull away from the dock. The lift truck could fall between the dock and truck or be left in the back of the moving trailer. Many trailer truck operators, however, are not accustomed to properly placing wheel chocks against trailer wheels. Lift truck operators erroneously assume that the wheels are chocked because that is the job of the trailer truck operator.

The responsibility to ensure wheel chocking lies with the powered equipment operator, who must physically check to ensure the wheels are chocked before entering the trailer. This may require a trip to the loading dock floor to check. If there is snow, ice, or water on the dock surface, the operator may be reluctant to go outdoors to chock the wheels. This oversight could easily result in a fall from the dock by the operator and the forklift. OSHA regulations require wheel chocking; this requirement makes sense when it comes to saving a life.

Several years ago an automatic trailer restraint was invented that allows for the trailer to be temporarily attached to the dock. An automatic trailer restraint is illustrated in Figure 6-1. When a trailer is spotted at the dock, a button on a panel within the warehouse is pushed and a bar/hook combination rotate upward from the dock floor to engage the Interstate Commerce Commission (ICC) bar, which then is secured by the restraint. It is estimated that over 95 percent of all trailers have an ICC bar.

When activated, a green light will begin flashing on a control panel mounted on the left side of the inside dock door. This light alerts the operator that the trailer is secure. On the outside of the building, a flashing red light alerts the trailer truck operator that the attachment is on the trailer and the trailer cannot be moved. A shear strength of 30,000 to 40,000 pounds is built into the device so that the trailer cannot be pulled away from the dock.

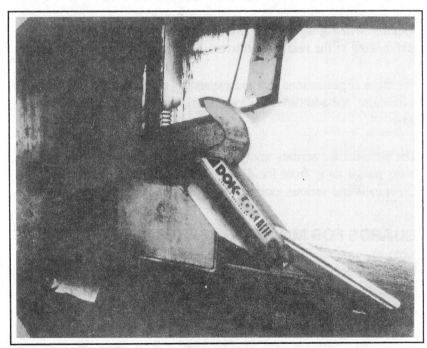

Figure 6-1. With an automatic trailer restraint system, a red light warns the operator not to enter the trailer and a green light shows that it is safe to proceed. The restraint hooks onto the trailer's ICC bar.

There are many advantages to automatic trailer restraints, and few disadvantages.

■ Advantages

- Ease of use—a button is pushed to activate or deactivate the trailer restraint.

- Flashing lights warn/alert both the lift truck operator and trailer operator.

- There is no need to go out into inclement weather to place a wheel chock.

- It keeps the trailer secure despite the condition of the dock well's surface area which could be covered with ice, snow, or water.

- The restraint is reliable, much safer than wheel chocks; and there is no lost time spent chocking, which saves money.

- It is highly unlikely that a trailer could be pulled away.

■ Disadvantages

- Cost is greater than standard wheel chocks.

- At times maintenance is required.

- Operator can still drive into a trailer when the red light is flashing (an obvious violation of warehouse safety rules).

An additional point is that warnings go beyond flashing green or red lights. Signage within the building tells operators when to enter or when not to enter the trailer. Also, signage on the outside of the building alerts the trailer truck operator that the device is engaged or disengaged. Red or green lights flash to warn the operator. The signage is also printed in reverse as that upon backing up, the sign can be read properly by just looking in the rear view mirror.

For those organizations that are expanding dock services at their warehouse or are considering a new warehouse, the addition of automatic trailer restraints will more than pay for themselves over a period of time.

The potential for serious injury is evident when looking at the OSHA data regarding dock safety. Trailers being pulled away from the dock or creeping are responsible for many injuries and fatalities each year. Close calls and serious incidents provide other high-risk exposures.

GUARDS FOR MOVING HAZARDS

Other than powered equipment, there are moving hazards within a warehouse that are overlooked at times but create serious exposures to pinching, shearing, cutting, or grinding actions. Areas to be considered can involve:

■ Conveyor systems—the hazards associated with moving wheels, drive belts, drive chains, sprockets, and conveyor rolls can seriously injure the hands or other body parts.

- Pulley belts on roll-up doors as seen in Figure 6-2 can create serious pinch points.

- The hazards of moving parts on a forklift can seriously injure the operator or other individuals.

- Elevator doors when closing expose workers to a serious pinch point.

- Wood-cutting table saws pose a serious hazard to the hands.

Many of the hazards listed above can be controlled through proper guarding, training, signage, and/or color coding. A hazard may be present yet go undetected because of a lack of awareness, neglect, or the machine and hazard may not be scrutinized for guarding because it is in an out-of-the-way location. Perhaps the machine is used only once or twice a year; this would cause workers to forget the need to inspect it. Mandatory inspections coupled with an understanding of machine hazards will help to ensure that the workplace is kept safe.

Figure 6-3 illustrates a small pulley belt guarded with wire mesh.

Conveyors

Conveyors have moving parts. Various pinch points exist in those areas that help the conveyor move product. A drive chain on a sprocket may move the rollers of the conveyor, but left unguarded this hazard can cause very serious hand injuries. The guard must be designed and mounted to completely seal off the hazards. This includes a full enclosure guard that does more than just cover the front of the drive chain. An employee could easily place a hand on the partial

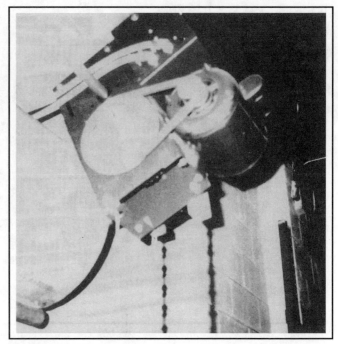

Figure 6-2. The drive belts on this roll-up door should be guarded.

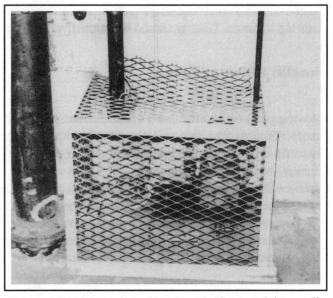

Figure 6-3. A barrier guard has been built around this small motor. The mesh should be anchored in place.

guard only to have the fingers caught in the drive chain on the open side. For greater visibility, paint guards yellow on the outside and orange on the inside. If a guard is left open in any way, the orange color serves as a reminder of the hazard.

In addition signs must warn of hand hazards, not to climb over a conveyor, and lockout/tagout hazards. A means of shutting off the power to a conveyor is needed, and the switch, button, or pull cord must be accessible to workers.

Figure 6-4. The pulley belts on this portable air compressor are safely guarded.

Pulley Belts

Pulley belts are a part of portable air compressors as well as drive motors for gates and roll-up doors. The guarding on the portable compressor in Figure 6-4 is excellent. A serious pinch point always exists on drive belts. In some cases, the pulley belts may be mounted eight or more feet from the floor and be considered safe because of distance. But it must be remembered that if maintenance is needed on the motor, someone must gain access to the motor and at

this point a serious injury could occur. Fixed barrier guards are needed and must provide complete coverage of the rotating parts both front and rear. Where wire mesh is used, the openings in the mesh must not exceed one-half inch. Openings larger than this would allow for a finger to be placed through the guard thus creating a hazard. Guards should be painted yellow on the outside and orange on the inside for visibility.

Forklift Moving Parts

Moving parts on forklift masts create serious pinch points. In one case, a forklift operator was lifting a maintenance worker on a pallet to an upper level so that a gas line fitting could be checked for leakage. To maintain his balance the maintenance worker placed both hands on the mast while standing on the pallet and leaning forward toward the operator. As the sectional mast began to operate, his small finger was caught between the roller and the mast. An amputation resulted from this unsafe practice. This serious injury could have been prevented. The safest method to gain access to an upper level is from a scissors lift. Had this device been used, the injury would never have taken place. A second means of gaining access to the gas valve would have been through the use of an approved lifting platform. It is important to note that some forklift manufacturers forbid the use of lifting platforms while using their equipment.

A lifting platform can be designed to protect everyone from moving parts. A proper lifting platform would consist of:

■ A high partition containing mesh with small holes that would keep any parts of the body from the mast area

■ Channels mounted at the underside of the platform to allow for maximum width on the forks. This long trough must fully enclose the fork but not be too large to provide play between the fork and channel.

■ A solid floor of nonslip metal

■ Handrail 42 inches high on three sides that is heavy duty to allow for maximum protection for the worker while elevated. Handrail must take the 200 pounds-plus deflection. A midrail and toeboard are also needed. Chain makes for poor handrailing because it sags in the center and because the correct strength factor of the chain is not considered.

■ A means of attaching and locking the platform to the mast of the forklift. The standard hook over chain method can be hazardous. A heavy-duty clevis should be used to attach the end of the chain to the back rest.

■ Signs mounted on the platform that inform workers to never stand on the railing, to keep the handrails in place, to securely anchor the platform to the mast, and to not enter the platform until a lift is about to take place.

■ Always storing platforms out of the way to prevent damage. Promptly tag and repair any defects on a lift platform. Needless to say, properly train employees in the care and use of lift platforms. Follow manufacturer's guidelines including those of the forklift manufacturer.

SAFETY LATCHES FOR CRANE HOOKS

Crane latches are needed on crane hooks to provide more safety for those handling loads with cranes or hoists. The purpose of the safety latch on the crane hook is to prevent inadvertent disconnection of the load. A falling load can be deadly. Immediate repair of defective latches is a must for proper employee safeguarding. Crane or hoist hooks that are not equipped with safety latches can be made safer by installing this device. Never weld, drill into, drill through, or modify a crane hook; this could cause failure of the hook. Contact the manufacturer of the hook so the proper size of latch can be mounted on the hook, or purchase crane hooks that include special swivel latches for maximum safety. Cranes and hoists can be used in a warehouse to lift product or batteries.

FIXED LADDERS

Access ladders to docks, roofs, and other areas of the warehouse must be properly designed and installed. OSHA regulations graphically outline the best design and application of fixed ladders. A few key points are:

■ Access ladders should be placed in areas where the likelihood of damage from powered equipment is minimized. Also, the person using the ladder should be separated from moving equipment; the ladder should be mounted in a safe area.

■ Never install a ladder by electrical wires or any other hazardous areas such as pits or balconies.

■ Doorways should never be located near the base of a ladder.

■ For straight ladders less than 20 feet in height, a cage may not be necessary. Ladders less than 20 feet may require a cage if the area below the ladder is hazardous. Cages are intended to prevent a worker from falling backwards off the ladder.

■ Ladders should not be made of wood because of possible defects as well as considerations for wood that will age and provide a false sense of security. Steel framework, rungs, and hardware provide the safest form of ladder. Never use reinforcing bars (re-bar) for rungs. Rungs are safest when they are first mounted in holes in the sides of the ladder, then welded on both sides.

■ Fixed ladders should be 16 inches wide with a 1-foot spacing between rungs. Rungs should be at least three-quarters-inch thick. The ladder should be kept at least 7 inches from the wall or fixed object to allow for the length of the foot of the climber. Anchor the base of the ladder to the floor.

■ Eliminate all sharp or hazardous protrusions or exposures on the rails and rungs.

■ Extend the side rails at least 3 feet above a landing so that gaining access to the ladder or egress from it is safer. Cages should also extend this same distance.

■ Minimize any open space between the ladder and any landing that will be used. This distance should be kept to several inches of opening wherever possible but must never exceed 12 inches.

■ For fixed ladders over 20 feet in length, a cage may be necessary. The cage must begin at the 7 foot level and continue the length of the ladder. This total length cannot exceed 30 feet.

■ Ladders at dock wells must contain the same provisions for width, height, and access. Jumping from a dock must be prohibited for employees gaining access to a dock well. Fractures of the ankle, knee, or wrist can be the result of jumping from a dock edge rather than using an access ladder.

TRASH COMPACTORS

Trash compactors are not uncommon in many warehouses. Newer models of these machines feature greater safeguards than those machines manufactured in the past. Fatalities have occurred in situations where the employee fell into the compactor while it was operating. To safeguard the machine:

■ All moving parts must be guarded. These moving parts would involve the usual pinch points for gears and drive mechanisms.

■ For buttons that are used to activate the machine, a constant pressure switch is needed. This button or switch must be designed so that it cannot be overridden. Operation of the machine must take place while the employee is not within reach of any machine hazards. When an employee can bypass a safety device such as this, serious injury or death could result. During routine warehouse inspections the operation of this machine must be evaluated.

■ Appropriate signage identifying how to safely use the compactor and prevent injury is needed.

■ Appropriate handrailing and other safeguards must be in place to prevent falls or contact with electricity.

■ The removal of the compacted material should be completed by a professional service or under close management supervision. Usually banding of cardboard or other bulk items is required. Banding can produce lacerations to the hands, arms, or face. Banding can also cause serious eye injury. Long-sleeve shirts, gloves, and goggles/glasses must be worn for protection.

■ Lifting the banded material cannot be done manually. Use powered equipment properly to complete this job.

■ Housekeeping in this area cannot be overlooked. Trash compactors can produce scrap that could be a fire hazard, as well as presenting a poor image to the warehouse and community.

■ Be sure to train employees for safe use of compactors.

SKYLIGHTS

Skylights help provide natural lighting and can be very beneficial to the working area. Skylights also provide a high-hazard risk to anyone walking or working on a roof. The fall hazard can endanger contractors as well as employees. The usual skylight is made of plexiglass or plastic and is usually not sturdy enough to support a worker. The size of the skylight is usually 3x3, 4x4, 5x5 or 4x8 feet.

A fall through a skylight can be the result of sitting on it or tripping on the raised skirt of the skylight. Workers will fall backward or forward through the opening to the floor below. Roofers, usually walking backwards with a machine or hot mop, can easily trip and fall backward.

OSHA reported the following incidents in 1995, all of which involved falls through skylights:

■ An employee working on a flat roof that was 27 feet high tripped while shoveling gravel and fell through a plastic dome skylight. The fall resulted in his death.

■ An employee was cleaning scrap materials from a roof and, while walking through the accumulation of debris, stepped on a plexiglass skylight that was concealed by the scrap. He fell 25 feet to the floor below and was killed.

■ A worker, who may have sat on the edge of a skylight to drink a cup of coffee, fell to the warehouse floor, some 23 feet, and was killed. The size of the skylight was 4 feet 6 inches wide by 8 feet 6 inches long.

■ A worker was performing a stripping operation on a roof and got a rock in his shoe. He sat down on a skylight to take off his shoe, the skylight gave way, and he fell to his death.

■ An employee was spray painting a wall of a new warehouse and may have tripped after becoming tangled in the spray air hose. He fell through a skylight to the floor below and was killed.

■ The owner of a painting company and another employee were walking across a roof when the owner stepped on a fiberglass covered skylight. The cover was not capable of supporting the weight of anyone walking on it, and the owner fell through the opening, struck his head, and was killed.

There are several methods to safeguard a skylight. A standard (metal) handrail 42 inches high with a midrail can be mounted on the frame of the skylight. The second method is to cover the entire face of the skylight with heavy-duty wire rods or grating. Such devices should be well secured against weather and tampering. When properly designed and installed, the surface area will prevent anyone from breaking through the skylight. OSHA has very specific guidelines for safeguarding skylights, but many employers either fail to realize a guarding requirement exists or fail to recognize skylights as a hazard. It is possible that a skylight has been painted over to match the color of the roof, and workers don't recognize them.

BARRIERS FOR GUARDING

Barriers to protect offices, walkways, racking, sprinklers, fire hoses, product, and other items are necessary in a warehouse. The time to install a barrier or protective device is before any damage takes place to the building, product, or employees. Visitors must also be protected while in the facility; many of the safeguards listed below will aid in injury prevention. Figure 6-5 identifies a barrier placed around the electrical equipment in this warehouse.

Figure 6-5. This warehouse installed a barrier around these electrical boxes.

■ Where offices or other administrative areas are adjacent to the movement of powered equipment, barriers must be erected to prevent building damage and injuries. Heavy-duty guardrails such as the one illustrated in Figure 6-6 help to provide a barrier between a 5-ton lift truck and a paneled office wall. The barrier should be out far enough from the walls so that the length of the fork cannot penetrate the office. Another alternative is to erect a solid barrier wall that keeps both lift truck and forks from striking the room.

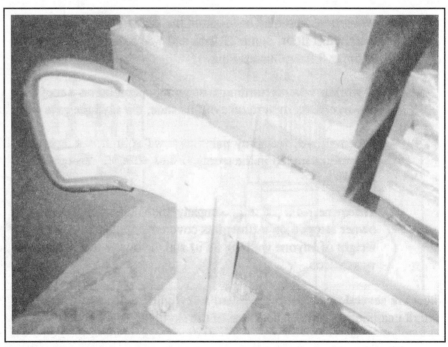

Figure 6-6. This barrier protects employees using the walkway. The edge of the barrier is padded to provide additional employee safety.

■ This same type of barrier can be used to protect anyone from the movement of powered equipment while using a warehouse walkway. Place signage on the railing at various intervals to warn of the dangers of having one's hand on the railing or barrier; amputations have been known to occur when a forklift struck a guardrail. Hands of employees, management, or visitors could easily be caught between the rail and lift truck. The barrier erected at this rear exit in the warehouse in Figure 6-7 keeps lift trucks and pedestrians from falling into the recess.

■ When a piece of powered equipment makes contact with racking in a warehouse, several things can take place. First, the racking will be damaged. If damaged severely, the entire section of racking could buckle and fall. Prior to collapsing, product could tumble down on anyone below. If in-rack sprinklers are present, the sprinkler heads and pipes could easily be damaged, which could cause major water damage to the facility and product. The sprinkler system would be made ineffective until the repairs were completed. Any fire within the building could not be controlled.

Effective supervision and employee training on all pieces of powered equipment will help prevent many serious incidents identified in the prior paragraph. Also, barriers to protect racking from lift truck damage provides effective safeguarding. It is more desirable that the powered equipment strikes the steel post or barrier rather than the racking. Racking is not designed to incur such abuse.

It is recommended that barrier posts be erected at the corners of each rack and aisle. Holes must be drilled into the concrete floor to accommodate the barrier posts. It should be noted that even barrier posts require maintenance. When posts are struck, the anchorage at the floor can shear off or the concrete may break apart. The damaged post must be removed, the holes correctly patched with a strong filler, and then the holes redrilled and the post remounted with new bolts. Yellow paint helps to highlight the barrier.

Sprinklers are necessary for the protection of property and employees in a warehouse. Valves, sprinkler heads, gauges, and pipes must be protected from damage caused by powered equipment. A survey should be made of the facility to determine where these safeguards are needed. If a new warehouse is being planned, consider proper placement of the above-mentioned items to prevent damage. Professionals like those representing the Factory Mutual System can offer good advice on this subject. Any fire insurance company wants to prevent loss and an effective sprinkler system offers such protection.

Significant water damage can occur before the water can be turned off

Figure 6-7. Hand railing has been placed around this stairwell to prevent lift trucks from going over the edge.

when sprinkler heads are struck by powered equipment. To help prevent these costly incidents; several safeguarding methods can be used:

Product must be stored at least 18 to 36 inches below sprinkler heads. This storage distance would be determined by local fire codes as well as the various commodities stored in the warehouse. A trained specialist should be consulted so that a set figure for proper clearance between product and sprinkler heads can be maintained. When product is being placed on racking or shelving, the sprinkler head can be protected by distance as well as the operator handling the load properly.

Figure 6-8. Sprinkler heads are protected from impact by metal guards.

Under mezzanines, walkways, and within rackings, protective guards can be placed over sprinkler heads to protect them from damage. Figure 6-8 identifies a protected sprinkler head. It is important to keep any piece of powered equipment away from low ceilings or low walkways. A part of the truck could easily shear off a sprinkler head. Some locations have been known to hang streamers or noise-producing metal strips from pipes and other parts of the building that could easily be struck by equipment or an elevated load. Painting of the hazards or adding yellow and black striped tape also helps to identify the area.

- Where possible, recess fire extinguishers, thermostats, outlets, power boxes, and conduits inside of a building support beam rather than mounting them on the outside. Powered equipment is prone to damaging these items. Metal frames can be built around fire hoses and other vital parts of the building for protection from impact. The thermostats and switches in Figure 6-9 have been guarded by metal brackets.

Figure 6-9. The electrical switch and thermostat are protected from forklift damage.

- Product that is of high value or prone to damage should be spotted up and out of the way of powered equipment. It can also be placed in an out-of-the-way area for protection. Metal mesh baskets can also be used to store valuable or delicate parts.

POWERED HAND TOOLS

Powered hand tools are used in warehouses as a matter of course. Hand drills, power saws, banding machines, and staple guns are typical power tools. Here are a few notes of interest regarding the safety of workers when using this equipment.

- Drills can be large, such as those that require significant power to drill through concrete, cinder blocks, or steel, and they can be dangerous if not handled properly. Assistance may be needed to safely use the large drill. Sharp drill bits can easily cut the hand. Employees sometimes fail to unplug the drill when changing bits only to have the drill activate while they are holding the bit. Rotating drill bits can easily cut the hand or cause an amputation; employees are to be warned about this danger.

- Eye protection is a must. Goggles, glasses, or a face shield will protect from sparks, dirt, rocks, wood, and steel shavings.

■ Powered hand saws are very dangerous because of the rotating saw blade. Employees must not block off or remove the circular blade guard. Be sure the electrical cord is out of the way when operating. Keep hands clear of the blade and cutting area. Eye protection is a must. Hearing protection may also be in order. The saw must be unplugged when changing the blade.

■ Banding machines are used to manually secure strapping around product to prevent movement. The metal or plastic bands can easily cut the skin or injure the eyes. Eye and hand protection is needed for this process.

■ Staple guns can be very dangerous. Earlier models lacked proper safety devices and it was not uncommon to see two workers having a duel while shooting staples at each other. Improved models require the staple gun to be pressed against the pallet or cardboard before the trigger will activate. Eye and hand protection is important when using this tool.

USE OF COLOR CODING

■ When using safety color-codes to mark physical hazards, OSHA requires that:

- Red is basic color to identify fire protection equipment and apparatus. Red shall be used to identify safety cans that contain liquids with a flash point at or below 80° F.

- Red is also used to color lights for barricades and as temporary obstructions. Stop buttons on machinery shall also be red.

- Yellow is the basic color for designating caution and for marking physical hazards such as stumbling, falling, tripping, striking against, or being caught in-between.

- Orange is used to designate "warning" for dangerous equipment that may crush, cut, shock or otherwise injure. As an example, machine guards should be painted yellow on the outside and orange on the inside.

- Green is used to identify safety and first aid equipment.

- Blue identifies the warning against starting, using, or moving equipment under repair.

- Black on yellow identifies radiation: x-ray, alpha, beta, gamma, neutron, or proton radiation.

- Black and white identifies boundaries of traffic aisles, stairways, and risers.

■ Guarding enhancement through the use of color helps provide awareness for a particular hazard. Color alone, however, will not prevent an injury. The employee must first recognize the color and make a decision in his/her mind as to what hazard it represents. The color could be on a fixed barrier or the color could be generated from a light. Color and lights to highlight hazards help make the warehouse safer.

■ Flashing amber lights on powered equipment help warn others of its approach. Where the aisles are busy and stacked with product a worker could easily walk into the path of a vehicle. Of course, horns and back up alarms on powered equipment offers additional safeguarding. The audio and visual effects of alarms and lights are intended to alert employees and visitors to the movement of powered equipment. Numerous injuries have been prevented because a conscientious employer took time to go beyond an OSHA regulation. OSHA currently does not require back-up alarms or flashing lights, but these devices are highly recommended. Figure 6-10 shows a sweeper in this warehouse that has a large flashing light to warn other workers.

It should be noted that there is no research to validate the 100 percent effectiveness of alarms and flashing lights. Back up alarms are usually reserved only for counter-balanced forklifts.

Figure 6-10. This sweeper is provided with an overhead guard and a warning light.

The use of yellow or a yellow/black striped combination of paint can be very effective in highlighting physical hazards. Consider painting edges of docks, perimeters of dock plates, barrier posts, walkway lines, machine guards, handrailing, edges of stairs, crane/hoist blocks, and corners of roll-up doors. In addition, red and white paint can be used to highlight fire protection equipment.

SUMMARY

Warehouses potentially contain many hazards that require some form of safeguarding as a means of preventing injuries. Barrier guards, handrails, fixed ladders, color coding, signage, and tool safety are all a part of injury prevention. A thorough department inspection should take place at least once a month, and hazards such as those included in this chapter must be evaluated. Creative thinking by both management and warehouse workers can generate problem-solving techniques to prevent injuries. The focus of this chapter is on the presence of physical hazards that are typical to warehouses, and various methods of corrective action to safeguard the hazards and keep employees injury-free.

REFERENCES

IMPO. "Machine Guards Prevent Serious Injuries." July 1996, p. 15.

National Safety Council. "Safeguards." *Accident Prevention Manual*. Itasca, IL, 1997, pp. 33 35, 131–158.

Plastecs, Inc. *FallGuard™ Skylight Screens*. Houston, TX 1998.

U.S. Department of Labor. *Concepts and Techniques of Machine Safeguarding*. OSHA #3067, 1980.

7

Lockout/Tagout Procedures

Up until the passage of OSHA's 1910.147, Control of Hazardous Energy, Lockout/Tagout Standard, very few organizations practiced the guidelines in this program. Large industry has used one form or another of a lockout program for many years. However, workplaces such as warehouses did not always consider the ramifications of such a program. Most of the repairs and maintenance to many buildings are not necessarily made by staff but by outside contractors. Many of these contractors have yet to grasp the need for a formal lockout/tagout (LOTO) program.

As an example of the lack of understanding, a potentially serious incident occurred recently that helps to drive this message home. A 90,000-square-foot warehouse had just opened and some electrical modifications were needed. The warehouse manager called the electrical repair company to complete the project.

The electrician, supposedly knowledgeable in his trade, had moved a set of circuit breakers to the "Off" position. The circuit breaker box was in a separate room in a hallway. When the switches were moved to the "Off" position, the lights in the hallway as well as the circuit in a room down the hallway were shut off. While the electrician busily worked on the revision, the warehouse supervisor found himself in a dark hallway. He had no knowledge of the repairs being performed.

He went into the room that held the circuit breaker box and, with the aid of a flashlight, moved the "Off" switches to the "On" position. At that point he heard a loud yell and ran down the hall into a room to discover the electrician flat on his back with a wooden step ladder on top of him.

After the unharmed electrician took several minutes to recover, the episode was discussed by everyone concerned. The circuit breaker box, being new, included a means of locking the door. The key was, in fact, in the door, having been left there by the warehouse manager in anticipation of the electrician. The electrician, apparently not taking his life or livelihood seriously enough, erroneously thought that he could rely on nobody going into the utility room and moving the circuits to the "on" position. For the matter of a few seconds, he put his life on the line.

Because this incident was potentially serious, the warehouse manager felt that he was partly responsible because he had not discussed the need for LOTO with the visitor. A reminder about safety in the warehouse, the key in the door, and the personal security of the electrician was in order.

This is not an unusual story nor is it a rare happenstance. Each year some 120 workers are killed as a result of not ensuring a zero-energy state on the process they are working with. In addition, some 60,000 injuries take place—many of them involving permanent disability. OSHA states that "approximately 39 million workers will be protected by this new rule." The electrician discussed above was only protected by the intent of the standard; he chose to follow his old habits and not take that extra moment to lockout.

LOTO GUIDELINES

The need for correct LOTO procedures in a warehouse is just as important as in a factory, chemical plant, or construction project. Take a quick look at the rather simple LOTO requirements.

Steps for Shutdown for Zero Energy

Prepare   Know how to control (bring to zero) the energy. Know all of the types of hazardous energy and associated hazards.

Shutdown   Turn the machine or equipment to the "off" position.

Isolate   Isolate the machine or process from the energy source.

Lockout   Apply the lockout, tag, and any other device to achieve zero energy.

Release   Release, disconnect, or block stored energy. Ensure that machinery that is coasting, rotating, or moving comes to a complete stop.

Verify/Ensure Attempt to start the process or machine. Ensure it cannot start.

Steps for Restart

Inspect   Ensure guards are back in place securely. Ensure tools, materials, hoses, wires, etc., have been properly removed. Ensure the process or machine is fully assembled.

Notify   Alert all affected employees of the start-up.

                Ensure everyone is safely positioned and out of danger.

                Double-check before activation.

Remove   Remove lockout devices, chains, clamps, blanks, tags, etc. Double

                check all energy sources, then restart.

Energy sources include:

- Electrical

- Mechanical

- Hydraulic

- Pneumatic

- Chemical

- Thermal

- Gravity

- Compression.

OSHA Requirements

Overall, the LOTO requirements are not very difficult and make a lot of sense. The OSHA standard
applies to the control of energy during maintenance
and/or the servicing of machines and equipment.

Under this LOTO program, OSHA requires that
employers must:

- Develop an energy-control program

- Use locks and other devices when equipment or processes can be locked out.
  Figure 7-1 illustrates a panel board with
  proper lockout hardware.

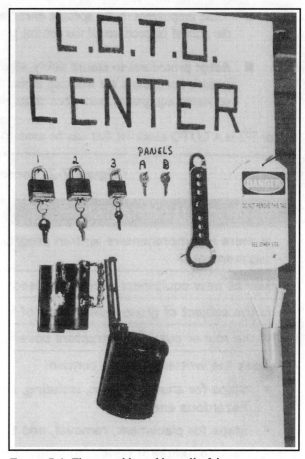

*Figure 7-1. This panel board has all of the necessary
hardware for lockout/tagout.*

- Identify and implement specific procedures in writing for the control of hazardous energy
  including preparation for shutdown, equipment isolation, lockout/tagout application, release of
  stored energy, and verification of isolation.

- Ensure that new equipment or overhauled equipment can accommodate locks.

- Employ additional means to ensure safety when tags rather than locks are used by using an
  effective tagout program.

- Institute procedures for release of lockout/tagout including machine inspection, notification and
  safe positioning of employees, and removal of the lockout/tagout device.

- Obtain standardized locks and tags that indicate the identity of the employee using them and that
  are of sufficient quantity and durability to ensure effectiveness.

- Require that each lockout/tagout device be removed by the employee who applied the device.

- Conduct inspections of energy-control procedures at least annually.

- Train employees in the specific energy-control procedures with training reminders as part of the annual inspections of the control procedures.

- Adopt procedures to ensure safety when equipment must be tested during servicing when outside contractors are working at the site, when a multiple lockout is needed for a crew servicing equipment, and when shifts or personnel change.

Figure 7-2 is a LOTO checklist that can be used to ensure compliance with the program.

Figure 7-2. Lockout / Tagout Checklist

A - PROGRAM CONTENTS	YES	NO
Is there a comprehensive written program that meets OSHA requirements?	☐	☐
Has all new equipment been purchased with LOTO hazards in mind?	☐	☐
Is the subject of group lockout part of the written program?	☐	☐
Is the role of outside contractors covered in the program?	☐	☐
Does the written program contain:		
• steps for shutting down, isolating, blocking, and securing all hazardous energy?	☐	☐
• steps for placement, removal, and transfer of LOTO devices?	☐	☐
• requirements for testing to verify the effectiveness of LOTO devices?	☐	☐
• are authorized employees identified?	☐	☐
• are affected employees identified?	☐	☐
B - TRAINING	YES	NO
Have the following employees been trained in LOTO:		
• supervisors?	☐	☐
• authorized employees?	☐	☐
• affected employees?	☐	☐
• maintenance personnel?	☐	☐
• other employees?	☐	☐
C - HARDWARE	YES	NO
Does the warehouse have the proper number of locks?	☐	☐
Are plug-lock devices available?	☐	☐
Are circuit breaker box switch lockouts available?	☐	☐
Are tags available that require name, date, and reason for lockout?	☐	☐
Are multihole lockout hasps available?	☐	☐

D - ENERGY CONTROL IDENTIFICATION	YES	NO
Has each switch in each circuit breaker box been identified for function?	☐	☐
Has a listing been made of all the machines, operations, or devices that would require LOTO?	☐	☐
Have individual guidelines been developed on how to isolate each form of energy?	☐	☐
Does the listing identify:		
▪ electrical?	☐	☐
▪ mechanical?	☐	☐
▪ hydraulic?	☐	☐
▪ pneumatic?	☐	☐
▪ chemical?	☐	☐
▪ thermal?	☐	☐
▪ gravity?	☐	☐
▪ compression?	☐	☐

EXAMPLES OF LOTO IN WAREHOUSES

These guidelines from OSHA are not as complex as they may seem. Use of LOTO in a typical warehouse is not difficult. The following scenarios could be properly used in most locations.

The following are examples of situations that would require the use of LOTO in a typical warehouse.

■ An overhead mercury vapor or fluorescent light has burned out. A scissors lift is used to gain access to the bulb(s). New bulbs do not solve the problem therefore, the ballast must need replacing.

The power to those particular lights in that aisle is most likely from a master circuit breaker box. To arrive at a zero energy state, the correct breaker box switch must be moved to the "off" position. At this time, a means of preventing someone from moving the switch to the "on" position is necessary.

Replacement of the ballast requires someone who is skilled and authorized to make these repairs, and LOTO must be used.

Two means of LOTO are available for this situation or any other that would require work on direct wiring from a machine or operation to the circuit breaker box:

1. A single, double, or triple pole breaker device can be placed on the switch while in the "off" position. A lock and tag must be added to the device.

2. The specific switch could be moved to the "off" position, and the door of the circuit breaker box would be locked. A tag identifying who locked it out, why, and when is also needed.

■ A large floor fan gave an employee a shock while the fan was being moved. The employee reports this incident to the supervisor.

The most effective means of protecting employees from this defective fan is to pull the plug on the fan and place the plug into a plug-lock device, which means it cannot be pulled out or pushed through so the defective fan could be plugged in. Once the plug is in the device, a lock is added along with a tag. Figure 7-3 illustrates how to lockout a defective floor fan.

This same procedure would hold true for any tool, device, or machine that receives its power from a plug. Items such as water fountains, power tools, appliances, machines, or any such device can be easily locked out by isolating the plug..

It is important to note that OSHA considers lockout to be a more reliable means of de-energizing equipment than tagout alone. Since safety programs that are recognized for excellence go beyond OSHA regulations, OSHA standards are minimum requirements. When an employer can exceed standards, safety performance will improve. Because OSHA may allow for a tag to be placed on the defective tool or appliance does not guarantee that if the tool is needed someone won't come along and use it.

For this reason, a plug-lock device is the best assurance that the hand drill, power saw, electric compressor, drop light, or any number of plug-in items won't be used.

■ Smoke is coming from a battery charger located near a group of electric forklifts. An employee immediately pulls down on the handle of the disconnect box and notifies his supervisor. The supervisor adds a lock and tag to the box. This is one of the more common means of lockout/tagout throughout industry. As a practical matter, and to satisfy OSHA regulations, ensure that all electrical boxes are marked for function and voltage.

In the case cited above, the smoking battery charger was numbered to correspond to the matching disconnect box. The employee was able to take immediate steps to prevent fire by matching the charger to the

Figure 7-3. The cord of this defective floor fan has been properly locked to prevent anyone from using it.

appropriate electrical box. Any repair, evaluation or modification to any piece of powered equipment must be completed by authorized, trained, and qualified employees. Processes such as fuse removal, wiring, or repair require great skill and must be left in the hands of professionals. The disconnect box in Figure 7-4 has been properly locked out.

It also bears mentioning that most people grasp the handle of a pull-down disconnect with their right hand. Since high-voltage boxes have been known to have a high-energy burst, it is advisable to pull the handle down with the left hand, thus putting the person's body away from the front of the panel box.

Figure 7-4. To lock out a disconnect box, pull down on the handle and attach a hasp, lock, and tag.

■ During a warehouse inspection a supervisor notes a large puddle of water directly below a water valve. The pipe below the valve will have to be repaired. The supervisor turns the valve to the "off" position and places a plastic, circular lockout device over the valve. He then adds a lock and tag.

Circular valves such as this can be used on any size valve; it is just a matter of purchasing the proper sizes and quantity to fit the valves.

■ A leak has developed in a compressed-air line that feeds an air-operated strapping machine. An in-line handle, lying parallel on the pipe, must be rotated clockwise from the air pipe. A special plastic device is added to the air line handle to keep it from being used. A lock and tag are then added to complete the job.

■ An employee, while placing a pallet on a rack, has struck a sprinkler head because the load was being carried too high. Product stored on the rack sustains water damage. Another employee alerts the supervisor to the problem. In order to shut off the water flow, the main sprinkler valve must be turned off. The supervisor unlocks the chain that keeps the water valve in the open position. The valve is then closed.

A new sprinkler head with the same rated temperature is placed in the system by the maintenance department. Once the main water valve to the sprinkler system was shut off, the security service that provided alarm service was notified of the down time. The alarm company is now contacted to report that the repair has been made and the water pressure has been restored to the system. The chain and lock is then placed back on the valve while it is in the open position.

■ During a prestart inspection of a forklift, an operator discovers that there is a problem with the brakes. He makes the proper notation on his inspection form and alerts the supervisor. The maintenance department immediately drives the lift truck to an open area of the warehouse where it is parked out of the way. The forks are lowered flat to the floor; the key is then removed and kept by the maintenance man. A tag is completed and placed on the steering wheel.

The brakes are properly adjusted and the forklift is placed back in service after another inspection. The tag is then removed.

This same process of removing the key and adding the appropriate tag can be used for any piece of powered equipment.

Some readers may question a few of the situations above and the need for lockout/tagout in each of the examples. It is important to isolate a hazard even if the end result will not necessarily cause injury; such as the sprinkler valve application. Each employee must understand that merely warning someone of a hazard or situation doesn't necessarily prevent someone from being affected by that hazard.

The examples cited:

- Overhead lights with defective ballast
- Defective floor fan
- Powered hand tools
- Battery-charger fire

- Leaking water pipe
- Leaking compressed-air line
- Broken sprinkler head
- Forklift with bad brakes

are typical for most warehouses and distribution centers. What is important is to recognize the hazard and the means of de-energizing the hazard. Many of the applications cited can be universal for any location.

TRAINING

For best results, there should be two levels of training for employees and supervisors.

1. Formal training is needed for all employees who use lockout/tagout for their own protection. These are the authorized employees. Only they can perform maintenance and service on the various operations and machines.

   It is highly recommended that supervisors be provided with this level of formal training. It stands to reason that if a department is to remain safe, the supervisor should know what rules, regulations, and safety procedures are required of the employees. One cannot enforce safety practices if one doesn't know what they are.

2. A general safety meeting is to be conducted at least once a year to alert all employees to the subject of lockout/tagout. Attendance at the meeting(s) should be mandatory for all directly affected employees as well as most facility employees. Essentially the training at this level covers awareness and overall safety knowledge regarding LOTO.

   Employees should be reminded during training that tampering with electrical boxes can result in injury to them or others. Figure 7-5 identifies an electrical box where three knockout plugs have been removed.

Both forms of training are to be performed annually. Document all of the training. Ensure that the requirements in the standard are understood by all employees, and that the company's written program reflects the requirements as well as meeting lockout/tagout standard.

Figure 7-5. Knock out plugs on electrical boxes should be checked periodically to ensure they are safe.

ADDITIONAL ITEMS

Outside contractors. The onsite employer and the outside employer must inform each other of their respective lockout or tagout procedures. Each employer must ensure that his or her personnel understand and comply with all restrictions and/or prohibitions of the other employer's energy-control program.

This interface is best accomplished by preplanning. The time to talk to the contractor is when a work order or contract is developed, prior to the work being done. The development stage, while the contractor and staff will be at the warehouse, is also a good time to discuss other safety issues.

Group lockout. This is a hasp on a disconnect box or other energy-producing item that allows for multiple locks. Each person servicing the piece of equipment must add his lock and tag. As each worker finishes the project, his lock is removed from the multiholed hasp.

Shift work. The written lockout/tagout program must take into account the possibility of shift work affecting the program. A particular project may have to be completed by the next shift. Employees should discuss the project and/or have the supervisor present so he/she knows the circumstances. Just because a shift ends is no reason for an employee to remove the lock and tag from the machine. Communication between employees will go a long way in preventing injuries.

Visuals. Color-coding of locks by group or department may help augment the program. Locks as well as tags must be durable enough to withstand the working environment.

Labels are very effective as reminders on circuit breaker boxes and disconnects. Lockout/tagout labels are readily available from many sources. Labels must be sturdy, durable, and clearly display the appropriate message. Tags must have a place on them for the signature of employee using the lockout, date, and reason for lockout.

SUMMARY

This chapter on lockout/tagout (LOTO) and the requirement for a zero-energy state is noteworthy. This is a common-sense program that will go far in protecting employees. The development of a written program is essential for meeting OSHA requirements for 1910.147; while this chapter does not provide a complete written program, it does provide valuable tips for coming into compliance in this important area.

OSHA recognizes that LOTO is very important. Next to the Hazard Communication Law (Right to Know for Employees), LOTO is the second most frequently cited standard. The enforcement process has resulted in substantial penalties for employers. In fiscal 1996, OSHA cited the following LOTO violations:

- No written LOTO program: 1,370 violations with $3,113,832 in penalties

- Lack of training: 859 violations with $2,949,493 in penalties

- Other: 1,255 violations for other parts of the 1910.147 program with $1,431,285 in penalties

This particular standard is heavily emphasized because, in many instances, someone's life is on the line, and statistics bear out the fact that many employees are injured or killed each year.

Considering the fact that this law has been in existence since 1990, it is surprising that so many employers have failed to implement it. Organizations, maintenance workers, and electricians are in agreement that it is a law that makes sense and is easy to understand.

Many of the recommended guidelines in this chapter may exceed those of OSHA in specific instances. But it is reasonable to assume that a facility uses the "best-practices" technique for problem solving, it will provide a safer environment for employees.

Key words in the 1910.147 standard are identified in the Glossary in the back of this book.

REFERENCES

Federal Register, Part IV, Occupational Safety and Health Administration, 29 CFR 1910. Control of Hazardous Energy Source (Lockout/Tagout) Final Rule. September 1, 1989.

National Safety Council. Electrical Safety, Accident Prevention Manual. pp. 257–259. Itasca, IL, 1997.

Occupational Safety and Health Administration, OSHA #3120. Control of Hazardous Energy (Lockout/Tagout). 1991.

8

Housekeeping

Good housekeeping goes hand in hand with safety, quality, and efficiency. Good housekeeping is a combination of orderliness and cleanliness. Warehouse housekeeping programs should not only promote visual orderliness, but management should insist that:

■ All unavoidable conditions that generate trash, debris, etc., must be cleaned up constantly.

■ All things are to be kept in their assigned spots when not in use.

■ All things have an assigned place for storage.

■ All things are to be stored properly.

■ All areas that are not clean are to be corrected.

PRACTICAL HOUSEKEEPING TIPS

Some practical tips for warehouse housekeeping programs include:

■ Mark walkways and storage areas with yellow guidelines. Figure 8-1 shows the neatness of this dock area. The painted lines outline planned product storage areas.

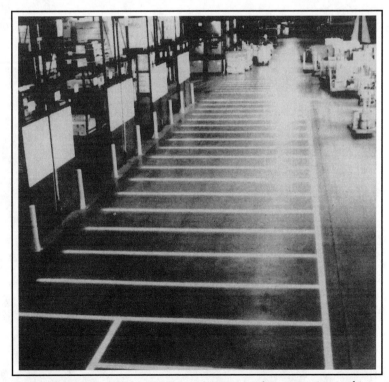

Figure 8-1. Note the excellent housekeeping and organization in this warehouse.

■ Change filters in heating and ventilation units to help control dust conditions.

■ Keep objects from protruding into aisles.

■ Keep walkways free of tripping or slip/fall hazards such as metal or plastic strapping, grease, oil, rope, scrap, and debris.

■ If cans, containers, cartons, or other parcels are potential fire hazards, keep them stored in an approved cabinet.

■ Keep stairs free of foreign objects and keep a nonskid surface on the stairs.

■ Keep handrails and midrails free of dirt, grease, and oil.

■ Keep materials sorted in an orderly manner. Store on racks only those materials and equipment intended for the racks. Figure 8-2 illustrates an orderly warehouse.

Figure 8-2. Another example of a well-organized warehouse.

■ Keep the areas under and between racks and bins free of dirt and debris.

Figure 8-3. This warehouse needs more basic housekeeping. The dumpster must be emptied more often so trash doesn't get piled along side it.

■ Do not allow product to hang out of bins or to be on the floor.

■ Provide for the ongoing discarding of wrappers, boxes, paper, strapping, and insulation. Proper receptacles must be available for this purpose. Figure 8-3 illustrates the need for improved housekeeping.

■ Empty trash containers on a regular basis.

■ Place signs on bins or other storage areas defining the product to be stored there.

■ Regularly clean up around dumpsters, trash compactors, bins, and also the perimeter of the warehouse. Pallet boards with protruding nails are not uncommon in warehouse operations.

■ Store products in neat rows with the identification facing out for easy visual access.

■ Never store flammables with combustibles. Keep separate storage areas for flammables based on fire codes.

■ Provide for a specific storage location for hand and powered tools. Keep tools in designated areas such as hooks or bins.

■ Keep powered and hand tools free of grease and dirt, and in good repair.

■ Smoking should not be allowed in a warehouse for obvious fire hazard reasons. Require special use of ash trays for cigarettes rather than allowing them to be discarded on the floor or around warehouse property.

■ Don't block fire-fighting and first aid equipment. Proper access can be aided by painting the areas below fire-fighting equipment with red squares and white striped borders.

■ To aid in the housekeeping duties, use a powered sweeper and floor scrubber for cleaner, neater aisles. Pedestrian aisles, such as those illustrated in Figure 8-4, require ongoing attention.

■ For chemical spills, use the proper cleanup procedures and dispose of the waste properly. Use all prescribed PPE while following EPA guidelines.

■ Keep floors free of water from leaks in the roof or water that has been brought in by mobile equipment. Slips and falls are common with wet floors. Powered equipment may have difficulty stopping on a wet floor. Use a squeegee to clear water in aisles and work areas when mopping may take too long.

■ Wipe off lights and reflectors for maximum visibility. Make sure to move overhead lights when racking configurations change to achieve for the best aisle and walkway lighting.

Figure 8-4. Portable hand rails seperate pedestrian walkways from storage space.

■ Properly patch holes in the warehouse floor as they occur. Doing this can help prevent a slip/fall injury, and it will help cushion the ride for powered equipment operators.

■ Replace burned-out lights on a regular basis.

■ Tops of work benches should be free of tools, cans, bottles, and debris.

■ Drawers in benches and tables should be kept neat. Items should be properly stored. Periodically purge the storage drawers to allow for more space.

■ Clean up scrap and materials as they are created so they aren't tracked to other parts of the warehouse.

■ If necessary, mark the floor where trash cans are to be placed.

■ Use a vacuum cleaner or fixed exhaust systems that capture dust and shavings to prevent uncontrolled debris from being tracked to various parts of the building.

■ Properly post signs and posters such as the one shown in Figure 8-5, reminding everyone of the need to maintain excellent housekeeping and to prevent falls. Change posters on a regular basis.

■ Periodically wipe off powered equipment, fire extinguishers, railings, shelves, barriers, mirrors, windows, and decks.

■ Periodically add a fresh coat of paint to the warehouse walls to cover up marks. Graffiti should be frowned on in any location. Do not allow graffiti to attract more graffiti.

■ Keep bases of columns, stairs, dock edges, fixed ladders, and other safeguards painted yellow for easy identification.

■ Keep tops of lockers free of dirt, debris, used gloves, etc. Periodically paint the inside of lunchrooms, rest rooms, and locker rooms.

■ Keep drawers closed on filing cabinets, tool boxes, etc.

■ Remove torn, obsolete, or defaced signs. Then replace with new signs.

Figure 8-5. A reminder to prevent slips and falls. (Courtesy of the National Safety Council)

- Assign someone to look after lunchrooms and break areas so that food scraps, bottles, wrappers, and cans do no accumulate.

- Empty garbage cans on a regular basis. Keep garbage cans covered properly to prevent attracting rodents and insects.

- Control the growth of weeds and grass on warehouse property.

NEW EMPLOYEES

During employee safety orientations, the subject of housekeeping must be discussed. This is the time to acquaint new employees with the importance of housekeeping, as well as the housekeeping duties they are to accomplish. If a supervisor waits too long before spelling out such responsibilities, some employees may think that something extra is being added to their jobs. Be sure to define the new employees' area of housekeeping responsibility. Point out where the trash bins are and where debris and refuse is to be placed.

BENEFITS OF GOOD HOUSEKEEPING

In any warehouse safety program, housekeeping should be viewed as a component that is beneficial to the bottom line. Productivity can be increased with housekeeping improvements. It is important to keep the following issues in mind regarding the overall benefits of housekeeping.

- Correct housekeeping portrays an image of a clean, neat, and tidy location. Potential customers should feel positive about coming into a warehouse and finding it clean and orderly.

- Good housekeeping reduces labor costs by requiring safe handling and storage of product. When tools and product are stored in an orderly fashion, they are less likely to be damaged and time is not lost looking for items that may be buried under debris.

- Poor housekeeping contributes to an estimated one-third of all workplace injuries. Improved housekeeping will result in fewer injuries, a significant benefit to an organization.

- Good housekeeping has a positive effect on employee morale. A clean workplace can help instill pride in a workforce. Taking pride in the working environment can help reduce employee grievances.

- Handling and storage can be enhanced through improved housekeeping. Storage capacity can be maximized by efficient organization of product for housekeeping purposes.

- Damage to racking, product, and the building are a by-product of poor housekeeping. Lift trucks can easily push overstacked product into racks and shelves. When debris or product is kept off the floor, the opportunity for damage is reduced.

- Many shipping errors result from product that is not staged correctly and at the time of shipment cannot be found. Good housekeeping can help reduce the space needed for shipping areas and increase accuracy.

- Good housekeeping aids in inventory control. Accuracy of inventory control is not possible without good housekeeping.

■ When products become difficult to find in a warehouse, many times this is a result of poor housekeeping. Profits are reduced when product becomes out-of- date or obsolete.

■ OSHA citations target housekeeping problems on a regular basis. A good way to avoid this type of citation is to practice good housekeeping.

■ Good housekeeping makes it possible to have an orderly evacuation of employees during an emergency.

SLIPS AND FALLS

The National Safety Council reported that slips and falls are the leading cause of death in the workplace, and the source of more than 20 percent of all disabling injuries. Falls cause more than 564,000 disabling injuries each year.

Slips and falls may be among the easiest incidents to isolate and prevent. Much of the corrective action involves safe housekeeping practices. The condition of the working floor surface is another area of importance.

Sometimes slips and falls are blamed on clumsy people and little thought is given to prevention. A slip and fall is usually the result of an abnormality in the environment that suddenly makes a routine act dangerous. A slip occurs when there is a sudden loss of traction between the shoe or foot and the walking surface. The normally dry surface of a floor or stair provides enough traction for people to move about without slipping or skidding.

A smooth, shiny surface on a floor looks terrific, but water, chemicals, oil, snow, ice, or grease can turn the surface very slick. All of this adds up to the high potential for a slip or fall. Steel, coated concrete, diamond plate, and tile can easily provide a very slippery surface if coated with any of the contaminants listed above.

Slippery surfaces can be temporarily corrected through the use of peel-and-stick tread tapes, sand added to paint, and chemical etches. But all of these remedies wear quickly and could possibly pose additional problems. Permanent coatings should not be applied until the floor has been meticulously cleaned of all grease, dirt, paint, oil, tar, glaze, surface hardeners, loose mortar, and cement. Light abrasive blasting and acid etching are two of the more common preparation techniques.

The most common floor coatings are epoxies, urethanes, and water-based epoxies. These coatings are reported to be environmentally friendly and can deliver long-term service on concrete floors. The recommendations from the coating manufacturers should be followed for mixing, reducing, and applying the floor coating.

Not only will floors look better, but the safety of workers should be enhanced. Coated floors look excellent and can be a real benefit to the housekeeping program. Before embarking on any floor improvement effort, check with the experts to be sure the project is feasible.

SUMMARY

Effective housekeeping programs play a major role in reducing injury and associated costs. Keeping floors clean and smooth greatly improves the appearance of a warehouse. Material handling equipment such as lift trucks and automatic guided vehicles will operate more efficiently and have fewer service problems. Clean floors reflect management's commitment to quality of the workplace. The customer's perception of the warehouse is improved through better housekeeping. The direct and indirect costs associated with injuries, product damage, and property damage are reduced through an effective housekeeping program.

Housekeeping is everyone's responsibility, and effective safety and health programs cannot be effective without this focus. Employees come to appreciate a clean and orderly workplace. Cleanliness and order are common to improved employee morale.

REFERENCES

Armco Steel Corporation. Five Kinds of Job Safety Training, Accident Prevention Fundamentals and Industrial Hygiene. Middletown, OH, 1976, p. 9-1.

Business and Legal Reports, Inc. Good Housekeeping, Supervisor's Safety Talks. December 1993, pp. 115.1–115.8.

Coban, Leon. "Good Housekeeping Makes Good Business Sense." Handling and Shipping Management. August 1985, pp. 54–56.

Feldman, Steven. "Total Traction. Occupational Health and Safety. April 1998, pp. 33–34.

Harper, Andrew, et al. "Curtin Industrial Safety Trial: Methods and Safe Practice and Housekeeping Outcomes." Safety Science. Vol. 24, No. 3, 1997, pp. 159–172.

Hart, Todd. "Selecting a Coating System for Concrete Floors." IMPO. September 1997, p. 76.

Larson, Melissa. "Light Your Way to Better Quality." Quality. January 1998, pp. 44–45.

OSHA 1910.22, General Requirements, Housekeeping.

The Safe Foreman. "Good Housekeeping = Good Safety." Vol. 65, No. 9, September 1994, pp. 4–7.

Shapiro, Joan. "Good Housekeeping Hampers Hazards." Today's Supervisor. December 1994, pp. 14–15.

Witt, Clyde E. "Productivity Through Floor Maintenance." Material Handling Engineering. September 1997, pp. 71–73.

9

Dock Safety

Warehouse docks are very busy departments that move many thousands of pounds of goods each day. Docks are a vital part of every distribution center—and they can be as dangerous as they are functional.

The main issues of dock safety begin with proper design, safeguarding, training, lighting, and employee communications. Docks expose workers to a variety of hazards, such as powered industrial trucks, chemicals, fire, material handling, trailer movement, and weather conditions. Visitors and their personal safety is also a concern. The potential for injury is a part of every dock operation and poor safety practices are responsible for some of most serious ones. The National Safety Council estimates that between 10 and 25 percent of all injuries occur on loading docks. Figure 9-1 illustrates the dangers of trailer creep. In this case the operator jumped clear. Movement of trailers and lift trucks is probably the most serious dock risk.

INJURY DATA

The most serious injuries involve powered equipment and the movement of trailers. Operators, employees, and visitors are vulnerable to injury. Pedestrians become victims of many dock injuries; more than twenty workers die each year after being struck by powered equipment or product being handled by this equipment. Many others are seriously injured or killed in adjacent areas of docks.

A comprehensive study of narrow-aisle truck injuries and fatalities by a major manufacturer of powered equipment was very descriptive of dock-related injuries and incidents. The study took place over a nineteen-year period. The data showed that:

- 72 lift trucks went off the dock.

- 127 lift trucks tipped over.

- 64 pedestrians were struck by lift trucks or product.

Figure 9-1. Trailer creep caused the gap between the dock and the trailer.

111

The study found that there were three subcategories involving off-the-dock incidents. The three categories were:

- Forklift traveling forward (forks leading)

- Forklift traveling in reverse (forks trailing)

- Falling dock plate.

Table 9-1 identifies the direction in which the narrow-aisle truck was traveling during the dock incident. Note that traveling in reverse (forks trailing) accounted for the most incidents in this study. The study, as identified in Table 9-2, further details the action of the operator during the off-the-dock incidents.

Table 9-1. Direction of Lift Truck Movement during Dock Incident

Incident Type	Incident Total	Percent
Rear direction	32	44
Forward direction	13	18
Dock plate fell	13	18
Direction unknown	14	19
Total	72	100

Table 9-2. Operator Action during Event at Dock

Operator Action	Incident Total	Percent
Operator jumped	29	40
Stayed with lift truck	13	18
Jumped or ejected	10	14
Partially ejected	4	6
No operator	2	3
Attempted jump	2	3
Unknown	12	17
Total	72	100

How serious were the injuries to the 72 employees of off-the-dock narrow-aisle truck incidents? Fortunately, one-third of the incidents did not involve an injury. Of course, the facility in which the incident occurred experienced significant economic losses as a result of work stoppages, damaged equipment, and most likely damaged product. Table 9-3 provides the details regarding the outcome of the off-the-dock incidents.

Table 9-3. Injury Severity versus Operator Action

Operator action	None	Minor	Major	Fatal	Unknown	Total
Attempted jump	0	1	1	0	0	2
Jumped	15	10	3	1	0	29
Jumped or ejected	0	0	5	4	1	10
No operator	2	0	0	0	0	2
Partially ejected	0	0	4	0	0	4
Stayed	2	8	1	0	2	13
Unknown	5	3	4	0	0	12
Total	24	22	18	5	3	72

A few of the more significant details for these off-the-dock narrow-aisle lift truck incidents are worth noting.

- Trailer pulled away, forklift fell rearward, operator jumped and suffered broken ribs and leg.

- Forklift drove off dock; employee had three fingers amputated.

- Forklift drove rearward off dock; driver ejected and had leg amputated below knee.

- Forklift fell rearward off dock; operator jumped or was ejected and sustained serious injuries to back, pelvis, and internal organs.

- Forklift fell rearward off dock; operator was partially ejected and suffered a broken back and collarbone.

- Forklift fell rearward off dock when truck pulled away; operator was pinned by falling lift truck and was killed.

- Forklift fell off the dock; operator was partially ejected and had two toes amputated.

- Forklift fell rearward off the dock; operator suffered a broken pelvis.

It is apparent from data in this study, as well as many other reports of serious injuries, incidents, and fatalities, that docks can be a dangerous department in a warehouse.

With up to one-fourth of all warehouse injuries occurring at the dock, hazards must be identified and eliminated. Employees must also be trained to recognize these hazards. Many dock hazards have a high potential for causing injury, but the most prevalent incident occurs when powered industrial trucks fall or are driven off the dock. One study revealed that 56 percent of all incidents at docks resulted from off-the-dock causes. Twenty percent of these incidents resulted in death. The graphic illustration in Figures 9-2 and 9-3 show the danger of trailer pull-away with the lift truck still in the trailer. In this case, no one was injured when the forklift came shooting out of the rear of the trailer.

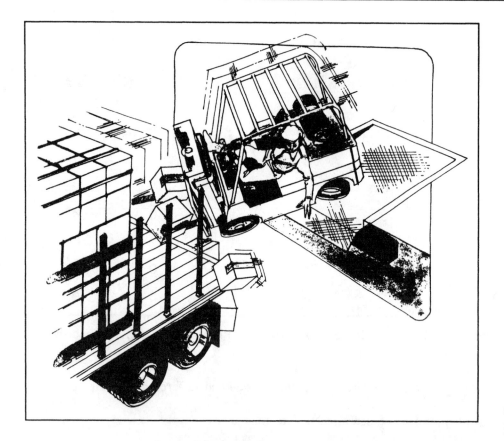

Figure 9-2. This trailer truck pulled away from the dock with the lift truck still inside. (Courtesy of the Rite-Hite Corporation)

Figure 9-3. This forklift fell out of the trailer and landed on the counterweight.

The dangers at docks were apparent in two articles regarding serious incidents that were reported in local newspapers. In one case a twenty-eight-year-old powered equipment operator was crushed to death when the piece of powered equipment turned over while loading a trailer. The truck driver began driving away from the dock, unaware that the forklift was still in the trailer. An unexpected movement of a trailer is not an uncommon event. In this particular case the truck's movement caused the forklift to topple, landing on top of the operator.

In another case, an employee was awarded nearly $1 million after losing a leg in a loading-dock incident. This employee, too, was entering a trailer with his forklift when the driver pulled away from the dock. The forklift dropped, pinning the employee to the front of the dock with the forklift prongs.

Wearing seat belts is essential for operator safety. Figure 9-4 illustrates wing seats and seat belts on this lift truck.

SAFE DOCK DESIGN

Since the dock area is a high-risk department in any warehouse, management must provide as many safeguards as possible. Much of the safety performance, as well as increased productivity, depends on proper design.

Planning a safe dock should not be undertaken without the assistance of professional planners. Docks must be designed to accommodate various heights and widths of trailers. Since April 1983, the federal government has approved trailer widths up to 102 inches.

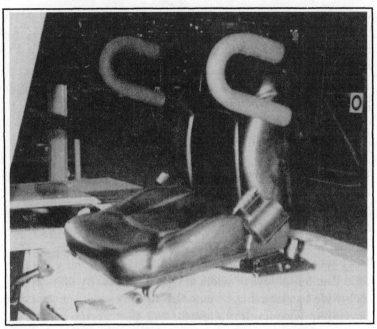

Figure 9-4. Lift trucks with wing-type seats offer more protection to operators. Always wear your seatbelt.

This width requires dock planners to allow more spacing between each dock door. Dock seals and dock shelters must be purchased or modified to allow for the trailer width. More maneuvering room outside of the dock area is also needed; trailers are now 48 feet and longer. Driveways, approaches, and turning areas must be properly designed for extended trailer size.

The potential for a trailer to have a lower floor must also be considered in planning. Conventional trailer heights from the ground to the floor level of the trailer are 48 to 52 inches. High cube trucks have dimensions as low as 36 inches. One way to accommodate this height difference is by installing 30-inch-high dedicated docks. However, these docks can only be used for trailers that are compatible.

Sloped approaches to docks can be a problem in the planning process. The correct dock height is important, and alternatives may have specific drawbacks. Portable ramps can elevate the trailer but serious consideration must be given to proper ramp size and safety. Truck levelers can be installed to adjust the trailer height to the dock. These installations are potentially expensive. Dock shelters, seals, and canopies must also be modified for new dock height design.

Dock planners have the following recommendations for truck traffic. Properly planned access to warehouse docks minimizes and reduces the hazards to employees and visitors entering the property. Safe zones for pedestrians and employee vehicle traffic must be considered.

Service roads should be no less than 26 feet in width. If possible, wider road access will pay greater dividends for future safety. Operators of trailers have approximately 2 feet of clearance when they are passing and approximately 1½ to 2 feet of side clearance. This amount of space may be adequate, but it adds a safety factor to have wider access.

One-way service roads may be an advantage and, if at all possible should be installed. Traffic circulation is better and safer. Widths of these service roads should be at least 12 feet. If the roadway will be used to provide pedestrian traffic, a 4-foot-added-width lane with a 4-foot-high protective barrier is needed.

The ideal flush dock has a level driveway, preferably slightly pitched away from the building to allow for proper drainage. When buildings are designed with a sloped driveway, backing trucks can easily strike and damage the building. Those employees that spot trailers must also be aware of the hazards involved with property damage when moving the vehicles.

Dock levelers are another aspect that must be planned properly. The length of the dock leveler is important. The usual guideline is that the longer they are, the longer the life of the unit. Dock levelers should be planned for a minimum lifespan of ten years. Lengths of dock levelers range for 2 feet 4 inches to 12 feet. Most are 8 feet in length.

Dock leveler widths, for recessed levelers, are usually in three basic widths: 6-foot, 6-foot 6 inches, and 7-foot. The 6-foot leveler width allows for access by 40-inch pallets on an 8-foot-wide trailer. The 6-foot 6-inch-wide leveler can accommodate 40-inch and 48-inch-wide pallets in an 8-foot or 8-foot 6 inches trailer. Seven-foot-wide levelers allow for two 48-inch side-by-side pallets in an 8-foot or 8-foot 6-inch trailer. If a 6-foot wide leveler is used for an 8-foot 6-inch trailer, a drop-off is created at the edge of the leveler. This can be hazardous to operators because it would be difficult to properly lift 48-inch pallets within these dimensions.

Dock leveler capacities should be based on the greatest impact that they will be subjected to from loads and powered industrial trucks. Greater-impact loading takes place on dock levelers that contain raised grades rather than being placed on a 0 percent grade. As an example, an 8,000-pound forklift carrying 4,000 pounds while traveling at 6 mph creates 30,000 pounds of impact force while traveling up an 11.5 percent grade.

Dockworkers must always be prepared for the unexpected. In Figure 9-5 a trailer door caught on the warehouse roll up door and pulled the entire door down, just missing several workers.

Figure 9-5. This trailer latch got tangled with the dock door rope. When the driver puller forward, he brought the entire dock door down. Fortunately, no one was injured.

VEHICLE RESTRAINTS

The unexpected movement of trailers at docks over the years has caused many injuries and deaths. To prevent movement of trailers, powered equipment operators can be protected by wheel chocks and various forms of mechanical trailer restraints.

A reminder sign attached to a cross-dock chain will deter operators from entering trailers at the wrong time, making the dock safer. This only acts as a warning device and will not stop a lift truck. Figure 9-6 illustrates this device.

Some thirteen dock equipment manufacturers provide vehicle restraints to industry. Many plant managers, safety professionals, and warehouse employees support the use of trailer restraints for many reasons. Most of all, these devices provide a much safer environment for powered equipment operators.

Manual wheel chocking is the traditional method of keeping the trailer safely in place for proper loading and unloading. Even though wheel chocks work in most cases, they are not the most effective trailer securing devices. Consider that the tractor trailer operator should be the person responsible for properly chocking the wheels when spotting a trailer, and powered equipment operators must not enter a trailer until they are assured that the wheels are chocked. If the wheels have not been chocked, then the powered equipment operator must take it upon himself to complete this task. There are warehouses that do not use wheel chocks; they may have used them at one time, but they were either lost or stolen and never replaced. It is not unusual to see wheel chocks lying unused on the dock. The facility should always have spare chocks on-hand.

If the dock-well surface area is covered with snow or ice, the wheel chocks may not be effective in providing security from trailer movement. If a sloped dock well has a drainage problem, the dock well could easily have 4 to 6 inches of water in it. This condition makes it less likely that anyone would venture out to install or remove wheel chocks.

When dock doors are being occupied by trailers, a visual check must be made of each trailer to ensure chocks are in place. Dock shelters can easily block the view of trailers' rear wheels. As a result, operators may have to physically check their particular trailers by going out-of-doors.

Chocks can easily slip away from the trailer wheel. The constant impact of powered equipment entering and exiting trailers can cause trailers to creep. Trailers prematurely pulling away from the dock cause many injuries and deaths each year. When wheels are not chocked, trailers pull forward more easily.

Figure 9-6. This sign alerts lift truck operators to stay out of the trailer.

Wheel chocks can be very effective in preventing trailer movement if the chocks are used properly. Some organizations assume that if the tractor is hooked onto the trailer, the driver will not pull away from the dock without checking to see if anyone is in the trailer. There have been cases where an operator had to remove only one pallet from a trailer and, through a lack of communication, was injured when the lift truck fell into the dock well when the trailer pulled away. All trailers that back into a dock must be chocked, even if a trailer is attached to the tractor with the air brakes set and the dock is sloped.

Vehicle restraints are more effective than manual wheel chocking. The restraint has a moveable steel hook, bar, or handle mounted onto the dock wall face. The hook, bar, or handle attaches to the ICC (Interstate Commerce Commission) bar, which is the horizontal bar mounted below the trailer bumper. This device is also called a rear impact guard.

When a trailer is backed into the dock, an employee activates the restraint by pushing a button on a control panel inside the building. Once the ICC bar is secured to the restraint, the trailer cannot move until loading or unloading is completed. The employee must push a button to deactivate the unit. Other units are activated when the trailer makes contact with a sensor on the restraint. If the ICC bar is missing or defective and the restraint can't lock onto the trailer, an alarm will sound to alert everyone to this condition.

Warning lights, like those in Figure 9-7 provide visual signals to powered equipment operators and truck drivers. When a trailer is secure, a green light flashes inside the building. Outside the dock door, a red light flashes to warn the truck drivers that the trailer cannot be moved because of the restraint device. When the device is released, a green light flashing outside of the building indicates that the trailer can be pulled away. The flashing red light inside the building alerts the operators not to enter the trailer. A flashing amber light warns of a malfunction in the system.

Figure 9-7. A red warning light inside the building warns operators to stay out of the trailer. A green light allows access.

The flashing lights and signage inside and outside of the building simultaneously alert operators of the powered equipment and the trailer operators that the restraints are being used. While backing into a dock well, the tractor trailer operator will be able to read the warning signs from his mirror—all of which are printed in reverse on the sign, but are readable in his mirror.

Not all trailers or trucks can be safely secured at docks. Trailers may not be equipped with ICC bars or the bar may be bent or missing. To mechanically secure these vehicles, a few new patented devices have been developed. For one specific unit, the process is as follows:

1. The trailer or truck is backed up to a dock door that is equipped with a special restraint device.

2. The vehicle backs over the low-profile "sled" in its low-profile stored position.

3. When the sled makes contact with the tires, it is activated.

4. Oval steel barriers rise up, much like an open clamshell. The barriers are then positioned against the truck's rear tires. Figure 9-8 illustrates this device called a *Wheel-Lok*.

Fully engaged, the device will secure a trailer against a 32,000 lb pullout force.

The mechanism consists of a simple, self-locking screw drive assembly and contains just three basic components.

Another mechanical wheel restraint system has been designed to allow for wheel chocking even if ICC bars are missing or damaged. Ultra low trailers, hydraulic lift gates, step vans, pickup trucks, and defective landing gears are not obstructions to this device. This system uses a single chock that inserts itself behind the first rear wheel it encounters. The trailer or truck can be equipped with a single pair or dual-double wheels.

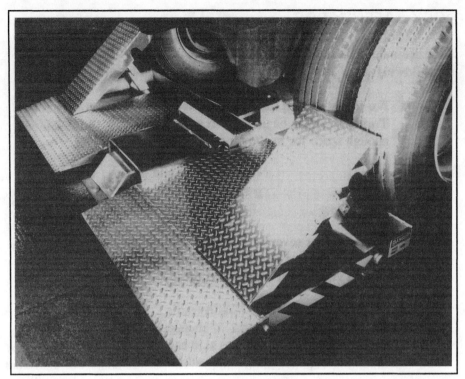

Figure 9-8. The Rite-Hite Corporation has developed a trailer restraint called the Wheel-Lok. It can be used on trailers with or without an ICC bar. (Courtesy of the Rite-Hite Corporation)

This hydraulic chock snugs the truck to the dock. A push button inside the building is activated to start the chock cycle. Appropriate lights alert those inside the building and outside. The parking pad allows the truck to place the trailer more easily at the dock. A look into the rearview mirror helps guide the operator.

For additional safety at a shipping or receiving dock, the Rite-Hite® Corporation has designed a safety barrier as a part of the dock plate. When the dock plate lip is in the stored position and not being used to gain access to a truck or trailer, a barrier is in place to prevent a dock incident. Figure 9-9 provides an illustration of this barrier. The dock plate is specially designed to operate hydraulically at the touch of a button at the dock. Should a trailer pull away from the dock, the dock plate folds back into a stored position with the "Safe-T-Lip" in its upright position.

Figure 9-9. This hydraulic dock plate is equipped with a safety lip, preventing the lift truck from driving off the edge of the loading dock. (Courtesy of the Rite-Hite Corporation)

DOCK SAFEGUARDS

There are numerous safeguards that can be implemented in a warehouse to make the dock a safer place. The following items should be considered for any facility safety program.

- For the most part, traffic control is more difficult at a dock than at other parts of a warehouse. Traffic lanes can be difficult to establish because of product and vehicle movement. Allow enough space for freedom of movement for lift trucks.

- Some important dock traffic rules would include: Vehicles must yield to any other piece of equipment approaching from another direction; always pass on the right; give the right-of-way to any piece of equipment backing out of a trailer.

- Material must never be stored on the dock where it can interfere with traffic movement or block the view of operators. Panoramic-style or convex mirrors can be a real plus for improved visibility of the working area.

- Signs such as "danger—forklift traffic," "caution—lift trucks," etc., can add to dock safety. Ice, rain, grease, oil, sand, or chemical spills can make the dock slippery, and a lack of traction can cause forklifts to skid and strike people, product, or the building. Operating speeds should be kept to a minimum to allow for full control of the vehicle despite the condition of the driving surface. Cones, signs, and barricades should be readily available to be placed where needed.

- The bridge between the dock and the trailer truck must be sturdy, secure, and capable of accepting capacity loads on powered equipment in use.

- When operating a powered walkie truck near the dock edge, never back the unit to the dock. Always have the load toward the dock for personal safety.

- Cross-traffic over dock levelers should be prohibited. A lift truck could easily fall through the gap left by a recessed ramp.

- Dock levelers must be chosen for length. Gentler grades provide for safer use. Grades for electric pallet trucks should not exceed 7 percent. Grades for electric forklifts should not exceed 10 percent. Gas-powered forklifts should not exceed a 15 percent grade. Low-slung material handling vehicles can easily hang up on the crown at the top of the slope. Excess slope also requires lift trucks to accelerate sharply going into or out of trailers. Loads could easily spill as a result of this acceleration.

- Before installing or redesigning dock areas, check with the product manufacturers to ensure safe design and overall safe working conditions in relation to the product. Always follow the manufacturer's guidelines for the care and use of the equipment.

- Safety stops are another feature of dock levelers, to keep the ramp from free-falling in case a trailer separates unexpectedly from the dock. Lift trucks crossing an unsupported platform can fall to the bottom of the leveler and possibly off the dock. Safety stops limit the free fall of the platform.

- Dock jumping by employees can be very dangerous. A dock ladder must be installed to accommodate anyone going down to the dock well. The rungs of the ladder should be at least 1 foot apart. The width of the ladder should not be less than 16 inches. Side rails should extend 3 feet above the dock landing for easy access or egress. Skid-resistant rungs must also be considered, especially where weather affects the dock area. Paint the ladder yellow for greater visibility

- Truck drivers should be alerted to dock safety rules both inside and outside of the facility. They should not have free access to the dock area, for their own personal safety. Truck drivers will most likely not be familiar with forklift traffic patterns at the dock. This unfamiliarity creates the potential for injury.

- Portable dock plates can be used to bridge the gap between the dock and trailer, but there are some inherent dangers. The capacity must be adequate to handle the weight of the lift truck and load. The overall condition of the plate must be assured through regular inspections. The plates may be difficult to install. Back injuries are possible as well as pinch points to the hands and feet of those manually handling the plates.

- Overlap of the portable dock plate must be at least 8 inches. This distance should be checked continuously to ensure that no slippage has occurred. Trailer creep could easily result in overlap shrinkage. Curbed edges on the plate help to ensure that the lift truck will not drive off of the plate. Legs that are attached to the bottom of the plate help to keep the plate from scooting backwards, when a lift truck accelerates on its surface. The grade of the ramp is also important; if too short, an extension ramp may be needed.

- Where possible, have a powered industrial truck lift the portable dock plate to prevent workers from being injured. Stay clear of the movement of the lift truck and plate. When not in use, store plates flat on the floor. If placed against a wall, the angle of the ramp must be proper to prevent a struck-by tipover incident.

- Lighting at the dock must be adequate to prevent incidents, injuries, and product damage. Quality and accuracy in handling the product are also issues related to proper lighting. Low level lighting can cause many problems. In addition to overhead lighting, there is always a need to provide lighting inside a trailer. This can be accomplished through fixed lights on the lift trucks and swing-away lights mounted on the dock adjacent to the dock doors.

- Employee training is essential for dock safety. Injuries are more likely, and productivity is affected, when management does not provide a comprehensive training program. Training should include manual material handling, powered industrial truck movement, the handling of chemicals or chemical spills, and ergonomic issues.

- Personal protective equipment is a must for warehouse employees, including those who work at the dock. Hard hats, gloves, and steel toe shoes/boots provide the bare essentials for protection. Hearing protection, eye and face protection, and rubber aprons (for battery care) are also important.

- In the event of a chemical spill, a chemical cleanup station should be easily accessible. Employees must be trained in the proper use of the materials as well as how to protect themselves from chemical hazards. Material safety data sheets must be available for all chemicals stored in the building, and those received at the dock. Compliance with any EPA disposal rules must be a part of the training program.

- An added measure of security for trailer safety is the positioning of jacks under the nose of the trailer. Landing wheels of trailers have been known to fail, which allows the trailer to tip nose-down at the dock. Trailer occupants could be injured by this incident.

SUMMARY

Rules and guidelines for dock safety are both broad and focused. The likelihood of serious injuries is ever-present at any warehouse if safety rules are not followed. Docks are a necessary part of every warehouse, and each employee must understand the necessity of safe behavior. Safety training should be provided to every employee and supervisor working at the dock. Visitors will also be in harm's way if proper safeguards are not taken. The high cost of dock-related injuries can be reduced through enforcement of safety rules, proper engineering controls, and employee training. Because the movement of product is often intense in a dock area, the attention given to safety must be constant. Figure 9-10 serves as a reminder of dock safety.

(An extensive dock safety checklist is included at the end of this chapter, courtesy of Rite-Hite Corporation. See Figure 9-11.)

Figure 9-10. This poster is a reminder that safety at the dock requires one's constant attention. (Courtesy of the National Safety Council)

REFERENCES

Feare, Tom. "New Wheel Restraints Advance Goal of Accident-Free Docks." *Modern Materials Handling*. February 1996, pp. 52–54.

Holzauer, Ron. "Loading Docks: Doorway to the Plant." *Plant Engineering*. August 1997, pp. 53–57.

Ketchpaw, Bruce. "The Loading Dock: Combating New Hazards." *Risk Management*. July 1986, pp. 44–48.

Rite-Hite Corporation. *Dock Design Guide*. Milwaukee, WI. 1990.

Rite-Hite Corporation. *Dock Safety Guide*. Milwaukee, WI. 1989.

Rite-Hite Corporation. *Dok-Lok Safety Systems*. Milwaukee, WI. 1991.

Schwind, Gene. "New Product Spotlight: Single Chock at the Dock." *Material Handling Engineering*. January 1998, p. 32.

Savart, J.B., P.E. *Analysis of 804 Crown Stand-Up Forklift Accident Reports. January of 1975 through December of 1993*. Report No: ATI-941002. Wichita, KS: Advance Technology, Inc., October 21, 1994.

Templer, Audrey. "Creating a Safe Loading Dock." *Plant Engineering*. April 1994, pp. 86–90.

"Hectic Warehouse Activity Increases Potential for Loading Dock Mishaps." *Occupational Health and Safety*. September 1993, pp. 111–115.

Loading Dock Safety Checklist

Provided as a service to industry by Rite-Hite Corporation.

Date _____

Company Name _____

Plant Name _____ Plant Location _____

Dock examined/Door numbers _____

Company representative completing checklist:

Name _____ Title _____

A. Vehicles/Traffic Control

1. Do forklifts have the following safety equipment?
   - ☐ Seat belt ☐ Load backrest
   - ☐ Headlight ☐ Backup alarm
   - ☐ Horn ☐ Overhead guard
   - ☐ Tilt indicator
   - ☐ On-board fire extinguisher
   - ☐ Other _____

2. Are the following in use?

	Yes	No
Driver candidate screening	☐	☐
Driver training/licensing	☐	☐
Periodic driver retraining	☐	☐
Vehicle maintenance records	☐	☐
Written vehicle safety rules	☐	☐

	Yes	No
3. Is the dock kept clear of loads of materials?	☐	☐
4. Are there convex mirrors at blind corners?	☐	☐
5. Is forklift cross traffic over dock levelers restricted?	☐	☐
6. Is pedestrian traffic restricted in the dock area?	☐	☐
7. Is there a clearly marked pedestrian walkway?	☐	☐
8. Are guardrails used to define the pedestrian walkway?	☐	☐

9. Comments/recommendations

_____
_____
_____
_____
_____

B. Vehicle Restraining

	Yes	No
1. If vehicle restraints are used:		
a. Are all dock workers trained in the use of the restraints?	☐	☐
b. Are the restraints used consistently?	☐	☐
c. Are there warning signs and lights inside and out to tell when a trailer is secured and when it is not?	☐	☐
d. Are the outdoor signal lights clearly visible even in fog or bright sunlight?	☐	☐
e. Can the restraints secure trailers regardless of the height of their ICC bars?	☐	☐
f. Can the restraints secure all trailers with I-beam, round, or other common ICC bar shapes?	☐	☐
g. Does the restraint sound an alarm when a trailer cannot be secured because its ICC bar is missing or out of place?	☐	☐

RITE·HITE

h. Are dock personnel specifically trained to watch for trailers with unusual rear-end assemblies (e.g. sloping steel back plates and hydraulic tailgates) that can cause a restraint to give a signal that the trailer is engaged even when it is not safely engaged? ☐ ☐

i. Are dock personnel specifically trained to observe the safe engagement of all unusual rear-end assemblies? ☐ ☐

j. Do the restraints receive regular planned maintenance? ☐ ☐

k. Do restraints need repairs or replacement? (List door numbers.)

_____

l. Comments recommendations

_____

_____

_____

2. If wheel chocks are used: Yes No

a. Are dock workers, rather than truckers, responsible for placing chocks? ☐ ☐

b. Are all dock workers trained in proper chocking procedures? ☐ ☐

c. Are chocks of suitable design and construction? ☐ ☐

d. Are there two chocks for each position? ☐ ☐

e. Are all trailers chocked on both sides? ☐ ☐

f. Are chocks chained to the building? ☐ ☐

g. Are warning signs in use? ☐ ☐

h. Are driveways kept clear of ☐ ☐ ice and snow to help keep chocks from slipping?

i. Comments recommendations

_____

_____

C. Dock Levelers and Ramps

   Yes No

1. Are the dock levelers working properly? ☐ ☐

2. Are levelers long enough to provide a gentle grade into trailers of all heights? ☐ ☐

3. Is leveler width adequate when servicing wide trailers? ☐ ☐

4. Do platform width and configuration allow safe handling of end loads? ☐ ☐

5. Is leveler capacity adequate given typical load weights, lift truck speeds, ramp inclines and frequency of use? ☐ ☐

6. Do levelers have the following safety features?
Working-range toe guards ☐ ☐
Full-range toe guards ☐ ☐
Ramp free-fall protection ☐ ☐
Automatic recycling ☐ ☐

7. Do levelers receive regular planned maintenance? ☐ ☐

8. Do levelers need repair or replacement? (List door numbers.)

_____

_____

9. Are dock levelers capable of helping prevent accidental falls of personnel or equipment from vacant loading docks? ☐ ☐

10. Are ramps kept clean and clear of debris, ice, snow or rain to prevent slipping and sliding during loading/unloading operations? ☐ ☐

11. Comments/recommendations_____

_____

_____

D. Portable Dock Plates

   Yes No

1. Is plate length adequate? ☐ ☐
2. Is plate capacity adequate? ☐ ☐
3. Are plates of suitable design and materials? ☐ ☐
4. Do plates have curbed sides? ☐ ☐
5. Do plates have suitable anchor stops? ☐ ☐
6. Are plates moved by lift trucks rather than by hand? ☐ ☐
7. Are plates stored away from traffic? ☐ ☐
8. Are plates inspected regularly? ☐ ☐
9. Do plates need repair or replacement? (List door numbers.)

_____

_____

10. Comments/recommendations

_____

_____

E. Dock Doors

	Yes	No
1. Are doors large enough to admit all loads without obstruction?	☐	☐
2. Are door rails protected by bumper posts?	☐	☐
3. Do doors receive regular planned maintenance?	☐	☐

4. Which doors (if any) need repair or replacement?

_____

5. Comments/recommendations

_____

_____

F. Traffic Doors

	Yes	No
1. Are doors wide enough to handle all loads and minimize damage?	☐	☐
2. Does door arrangement allow safe lift truck and pedestrian traffic?	☐	☐
3. Are visibility and lighting adequate on both sides of all doors?	☐	☐

4. Which doors (if any) need repair or replacement?

_____

5. Comments/recommendations

_____

_____

G. Weather Sealing

	Yes	No
1. Are the seals or shelters effective in excluding moisture and debris from the dock?	☐	☐
2. Are seals or shelters sized to provide an effective seal against all types of trailers?	☐	☐
3. Are seals or shelters designed so that they will not obstruct loading and unloading?	☐	☐

	Yes	No
4. Are dock levelers weather sealed along the sides and back?	☐	☐
5. In addition to seals or shelters, would an air curtain solve a problem?	☐	☐

6. Do seals or shelters need repair or replacement? (List door numbers.)

_____

7. Comments/recommendations

_____

_____

H. Trailer Lifting

1. How are low-bed trailers elevated for loading/unloading?
   ☐ Wheel risers   ☐ Concrete ramps
   ☐ Trailer-mounted jacks
   ☐ Truck levelers

	Yes	No
2. Do lifting devices provide adequate stability?	☐	☐
3. Are trailers secured with vehicle restraints when elevated?	☐	☐

4. Do lifting devices need repair or replacement? (List door numbers.)

_____

5. Comments/recommendations

_____

_____

I. Other Considerations

	Yes	No
1. Dock lights		
a. Is lighting adequate inside trailers?	☐	☐
b. Is the lift mechanism properly shielded?	☐	☐
2. Scissors lifts		
a. Are all appropriate workers trained in safe operating procedures?	☐	☐
b. Is the lift mechanism properly shielded?	☐	☐
c. Are guardrails and chock ramps in place and in good repair?	☐	☐

3. Conveyors
   a. Are all appropriate workers trained in safe operating procedures? ☐ ☐
   b. Are necessary safeguards in place to protect against pinch points, jam-ups and runaway material? ☐ ☐
   c. Are crossovers provided? ☐ ☐
   d. Are emergency stop buttons in place and properly located? ☐ ☐

4. Strapping
   a. Are proper tools available for applying strapping? ☐ ☐
   b. Do workers cut strapping using only cutters equipped with a holddown device? ☐ ☐
   c. Do workers wear hand, foot and face protection when applying and cutting strapping? ☐ ☐
   d. Are all appropriate workers trained in safe strapping techniques? ☐ ☐

5. Manual handling
   a. Is the dock designed so as to minimize manual lifting and carrying? ☐ ☐
   b. Are dock workers trained in safe lifting and manual handling techniques? ☐ ☐

6. Miscellaneous   Yes   No
   a. Are pallets regularly inspected? ☐ ☐
   b. Are dock bumpers in good repair? ☐ ☐
   c. Is the dock kept clean and free of clutter? ☐ ☐
   d. Are housekeeping inspections performed periodically? ☐ ☐
   e. Are anti-skid floor surfaces, mats or runners used where appropriate? ☐ ☐

   f. Are stairways or ladders provided for access to ground level from the dock? ☐ ☐
   g. Is the trailer landing strip in good condition? ☐ ☐
   h. Are dock approaches free of potholes or deteriorated pavement? ☐ ☐
   i. Are dock approaches and outdoor stairs kept clear of ice and snow? ☐ ☐
   j. Are dock positions marked with lines or lights for accurate trailer spotting? ☐ ☐
   k. Do all dock workers wear personal protective equipment as required by company policy? ☐ ☐
   l. Is safety training provided for all dock employees? ☐ ☐
   m. Are periodic safety refresher courses offered? ☐ ☐

J. General Comments/Recommendations

_____
_____
_____
_____
_____

For additional copies of this Loading Dock Safety Checklist, write to Rite-Hite Corporation, 8900 Arbon Drive, P.O. Box 23043, Milwaukee, WI 53223-0043.
For more information on loading dock safety, write for a complimentary copy of Rite-Hite's Dock Safety Guide.

This loading dock safety checklist is provided as a service by Rite-Hite Corporation, Milwaukee, Wis. It is intended as an aid to safety evaluation of loading dock equipment and operations. However, it is not intended as a complete guide to loading dock hazard identification. Therefore Rite-Hite Corporation makes no guarantees as to nor assumes any liability for the sufficiency or completeness of this document. It may be necessary under particular circumstances to evaluate other dock equipment and procedures in addition to those included in the checklist.
For information on U.S. loading dock safety requirements, consult OSHA Safety and Health Standards (29 CFR 1910). In other countries consult the applicable national or provincial occupational health and safety codes.

RITE·HITE®

Contact: Rite-Hite Corporation, 8900 N. Arbon Drive, P.O. Box 23043, Milwaukee, WI 53223
(414) 355-2600 ● 1-800-456-0600 ● FAX (414) 355-9248
Rite-Hite® is a registered trademark of the Rite-Hite Corporation

10

Powered Industrial Trucks

Powered industrial trucks play an important role in warehouse operations. The backbone of the material handling effort lies with the forklift; these pieces of powered equipment can also cause their share of incidents and injuries. Because the subject of powered equipment in a warehouse is a broad one, this chapter will deal with a variety of issues concerning the safety of the employee and the proper handling of the equipment.

OSHA STATISTICS

Powered industrial trucks can be dangerous pieces of equipment if operators are not properly trained, if the machines are not properly maintained and if management fails to enforce safety rules. Statistics show that more than 100 employees are killed each year as a result of powered industrial truck incidents. Some 34,900 suffer serious injuries that include fractures, amputations, and permanent disability. An additional 61,800 experience minor injuries. There are no statistics to identify the daily costs of incidents that cause product damage, property damage, fires, and delayed shipments. In all likelihood many thousands of these potentially serious incidents or events take place each day in the workplace, but they are often considered commonplace occurrences by workers and management.

An analysis of contributing factors in Table 10-1 identifies the causes of the annual toll of fatalities for powered industrial truck operators. Management should focus on the causes in an effort to prevent loss of life in their own facilities.

These percentages were taken from an OSHA study titled, "First Report of Serious Accidents, 1985–90."

Table 10-2 identifies an additional study by the Bureau of Labor Statistics and OSHA for the years 1991–92 evaluated 170 powered industrial truck fatalities.

Additional studies on forklift incidents have taken place in specific states as well as nationally. OSHA completed a computer search of data to identify the bank of information available on powered industrial truck injuries. The study identified 4,268 reports in the system search using the key word "industrial truck." Within the study, 3,038 fatalities, 3,244 serious injuries and 1,413 nonserious injuries were identified. It is important to note that some of the reports indicated multiple injuries and/or fatalities per incident.

127

Table 10-1. Causes of Forklift Incidents

Rank Order	Item	Percentage
1	Tipover	25.3%
2	Struck by powered industrial truck	18.8%
3	Struck by falling load	14.4%
4	Elevated employee on truck	12.2%
5	Ran off dock or other surfaces	7.0%
6	Improper maintenance procedures	6.1%
7	Lost control of truck	4.4%
7	Truck struck material	4.4%
7	Employees overcome by CO or propane fuel	4.4%
10	Faulty powered industrial truck	3.1%
10	Unloading unchocked trailer	3.1%
10	Employee fell from vehicle	3.1%
13	Improper use of vehicle	2.6%
14	Electrocutions	1.0%

Table 10-2. BLS Study of Forklift Fatalities - 1991/92

Cause of Fatality	Number	Percentage
Forklift overturned	41	24%
Worker struck by material	29	17%
Worker struck by forklift	24	14%
Worker fell from forklift	24	14%
Worker pinned between two objects	19	11%
Forklift struck something or ran off dock	13	8%
Worker died during forklift repair	10	6%
Other injury cause	10	6%
Totals	170	100%

OSHA Computer Search: Key Word "Industrial Truck"

Specific Injury/Fatality Causes (Listed by ranking)

- Operator inattention
- Overturn
- Unstable load
- Operator struck by load
- Elevated employee falling
- No training
- Overload, improper use of machine
- Injured during maintenance
- Obstructed view of operator
- Improper equipment being used
- Falling from platform or curb
- Not powered industrial truck injury
- Other employee struck by load
- Carrying excess passenger
- Vehicle left in gear
- Falling from trailer
- Speeding.

As demonstrated by the statistics, there are many ways in which an employee or pedestrian can be injured or killed by a piece of powered equipment. How do these injuries occur? What can we teach employees to safeguard them from injury?

TIPOVER

Statistics indicate that forklift tipover claims at least twenty-five lives each year in the United States. How does tipover occur, what are the causes, and how can it be prevented?

The OSHA results of the study presented in Table 10-3 list the following causes:

Another study of forklift tipover in California showed this incident to be the leading cause of powered industrial truck fatalities from 1966 to 1980. This research revealed that 66 fatalities occurred as a result of tipover. Table 10-4 highlights the data from this study.

In a 1995 study conducted in Ontario, Canada, some 6,000 recorded injuries associated with forklift trucks were identified. In 60 percent of the cases, the operator of the lift truck was involved in the incident. According to the data, 17 workers died and 143 were critically injured. Primary injury causes included:

- Collisions
- Falls from docks
- Falling or jumping from the lift truck
- Carbon monoxide exposure
- Tipover
- Rollover
- Explosions.

Table 10-3. OSHA Study of Tipover Incidents

Causes of Tipover	Number	Percentage
Elevated load on the vehicle was not controlled: speeding, mechanical problems, etc., were the cause.	7	13%
Lift truck ran off or over the edge of a dock, roadway, etc.	4	8%
Operator attempted to make too sharp of a turn in addition to excessive speed, unbalanced load, etc.	4	8%
Employee jumped from overturning lift truck while truck was being pulled by another vehicle.	2	4%
Lift truck skidded or slipped on a slippery surface.	2	4%
Wheels on lift truck on one side of the vehicle ran over a raised surface or object.	2	4%
Forklift tipped over when struck by another vehicle.	1	2%

Table 10-4. Causes of Forklift Tipover Fatalities in California 1966–80

Cause	Fatalities
Turning at excessive speed	15
Excessive or unbalanced load	7
Falling off loading dock or truck	6
Wheels falling into holes on soft ground	5
Running off ramps or up walls at end of ramps	4
Collision (mast/forks struck overhead obstacle)	3
Losing control on steep slope	3
Machine failure	3
Skidding on oil while turning	2
Running off road; steering sharply to get back on	1
Driving forks into hill at side of road	1
Driving in reverse along farm road, hit power pole, over-turned in irrigation canal	1
Worker riding on load of dry wall, load unbalanced, worker fell, load fell on him	1
Unknown	10
Total	66

A 1992 study of forklift incidents in Victoria, Australia, recorded the following as the predominant causes of worker injuries:

- Driving into coworkers

- Dropping loads

- Collisions

- Tipover.

Narrow-Aisle Trucks and Tipover

In a study of 804 injuries and incidents involving narrow-aisle lift trucks, tipover accounted for 127 of the reported claims, or 16 percent of the total. In the case of a narrow-aisle truck tipover incident, the truck can tip three different directions: forward, rearward, and onto its side. Of the 127-tipover incidents, 64 percent involved tipover onto the side of the lift truck, 12 percent were forward tipovers, and 11 percent were rearward tipovers. Those that occurred in an unknown direction accounted for 13 percent of the total incidents.

During tipover, operators take a certain action. This study revealed that four actions were commonly performed: ejected, jumped, jumped/ejected, and stayed. Operators jumping during narrow-aisle truck tipover occurred the most often; note the data in Table 10-5.

Twenty-six of the twenty-nine operators that stayed in the operator's compartment during tipover incidents reportedly received minor or no injuries. In three of the incidents the injury severity was unknown. The minor injuries were superficial, i.e., cuts, bruises, and scrapes. Those incidents where the operator did not remain in the operator's compartment accounted for all of the injuries major or fatal.

The direction of the tipover and the associated severity of the injury is identified in Table 10-6. This portion of the study shows that in the cases where the operator stayed within the confines of the operator's compartment, no major or fatal injuries were reported to have occurred.

Descriptions of the more serious narrow-aisle tipover incidents are identified below.

- Rearward tipover occurred; employee jumped and was pinned by the forklift; he suffered a broken leg.

- Lift truck tipped over and operator was ejected. He suffered a major back injury.

- Lift truck struck mezzanine and tipped over onto its side; operator fractured his pelvis.

- Lift truck tipped over onto its side; the operator jumped or was ejected and paralyzed his back.

- Lift truck struck overhead beam and tipped over; operator jumped from truck and was pinned by the unit. The operator was killed.

- Lift truck struck a door with the mast, tipped rearward, operator jumped and was pinned; his foot had to be amputated.

Table 10-5. Operator Action versus Direction of Tipover

Operator Action	Unknown	Forward	Rearward	Side	Total
Ejected	3	4	0	1	8
Jumped	6	2	9	46	63
Jumped/Ejected	0	0	0	1	1
Stayed	0	6	1	22	29
Unknown	7	3	4	12	26
Totals	16	15	14	82	127

Table 10-6. Direction of Tipover versus Injury Severity

Direction of Tipover	Operator Action	None	Minor	Major	Fatal	Unknown	Total
Forward		9	6	0	0	0	15
	Stayed	4	2	0	0	0	
	Other	2	4	0	0	0	
Rear		8	3	3	0	0	14
	Stayed	0	1	0	0	0	
	Other	5	2	3	0	0	
Side		60	16	2	1	3	82
	Stayed	11	8	0	0	0	
	Other	41	4	2	1	0	

(Circumstances associated with unknown operator actions not included in the above data)

Additional information on tipover incidents:

The OSHA Management Information System identified the following data as illustrated in Table 10-7.

Of the 93 tipover fatalities in this study, being pinned by the mast and overhead guard was the cause of more than half the deaths. Table 10-8 identifies the details in this phase of the study.

Tipover training must be a part of an operator's educational program. It is apparent that every effort must be made to prevent tipover in any warehouse or other industrial setting. Management has an obligation to train operators to save lives and prevent injuries. Those elements that are responsible for tipover—transporting a load improperly, speeding, violating the stability triangle—must be a part of training.

When a lift truck tips over onto its side like the incident shown in Figure 10-1, or goes forward or backward off a dock, the operator can be ejected. When this occurs the operator can easily be crushed by the

Table 10-7. Fatal Work-Related Injuries Investigated by OSHA 1984-89*

Involving Lift Truck Tipover or Rollover

Industry	Same-Level Tip Over	On Ramp, Incline or Ditch	Total
Agriculture/Forestry/Fishing	0	2	2
Construction	5	8	13
Manufacturing	18	23	41
Mining/Oil and Gas	1	0	1
Services	2	2	4
Wholesale and Retail Trade	14	5	19
Transport/Utilities	4	6	10
Other	2	1	3
Total	46	47	93

California, Washington, and Michigan were not in the data base

Table 10-8. Fatal Work-Related Injuries Involving Lift Trucks Investigated by OSHA

1984-89 — Mechanism of Physical Injury from Tipover or Rollover

Cause of Injury	Fatalities
Operator head slapped against floor; it was not struck by forklift	3
Mast or overhead protection structure struck victim	48
Part of lift truck other than the mast or overhead guard struck victim	12
No mention of what victim struck or what struck victim	30
Totals	93

overhead guard or mast. The operator could be caught between stationary objects during this process. Even when an operator takes the chance of jumping clear, the statistics show that he could easily be crushed. This list of the causes of tipover, though not all-inclusive, is illustrative:

■ Operator is traveling up or down a ramp or incline and decides to turn the lift truck and travel in the opposite direction.

■ Operator fails to check for wheel chocks at a trailer; the trailer creeps forward or pulls away from the dock.

■ Operator is traveling with an elevated load, or elevated empty mast, and makes a sharp turn.

■ Operator runs over a rut, block of wood, edge of a roadway, or dock.

Figure 10-1. This lift truck tipped over on a ramp. Fortunately the operator was not injured.

■ Operator drives into a hole, ditch, or off a roadway.

■ Operator turns sharply with a container of liquid; a simple tipover becomes an environmental issue

■ Operator is driving a lift truck with underinflated tires or tires that are in poor condition.

■ Lift truck is struck by another lift truck.

■ Lift truck drives off the edge of a flatbed truck.

■ Lift truck is inside a trailer when it pulls away from the dock. The lift truck and operator move out of the rear of the moving trailer and the forklift upsets.

■ Horseplay can be another cause of forklift tipover. One investigation of a fatality revealed that two employees were racing their forklifts while working in a brickyard. During the drag race, one forklift bumped into the other forklift, causing it to tip over. The employee tried to jump clear of the tipping lift truck only to have the overhead guard come down on his back, killing him.

Most lift trucks have four wheels; however, the stability of the lift truck is controlled by the two front wheels and the center of the rear axle. The front wheels carry the load; the rear wheels are for steering. The center of gravity is one of the major problems with forklifts. Speeds as low as 5 mph can tip a lift truck. Forklifts have a narrow wheel base, which contributes to tipover.

For operator protection, the lift truck manufacturers recommend the following operator guidelines in the event of tipover:

- Don't jump from the lift truck.

- Hold on tight (steering wheel, overhead guard).

- Brace your feet.

- Lean away from the side that is lowest during the tip.

- Wear the seat belt at all times.

For a stand-up-operated lift truck, the manufacturers recommend that the operator step out of the rear of the lift truck in event of a tipover. The entrance for the operator in a narrow-aisle truck would provide an open access to an immediate exit. However, there may be a few situations where exiting the truck could provide for more danger to the operator.

It is difficult to imagine the reaction of an employee when a tipover begins. There aren't any devices or methods to duplicate the experience of a tipover in training. One equipment manufacturer's safety literature recommends that when a tipover begins, the operator should brace his feet and reach up to grasp the overhead guard. This process requires serious thought, and it is difficult to imagine that every employee operating a narrow-aisle truck would be capable of this disciplined thinking as well as physical reaction. It is almost instinctive to jump clear of the tipping lift truck.

For this reason, seat belts on counter-balance trucks have become the norm. In addition to a seat belt is a modified operator's seat that includes a wrap-around shoulder support system, referred to as a wing seat. On other models, the base of the seat may be modified to include bolsters on each side to prevent the body from sliding out of the seat during tipover. The operator would still have to brace his feet, hold onto the steering wheel, and lean away from the tilt. It should be noted that a tipover occurs in approximately 1.5 seconds. This does not provide much time for anyone to plan response actions once the tipover has begun. As a result of the seat and seat belt improvements, the operator is provided with an added margin of safety.

The wing seat concept was first developed by Clark Equipment Company in the early 1980s. They funded research to determine what could be done to prevent tipovers. They began the research with ideas about what devices should be placed on lift trucks to protect operators during tipover.

As a result of this company's research and efforts, the forklift manufacturers have adopted the installation of seat belts and some form of seat restraint on their units. There is a lot of evidence indicating that these modified seats and seat belts have provided protection for operators.

Perhaps the most dramatic evidence to date supporting the use of forklift seat belts is the survival of a lift truck operator after a 40-foot fall. The operator was moving a pallet load of air compressor motors on the fourth floor of a warehouse when the floor collapsed. The forklift came to rest on its side. The overhead guard and the fact that the seat belt on a winged seat was used is credited with saving the life of the operator. The debris of the falling floor completely covered the lift truck. It took rescue personnel four and one-half hours to free him from tangled concrete and steel.

In another situation an operator at a warehouse dock was saved from serious injury because of a wing seat. A trailer pulled away from the dock too soon, before the last pallet was loaded. The front wheels of the lift truck were inside the trailer when the trailer pulled away. The lift truck fell to the dock well and bounced three times. The impulse of the operator who was not wearing a seat belt, was to jump off the lift truck, but the wing seat prevented him from doing so, and possibly saved his life.

Some have argued that operator training is the key to preventing injuries and fatalities during tipovers. Is training more basic than seat belts and wing seats? Can an employer rely on each operator to follow prescribed safety rules provided in the classroom? Many safety professionals insist on both training and the use of safety equipment.

There are a few studies that have indicated that seat belts are not always practical. In 1988 the Advanced Safety Studies Institute spent over $100,000 in grant money to determine if seat belts are practical, necessary, or advisable safety devices on forklifts. The testing used 4,000 - and 6,000 –pound-capacity counterbalanced remote controlled forklifts and anthropometric (humanlike) dummies—the kind used in auto crashes.

The conclusions of the institute's studies were:

- Lift trucks are not that easy to tip over.

- Properly trained operators seldom operate their trucks in a reckless manner.

- Providing seat belts does not mean that the operator will use them. Use of seat belts would be difficult to monitor and enforce.

- Seat belts can be restrictive and unsafe when the operator must also turn in the seat to operate the truck in reverse. This position is a very common operator's method of looking in the direction of travel.

- Visibility considerations override safety considerations when operators must turn their heads and upper bodies in the direction of travel.

- A belted-in operator will sustain more head injury from hitting the floor, and as much as an unbelted operator sustains from hitting the overhead guard.

- Belt enforcement is a great effort for an accident that is infrequent, although often severe, and one that training can prevent far more easily.

- Some street delivery trucks and postal drivers are exempt from state seat belt regulations for the same reasons they do not prove practical in lift truck operations, i.e., the driver is on and off the seat many times in the course of his work cycle.

- If you add seat belts, then you must enforce their use and enforcement implies safety.

Tipover usually occurs because of operator error. As an added safeguard to counter operator error, the wearing of seat belts and the use of wing seats make sense. Despite the fifteen years of operator-seat modifications and seat belt installations on counterbalance lift trucks, the toll of injuries and fatalities continue. The seat belt may not be a perfect device that is readily accepted by operators and management, but the use of such safety devices surely contributes to reducing the numbers of injuries and deaths. The use and enforcement of these devices should be a part of every operator's training.

FORKLIFT TRUCKS—GENERAL SAFETY GUIDELINES

The operator of a powered industrial truck must know and understand a myriad of safe operating rules and guidelines. All of the following guidelines can be a part of a comprehensive training package.

All operators must be thoroughly trained in the safe handling and use of their equipment. All employees should familiarize themselves with the manufacturer's guidelines for each specific vehicle or model of truck. Most powered industrial equipment requires operator safety instruction.

- Each piece of equipment must be evaluated prior to each work shift. Forms should be used to document the inspections.

- Management should review the inspection forms each day and provide corrective action on each deficiency.

- Only one person shall be on each piece of powered equipment at a time—no riders.

- Wear the required personal protective equipment. This could consist of hard hats, gloves, steel toe shoes or boots, safety glasses, or goggles.

- Know the locations of fire extinguishers and how to properly use an extinguisher if necessary.

- Report any defects or malfunctions to management as they are discovered.

- Never operate a malfunctioning lift truck. Properly secure the truck and hang an "out of service" sign or tag on it.

- Never overload the lift truck. The rated capacity is shown on an identification plate permanently mounted on the truck. Keep loads within the rated capacity.

- Always wear your seat belt when on a sit-down lift truck. Figure 10-2 illustrates the use of a seat belt.

- Always look in the direction of travel. If loads are too high, drive while in reverse.

- Before lifting a load, ensure that the product is stable and secure, that the load is within the capacity of the truck, that the pallet or container being used is not defective, and that the size of the load allows it to be driven to a prescribed location. The operator shown in Figure 10-3 is attempting to lift four containers of product rather than only two as required by the rules in the warehouse. These four containers could easily topple over.

- Keep forks approximately 6 inches off the floor when traveling. Figure 10-4 serves as a reminder for fork height.

- Ensure the forks are wide enough when lifting a pallet; keep forks as wide as possible for any load.

- When approaching corners or blind spots, or when going from a bright area into a darkened area, stop, look, and sound the horn before proceeding.

Figure 10-2. This forklift operator is correctly wearing his seat belt and looking in the direction of travel. (Courtesy of Clark Material Handling Company)

Figure 10-3. This operator is preparing to lift four pallets at one time. The company rule in this case is two at a time; as it should be.

■ When traveling, keep focused on the direction of the lift truck, watching for any hazards in the working area. Also, for maximum safety, be sure to maintain the stability of the load. The illustration in Figure 10-5 serves as a reminder to look before backing.

■ Never raise or lower a load while the vehicle is in motion.

■ Use shrink wrapping and product banding for security and prevention of collasping of product. Where banding or shrink wrapping is broken or missing from elevated loads, lower the loads and secure them.

■ Do not speed. Adjust driving speed according to conditions. When people are present, expect the unexpected—slow down. Place traffic cones, barricades, or signs on slippery areas within the warehouse to warn workers of the hazard.

■ If possible, drive in the middle of an aisle to allow for reaction time if anyone steps out into the path of travel.

■ Keep to the right and observe proper safe-driving principles.

Figure 10-4. This graphic reminds operators to keep forks low, with or without a load. (Courtesy of the National Safety Council)

■ Never turn on a ramp. Be alert to potholes, drop-offs on roadways, and other obstacles that could tip the truck. Never travel with an elevated load, and never turn with an elevated load because of the high potential for tipover.

■ Be alert for materials protruding into aisles and overhead obstructions.

■ Remove blocks of wood or other obstacles in the path of travel as they are discovered. Place trash in the proper receptacle.

■ Long loads reduce the truck's capacity because of the lengthened load center.

Figure 10-5. This illustration is a reminder to look before backing. (Courtesy of the National Safety Council)

■ Take advantage of mirrors, signs, alarms, and other warning devices to protect pedestrians. If any of these devices are found to be defective, alert the supervisor. A mirror, mounted high on the racking in Figure 10-6, makes it possible for operators to see pedestrians.

■ Beware of the rear-end swing of the vehicle. The powered industrial truck is different from an automobile in that it has a very tight turning radius. Other workers or pedestrians can easily be struck by the vehicle. Figure 10-7 illustrates the tight turning radius of a lift truck.

■ Be observant of the forklift's lift chains. If they go slack, raise and lower the load again to correct the problem. Never attempt to repair chains, uprights, carriage, or attachments; these are jobs for trained professionals. Never climb onto or reach into this part of the machinery.

■ Always alert pedestrians of your presence and intentions. Make eye contact with an individual before moving the vehicle.

■ Use wheel chocks designed for the purpose. Do not use lumber, rocks, concrete blocks, chunks of asphalt, or any other nonapproved chock device. Wheel chocks are frequently removed from dock wells by snow plows; use care when the storing the chocks.

■ Keep product stored at least 36 inches from sprinkler heads. Keep loads clear of sprinkler heads when moving product so that they aren't struck. Damaged sprinkler heads could cause a major water leak.

■ Steer clear of oil and grease spots so they aren't tracked to other areas. Wipe up spills if possible. Report spills to the supervisor.

Figure 10-6. A mirror mounted at a corner on the racking provides operators with a margin of safety.

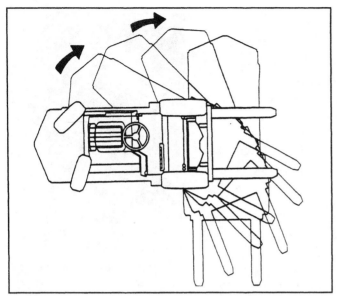

Figure 10-7. Operators and pedestrians must be trained to stay clear of the rear swing of a forklift. (Courtesy of Clark Material Handling Company)

- Make turns smoothly; slow down for turns in advance.

- Know the locations of chemical spill cleanup kits. Training is necessary in spill cleanup to protect the worker and environment.

- Always chock both sides of the wheels of trailers and trucks before entering them. It is the responsibility of the operator to check on this safeguard. If the truck driver has not chocked the wheels, it is incumbent on the operator to do the chocking. If the driveway is slippery, constantly check the placement of the wheel chocks.

- Never enter a trailer when the electronic signals of a trailer-restraint system show that the trailer is not restrained to the dock face.

- Management must ensure that all dock employees know how to work and use the restraints and report any malfunctions.

- Use steps or ladders to gain access to dock wells; never jump off a dock.

- Be sure the dock plate and trailer floor are secure and sound before entering the trailer. A preinspection of each trailer should take place prior to loading.

- Check dock plates, ramps, and levelers before crossing; always go straight into and straight out of trailers or railcars.

- For internal combustion engines, never leave the truck idle inside a trailer; these situations could produce high levels of carbon monoxide gas.

- When stacking material, always place heavier material on the bottom and lighter material on the top. Figure 10-8 serves as a reminder for safe material stacking.

- Take advantage of trailer lighting for improved dock and trailer safety.

- Use running lights if operating outdoors. Follow the same safe driving principles used on the highway. Reflective signs, lights, additional assistance from other employees, and a reflective vest are needed for safeguarding when outdoors.

- A fire extinguisher must be mounted on the lift truck if the truck must operate outdoors or in remote areas.

Figure 10-8. Stack materials straight to avoid accidents and injuries. (Courtesy of the National Safety Council)

- Overhead guards are designed to protect operators from falling loads such as boxes, bags, etc. It is not intended to protect an operator from a falling capacity load. In addition, the overhead guard must not be considered as a rollover bar. Do not place product on the overhead guard.

- Never overload racks, bins, boxes, or pallets with product or materials.

- At railroad tracks, slowly cross at an angle so that the lift truck is not damaged and that the load is not affected.

- If parking near railroad tracks, keep at least 8 feet from the track.

- Fueling a vehicle with gasoline, diesel fuel, or propane must be done outdoors. Ensure that the proper OSHA and fire regulations have been followed. Observe all specific safety rules, including a no-smoking policy.

- Never lift anyone on the forks. Many of the manufacturers of forklifts strongly recommend that a lift truck not be used with a lifting cage so that a worker can gain access to a working elevation. Utilize a scissors lift or other suitable means of elevation. Follow all of the prescribed safety rules if a person will be working aloft.

- Never modify or misuse a lift truck. Figure 10-9 identifies a serious misuse of a forklift. An order-picker broke down and the lift truck driver began pushing it. One of the forks went under a metal barrier and struck the operator on the ankle. This resulted in a serious injury.

- When driving keep at least three truck lengths behind the vehicle in front of the truck.

- Pedestrians always have the right-of-way.

- When traveling up a ramp, have the load leading; when going down a ramp, have the load trailing. If a malfunction of the equipment occurs on a grade and the lift truck must be parked, block the wheels and add a sign or tag indicating what the problem is. Be sure to set the parking brake, lower the load to the floor, set the gears in neutral, and remove the key. Figure 10-10 illustrates the proper method for ramp access and egress.

Figure 10-9. Mis-use of equipment can cause serious injury.

Figure 10-10. Keep a load upgrade; and the forks pointed downgrade when no load is present. (Courtesy of the Clark Material Handling Company)

■ Never indulge in stunt driving or horseplay.

■ Never leave a truck unattended. When stopped, always park out of the way, lower the forks until they are flat on the floor, apply the parking brake, neutralize the controls, turn off the key, and remove it from the ignition.

■ Report any injuries to the supervisor as soon as possible.

■ Keep empty wooden pallet stacks at a 6-foot height because of fire code restrictions.

■ Never drive up to an attended fixed object without asking the employee to move first.

■ Always wait for the powered equipment to come to a complete stop before getting off.

■ If a portable dock plate must be used, allow a lift truck to put it in place at the dock rather than manually handling it.

■ Stabilizer posts may be necessary in the front of the trailer to keep the landing wheels from collapsing.

■ Keep loads cradled against the backrest while tilted. This helps the center of gravity on the forklift as well as helping to prevent the load from sliding off the forks. The backrest is designed to protect the operator from spilled loads.

■ Never allow employees to ride on loads or help to balance loads.

■ Never allow employees to walk or work under a suspended load.

■ Where lift trucks are equipped with front-end attachments, the weight allowed to be lifted must now be reduced per manufacturer's guidelines.

■ The atmosphere in the facility shall be classified as hazardous or nonhazardous, and the appropriate powered industrial trucks must be used.

■ Battery-charging installations shall be located in areas designated for that purpose.

■ An overhead hoist, conveyor, or equivalent material handling equipment shall be used for handling batteries.

■ Both eye wash and body showers must be located in battery-charging areas. Eye wash stations must allow for at least 15 minutes of eye flushing to satisfy the OSHA code.

- In the battery-charging area, protective clothing consisting of rubber gloves, apron, and face shield must be available.

- Keep battery covers and protectors in place.

- A means of neutralizing spilled battery acid is needed. Cleanup procedures must comply with EPA regulations.

- Fire extinguishers, such as CO_2 and dry chemical, must be available at the recharge area. In addition, a completed job hazard analysis and the manufacturer's posted guidelines for battery charging must be available.

- A powered industrial truck is considered unattended when the operator is 25 or more feet away from the vehicle which remains in his/her view, or whenever the operator leaves the vehicle and it is not in his/her view.

- Ensure that there is proper lighting in the warehouse to perform daily operations safely.

- Users of powered industrial trucks shall comply with the recommendations set forth by the lift truck manufacturer regarding the care and use of the equipment.

- Operators must keep their arms, legs, and head clear of the mast and uprights at all times. Figure 10-11 illustrates an operator in a narrow-aisle truck with his foot dangerously sticking out of the lift truck.

- A safe distance shall be maintained from the edge of ramps or platforms while on any elevated dock, platform, or freight car.

- Lift trucks shall not be used for opening or closing freight doors.

- Approach elevators slowly. Enter the elevator evenly and squarely after the elevator car is leveled. Once on the elevator, lower the forks, set the brake, neutralize the controls, and turn off the ignition.

- The load backrest extension shall be used whenever necessary to minimize the possibility of the load or part of the load falling rearward onto the operator.

- Operators shall not pass other trucks going in the same direction at intersections, blind spots, or other dangerous location. To prevent a cross-aisle collision, this warehouse uses nylon strips as shown in Figure 10-12 to alert operators that equipment is being operated here.

- An elevated load must only be tilted forward when it is directly over a stack racking or the location where the load will be deposited.

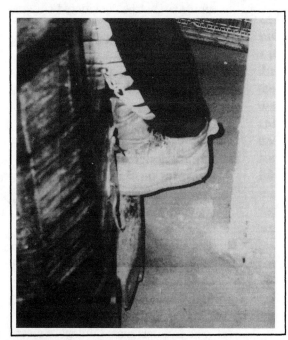

Figure 10-11. Always keep your feet inside the equipment.

- No truck shall be operated with a leak in the fuel system until the leak has been corrected.

- All parts replacement on a powered industrial truck shall be replaced only by parts equivalent as to safety with those used in the original design.

- Never remove or alter any parts on the truck. Never tamper with a safety device.

Figure 10-12. Block aisles with nylon safety strips to safeguard operators.

The following classifications for lift trucks identifies those that are listed in OSHA 1910.178.

Designations. For the purpose of the 1910.178 standard there are eleven different designations of industrial trucks or tractors as follows: D, DS, DY, E, ES, EE, EX, G, GS, LP, and LPS.

- The D designated units are units similar to the G units except that they are diesel engine powered instead of gasoline engine powered.

- The DS designated units are diesel-powered units that are provided with additional safeguards to the exhaust, fuel, and electrical systems. They may be used in some locations where a D unit may not be considered suitable.

- The DY designated units are diesel-powered units that have all the safeguards of the DS units and in addition do not have any electrical equipment, including the ignition, and are equipped with temperature-limitation features.

- The E designated units are electrically powered units that have minimum acceptable safeguards against inherent fire hazards.

- The ES designated units are electrically powered units that, in addition to all of the requirements for the E units, are provided with additional safeguards to the electrical system to prevent emission of hazardous sparks and to limit surface temperatures. They may be used in some locations where the use of an E unit may not be considered suitable.

- The EE designated units are electrically powered units that have, in addition to all of the requirements for the E and ES units, the electric motors and all other electrical equipment completely enclosed. In certain locations the EE unit may be used where the use of an E or ES unit may not be considered suitable.

- The EX designated units are electrically powered units that differ from the E, ES, or EE units in that the electrical fittings and equipment are so designed, constructed, and assembled that the units may be used in certain atmospheres containing flammable vapors or dust.

■ The G designated units are gasoline-powered units having minimum acceptable safeguards against inherent fire hazards.

■ The GS designated units are gasoline powered units that are provided with additional safe-guards to the exhaust, fuel, and electrical systems. They may be used in some locations where the use of a G unit may not be considered suitable.

■ The LP designated unit is similar to the G unit except that liquefied petroleum gas is used for fuel instead of gasoline.

■ The LPS designated units are liquefied petroleum gas-powered units that are provided with additional safeguards to the exhaust, fuel, and electrical systems. They may be used in some locations where the use of an LP unit may not be considered suitable.

For more information on lift trucks and the locations in which they are allowed to operate, contact your powered industrial truck dealer or OSHA for clarification. Also, 1910.178, the powered industrial truck standard, can provide necessary information.

HOW LIFT TRUCKS WORK

Operating a lift truck takes a great deal of skill and knowledge. Operators need to possess an understanding of the various operating principles to perform their jobs safely. The biggest error that many employers and operators make is that they assume that if one can operate a car, then one can operate a piece of powered equipment. A state driver's license does not grant the privilege of operating a forklift.

Industrial trucks can be powered by electric batteries, liquid propane gas (LPG), gasoline, diesel fuel, and compressed natural gas (CNG). Some types of lift trucks should not be used in the presence of certain chemicals or conditions. The current OSHA regulation, 1910.178 for powered industrial trucks, contains descriptions of the various divisions, classes, and groups of classified hazardous areas. The hazardous materials that determine which lift trucks can be used are also listed in the regulation. Since OSHA was promulgated, the number of substances that contribute to fire and/or explosion has greatly increased.

STABILITY OF POWERED INDUSTRIAL TRUCKS

Operators should be trained in the following subjects regarding the principle of stability:

■ Load center

■ The stability triangle

■ Lateral stability

■ Dynamic stability

■ Longitudinal stability.

Load Center

Operators may encounter loads that are unbalanced, loose, or not level, straight, or secure. Operator training must include information on how to handle unstable loads. Loads may be asymmetrical; operators must also be trained to handle such loads. As a result of the need for safe handling of a variety of loads, load center and the principles of moment must be a part of the education process.

The capacity of each forklift is identified on the manufacturer's data plate; the load center is also identified on the nameplate. Load centers are usually 24 inches forward from the mast. If a load is within the capacity of the lift truck but its

Figure 10-13. Keep the center of gravity low where operating fork lifts. (Courtesy of Clark Material Handling Company)

load center is greater than 24 inches, the lift truck may not be able to safely handle the load. Overloads are another problem for lift trucks. Damage to chains, truck components, and other truck parts can easily occur if overloaded. The truck can tip forward, as demonstrated in Figure 10-13, with the counterweight raised off the floor, which could injure employees and damage property.

Stability Triangle

Operators must be taught the principles of the stability triangle. This principle can be compared to a see-saw. If one end of the see-saw has a heavier load than the other, the heavy load will go downward. The determination of whether an object is stable is dependent on the moment of an object at one end of the system being greater than, equal to, or smaller than the moment of the object at the other end of the system.

The stability triangle is illustrated by using an invisible dot situated within a triangle under the lift truck. The triangle is formed by three imaginary lines between the center of the two front wheels and the center of the rear axle. By following the proper driving rules and handling loads correctly, the invisible dot will remain inside the triangle. If the operator travels too fast and makes a sharp turn, the invisible dot will travel outside of the triangle. At this point the lift truck is unstable and could tip over. Figure 10-14 provides a graphic illustration of the three points of the triangle.

There are several additional situations where operators could lose stability.

- If an operator places a load on a section of high racking or retrieves an elevated load, the truck could easily lose stability if the operator continues to move the lift truck without lowering the mast. A sharp turn to the right or left and an elevated mast with or without a load could easily tip the equipment.

- Any turning while going up or down a ramp or incline has a high potential of tipover. The weight of the load and the truck combined with the slope of the incline can easily cause a loss of stability. Figure 10-15 illustrates the movement of the invisible triangle dot when making a turn with a load while going too fast.

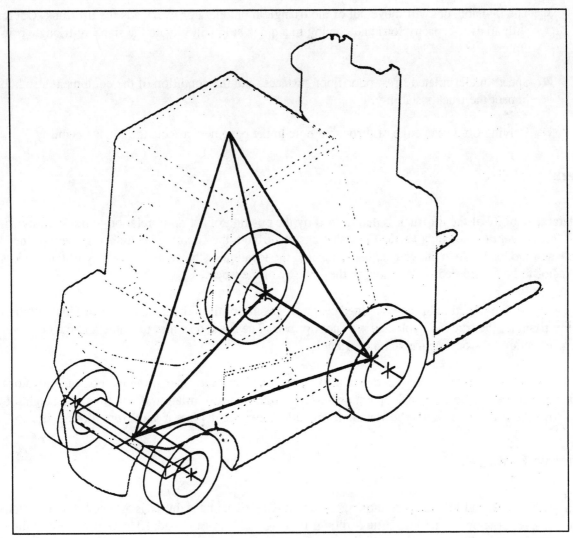

Figure 10-14. Any change to the truck's weight load capacity or certain components, alters the stability triangle. (Courtesy of Clark Material Handling Company)

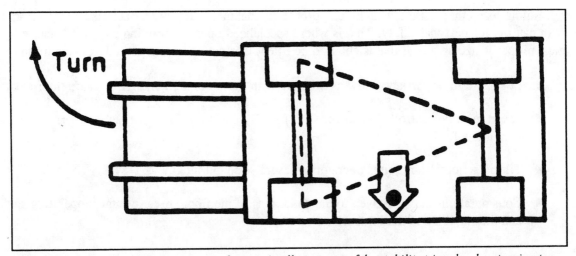

Figure 10-15. The invisible dot (center of gravity) will move out of the stability triangle when turning too fast with a load.

- The invisible dot will move out of the triangle if an operator overloads the lift truck. Operating with an over-capacity load and coming to a quick stop will violate the stability-triangle principle.

- Speed, underinflated tires, poor floor surfaces, and the condition of the equipment also help to impact the truck's stability.

- Driving off a road edge or through a hole in the pavement affects the truck's stability.

Lateral Stability

The lateral stability of the lift truck is determined by the position of action in relation to the stability triangle. This is represented by a vertical line that passes through the combined center of gravity of the vehicle and the load. When the vehicle is not loaded, the location of the center of gravity of the truck is the only factor to be considered in determining the stability of the truck.

As long as the line of action of the combined center of gravity of the vehicle and the load falls within the stability triangle, the truck is stable and will not tip over. The truck becomes unstable and may tip over if the line of action falls outside the stability triangle.

Factors that have an effect on the lateral stability of the truck include: speed, the method the operator used in placing the load on the truck, the operating surface, condition and inflation of the tires, the height of the load above the surface on which the vehicle is operating, and the degree of lean from the vehicle.

Dynamic Stability

When the lift truck and load are put into motion, the truck's dynamic stability is affected. Stability considerations involve: braking, cornering, lifting, tilting, moving and lowering loads. The transfer of weight and the resultant shift in the center of gravity is due to the dynamic forces created by the movement of the lift truck.

When handling loads that cause a vehicle to approach its maximum design characteristics, operators must use extra caution for personal safety. This is where specialized operator training pays off because operators must properly size up a load that is about to be lifted. Correct operating procedures require that:

- Loads are to be carried as low as possible with the forks high enough for safe floor clearance.

- Speed must be controlled at all times, especially during turns. Approach corners cautiously with a low load.

- Tilting action also requires operators to exercise sound judgment.

- Considerations must be given to the conditions of the floor, tires, weather, operating surfaces, and the condition of the lift truck.

Longitudinal Stability

A load that is heavier than the rated capacity of the lift truck will cause the lift truck to tip forward. The distance between the backrest to the center of the load determines if a load can be lifted safely. If a load is within the capacity of the lift truck but too far out on the forks, the lift truck can tip forward. Forks must be placed completely under a load and the mast must be tilted back for load stabilization. When the load moment is greater than the vehicle moment, the greater load moment will force the truck to tip forward.

FEATURES OF POWERED INDUSTRIAL TRUCKS

Each powered industrial truck model and type has its own operating characteristics. When the training of operators is taking place, it is important to discuss the models and types of lift trucks that they will be operating. Controls and safety features may not be the same for each manufacturer's models. Functions, controls, and placement of controls can vary from manufacturer to manufacturer.

Lift trucks are designed to carry, lift, load, stack, push, or tier product and material. It takes a great deal of skill and ability to be able to efficiently and safely operate equipment.

Many employers foolishly assume new operators are qualified to drive a forklift because they have an automobile driver's license. Many rookie operators experience serious injuries and incidents each year. The lift truck does not function like an automobile. The only comparison is that they all have steering wheels and the majority of lift trucks have four wheels. This is where the similarity ends.

Forklifts have a narrower wheelbase than a car and a much higher center of gravity; this is why forklifts can easily be tipped over. Forklifts operate on a teeter-totter principle. A counterweight on the rear helps balance the load on the front. Forklifts that are empty are still potentially dangerous. A car handles and carries its load on the inside of the vehicle; a forklift carries its load on the outside. This load can be unstable because of its height, weight, width, shape, or the load not being properly secured.

A car can turn over under certain circumstances, i.e., a hole in the pavement, a sharp turn on a grade or ramp. A tipover can also occur while turning on ice, loose gravel, and even on dry pavement if operating at a high speed. A lift truck can turn over much easier and at much lower speeds. Speeds as low as five miles per hour can cause a tipover. Lift trucks when empty have the ability to turn over. Operating environments that could cause or contribute to tipover include: underinflated tires, holes in pavements, obstacles on the roadway, speeding, turning on a ramp, driving off the edge of a roadway, railroad tracks, uneven surfaces, and an elevated mast.

Lift trucks have unique operating capabilities, which include braking. A forklift, when fully loaded and at a slow speed, is not easily stopped. When the reaction time of the operator is combined with stopping distance, it is very possible that even an experienced operator would not be able to quickly stop. The small wheels on a forklift combined with only two braking wheels don't always allow for a sudden stop. Maintenance on the vehicle may be lacking, which could allow the braking system to fail. The braking system may not have a backup system to provide stopping ability.

ANSI B56.1 RECOMMENDATIONS FOR OPERATOR TRAINING

The American National Standards Institute (ANSI) provides the following recommendations for safety-training principles for powered industrial truck operators.

Operator Qualifications

The ANSI standard recommends, (as well as OSHA), that only trained and authorized persons be permitted to operate a powered industrial truck. It is not unusual for any employee to climb aboard a forklift or grab onto the handle of a powered pallet jack to test his skills or to complete a task. This often results in serious incidents or injury to others. This is why it is important to have a safety rule in a warehouse, or wherever, that only *trained* and *authorized* employees have permission to operate the equipment. In addition, operators shall be qualified based on visual, auditory, physical, and mental ability to operate the equipment safely according to the data below.

Operator Training

Personnel who have not been trained to operate powered industrial trucks may operate a truck for the purposes of training only and only under the direct supervision of the trainer. This training should be conducted in an area away from other trucks, obstacles, and pedestrians.

The operator training program should include the user's policies for the site where the trainee will operate the truck, the operating conditions for that location, and the specific truck the trainee will operate. The training program shall be presented to all new operators regardless of previous experiences.

The training program shall inform the trainee that:

- The primary responsibility of the operator is to use the powered industrial truck safely, following the instructions given in the training program.

- Unsafe or improper operation of the powered industrial truck can result in death or serious injury to the operator or others, and damage to the vehicle or other property.

The training program shall emphasize safe and proper operation to avoid injury to the operators and others and prevent property damage and shall cover the following areas:

- Fundamentals of the powered industrial truck(s) the trainee will operate, including:

  - Characteristics of the powered industrial truck(s), including variations between trucks in the workplace

  - Similarities to and differences from automobiles

  - Significance of nameplate data, including rated capacity, warnings, and instructions affixed to the truck

  - Type of motive power and its characteristics

- Operating instructions and warnings in the operating manual for the truck, and instructions for inspections and maintenance to be performed by the operator

- Method of steering

- Braking method and characteristics with and without loads

- Visibility with and without load, forward and reverse

- Load handling capacity, weight, and load center

- Stability characteristics with and without load and without attachments

- Controls, locations, function, method of operation, identification of symbols

- Load handling capabilities, forks, attachments

- Fueling and battery charging

- Guards and protective devices for the specific type of truck

- Other characteristics of the specific truck.

■ Operating environment and its effect on truck operations, which includes:

- Floor or ground conditions including temporary conditions

- Ramps and inclines with and without load

- Trailers, railcars, and dockboards (including the use of wheel chocks, jacks, and other securing devices)

- Fueling and battery-charging facilities

- The use of "classified" trucks in areas classified as hazardous due to risk of fire or explosion as defined in ANSI/NFPA 505, Powered Industrial Trucks

- Narrow aisles, doorways, overhead piping, and other areas of limited clearance

- Areas where the truck may be operated near other powered industrial trucks, other vehicles, or pedestrians

- Use and capacity of elevators

- Operating near edge of dock or edge of improved surface

- Other special operating conditions and hazards that may be encountered.

■ Operating the powered industrial truck including:

- Proper preshift inspection and approved method for removing from service a truck that is in need of repair

- Load handling techniques, lifting, lowering, picking up, placing, and tilting

- Traveling with and without loads, turning corners

- Parking and shutdown procedures

- Other special operating conditions for the specific application.

■ Operating safety rules and practices, including:

- Provisions of the consensus standard regarding safety rules and practices

- Provisions of the consensus standard addressing care of the truck

- Other rules, regulations, or practices specified by the employer at the location where the powered industrial truck will be used.

■ Operational training practices, including:

- If feasible, practice in the operation of powered industrial trucks shall be conducted in an area separate from other workplace activities and personnel.

- Training practices shall be conducted under the supervision of the trainer.

- Training practices shall include the actual operation or simulated performance of all operating tasks such as loading, maneuvering, traveling, stopping, starting, and other activities under the conditions that will be encountered in the use of the truck.

■ Testing, retraining, and enforcement:

- During training, performance and oral and/or written tests shall be given by the employer to assure the skill and knowledge of the operator in meeting the requirements of the standard. Employers shall establish a pass/fail requirement for such tests. Employers may delegate such testing to others but shall remain responsible for the testing. Appropriate records shall be kept.

- Operators shall be retrained when new equipment is introduced, existing equipment is modified, operating conditions change, or an operator's performance is unsatisfactory.

- The user shall be responsible for enforcing the safe use of the powered industrial truck according to the provisions of the standard.

WALKIE TRUCKS

The walkie or pallet truck is one of industy's most versatile pieces of equipment. It is designed to transport, load, unload, lift, pick, stage, and store materials or product. These units can be found in just about any facility that moves product. They are relatively inexpensive and don't require the same degree of maintenance, operating expense, or operator training as forklifts. Walkies can easily move product around at any small business where material handling needs are small.

Walkies are very versatile but can also be very dangerous. The simplicity of design and controls are deceiving to the unsuspecting. Workers operating walkie trucks may be injured in a number of ways: The feet can be run over by the unit, hands can be caught between the operating handle and a fixed object, and product can easily fall on operators. Other workers could be injured by being struck by the machine or loads.

Many employers do not provide operator training on these units because they appear to be easily operated. Many workers, including untrained office staff and visitors, will all try their hand at operating a walkie. Many are surprised when the unit runs into another person, damages racking or product, or drives off a dock.

To safely operate a walkie truck, basic safety principles must be taught to workers and then enforced. The following safe-working guidelines can be very useful in training operators to handle walkie trucks.

- Read the literature from the manufacturer before operating the unit. Each model may have different guidelines as well as different controls and functions. Focus on the safety features of the model being operated as well as the necessary safety guidelines. A specific training program for powered walkie safety may be available from the equipment manufacturers or their representatives. The OSHA operator training standard requires specific training for each piece of powered equipment.

- Operators must be thoroughly trained and authorized to operate these units. A comprehensive training program must be in place to ensure operator safety.

Before using the walkie, check the main functions of the machine including:

- Load wheels
- Steering handle
- "Belly button" reverse switch
- Operating controls
- Battery connections and cables
- Horn
- Load backrest and extension

- Gauges
- Directional and speed controls
- Load data plate
- Safety signs and labels
- Braking mechanism
- Other safety and operating devices.

While Operating a Walkie

- The operator must always face the direction of travel.

- Never walk faster than the speed of the unit being operated.

- Only one person must operate the unit at one time. There must be a "no riders" rule.

- To prevent being struck or having one's foot run over by the truck, walk to one side when the load is trailing the operator.

- Focus on the movement of the equipment near workers, other powered equipment, and obstacles in the path of travel. Always be aware of the position of the load and forks.

- Be aware of floor surface conditions. Oil, sand, grease, ice, water, or any other slippery substance can cause the equipment to skid or be difficult to stop. A rider-walkie can provide a greater hazard to the operator traveling on a slippery surface.

- Hands can easily be pinched between the handle and a stationary object. This is a very common injury-producing situation. Allow for sufficient clearance when moving the pallet truck.

- Keep hands, feet, and other body parts confined to the running lines of the rider-walkie truck.

- Be sure the hands and soles of shoes are free of grease and oil. Nonskid paint on the standing surface of a walkie-rider unit will help the operator to keep from slipping.

- Wear personal protective equipment as required.

- Sound the horn to alert others of the truck's position and motion.

- Never speed; an empty walkie unit can tip over if traveling too fast while negotiating a sharp turn.

- Never use a second piece of powered equipment to push, pull, or lift the unit.

- Keep employees and visitors away from the area where a load is being lifted or deposited. Always warn others of your intentions. Make eye contact with others before moving the powered walkie truck.

- Avoid sudden starts and stops. It is not uncommon for an operator to be thrown off a walkie-rider unit as a result of acceleration changes or while rounding curves. Loads can easily become dislodged when making a quick stop.

- Avoid ruts, bumps, blocks of wood, nails, plastic wrap, or other debris that may be on the floor. A load can be spilled if one of these obstacles is struck. Be alert for wet floors, as well as oil and grease spots. The walkie will be more difficult to stop as a result of reduced traction.

- To avoid collisions, come to a complete stop at all blind corners, stop signs, and aisle intersections. Sound the horn where necessary.

While Stacking Loads

■ Never permit anyone to stand or walk under the load-engaging mechanism of the walkie trucks. Keep the arms, hands, feet, legs, and head away from the upright mast at all times.

■ Stack product securely on the forks. Restack an unbalanced load before moving it. Loads that are not secured should be equipped with metal or plastic banding or plastic shrink wrapping.

■ Never overload the walkie. The manufacturer's data plate identifies the capacity. Capacity can easily be made more visible to all operators by stenciling the numbers on the sides of the powered equipment.

■ Keep loads stacked as low as possible. Overloaded pallets can easily strike the top of a trailer while entering. Dislodged product can easily fall back onto the operator or someone else.

■ Allow for proper turning and positioning clearances when moving loads. The stacked product can easily strike other product, racking, electrical equipment, sprinkler pipe, or parts of the building structure.

■ Only raise the load high enough for adequate floor clearance. Never travel with an elevated load. Never raise or lower a load while the truck is in motion.

■ Use care and caution when operating near sprinkler heads, water pipes, electrical wiring, heaters, steam pipes, or any other fragile or dangerous material or equipment.

■ Walkie trucks do not have overhead guards; therefore, the security of the load is important. Never remove the protective backrest from the mast. This metal bracket device helps to secure product from falling back onto the operator.

While At the Dock

■ Be sure the trailer's wheels are chocked or the trailer is secured with an automatic trailer restraint, before entering. Figure 10-16 illustrates the dangers in trailer pull-away while using a walkie.

■ Go slowly on dockboards and dockplates. Be sure they are secured before traveling on them. In addition, the capacity of the dockplate must allow for the weight of the walkie truck and the load being carried. The lip of the dockplate

Figure 10-16. Always chock the wheels before entering a trailer with a walkie truck. (Courtesy of Clark Material Handling Company)

should be fully extended onto the back of the trailer. The trailer should be parked flush against the building with the engine turned off.

■ Keep clear of dock edges, especially with rider units. Never back up toward a dock edge. Paint dock edges yellow to provide for a visual warning to operators and pedestrians.

■ Know and observe floor and trailer floor load limits. Properly inspect the trailer floor for security before driving into the trailer.

Batteries

■ If operators are responsible for charging the batteries in pallet trucks, safe procedures must be followed. When disconnecting the battery cord from the charger, first turn the charger to the "off" position, then disconnect the battery. Be sure to wear all of the required PPE.

■ Batteries should be serviced or recharged only in designated areas. Those individuals performing this service must be thoroughly trained and authorized to do so. Observe the no-smoking rule.

■ Make note of the proper job hazard analysis and battery manufacturer's guidelines when performing any maintenance on batteries.

Ramps and Inclines:

■ When moving a load up or down an incline, the load should be facing uphill. When the unit is empty, the forks should be facing downhill at all times.

■ Never turn a walkie truck on a ramp or incline; the unit could easily tip over.

■ If the pallet truck breaks down on a ramp or any other sloped surface, the wheels should be blocked to prevent movement. Place a warning tag on the operating handle to alert others of the mechanical problems. Remove the key to ensure no one uses the truck.

Elevators

■ If using a freight elevator, be sure that the combined weight of the walkie and the load does not exceed capacity.

■ While waiting for an elevator, keep your powered equipment parked at least 6 feet away from the elevator. When driving into an elevator, drive in forks-first and center the pallet truck and load in the space available. No one should be in an elevator when the pallet truck is entering or leaving.

Additional Guidelines

- Pedestrians always have the right of way. Always be alert for pedestrians that step out into aisles or who are not paying attention to where they are walking.

- Notify your supervisor if any problems or questions arise from the operation of your pallet truck.

- When on a rider model, always come to a complete stop before getting off.

Figure 10-17. Do not reach under a pallet truck unless there is a zero energy condition. (Courtesy of Clark Material Handling Company)

- Never reach under the walkie truck to clear a jam or to search for foreign objects. Injury can occur when someone else moves the truck. Always turn the key off when inspecting the walkie unit. Figure 10-17 serves as a reminder of this safety rule.

- When parked, shut off the key and lower the load. Be sure the unit or load is not blocking a doorway, emergency equipment, or an aisle. Be sure to remove the key to prevent unauthorized use of the walkie truck.

- Take advantage of mirrors mounted on walls, beams, etc., to prevent incidents. Obey safety signs posted throughout the building.

- Ensure regularly scheduled maintenance is performed on the truck.

- Operators should not wear headsets to listen to music.

FINE-TUNING OPERATOR TRAINING

Studies have shown that effective forklift operator training programs can improve safe performance by as much as 70 percent. Safety advantages and special features and options included in newer models of lift trucks are operator friendly. These features include:

- Maintenance diagnostics available to the operator

- Programmability of functions

- Automatic adjustment of travel or load-lowering speeds based on the weight of the load

- Automatic accountability of an operator for a hit by the truck

- Inoperability of the trucks if operator is not standing inside compartment (in some narrow-aisle models)

- Operator controls and panel identification easier to use and read

- Brake lights, seat belts, wing seats for operator safety

- Redesign of the mast for greater operator visibility

- Improved ergonomics for operator comfort and vision.

Operator training is the one area that continues to lack focus in the workplace.

The statistics involving operator injury and death in the United States are alarming. Many of these statistics were identified earlier in this chapter. In Canada, 19 lift truck-related deaths occurred in 1995. Many of these deaths were attributed to a lack of operator training. To help reduce the toll of injuries and incidents, both the U.S. Department of Labor—OSHA and Ontario Province have developed extensive requirements for operator training.

The training of operators must include classroom interaction and the use of visual aids. Many of the various details of lift truck movement such as tipover, tip forward, counterbalance, stability triangle, lateral and longitudinal stability must be discussed. Trainees must know each model's specific details for operation. Couple this with the different kinds of lift trucks: counterbalance, narrow-aisle, walkies, stock-chasers, etc., and it's obvious that there are many details involved in operating a powered industrial truck.

Operators must be quizzed both orally and in writing to ensure they are absorbing the details of the program. Electronic interactive programs can provide training on a one-to-one basis. If the operator selects the incorrect response to a question, the program provides the details of a consequence based on the response. There are many different types of programs available on the market and they should be used to train operators and supervisors. If supervisors are going to enforce the safety rules on the warehouse floor, then they should be knowledgeable on the subject.

Manufacturers of powered industrial trucks have developed top-quality, comprehensive, operator training programs—many of which are broad in nature, covering various models of machines and operating instructions. The new OSHA standard on operator training will generate much interest in training. If injuries are to be reduced, more training must take place. Some industry veterans claim that only about 25 percent of all lift truck operators are properly trained.

Training in the daily evaluation of the lift truck is necessary. Every lift truck must be inspected prior to the start of the shift. A detailed form is required to assist the operator. Supervisors can easily evaluate the correct procedure involved in daily inspections by observing each operator at the beginning of a shift. This serves as a reminder that the process is important and that it must be done correctly.

Operator skills are also important in the training and evaluation process. Evaluations can take place several different ways.

■ An obstacle course provides all of the challenges that the operator faces each work day. Pallets, racking, and obstacles can be laid out to help determine operator skills in stacking, retrieval, cornering, backing, steering, stopping, and loading processes.

■ Evaluate operators one at a time by using a specific evaluation list. Operators should be performing their jobs of material handling, and each operational point can be checked for safe performance. A point system should be used to determine if the operators have followed all of the prescribed operating rules. If a pallet is bumped or placed improperly, if the operator failed to look on both sides before backing, if he/she failed to use the horn at an intersection, etc.; then prescribed points should be deducted from the items on the evaluation sheet.

■ Competitions such as a forklift rally or rodeo provide an excellent opportunity to test operator skills. These programs are known for promoting safety, boosting morale, improving labor relations, decreasing workers' compensation claims, and enhancing the status of the forklift operator. A rally provides an opportunity for operators to demonstrate their skills at maneuvering various pieces of powered equipment through a challenging course. The event stresses safety and the winners of the competition will receive scores from several judges to reflect their true abilities. A program such as this should include:

   • Written tests on operator knowledge

   • Verbal tests regarding daily lift truck inspections

   • Requirements for prerun safety checks

   • Skills requirements for lifting, stacking, operating in forward and reverse, trailer unloading, narrow-aisle maneuvering, and abiding by all safety requirements.

Points can be deducted for failure to perform specific functions. All of the contestants would be equally judged through the use of master score cards. Each contestant would be shown copies of these forms in advance so they would know what is expected of them. Employee interest in forklift skills driving is high.

OSHA CITATIONS

What happens when an employer neglects operator training and does not enforce the safety rules? Obvious answers include higher workers' compensation claims, increased damage to product and property, and an increase in management's liability. An often-neglected area of concern by employers is that of OSHA citations. A few examples of OSHA citations highlight the need for operator training and rules enforcement.

■ An employer in New York was cited for two serious operator training issues. The $8,400 penalty was issued for the failure to train operators and for handling loads that exceeded the trucks' capacities.

■ For failure to train operators, for operating defective lift trucks, lack of a maintenance program, and for high carbon monoxide levels, some 3,200 citations were written against an employer in Maine. Penalties of $245,000 and $292,000 resulted from the inspection.

■ A firm in Wisconsin was cited for exceeding the rated capacity of industrial trucks; the penalty was $49,500.

■ An employer in Virginia was cited for $112,000 in penalties following the death of a forklift operator. The operator was performing the duties of an electrician and was not qualified to do so.

■ In Michigan, a forklift operator died after hitting an overhead beam. Proposed penalties were $74,700.

■ In Ohio, an employer was cited for four violations of the powered industrial truck standard: failure to remove defective trucks from service, not repairing defective trucks, not having a daily inspection program, and removing the manufacturer's nameplate. The proposed penalties amounted to $8,500.

■ An employer in Missouri was cited for allowing lift truck drivers to operate their equipment without wearing seat belts. Section 5(a)(1) was used for the willful citation. The employer was contesting the $140,000 penalty.

■ An employer was cited for allowing an employee to work off an elevated platform. The employee fell 15 feet and sustained fatal head injuries. The proposed penalty was $211,900.

■ An employer in Nebraska was cited for $140,000 for allowing employees to ride on elevated forks. An additional $7,000 was proposed for not providing adequate training for operators.

Attachments Require Training

Hydraulically powered lift truck attachments are very versatile and can do everything from reaching deep into a rack to remove a pallet, to lifting, turning, stacking, and transporting paper rolls weighing some 10,000 pounds.

Many attachments have four primary effects on a lift truck:

■ The attachments downrate the capacity of the truck or require a greater capacity truck.

■ The attachments may change the center of gravity or the stability triangle of the truck.

■ They can add simple or extensive complexity to electrical and hydraulic control systems.

■ All of the attachments require detailed and individual operator training and sometimes certification.

No attachment should be added to a lift truck unless that attachment is marked for use only with a particular kind, size, or brand of lift truck. Operator training is rather limited with most organizations; safety training for fork-mounted attachments is even more scarce. Any attachment, permanent or detachable, other than the standard forks, that is added to a lift truck must be approved by the lift truck manufacturer in writing. An appropriate revised or additional data plate must be furnished. Employees or contractor workers require special training to handle maintenance issues for attachments.

WHEN FORKLIFTS MAKE THE HEADLINES

Often serious workplace injuries and fatalities are reported in local newspapers. These tragic events are reminders that the workplace, just like the highway, can take a life or cause an operator or pedestrian to be forever maimed. Forklifts share this spotlight many times, usually as a result of some bizarre or unusual occurrence with the equipment. The following headlines from various newspapers are some of the more serious forklift incidents.

"Forklift Kills Trucker at City Recycling Plant"

A truck driver delivering a load of recyclable material at a plant in Montreal, Canada, was killed after being hit by a forklift.

"Boy, 15, Crushed at Family Business"

A fifteen-year-old boy, while assisting with duties on the weekend at his family's business, was killed when his forklift tipped over after he turned too sharply.

"Pedestrian Killed by Steel Frame"

A welder and father of two was killed in a Missasauga, Ontario, plant when a 1,000-pound steel frame being transported by a forklift struck and killed him.

"Man Crushed by Forklift"

A Sacramento, California, man was killed when his forklift drove off a warehouse dock. The operator was trapped between the lift truck and dock well.

"Worker Hit by Lift Truck"

In Southern Ontario, a lift truck operator parked his vehicle close to a worker who was at his station. The operator then climbed back into his lift truck from the wrong side, hit the controls, and backed into the worker.

"Pedestrian Killed by 8-Ton Forklift at Construction Site"

At a downtown Chicago construction project, an 8-ton forklift carrying a load of mortar made a right turn and ran over a passing pedestrian who was on her way to a dental appointment.

"Oshawa Youth Injured in Forklift Accident"

A seventeen-year-old was learning how to drive a forklift in a parking lot; the lift truck tipped over and pinned the youth. Injuries occurred to his head, which was struck by the overhead guard.

"Store Owner Found Guilty, Fined $60,000"

A forklift transporting topsoil tipped over while turning and a young man was crushed when he attempted to jump clear. A 4,000-pound car jack was needed to free the victim's body. The guilty verdict was leveled against the employer for not providing operator training and for not teaching the employee not to jump from a tipping lift truck.

"Forklift Crushes Worker to Death"

A Michigan man was crushed under a forklift when he disconnected a hydraulic hose while making a repair. The lift mechanism and load collapsed on the worker when he pulled the hose, causing a loss of pressure in the machine's hydraulic system.

"Man Critically Hurt in Forklift Accident"

A thirty-six-year-old mechanic was seriously injured at a garage in a Chicago suburb. A lift truck rolled onto the worker's leg and torso after he fell. The 22,000-pound forklift had to be lifted off the man by another forklift.

"Sudbury Inquest Hears Mother's Urge for Worker Safety"

A mother of a twenty-year old worker pleaded for improved worker safety during a coroner's inquest looking into the death of her son. The worker drove his forklift into the path of an oncoming ladle full of molten iron.

"Worker Killed in Freak Accident"

A fifty-seven-year-old Missassauga, Ontario, father was killed when an 1,800-kilogram crate fell on him from a forklift.

"Worker Dies After Pillar Crushes Him"

A worker at a construction site in Denver was killed when a 4,000-pound pillar rolled off a forklift and crushed his leg. Attempts to free the man's leg resulted in the pillar rolling again and crushing him.

"Kitchener Faces Charges"

The city of Kitchener, Ontario, was cited for the death of a worker killed by a 1,400-pound fruit drink machine that slid off a forklift.

"Forklift Driver Hits Pillar, Dies in Collapse"

A forklift operator for a plumbing and heating firm drove has forklift into a supporting pillar of a building and died when a section of the second floor collapsed on him.

"Fatal Forklift Had No Brakes, Jury Told"

While operating a lift truck, the brakes seized and the worker was killed when his neck was pinned between the controls and falling crates.

"58 at Company Overcome by Carbon Monoxide Fumes"

Fifty-eight people from a factory near Chicago were admitted to area hospitals because of high levels of carbon monoxide gas. An additional 100 employees were forced to leave the warehouse as a result of a faulty forklift truck using propane as a fuel.

PEDESTRIAN SAFETY

In any powered industrial truck training program, the safety of pedestrians must be considered. More than twenty pedestrians are killed each year as a result of being struck by a forklift or by a falling or moving load. Many very serious injuries occur that result in fractures, amputations, paralysis, and permanent disabilities. Much can be done by industry to protect the pedestrian. It starts with a comprehensive training program for every employee in the warehouse. Safeguards within the facility must also be improved. Management must enforce safe-driving practices and correct deficiencies in the maintenance program to further protect the person on foot. A pedestrian was almost struck by falling cartons when a lift truck operator pulled them over. He had set down a load and was backing away. Figure 10-18 illustrates the results of this incident.

There are many industrial injury reports that identify some of the more serious injuries and incidents that occur to pedestrians. One specific study on narrow-aisle lift trucks cited the following brief list of significant incidents involving pedestrians:

- Pedestrian suffered fatal injuries when he was pinned against a wall.

- Pedestrian's head was crushed when pinned by the lift truck.

- A child was struck by a lift truck and had four fingers amputated.

- Pedestrian was standing by a desk when struck by the lift truck; he suffered major kidney damage.

- Pedestrian was struck and killed by a falling load from a lift truck.

- Pedestrian was run over by lift truck—leg was amputated.

The list of incidents to pedestrians from other studies would be quite similar to this study of narrow-aisle trucks. Some of these claims involve lawsuits in addition to the workers' compensation issue. Pedestrian injuries occur as a result of being involved in incidents from a variety of pieces of equipment. Counterbalanced forklifts, narrow-aisle units, powered pallet trucks, stock-chasers, and order-pickers all play their parts in contributing to pedestrian injury. The individual can be struck by the counterweight, the forks, a falling load from the vehicle, loads which were knocked off racking or knocked over, and moving loads.

Figure 10-18. As a result of poor stacking, a large group of pallets fell, nearly hitting a pedestrian, and requiring extensive clean-up.

There is much that can be done to reduce and eliminate injuries to pedestrians; however, many basic principles must first be understood by equipment operators. Basic operating principles involving the lift truck must be pointed out to the forklift operators, supervisors, and all other employees. Note the following issues that involve lift truck movement.

- Lift trucks usually travel at speeds of five to ten miles per hour. This is much faster than someone on foot. The weight of a lift truck can be at least twice as heavy as an automobile and can easily weigh four to five times as much. When considering the speed of the truck, the time it takes to stop, operating surfaces, the weight of the truck, condition of the truck, the load being carried, and the fact that two pointed forks are leading the load, injury can take place quite easily.

■ The size of the loads being carried can contribute to an injury. Loads may be too high, too long, too heavy, or insecure on the forks. If the operators can't see where they are driving, a collision could easily take place. Any quick stop could cause a load to continue to move forward and strike someone. Since there are only two braking wheels on most lift trucks, stopping distances are easily affected.

■ Maintenance and regular inspections of each lift truck is important. Operators should use an inspection checklist prior to the operation of the truck. Defects in steering, brakes, horn, vehicle structure, tires, backup alarm, hydraulics, and lights are to be reported to management. When contractors come into the warehouse to perform preventive maintenance on lift trucks, all safeguards are to be checked and corrected where necessary. This process protects the operator, prevents damage to product and the building, and safeguards the pedestrian.

■ Powered equipment, when not in use, is to be parked out of the way with the forks flat on the floor, parking brake on, and gears placed in neutral. Pedestrians have been injured by walking into raised forks or tripping over forks that are not flat on the floor's surface.

■ The rear-end swing of a lift truck can be deceptive to a pedestrian. Unlike an automobile, the rear wheels do the steering on a lift truck, which allows it to turn sharply. Movement of the lift truck is quick and could easily strike the unwary pedestrian.

■ The use of backup alarms on counterbalanced trucks is a plus for the pedestrian as well as the operator. This warning device does much to help in alerting those on foot. In a noisy department the alarm may be difficult to hear. The alarm's volume should always be adjusted for the department in which the equipment is located. The equipment must not be tampered with. Backing incidents injure many employees each year. Figure 10-19 is a reminder to both operator and pedestrian.

■ Mirrors on the lift truck as well as those mounted at blind corners, walkways, and dock areas are necessary. Also, any areas where red or yellow flashing lights could be mounted will warn the pedestrian of an approaching lift truck. These should be used where visibility is limited and pedestrian safety requires visual and audible warnings. Even the horn of the forklift can provide a warning to those on foot.

■ Where equipment operates out-of-doors, in remote areas, or along roadways, proper lighting, both on the roadway and vehicle, signage, protective barriers, road maintenance, and employee training are necessary.

■ Established walkways should be at least 3 feet wide on each side of the widest load being carried.

Figure 10-19. Be alert for pedestrians while backing. (Courtesy of the National Safety Council)

Additional Pedestrian Safeguards

Figure 10-20. Labels such as these should be placed on the floor where pedestrians will be entering the warehouse.

- Pedestrians should not be permitted in departments with unpredictable traffic patterns and no traffic lanes.

- Workers and visitors should never challenge a piece of powered equipment. A load could easily be lost or could strike the person if a truck swerves to avoid them.

- Pedestrians are to obey signs, take advantage of barriers, and use fixed crosswalks and designated walkways. Where walkways are not provided, pedestrians must exercise extreme care for their well-being. This includes being alert on ramps, roadways, main aisles, storage areas, and docks. Large warning labels for the floor, such as the one illustrated in Figure 10-20, help to alert pedestrians before entering a hazardous area.

- Use reflective vests, flashlights, or brightly colored apparel to improve individual visibility if out-of-doors or where lighting is impaired.

- Use pedestrian-designated doors at docks if available. If heat curtains are installed at large doorways as illustrated in Figure 10-21, vehicle and pedestrian traffic using the same doorway could be a problem. Heat curtains tend to discolor and become scratched, which can limit visibility.

Figure 10-21. Pedestrians should have separate access to the loading dock and not use doors designated for powered equipment. (Courtesy of the Rite-Hite Corporation)

- Everyone on foot must stay away from the rear-end swing of the truck. Do not walk between the lift truck and a fixed object.

- Cluttered aisles and the storage of product can many times hide the pedestrian. Pedestrians must make every effort to let the lift truck operator know of their presence. Proper housekeeping practices will aid in facility safety.

- Pedestrians must not operate powered equipment unless they are trained and authorized to do so. Also, pedestrians must not ride on equipment as passengers.

- Never walk or work under a suspended load or mast. Keep clear of a fixed object if a lift truck is approaching a work station.

- Areas of the docks should be designated for truck drivers to prevent them from wandering around the dock areas or into the warehouse. Signs should be posted for this control.

Operator Guidelines

- Operators should anticipate workers stepping out into the aisle, roadway, around blind corners, and in those areas where designated walkways aren't defined. Be especially alert for visitors; some visitors may be in an industrial facility for the first time. Operators should expect the unexpected.

- Do not speed. Always maintain control of the lift truck. Follow safe-driving rules prescribed by OSHA and the lift truck manufacturers.

- Operators must not drive with unstable loads. Use banding or nylon binders on loads to prevent them from falling. Do not use pedestrians to balance or hold onto loads.

- Keep pedestrians away from battery and fuel charging areas. Only authorized employees are allowed to perform these operations.

- Operators must never jump off moving equipment. Wait for the equipment to come to a complete stop before getting off. Pedestrians have been struck by unoccupied moving equipment.

- Operators should take advantage of lift trucks' alarms and mirrors. However, looking in the direction of travel is very important; operators should make eye contact with pedestrians before moving the truck.

- Where blind spots or areas exist that require special attention, use spotters as guides. Do not move the lift truck unless cleared by a spotter and the spotter is physically clear of the load.

- If coming in after operating out-of-doors in the bright sun, allow the eyes to adjust to the light inside the building before proceeding. Stop at the building entrance before proceeding.

OSHA'S NEW FORKLIFT OPERATOR TRAINING STANDARD

OSHA has revised its existing requirements for powered industrial truck operator training, 1910.178 (1), and has issued new requirements on December 1, 1999 to improve the training of these operators. The new requirements are intended to reduce the average of 101 annual fatalities caused by lift trucks by 10%. Injuries total 94,570 each year and are expected to decline by 9,422 as a result of the new requirements. (See the full text in Appendix A)

SUMMARY

The prevention of injuries and damage to property and product is in the hands of management. Powered industrial trucks require ongoing maintenance to ensure they are safe to use. Operators must be formally trained to drive their specific pieces of equipment. Management must never assume that an automobile driver's license qualifies operators to drive lift trucks; this is a common mistake throughout industry.

Operator training can pay off with fewer injuries and incidents in the warehouse. The money invested in training will return dividends. Training programs are to include classroom instruction, audio-visuals, quizzes, and skills-driving evaluation.

OSHA requires training programs for operators. The former OSHA regulation for operator training was very nebulous and did not provide any guidance for assuring that operators were properly trained. The new OSHA standard requires that operator training takes on a new dimension resulting in greater skills, fewer injuries, and less damage to property. The Province of Ontario, Canada has yet to pass their final operator training requirements.

REFERENCES

Clark Equipment Company. *Operators Instruction Manual, Book 01-321*. September 1983.

Cravens, Catherine P. *Getting In Step, Occupational Health and Safety*. April 1998, pp. 68–69.

—. *Help for Hands and Feet, Workplace Ergonomics*. March/April 1998, pp. 25–26.

Deere and Company. *Moving Material with Walking Powered Lift Trucks*. Deere and Company, Occupational Safety Department.

Dessoff, Alan L. "OSHA Looks at Powered Hand-Truck Safety." *Safety and Health*. October 1994, pp. 72–76.

Entwisle, Frank "Preventing Lift Truck Overturns." *Modern Materials Handling*. January 1995, p. 19.

J. Keller. "OSHA Clarifies Seat Belt Use for Forklift Operators." *Keller's Industrial Safety Report*. Volume 7, Number 6, June 1997, p. 3.

Kuleviec, Roy. "Needed: Greater Lift Truck Safety." *Modern Materials Handling*. February 1996, p. 3.

Lovested, Gary. "Backtalk, Using Motorized Hand Trucks Safely." *Plant Engineering*. July 10, 1995, p.21.

Modern Materials Handling. "Lift Truck Safety Belts—A Good Idea." February 1992, p. 17.

—. "Operator Rodeos: Big Investment, Even Bigger Payoff." January 1995, pp. 12–17.

—. "Wing Seat Deters Injury." April 1991, p. 17.

Occupational Hazards. "Achieving Safe Sight 24 Hours a Day." April 1998, pp. 71–72.

Occupational Health and Safety. "Forklift Cage Saves Operator" November 1997, p. 14.

Robertson, Robert. "Is Your Lift Truck Trainer Qualified*?" Materials Management and Distribution.* January 1997, p. 7.

—. "Load Lifters." *Materials Management and Distribution.* January 1996, pp. 24–27.

Savart, J. B. *"Analysis of 804 Crown Stand-Up Forklift Accident Reports January of 1975 through December of 1993."* Wichita, KS: Advance Technology, Inc. October 21, 1994.

Schwind, Gene F. "Can Training Replace Seat Belts?" *Material Handling Engineering.* October 1987, p. 22.

—. "Every Attachment Needs Special Training." *Material Handling Engineering.* December 1996, p. 14.

—. "Improved Attachments Challenge Users." *Material Handling Engineering.* December. 1996, pp. 43–46.

—. "Narrow Aisle Lift Trucks: Operator Friendly and More." *Material Handling Engineering.* June 1998, pp. 58–63.

—. "Powered Walkie Trucks: New Designs Stretch Applications." *Material Handling Engineering.* December 1995, pp. 47–55.

—. "A Real World Look at Lift Truck Seat Belts." *Material Handling Engineering.* July 1988, p. 20.

—. "To Belt or Not to Belt." *Material Handling Engineering.* September 1987, p. 14.

—. "What Happens If You Ignore Training?" *Material Handling Engineering.* April 1998, p. 22.

—. "Workhorse Walkies." *Material Handling Engineering.* June 1997, pp. 55–61.

Suruda, Anthony, *et al*, "Avoiding Rollover/Tipover." *Material Handling Engineering.* June 1997, pp. 71–75.

Swartz, George. "Forklift Tipover: A Detailed Analysis." *Professional Safety.* January 1998, pp. 20–24.

Swartz, George. "Powered Walkie/Rider Pallet Trucks." *Forklift Safety: A Practical Guide for Preventing Incidents and Injuries.* Rockville, MD: Government Institutes. 1997. pp.59–68.

Torok, Douglas B. "Lift Truck Safety: It Pays to Train." *Material Handling Engineering.* August 1990, pp. 52–58.

Von Holt, Dirk. "Selection Guide for Walkie Hand Trucks." *Plant Engineering.* December 11, 1995, pp. 77–78.

11

Materials Handling

The movement of product in and out of a warehouse is one of the major sources of revenue for an organization. The need to unload product from trucks, trailers, and railroad cars is essential to production. Product arrives at a warehouse, is unloaded, and then placed in storage. At a later time the product is collected by workers for shipment out of the building. Without the movement of product very little would be accomplished in industry.

This very same movement of product is a contributor to many workplace injuries. This chapter will focus on the manual handling of product and the use of back belts, conveyor safety, crane safety, and hoist safety. Guidelines for materials handling with powered industrial trucks can be found in Chapter 10.

BACK INJURIES AND BACK SUPPORT BELTS

The subject of lower-back injuries and back supports is usually included in any discussion on material handling safety. Much has been written on this subject in recent years, including the pros and cons of back belts. Various studies sometimes contradict each other. The main points of the lower-back injuries/support belts issue will be discussed here.

Back Injuries

Back injuries are very common throughout the workforce, although some industries and occupations have more back injuries than others. Back injuries account for nearly 20 percent of all workplace injuries and are the leading cause of injuries to workers under the age of forty-five. The costs associated with back injuries are estimated at $20 to $50 billion per year.

Surgeries for some 350,000 spinal injuries are performed each year on all kinds of people. The most common operation, called a diskectomy, entails removing one or more of the jelly-doughnut-like cushions that separate the vertebrae and serve as shock absorbers. Many of these surgeries cost about $30,000 and include at least eight days' hospitalization.

169

Approximately 80 percent of the U.S. population will be laid low sometime by an episode of back pain. Poor posture is listed as a big factor in back problems. Nutrition and exercise are key factors in good back care. Strong back and stomach muscles are the guy wires that support a spine. Being in good physical condition also speeds up a recovery process should one need a back operation.

The Bureau of Labor Statistics reported that in 1996, of the 6.6 million nonfatal injuries and illnesses, 900,000 cases of back injury were reported. Low-back pain accounts for 18 percent of all workers' compensation claims at Liberty Mutual Insurance Company and nearly one-third of the costs. It is estimated that 25 percent of all workers' compensation cases in California involve the treatment of lower-back problems.

A survey of workers' compensation programs was completed by the National Association of Wholesale Grocers Association (NAWGA) and the International Foodservice Distributors Association (IFDA) for 1990. The survey revealed that back sprains and strains among food warehouse workers accounted for 30 percent of all injuries. The report also indicated that in one case more than 54 percent of the back injuries were attributable to manual lifting.

In Canada, the warehousing industry has one of the highest rates of back injury. Researchers have connected this to the heavy lifting, awkward postures, and fast-paced work being driven by production. Injuries in warehouses are typically not caused by one traumatic event, or one "bad" lift. More commonly, the back injuries are a result of repeated microtears to the muscles and ligaments in the back, shoulders, and neck.

Injuries to the back can be caused by faulty lifting methods, perhaps brought about by the unsuitable storage of product. Most warehouses store products on pallets that are about 4 inches off the floor. As product is removed from a pallet, the worker is forced to bend over more to reach the load. Product is stored within racking stations in this manner to conserve space. Any picking station which is under 6 feet in height can result in poor lifting techniques, which increase the chance for injury.

Back Belts

There continues to be a serious debate over the merits of back belts. Some rate back belts as very effective while others rate them as having no benefit whatsoever. However, when back belts are used with an overall program of injury prevention which includes the correct application of ergonomics, back injuries can be reduced.

Some of the comments regarding the improper use of back support belts include:

■ The belt is worn improperly by the user. Most of the back support manufacturers design the back belts to be worn below the navel. When improperly worn, the belt is usually placed too high, around the waist.

■ The belt is not sized correctly. Manufacturers make the belts in various sizes and often the wearer of the belt has not had a proper fitting.

■ Workers wear the belt tightly at all times rather than tightening them when lifting is required and loosening after the lift. By constantly wearing a back belt in a tight position, back exercise is limited.

- Workers believe that by wearing a back belt, they can lift more. This erroneous belief often results in back injuries.

- Workers who wear a back belt all day can injure their backs at home. The tightness of the back belt during the day and the absence of the belt at home can result in an injury while lifting a child or other object after work hours.

- When workers ignore the basics of safe lifting, injuries to the lower back can occur.

- When proper ergonomic principles aren't practiced on the job, injury can occur at any time.

- Some scientific reports note increased blood pressure and heart rate in some back belt users due to increased intraabdominal pressure.

Several recent studies were conducted on the use of back belts, and the results were surprising. In the March 1997 issue of *Material Handling Engineering*, back supports proved effective in an extensive study at Home Depot. This six-year study took place from January 1, 1989, through December 31, 1994. Details of the study indicate that:

- A 34 percent reduction in the rate of low-back injuries occurred during the study.

- With 99,891,164 hours worked, 2,152 back injuries were reported, at the rate of 21.5 incidents per million hours worked.

Note the data from this study in Tables I, II, and III (Courtesy of Material Handling Engineering).

Home Depot Stores Low-Back Injury Study 1989–94

Table I - Reduction in the Rate of Low-Back Injuries Was 34%

Back Support Uses	Working Hours*	Number Injured*	Rate Per Million Hours	Rate Ratio and 95% CI	Prevented Fraction (%) a-b/a X 100
No	12,812,726	392	30.6(a)	1.52 (1.36-1.69)	34.0
Yes	87,078,438	1,760	20.2(b)		
Total	99,891,164	2,152	21.5		

* Excludes hours and injuries occurring during store transaction to back support use policy implementation.

Table II - Best Rates of Injury Reduction: Under 25 and Over 55

| | Working Hours (X1.000) | | Number Injured | | Rate Per Million Hours | | | |
	No Back Support	Back Support	No Back Support	Back Support	No Back (a) Support	Back (b) Support	Rate Ratio and 95% CI	Prevented Fraction (%) a-b/a X 100
Gender								
Women	4,056	28,380	78	414	19.2	14.6	1.32 (1.03-1.68)	24.0
Men	8,756	58,698	314	1,346	35.9	22.9	1.56 (1.38-1.77)	36.2
Age Group								
<25	4,197	25,594	184	555	43.8	21.7	2.02 (1.72-2.40)	50.5
25-34	4,888	33,869	127	683	26.0	20.2	1.29 (1.06-1.55)	22.3
35-44	2,121	15,588	43	330	20.3	21.2	0.96 (0.69-1.31)	—
45-54	993	7,662	15	125	15.1	16.5	0.91 (0.53-1.55)	—
55+	612	4,465	23	67	37.5	15.0	2.50 (1.64-4.16)	60.0

Prevented fractions reported only with positive confidence intervals.

Table III - High, Low Intensity Lifters Reduced Back Injuries

| | Working Hours (X1.000) | | Number Injured | | Rate Per Million Hours | | | |
	No Back Support	Back Support	No Back Support	Back Support	No Back Support	Back Support	Rate Ratio and 95% CI	Prevented Fraction (%) a-b/a X 100
Lifting Intensity								
Low	2,565	15,874	49	72	19.1	4.5	4.21 (2.93-6.06)	76.4
Mod.	2,403	17,579	43	284	17.9	16.2	1.11 (0.08-1.53)	—
High	2,845	53,628	300	1,404	38.2	26.2	1.46 (1.29-1.65)	31.4
LOE (Years)								
<1	5,390	32,345	146	901	27.1	27.9	0.97 (0.82-1.16)	—
1-2	2,914	19,864	177	376	60.7	18.9	3.21 (2.68-3.84)	68.9
2-3	1,789	12,951	35	188	19.6	14.5	1.35 (0.94-1.93)	—
2-4	1,170	8,675	21	146	17.9	16.8	1.07 (0.67-1.68)	—
4+	1,549	13,243	13	149	8.4	11.3	0.73 (0.42-1.31)	—

Table 1. Number of employee working hours, number injured, incidence density rates, rate ratios, 95% confidence intervals (CIs) and prevented fraction for back support use, Home Depot Stores, California 1989–94.

Table 2. Number of working hours, number injured, incidence density rates, rate ratios, 95% confidence intervals (CIs) and prevented fractions for back support use by gender and age, Home Depot Stores, California, 1989–94.

Table 3. Number of working hours, number injured, incidence density rates, rate ratios, 95% confidence intervals (CIs) and prevented fractions for back support use by gender and age, Home Depot Stores, California, 1989–94.

The Fleming Companies, a major warehousing and food distribution center with more than 4,500 employees in thirty locations, support back belts. The belts have proven to be an integral part of their injury-prevention program. Fleming experienced a 58 percent reduction in low-back injuries per each 200,000 hours worked. The rate of disabling injuries fell by 52 percent. The rate of lost work days per 200,000 hours worked for the first nine months of 1992 was reduced by 74 percent when compared to the same period in the prior year.

In addition to the extensive Home Depot studies, other supporters of back belts offer some favorable comments on this subject.

- Some researchers believe that if back supports increase the support to the spine, the belts would also decrease back muscle activity, or loading on the spine. This would tend to decrease the risk of damage to the discs in the lower back.

- Users of back belts are restricted in forward bending to 30 degrees or less, which aids in correct lifting techniques.

- The wearing of the back belt may, by itself, be a reminder to workers to lift properly.

There are other organizations that have registered success with the use of back belts. A reader survey conducted by *Material Handling Engineering* in 1994 showed the following results:

- 66.9 percent of the companies allow the use of back-support belts and will pay for them.

- 19.6 percent of the companies allow the use of back-support belts but will not pay for them.

- 14.2 percent of the companies require that workers use back-support belts.

- 3.6 percent of the companies forbid the use of back-support belts.

When back-support belts are used in a company, the following applications are the most common:

- 69.0 percent: Shipping/receiving docks

- 62.9 percent: Warehousing

- 41.0 percent: Orderpicking

- 34.5 percent: Assembly operations

- 30.6 percent: Storeroom

- 25.8 percent: Fabrication

- 12.7 percent: Machining.

Questionnaires were sent to 1,500 readers; the back support questions were answered by 253. Responses add to more than 100 percent due to multiple answers.

It's apparent from this survey that back belts are still not a mandated piece of protective equipment. Only those organizations that have achieved success in reducing lower-back injuries fully endorsed them. Only 14 percent of the 253 responses actually require the use of back belts. Most organizations will pay for them, but not mandate their use. Only 3 percent forbade their use, thus giving credence to the fact that most industries accept them.

The following guidelines will help reduce the incidence of low-back injuries:

■ Design the material handling system to eliminate or mechanize the lift or push/pull motions.

■ If the worker is essential to the material handling operations, provide mechanical assistance such as hoists, manipulators, walkie trucks, lift tables, work positioners, and similar systems or devices.

■ If the modification or purchasing of material handling equipment cannot be economically justified, consider changes in load weights, positioning and size of loads, as well as worker training. Ergonomic assessments should be completed on warehouse jobs to ensure that work activity can be accomplished without exceeding the physical capabilities and/or capacities of the workers.

■ A medical management program can be beneficial. Since 80 percent of adults will experience an episode of low-back pain during their lifetime, it follows that a large portion of the workforce will lose work days or have to modify work activities at some point for this reason. The vast majority of people recover from back injury quickly: 50 percent recover in one week, 70 percent in three weeks, and 90 percent in three months. The employees may not be 100 percent pain free, but they will be functioning at work. The 10 percent that do not recover from back pain will account for approximately 90 percent of the back-injury costs. If back belts are chosen as a part of personal protective equipment, the devices must serve as only one element in the material handling system. A reminder that:

  • Back belts must be properly fitted to the individual.

  • Workers must be trained in the use of the back belts and the use of mechanical handling equipment.

  • Safe lifting techniques must be followed.

  • Weight, size, and shape of all loads being lifted must be a part of training.

  • Contributing factors to back problems such as chronic poor posture, faulty lifting, overexertion, lack of exercise, and the process of aging must be discussed with workers.

  • Treatment of back injuries can include immediate application of ice and muscle therapy, exercise programs, limited days of bed rest, and a return-to-work strategy.

  • Include a job hazard analysis for task evaluation.

  • Strive to stay below the 13.8-pound limit established in the NIOSH tables for reaching while bending motions are taking place.

  • Workplace ergonomic improvements are the key in injury prevention.

It is important to point out that overexertion is a key factor in all back injuries. A one-time overexertion injury is caused by a worker who lifts an object that is too heavy. The majority of back injuries come on gradually from repeated bending and lifting, regardless of the object being lifted. Body fatigue can result in a fatigue-related overexertion injury. Other contributing factors are awkward postures, job demands, and at times something as simple as climbing a ladder or getting out of a vehicle.

CONVEYOR SAFETY

Conveyors are involved in more than 9,000 injuries each year. Causes of the injuries are the disabling, removal, or modification of equipment safety devices; failure to follow proper lockout/tagout procedures; lack of training, and failure to enforce safety rules. Powered conveyors were also the primary source of injury in twenty-three workplace fatalities, 12.2 percent of all plant equipment-related deaths in 1995. Powered and gravity conveyors were a secondary source of injury in fourteen additional workplace fatalities that year.

Some individuals in the material handling industry argue that the improvements in conveyor safety have not kept pace with improvements in other machines and processes. Some of the noticeable improvements, however, include: full enclosures of pinch points such as chain and sprocket transmissions, perimeter pull cords for emergency stops, audible alarms and a delayed start-up function, pop-out rollers, improved warning labels, and interlock guards that are designed to shut off the power if removed.

Many conveyor injuries are the result of missing or defective guarding. Typical conveyor hazards that may require guarding include:

- Power transmission interfaces such as drives, gears, couplings, and shafts

- Nip points (or pinch points) where a moving object in a line or a rotating object meets a similarly moving object, such as belts and pulleys, and the meshing of gears

- Spill points, formed where material could spill from a conveyor, which could be guarded by side rails and netting on overhead conveyors

- Exposed edges of conveyors, because of sprocket meshing

- A transfer mechanism, a device that transfers materials onto or off a conveyor, or from one conveyor to another

- Counterweights, which should be enclosed in the areas where injuries can occur.

- Exposure to energy of any kind which can be harmful to maintenance personnel, workers, and contractors. Lockout/tagout procedures may be lacking.

Despite the improvements in conveyor safety, guards and other safeguards are sometimes removed, thus disabling these safety devices. In one case, a maintenance worker bypassed a safety limit switch by using a jumper wire to disengage the switch. A serious injury occurred because the maintenance worker failed to remove the temporary wire.

Following basic rules will help to prevent conveyor-related injuries.

- Since many conveyor injuries occur because of poor initial layout of the system, be sure to consider auxiliary hazards when installing the unit. These include guarding, electrical, exits, side-hinged gates, alarms, lights, and hidden pinch point hazards.

- Never attempt to service or repair a conveyor without following procedures for locking and tagging. Bring the unit to a zero-energy state.

- Never walk, ride, sit, or climb on a conveyor not intended for that purpose.

- Never operate any conveyor unless all safety guards, interlocks, guards, covers, maintenance panels, and warning devices are in place.

- Keep all body parts away from moving parts of the conveyor.

- Wear proper clothing around conveyors so loose shirts, jewelry, belts, ties or other apparel are not caught on moving parts.

- To avoid slips and falls, be sure all working surfaces are free of oil or grease.

- Use rubber floor mats to prevent foot fatigue. Keep floor mats flat; curled or loose mat ends can create tripping hazards. Torn bags may allow product to spill on the floors causing slip/fall situations.

- Never overload any conveying equipment.

- Never operate any conveyor until proper training has been provided.

- Allow for ongoing inspections of conveyors to ensure safe operating equipment. Check signs, alarms, guards, wiring, walking surfaces, and other working/safety features. When installing new or used conveyors, utilize the services of trained professionals. Always follow manufacturers' guidelines and recommendations.

- Place netting or other barriers below conveyors to prevent product from falling to lower levels and striking employees. Figure 11-1 illustrates the use of wire mesh guarding to prevent boxes from falling to a lower level.

- Maintenance must be performed by only trained and qualified personnel.

Figure 11-1. This overhead conveyor is equipped with metal mesh to prevent product from falling to the lower level. The striped tape alerts lift truck operators to the overhead hazard.

Figure 11-2. If workers must cross over conveyors, add approved walkway and staris for safe passage. (Courtesy of Rite-Hite Corporation)

■ Where a conveyor passes over a walkway, roadway, or workstations, all moving parts are to be guarded regardless of the height from the floor. Figure 11-2 illustrates the method for safe access over a conveyor.

■ Every belt conveyor must have either an emergency stop cable extending the length of the conveyor so that it may be stopped from any location along the line or have stop buttons within 10 feet of a work station.

 ■ For information on conveyor safety, see ANSI B20.1 and OSHA 1910.212 on guarding applications.

■ Only use a conveyor that has specifically been designed for a particular application. The manufacturer can be of assistance.

Figure 11-3 is a conveyor inspection form that can be used in the safety program.

Figure 11-3. Conveyor Safety Inspection Checklist

Item	Yes	No	N/A
Are the *start* and *stop* buttons clearly marked?	☐	☐	☐
Is the area around the start and stop buttons free of clutter, product, etc?	☐	☐	☐
Are labels and signs in place to warn of hazards?	☐	☐	☐
Are chain drives guarded on all sides?	☐	☐	☐
Are pulley belts guarded on all sides?	☐	☐	☐
Are the ends of rotating shafts properly guarded?	☐	☐	☐
Are support legs undamaged?	☐	☐	☐
Are sideboards properly fixed in place?	☐	☐	☐
Are overhead conveyors properly guarded to prevent product from falling to a lower level?	☐	☐	☐
Are limit switches functional at conveyor ends?	☐	☐	☐
Are handrails in place for crossover stairs?	☐	☐	☐
Are pull-cords readily available along the length of the conveyor?	☐	☐	☐
Are warning alarms functional to announce start-up?	☐	☐	☐
Is housekeeping along conveyor sides acceptable?	☐	☐	☐
Are employees wearing prescribed safety equipment?	☐	☐	☐
Is lighting functional throughout the conveyor area?	☐	☐	☐
Are employees dressed properly, i.e., no loose shirts, sleeves, or jewelry?	☐	☐	☐
For those employees with long hair, is it tied back or tucked under a hard hat?	☐	☐	☐
Is the product being handled within the posted limits of the conveyor?	☐	☐	☐
Has the conveyor received the correct preventive maintenance?	☐	☐	☐
Were any employees observed climbing under or over the conveyor?	☐	☐	☐
Are working heights of tables, conveyors, etc. correct to satisfy ergonomic considerations?	☐	☐	☐
Are floor mats in place to prevent fatigue?	☐	☐	☐
Is the lockout/tagout program readily available for use if needed?	☐	☐	☐
Are employees using safe lifting techniques when manually handling product?	☐	☐	☐

Extendible Conveyors

Many warehouses have used extendible conveyors to move products into trailers for many years. A fixed conveyor system may be designed to have an additional extendible portion. Extendible units are often used at the loading dock. A commonly used one is the skatewheel type with accordion sides. These come in either nonpowered or powered models, as do roller conveyors. The nonpowered models use gravity to move cartons. The conveyor is pulled onto a trailer and retracted as the trailer fills.

Extendible conveyors can be equipped with casters and moved to various fixed conveyor or loading dock positions as required. Ergonomics is improved when a powered conveyor can be extended some 60 or 70 feet and stretched out into a trailer.

Proximity switches on the power conveyors can be used to keep cartons separated and to halt rollers when a carton reaches the end of the conveyor. The operator may not be prepared to lift the carton when it arrives. Extendible conveyors, like any other piece of equipment, must be properly maintained and used per manufacturers' guidelines.

Conveyor Noise

Anytime industrial noise can be reduced it is a plus for the workers. Each noise source contributes to the total level of noise to which a worker may be exposed. The installation of any new roller conveyor systems should include noise control as part of the purchase.

There are some options available for noise control and noise reduction.

- The noise does not have to be created at all.
- Modify or substitute processes and components that generate less noise.
- Use vibration isolation or clamping.
- Absorb acoustic energy.
- Shield or enclose the noise source or the receiver.
- Combine or integrate systems.

The first attempt at control should be to reduce the noise at the source. Many times simple, basic design changes will help.

Another approach involves the modification or substitution of components. Belts can be substituted for gears, or free-fall processes can be avoided. Cushioning the impact points or substituting plastic parts for metal parts are effective methods of dampening sound or isolating the vibration.

Acoustical materials installed within housings and enclosures will help to absorb sound. Manufacturers of conveyors should be asked to offer conveyors that generate 80 decibels or less.

To quiet roller-tube ringing, lined or covered tubes could be used. Some manufacturers don't line the tubes but use a specially designed drive belt that has a dampening effect on the ringing sound. To prevent frames from transmitting noise, use dampening pads, nonmetallic hangers, or vibration absorbers.

CRANES AND HOISTS

A U. S. Department of Labor and Bureau of Labor Statistics study identified cranes and jacks as responsible for more than 41 percent of all plant equipment-related deaths in 1995.

There are some warehouses that utilize overhead cranes or hoists to handle and move product. Along with forklifts in these facilities, cranes are used to move many thousands of pounds of product. With lifting equipment, workers must maintain high production levels as well as observe safe operating procedures.

Operator Training

The American National Standard B30.2 sets minimum standards for training operators of overhead cranes. The goal is to have prospective operators demonstrate that they can safely operate cranes and hoists. Part of the ANSI B30.2 standard identifies some of the items required for operator training. Operators must pass an oral or written exam, and practical examinations on the specific equipment they will operate.

A few basic requirements for training include acceptable vision and depth perception, manual dexterity, overall good health, and passing written and practical exams that test the workers' judgment.

Many of the same issues regarding crane operator training parallel those of forklift operator training. Many operators of cranes have no formal training. Operators must be trained in how a crane operates; hooking onto loads; how chains, slings, and hooks function; and how to use hand signals and pendant controls. Lifting loads and transporting product and equipment involves experience and sound judgment.

Crane Safety Guidelines

Crane operators can improve safety in their departments by adhering to basic guidelines. The following rules apply only to floor-operated cranes.

- Follow crane manufacturer's operating procedures and safety guidelines.
- If an employee believes that there is any problem with the crane, the problem must be reported to the supervisor. Do not operate the crane until the problem is corrected.
- Employees should receive hands-on training and have a thorough working knowledge of the crane control functions and operations before starting in this job.
- When operators are being tested, for safety reasons the crane and operator should not be near any other workers. Always stand clear of loads being lifted.
- Operators and maintenance staff must know and understand how to disengage the power to the crane in the event of malfunction or fire.
- At the start of each shift a checklist is to be used to evaluate:
  - Brakes
  - Limit switch
  - Crane hook

- Safety latch
- Visual check of cables/wire rope
- Alarms
- Hook attachments
- Labeling on pendant controls.

■ Management must review the checklist daily to ensure it has been completed and to correct deficiencies as noted on the form.

■ Under no circumstances are any employees allowed to ride on the load or crane hook.

■ When testing the limit switch, stand to the side and away from other workers and machines. Push the "up" button on the pendant control and allow the block to travel. Stop the block several inches from the limit switch. Slowly inch up the block until it touches the limit switch. At that point the crane block should not travel upward. The block can now be lowered. This process should be repeated at the start of each work shift.

■ Never lift more than the allowed capacity of the crane. Load limits should be marked on the bridge of the crane. It is also a good idea to identify the capacity on the sides of the crane block. If a two-block crane is being used, each block must be identified for its capacity.

■ Utilize safety latches on crane hooks. Ensure that all lifting devices are seated properly on the hook and that the safety latch is in place.

■ Any attachment used for lifting must be inspected on a regular basis to ensure it is not defective in any way. This would apply to hooks, spreader bars, chains, cables, and clamps. Never alter a lifting device. All attachments must be properly sized for the crane.

■ Never point-load a hook.

■ Periodically check how the cable is wound on the drum. The cable must always seat properly in the grooves on the brake drum.

■ When lifting, take up the slack slowly. Hold onto an edge of a load to keep it from swinging. Warn others that you are lifting a load and moving it. Use crane warning alarms if available.

■ Never use twisted, kinked, knotted, worn, or frayed cables or chains. By adding wires, bolts, or other devices to a chain or cable, serious injury could occur. Follow the guidelines established by manufacturers of lifting devices.

■ When a load is about to be lifted, spot the crane and block directly above the load. The purpose of this is to prevent any swinging of the load when it is being lifted, as well as the need to have the cable wind properly on the drum.

■ Never make a side pull. Side pulls are the result of the crane trolley not being directly over the load, or the crane block and hook are attached to a load beyond the perimeter of the crane's access. When side pulls occur, the crane's cable usually winds improperly on the drum, which means the cable can be damaged by the drum's cable grooves.

■ Ensure that proper hand signals are used between crane operators and other workers.

■ If two cranes are on the same runway and a maintenance problem exists, spot one crane at the end of a runway to keep it from being struck by the other. Rail stops should be added to the rails in front of the defective crane. A banner could also be hung from the bridge to identify the crane as being in need of repair. Hang special caution or danger tags on pendant controls. Only trained technicians should be allowed access to cranes and to perform maintenance on them.

■ Compliance with OSHA standard 1910.179, Overhead and Gantry Cranes, is very important to crane safety.

■ Each crane should undergo an annual evaluation by trained professionals.

HOISTS

Hoists can also be used in a warehouse to handle product. Using hoists rather than manually handling boxes, bags, and other storage containers can help increase productivity. Safety controls must be developed to protect hoist operators. Some of the same applications associated with overhead cranes also apply to hoists.

■ Never lift more than the rated capacity of the hoist.

■ Learn and understand all of the proper operating procedures, warnings, manufacturer's guidelines, and maintenance requirements.

■ Check the limit switch at the start of the shift. Push the "up" control on the pendant control and stop the block before it touches the limit switch. Gently push the "up" control until the limit switch stops the block. Lower the block when complete. Stand away from the hoist block.

■ Never use a damaged or defective hoist. Report the problem to the supervisor.

■ Pendant control buttons must be approximately marked to identify direction.

■ Never use twisted, kinked, knotted, or worn chains or wire ropes. Never modify a chain with bolts, wires or special attachments. Follow manufacturer's instructions for safe use of any lifting device.

■ Utilize a safety latch on the hook of the hoist.

■ When lifting, ensure the load slings or other approved attachments are properly sized and seated in the hook saddle.

■ Never perform side pulls with the hoist and always position the block and hoist directly over the load.

■ Never lift a load unless the chain is properly seated in wheels or sprockets or wire rope is properly seated in drum grooves.

■ Never lift loads over the top of fellow workers or visitors.

■ The operator must focus on the job at hand and not have his attention diverted while operating the hoist.

■ Take up slack gently before lifting. Do not allow the load to swing. Keep the load in balance and check the security of the load before moving it.

■ Warn workers of an approaching load. Never stand under a load.

■ Use only original equipment manufacturer's parts for repair.

■ Regularly inspect hoists; ensure worn defective or damaged parts are corrected. Maintain appropriate maintenance records.

■ Chains, wire ropes, slings, and attachments must be inspected annually. Follow manufacturer's guidelines for care and maintenance.

■ Provide current overload protection and grounding on branch circuits of electric hoists.

■ Never point-load a hook.

■ Never alter or attempt to repair chains, slings, or wire rope.

■ Keep warning labels and other signage in place.

■ Don't allow two hoists to collide.

■ Never leave a load suspended overnight, unless absolutely necessary. Do not leave suspended loads unattended.

SUMMARY

Workers are vulnerable to injury in warehouses when they are manually or mechanically handling product and equipment. Back injuries occur to over 900,000 workers each year. Many of the injuries are disabling, which costs industry billions of dollars each year. Using cranes, hoists, conveyors, or forklifts to move product does help to prevent wear and tear on workers, but these devices pose hazards that can maim or kill if proper safeguards are not followed.

The correct use of back belts is still hit-and-miss throughout industry. If workers are not instructed properly and the correct use of these devices isn't rigidly enforced, back belts can actually do more harm than good. The Home Depot study appears to be the most in-depth analysis of back belts to date. The program was successful because of training, proper supervision, and management commitment.. More study is needed on the subject of back belts if industry is to move ahead in reducing back injuries.

Powered equipment in the form of cranes, hoists, conveyors, and lift trucks also require specific employee training to prevent injuries. One must rely on the manufacturer's expertise to identify all of the safety guidelines associated with the use, care, and maintenance of their equipment. This chapter only touched on the highlights associated with the equipment; much more information should be sought from those organizations that design, build, and install powered equipment. It is also important to reference OSHA standards 1910.179, Overhead and Gantry Cranes; 1910.178, Powered Industrial Trucks; 1910.184, Slings; 1910.212, General Requirements for all Machines (Guarding); and 1910.219, Mechanical Power Transmission Apparatus.

Since the handling of materials is the lifeblood of a warehouse, the pace of materials movement can be dangerous. Training of workers to recognize hazards and take precautions is essential in preventing injuries. Safe materials handling must be given daily attention in the workplace. Supervisors and safety committee representatives must continually observe movement of product in their departments and make corrections as needed. New employees must be properly trained before being placed in a high-risk job. Maintenance must also be a priority; take the time and opportunity to repair powered equipment, where and when needed. Where automated systems for material handling are present, training and proper maintenance are essential to the operation.

REFERENCES

Arnold, Anne-Kristen. "No Pain, More Gain." *Materials Management and Distribution*. September 1995, pp. 22–23.

Auguston, Karen. "You Can Prevent Conveyor Accidents." *Modern Materials Handling*. November 1996, pp. 35–37.

Brown, Stuart F. "Ridding Production Work of Strain and Pain." *Fortune*. July 6, 1998, pp. 166(B)–166(N).

Bureau of Business Practice, California. *Guidelines Adopted for Medical Treatment of Industrial Back Injuries*. #2290, September 25, 1997, p. 8.

Conveyor Product Section, Material Handling Industry. *Noise Considerations for the Design, Specification, and Installation of Roller Conveyor Systems*. Charlotte, NC. 1997, 12 pp.

Farnham, Alan. "Backache." *Fortune*. December 14, 1992, pp. 132–141.

Fernberg, Patricia M. "Return-to-Work Combats Back Injuries." *Occupational Hazards*. March 1998, pp. 53–56.

Hermanowski, David. "Don't Overlook Overhead Crane Safety." *Plant Services*. May 1997, pp. 105–106.

Holzhauer, Ron. "Comparing Powered Hoist Options." *Plant Engineering*. September 1996, pp. 76–81.

Knill, Bernie. "Ergonomic Tools for Home Improvement." *Material Handling Engineering*. March 1997, pp. 46–51.

Knill, Bernie. "The Material Handling Solution to Back Injuries." *Material Handling Engineering*. February 1996, p. 7.

—. "New Champion on Back Belt Research." *Material Handling Engineering*. March 1997, p. 9.

—. "Readers' Companies OK Back Support Belts." *Material Handling Engineering*. October 1994, p. 26.

Kulwiec, Roy. "How to Select the Right Crane for the Job." *Modern Materials Handling*. April 1995, pp. 70–72.

Material Handling Engineering. "Back Support Study Gains Momentum in Media." March 1997, p. 34.

Material Handling Engineering. "Overhead Cranes: A Dozen Paths to Better Performance." August 1997, pp. 48–53.

Megan, Graydon P. "Back Belts: The Debate Continues." *Safety and Health*. June 1996, pp. 38–41.

Modern Materials Handling. "Back Belts: Approach With Caution." August 1997, pp. 14–15.

Schultz, George A. "Planning for Conveyor Safety." *Modern Materials Handling*. March 1998, pp. 53–55.

Schwind, Gene. "Crane Operators Need Training, Too." *Material Handling Engineering*. August 1997, p. 20.

Trunk, Christopher. "Lifting Right With Packaged Hoists." *Material Handling Engineering*. May 1998, pp. 58–63.

Waters, Thomas R., Ph. D. "Workplace Factors and Trunk Motion in Grocery Selector Tasks." *Proceedings of the Human Factors and Ergonomics Society 37th Annual Meeting*. 1993, pp. 654–58.

Witt, Clyde E. "Extendible Conveyors Tighten the Supply Chain." *Material Handling Engineering*. June 1998, pp. 66–70.

12

Warehouse Inspection Process:

The Building and Industrial Trucks

Inspections are one means of assuring compliance with company and OSHA safety programs. Compliance with guidelines issued by manufacturers of products and equipment must also be monitored. One key element in any safety program is the comprehensive inspection program and its associated forms. This chapter will focus on the inspection process for the warehouse, powered industrial trucks, and other powered equipment. Sample forms are provided within the chapter to assist in the inspection program. Using the guidelines in this chapter, a program for detailed inspections can be developed if one does not exist.

The main reason that safety inspections must be conducted on a regular and systematic basis is that unsafe conditions are continuously being created in the warehouse. Normal "wear and tear" results in things wearing out after a period of time. The actions of employees can create unsafe conditions, and management could fail to insist on corrective actions. Unless unsafe conditions are identified and corrected on an ongoing basis, they could continue to build up. Injuries would soon follow and more employees would pay the price of uncorrected hazards.

POWERED INDUSTRIAL TRUCKS

The equipment being used in the workplace must be mechanically sound. A machine with faulty brakes, defective steering, or any other mechanical problem can cause serious injuries to fellow workers. A typical day in a warehouse or distribution center places a significant amount of wear and tear on powered equipment. A checklist should be developed for each model of powered equipment in the building. Once developed, operators should be trained in the use of the forms. The operator in Figure 12-1 is using a clipboard and a detailed inspection form to evaluate his lift truck. Management should insist on compliance with inspection programs and ensure that:

- The proper forms are being used for each piece of equipment.

- The forms are completely filled out and the inspection is thorough.

- Defective parts are identified properly.

- Maintenance is alerted for proper repair.

185

- Ongoing maintenance is being performed on the vehicles.

- Manufacturers' guidelines are being adhered to.

- OSHA requirements are being satisfied.

Pre-Use Inspections

When an operator is ready to inspect the powered equipment, he/she should use the proper form and systematically proceed. Each piece of equipment must be inspected at the start of each work shift. Figure 12-2 provides a full month's inspection on a single form. With clipboard in hand, the following items are typical of those found on inspection forms:

Figure 12-1. This operator is doing a thorough job of inspecting his lift truck.

- Horn
- Brakes
- Raise, lower, tilt
- Steering
- Gauges
- Lights
- Seat and seat belt
- Back up alarm

- Fuel level/power level
- Oil level
- Hydraulic hoses
- Coolant level
- Fire extinguishers
- Overhead guard
- Tires
- Load-limit plate.

Most of these items are a part of each forklift inspection program. Following is a detailed description of these key inspection points.

Horn. The horn on the piece of powered equipment must be functional. OSHA can cite an organization for a defective horn because this is classified as a serious violation. Without a horn, pedestrians and others are vulnerable to being struck by the equipment. If pedestrians cannot be warned, the potential for injury increases.

Figure 12-2. Forklift Daily Record
(All Trucks)
This Form Is To Be Completed Daily For Each Powered Industrial Truck

Truck Asset Number:

Make and Model:

Fleet Number:

Dept:

Date:

Warehouse Number:

Exception Codes:

Safety Checks:

1. B-Meter
2. 1-Available Equipment Idle
3. T-Meter Turned Over or Replaced

1. ✓ OK
2. X - Needs Service

Equipment Meter Readings

In Service Hours

Downtime Hours

Exception Cod

Equipment Safety Checks - Operators

Maintenance Checks

Week-End --->	Day --->	Start	End	Total	B-I-T --->	Brakes	Horn	Lift Tilt	Lights	Oil Leaks	Reach & Forks	Steering/Seat Belt	Tires	Engine Oil	Backup Alarm	Overhead Guard	Lift Chains	Battery	Coolant	Operator	
	1																				
	2																				
	3																				
	4																				
	5																				
	6																				
	7																				
	8																				
	9																				
	10																				
	11																				
	12																				
	13																				
	14																				
	15																				
	16																				
	17																				
	18																				
	19																				
	20																				
	21																				
	22																				
	23																				
	24																				
	25																				
	26																				
	27																				
	28																				
	29																				
	30																				
	31																				

Brakes. The service brakes on counter-balance trucks are tested by pushing in the pedal. There should be a solid feel to the pedal, not a spongy feel. The brakes should not fade or drift. It is recommended that operators push in on the pedal and hold it for 10 seconds. The parking brake handle should be applied and released to check its quality and reliability.

Raise, lower, and tilt. While in the operator's seat, the controls are to be used to tilt the mast forward, backward, up, and down. Check for slackness in the chain. Is the movement smooth? The forks should be flat on the floor when looking at the condition of the chain. A thorough check of the chains should be completed with a gloved hand and rag for personal protection. All of the knobs, controls, handles, and markings should be in place.

Steering. With power on, turn the steering wheel to the left and right. Squealing noises from the steering pump would indicate that there is a problem. The steering wheel should feel normal and not loose.

Gauges. All gauges should be functional. The glass or plastic facing should not be cracked. Where required, log the proper information from the gauges on the daily inspection form.

Lights. Auxiliary lights must be functional. Check the overhead flashing light and any brake lights.

Seat belt and seat. Ensure the seat belt is functional and intact. The seat should be secure and equipped with wings or hip bolsters to aid the operator in event of a tipover.

Back up alarm. Put the lift truck in reverse and listen for the back up alarm. This device should be functional but not offensively loud. Ensure that the forward and reverse controls are working.

Fuel level/power level. Gauges will identify fuel or power levels. Gasoline or diesel fuel-powered vehicles will have a fuel gauge similar to that of an automobile. Liquid petroleum gas (LPG) gauges are a part of propane tanks. Propane tanks are strapped onto the back of a forklift with metal bands and locking devices. If there is a need to connect or disconnect an LPG hose, eye and hand protection must be worn.

For battery levels, remove caps while wearing rubber gloves and a face shield. Slowly add water, preferably with an automatic water-feed device. For compressed natural gas (CNG) check the gauges on the storage tank on the back of the lift truck. Follow manufacturers' guidelines on charging time, maintenance, and safety rules for batteries.

Oil level. Check the oil in an internal combustion engine by using the same procedure as one would for a personal car. Be sure the engine is turned off. Be alert for hot surfaces. Use a rag to wipe off the dipstick.

Hydraulic hoses. Check for the condition of hydraulic hoses. Are there any cuts or abrasions? Are hoses worn in spots as a result of rubbing action? Are there any leaks?

At the same time check under and around the lift truck for oil or hydraulic leaks.

Coolant level. Where applicable, check the coolant level of the lift truck. Check this at the beginning of the work shift when the engine is cold. Use gloves for this process. For multiple work shifts be sure to allow a cooldown before checking the fluid. Personal protective equipment such as a face shield and heavy-duty gloves must be worn; when burned with antifreeze from a coolant system, it will bond to the skin and cause more harm than boiling water.

Fire extinguisher. The fire extinguishers that may be located on lift trucks must be inspected and serviced as necessary. Are the pin, seal, and inspection card in place? If it is a dry chemical unit, does the gauge read "full"?

Overhead guard. The overhead guard is in place to protect the operator from the hazards of falling bags, boxes, and product. It is not intended to protect from a falling capacity load. Check the guard for loose bolts, cracked welds, or any structural damage. Notify management of any defects.

Tires. Check for cuts, tears, signs of wear, and missing chambers of rubber. Do the lug nuts on the tire rim look tight? While wearing gloves, check the surface of the tires for protruding objects.

Pneumatic tires must be checked correctly with a gauge to ensure the proper pressure is in the tire. Low air pressure can have an effect on the stability of the lift truck as well as steering and stopping distance. Maintenance must be summoned to work on tires. Split rims can be very dangerous, and professionals must use safeguards such as cages or security chains during servicing or maintenance. Follow manufacturers' guidelines for care and maintenance. Stand to the side when checking pneumatic tires.

Load-limit plate OSHA requires that the manufacturer's load-limit plate be permanently mounted on the lift truck. Some states, such as California, require that the truck's capacity be stenciled or identified on the sides of the truck for easier visibility and greater safety.

During this time in the inspection process, it is a good idea to check any other items on the lift truck such as the condition of pedals, loose bolts, or other safety-related features. Figure 12-3 illustrates an operator performing an inspection of the tires, etc.

This chapter contains inspection forms for several different types of powered industrial trucks.

The forms are here to assist the reader in an overall warehouse safety program. The manufacturers of powered equipment can assist in developing more comprehensive programs, if needed, for powered equipment.

FACILITY INSPECTIONS

There are many individual items to evaluate in a warehouse.

To help in the evaluations, custom-made inspection forms should be developed. The safety committee in the warehouse could easily create a comprehensive list by walking through the various departments and observing. Both employees and supervisors can assist in this process.

Inspections may be informal, routine, or programmed.

Figure 12-3. This operator is doing a thorough inspection of the lift truck, including the tires. (Courtesy of the Rite-Hite Corporation)

- *Informal* inspections are a result of day-to-day observances in a department. By being more observant, unsafe conditions can be corrected on the spot or reported to management for correction. Each employee is responsible for helping to identify hazards in his/her department. The hazard should be personally corrected when possible. A form is not usually used for the informal process. Incident reports can also be used to document unsafe conditions.

- *Routine* inspections are inspections that take place on a regular basis. A form is used to document the department tour, which is usually assigned for a specific date. The scope of the inspection is determined by the form being used. As with all inspections, where discrepancies are discovered, they should be corrected immediately, if possible. Those items that require maintenance should be assigned to someone for correction. A part may have to be ordered, welding may have to take place on a broken handrail, ballast lights may be defective, etc. The back of the inspection form should state, in narrative form, the items corrected during the inspection. Inspection forms shown in Figures 12-4 and 12-5 provide samples for use in warehouse evaluations each month.

- *Programmed* inspections are less frequent and involve and in-depth look at department safety. A consultant or someone from another department or facility can complete the inspection. A new pair of eyes may spot specific conditions that could be missed by local personnel. The written reports from programmed inspections are usually more detailed and more specific.

The collection of miscellaneous items listed in the various departments are recommendations and reminders of what to inspect for in a warehouse. There may be additional unmentioned items that should be a part of a specific inspection checklist. Checklists should be designed to be specific for a particular department and should not include items that do not exist in the area. Develop the checklist based upon knowledge of what, where, and how unsafe conditions have occurred in the past. An evaluation of departmental injury reports also provides a good source of ideas about which items require regular inspection. Employees are also helpful in recommending items that should be on the inspection list. When looking at a tool, machine, structure, or piece of equipment, direct the attention to those parts that are subject to developing unsafe conditions.

Another element of the inspection process is to decide and specify exactly which unsafe conditions are to be checked. Give a brief description of a defective condition, using words such as broken, cracked, loose, leaking, protruding, unstable, sharp-edged, frayed, crooked, or deteriorated. Comments such as these could also be used on the reverse side of the inspection form for items not covered in the checklist.

There are advantages to using a tailored inspection checklist.

- The person inspecting knows and understands the department and the specific items requiring inspection.

- The checklist makes it less likely that items will be overlooked. It highlights items yet to be inspected because they are not checked off.

- The completed form facilitates recording and reporting of findings to upper management.

- The completed checklist provides a means for upper management to help eliminate deficiencies.

- The checklist helps reduce inspection time.

- Properly completed checklists aid in OSHA compliance.

Figure 12-4. Warehouse Safety Inspection Form

Each warehouse should be thoroughly inspected at least once each month. Use safety committee representatives where possible to assist in the inspections.

Item	Good	Improve	N/A	Inspection Item	Good	Improve	N/A
Condition of Racking	☐	☐	☐	**Personal Protective Equipment:**			
Mirrors	☐	☐	☐	Hard Hats	☐	☐	☐
Conveyor	☐	☐	☐	Steel Toe Shoes	☐	☐	☐
Material Storage	☐	☐	☐	Gloves	☐	☐	☐
Dock Plates	☐	☐	☐	Goggles/Glasses	☐	☐	☐
Dock Lights	☐	☐	☐	Hearing Protection	☐	☐	☐
Wheel Chocks	☐	☐	☐	Daily Lift Truck Inspections	☐	☐	☐
Pallet Conditions	☐	☐	☐	Overall Housekeeping	☐	☐	☐
Condition of Floor	☐	☐	☐	Sanitation	☐	☐	☐
Condition of Corner Posts	☐	☐	☐	Locker Room	☐	☐	☐
Elevator	☐	☐	☐	Trash Compactor	☐	☐	☐
Warehouse Lighting	☐	☐	☐	Emergency Oxygen	☐	☐	☐
Aisle Marking	☐	☐	☐	First Aid Kit	☐	☐	☐
Electric Boxes	☐	☐	☐	**Battery Recharge Area:**			
Fire Extinguishers:				Clean Up Kit	☐	☐	☐
Tags	☐	☐	☐	Gloves	☐	☐	☐
Seals	☐	☐	☐	Apron	☐	☐	☐
Current Date	☐	☐	☐	Face Shield	☐	☐	☐
Not Blocked	☐	☐	☐	Eye Wash	☐	☐	☐
Signs	☐	☐	☐	Power Equipment	☐	☐	☐
Delivery Cages	☐	☐	☐	Drivers Driving Safely	☐	☐	☐
Condition of Fans	☐	☐	☐	Sprinkler Testing	☐	☐	☐
Sprinkler Head Clearance	☐	☐	☐	Guard Rails	☐	☐	☐
Propane Storage	☐	☐	☐	Other	☐	☐	☐
				Other	☐	☐	☐

Inspected by: _____   Date: _____   Location: _____

Safety Committee Representative: _____   Date: _____

Comments:

_____

_____

Figure 12-5. Warehouse Safety Inspection Checklist

Rate each of the following inspection items accordingly:

Inspection Item	Good	Improve	N/A
Safety Policy Posted Behind Plastic	☐	☐	☐
OSHA Poster Posted on Bulletin Board	☐	☐	☐
Safety Posters Changed Regularly	☐	☐	☐
Emergency Plan Posted, Listing of Assignments, Hazards Identified	☐	☐	☐
Monthly Reporting of Incidents, Damage, Fires, etc.	☐	☐	☐
New Employee Orientation Program in Place	☐	☐	☐
Monthly Facility Safety Inspections	☐	☐	☐
Monthly Evaluation/Testing of Fire Protection Systems	☐	☐	☐
Safety Committee Meetings Being Held	☐	☐	☐
Safety Films Being Shown	☐	☐	☐
Forklift Training Programs/ Employee Testing Being Conducted	☐	☐	☐
Job Safety Observation Program	☐	☐	☐
Dock Plates, Dock Lighting, and Wheel Chocks	☐	☐	☐
Battery Charging	☐	☐	☐
• Eye Wash Units (changing, cleanliness)	☐	☐	☐
• No Smoking Signs	☐	☐	☐
• Housekeeping/ Appearance	☐	☐	☐
• Rubber Gloves	☐	☐	☐
• Face Shields	☐	☐	☐
• Rubber Apron	☐	☐	☐
• JSA/ Procedure Posted	☐	☐	☐
Daily Forklift Inspection and Repair Program	☐	☐	☐
First Aid Certification/ Training	☐	☐	☐
CPR Certification/ Training	☐	☐	☐
First Aid Log and Emergency Oxygen	☐	☐	☐
Pipes, Exits, Hazards Marked and Identified Properly	☐	☐	☐
Fire Protection:	☐	☐	☐
• Extinguishers - Accessible	☐	☐	☐
• Tagged	☐	☐	☐
• Charged	☐	☐	☐
• Monthly Inspections	☐	☐	☐
• Fire Hoses Clear of Product	☐	☐	☐
Safety Handbooks and Manuals Being Used	☐	☐	☐
Overall Facility Housekeeping (Housekeeping Plan)	☐	☐	☐
Overall Facility Product Storage Practices, Open Aisleways	☐	☐	☐
Rubber Tips on Ladders	☐	☐	☐
Employee Equipment Being Worn:	☐	☐	☐
• Steel Toe Shoes	☐	☐	☐
• Hard Hats	☐	☐	☐
• Gloves	☐	☐	☐
• Glasses / Goggles (for banding)	☐	☐	☐
• Hearing Protection	☐	☐	☐
• Respirators/Dust Masks	☐	☐	☐
Sanitation of Rest Rooms, Lunch Room, Offices	☐	☐	☐
Facility Lighting	☐	☐	☐
Voltage Identified and Labeled Properly	☐	☐	☐
Product Stored Securely, Properly Blocked	☐	☐	☐
JSA Programs, Postings of Special JSAs	☐	☐	☐
Outside Sources for Health Training (i.e., Emergency Oxygen, Battery, Respirators)	☐	☐	☐
Injury Investigation	☐	☐	☐

Inspected by: _____ Date: _____

The narrative required on the back of the inspection forms makes it possible to identify only specific items needing additional attention.

Inspecting anything more often than necessary is costly. Inspecting less often than necessary is taking chances. The potential for serious injury could be the result of failure to inspect on a regular basis. The greater the injury potential, the more frequent should be the rate of inspection. Some individuals prefer the completion of an inspection at the beginning or end of the week. If a monthly inspection is planned and there are many items on the checklist, the inspector may wish to spread the task over several weeks to ensure compliance with the program.

WAREHOUSE ITEMS TO INSPECT

Docks

- Fixed ladders to the dock well

- Stairs to dock well—nonskid, sturdy railings

- Fire extinguishers

  - Charged

  - Tagged (current date)

  - Seals, pins in place

  - Not blocked

- Wheel chocks being used

- Trailer restraints

- Housekeeping

  - Dockwells

  - Under dock plates

  - General housekeeping

- Signage in place

- Emergency lights functional

- Sprinklers not blocked with product

- Overhead lighting functional

- Auxiliary trailer lights functional

- Walkway lines visible

- Propane lift trucks not operating while parked in trailers

- Dock plates functional

- Chemical spill cleanup kits available

- Exits properly identified and not locked

- Aisles and passageways free of clutter

- Overall housekeeping adequate

- PPE being worn as required

- Stop signs visible and in place

- Convex mirrors clean, visible, and in place

- Guardrails and barriers in place

- Conveyors

  - Properly guarded

  - Safety switches operational

  - Warning signs in place

  - Alarms, lights, and buzzers functional

  - Overhead netting in place

- Pedestrians protected with walkways, barriers, and signs

- Safety bulletin board up-to-date

- Machines properly guarded

- Racking secure, sturdy, and safe

- Product stored on the racking, secure, and straight

Battery-Charger Area

- No-smoking signs present

- Job hazard analysis forms posted

- Fire extinguishers

  - Charged

  - Tagged (current)

  - Sealed with pins

  - Not blocked

  - ABC or CO_2 type

- Ventilation fans working

- Manufacturer's guidelines for battery care posted

- Eye wash unit clean and functional

- Proper PPE available for use

  - Face shield

  - Goggles

  - Rubber gloves

  - Rubber apron

  - Rubber boots

- Overall housekeeping adequate

- Acid neutralizer available

- Cell watering device available

- Battery pulling device available

- Emergency phone numbers posted

- Appropriate MSDSs available

- Battery chargers properly labeled to match the power disconnects in event of emergency

- Electrical cord retractors or springs in place

- Racking for the battery chargers secure and safe

Small-Parts Storage

- Vertical lift functioning properly

- Vertical lift inspected

- Safety signs on the vertical lift

- Pinch points guarded on the lift

- Racking shelves sturdy and intact

- Racking free of damage

- Product stored straight and secure

- Aisles free of clutter

- Heavy, bulky products stored between knee and shoulder height

- Floor free of cracks and defects

- Proper lifting techniques used by employees

- Proper PPE worn as required

- Lift trucks operating safely in the aisles

- Fire extinguishers

  - Charged

  - Tagged (current)

  - Sealed with pin intact

  - Not blocked

- Fire hoses unobstructed

- Overhead lights working

- Portable ladders free of damage

- Portable ladders used safely

- Aisles properly identified with lines

- Safety signs available

- Machines properly guarded

- Conveyors used properly

- Conveyors properly guarded

Mezzanine Storage

- Access steps free of debris

- Handrailing and fixed stairs safe

- Movable access gates closed

- Sprinkler heads at least 18 inches from product

- Fire hoses clear of obstructions

- Stored shelves sound and free of defects

- Storage bins and shelving secure and free of defects

- Weight-capacity signs posted

- Portable carts free of damage

- Exits properly identified

- Emergency lights functional

- Movable ladders free of damage and defects

- Heavy, bulky parts stored between knee and shoulder height

- Overall housekeeping acceptable

- Machines properly guarded

- Exhaust fans functional

- Fire extinguishers
  - Charged
  - Tagged (current)
  - Sealed with pin intact
  - Not blocked

- Vertical lift functional

- Lift safety signs in place

- Vertical lift inspected

- Pinch points on the lift properly guarded

Main Warehouse

- Powered industrial trucks inspected every day

- Operators properly trained

- Operators driving safely

- Racking free of damage

- Storage shelves safe and secure

- MSDSs available for chemicals in storage

- Wheels on carts functioning properly

- Portable ladders free of defects

- Product stored at least 18 inches from sprinkler heads (determined by codes)

- Fire hoses clear of obstructions

- Walkways clearly identified with stripes

- Overall housekeeping adequate

- Overhead lighting working

- All electrical wire and connections meeting code requirements

- Safety signs properly posted

- A safe place for delivery truck drivers to wait

- Are machines properly guarded

- Trash compactor controls and safety features functional

- Wheel chocks being used

- Are skylights properly guarded to prevent a person from falling through

- Chemicals stored safely

- Proper chemical labels being used

- Lockout/tagout program and hardware available for use

- Bulletin boards current and material posted properly

- Employees wearing required PPE

- Fire extinguishers

  - Charged
  - Tagged (current)
  - Sealed with pin intact
  - Not blocked
  - Mounted properly

- Correct ergonomic practices being used

- Sprinklers drain-tested each month

Maintenance

- Compressed-gas cylinders properly stored

- Required PPE being worn

- Trash containers for enough away from the building

- Machines properly guarded

- Overall housekeeping adequate

- Ventilation functioning properly

- Power tools free of defects

- Lockout/tagout program and hardware used properly

- MSDSs available for chemicals in use

- Wiring within code requirements

- Extension cords free of defects and properly grounded

- Overhead lighting functional

- Raw material safely stored

- Safety signs in place

- Emergency lights functional

- Torch-cutting permits available for fire prevention.

SAFETY AUDITS

Safety programs that are the most successful periodically perform formal safety audits. Audits usually go beyond OSHA compliance and include many different components from the safety program. What should be included in an audit, when should it be conducted, how long should an audit take, and who should conduct it are issues that need defining. Figures 12-6 and 12-7 identify two pages from a comprehensive safety audit program that contains sixty-six total pages.

Figure 12-6. A Single Page From A Comprehensive Audit

Condition of Overall Building and Structure:

Auditor: Deduct (1.0) for each item that is found defective from this list.

	Yes	No	N/A
Are all panel boxes, electrical boxes and plug-type machines/devices capable of LOTO?	☐	☐	☐
Are circuit breaker boxes and disconnects equipped with voltage and function labels?	☐	☐	☐
Are yellow protective corner posts firmly anchored?	☐	☐	☐
Are there any broken windows?	☐	☐	☐
Are hand railings in place and functional?	☐	☐	☐
Is hand railing equipped with a top rail, middle rail and toe board?	☐	☐	☐
Are toe boards installed where necessary?	☐	☐	☐
Are there any unguarded floor openings?	☐	☐	☐
Are docks, dock wells, dock plates in need of repair?	☐	☐	☐
Is product racking safe and not damaged?	☐	☐	☐
Are steps and ramps intact?	☐	☐	☐
Are seat belts installed on all sit-down lift trucks?	☐	☐	☐
Is each lift truck seat equipped with wings or hip guards?	☐	☐	☐
Are there any significant cracks in the floor?	☐	☐	☐
If so, are you planning to repair the cracks?	☐	☐	☐
Are facility overhead and wall pipes and other material sources labeled?	☐	☐	☐
Are yellow or white lines painted on the floor where necessary?	☐	☐	☐
Are the perimeter of dock plates highlighted in yellow?	☐	☐	☐
Does the roof of this facility leak?	☐	☐	☐
If so, are there plans to have the roof repaired?	☐	☐	☐

Figure 12–7. Scoring System - Corporate Audit Program - For Distribution

Each section is scored by circling the number located under the appropriate rating heading.

Group B - Controlling Hazards		None	Fair	Good	Excellent
a.	Control of Flammables, Gases and Chemicals	0	1	2/4	5
b.	Guarding of Machines/Safeguards for Operations	0	1 / 3	4 / 8	9 / 10
c.	Lockout/Tagout Compliance	0	1 / 3	4 / 8	9 / 10
d.	Availability/Use of Material Safety Data Sheets	0	1	2 / 4	5
e.	Condition of Overall Building and Structure	0	1	2 / 4	5
f.	Warehouse Safety Inspections	0	1 / 4	5 / 10	11 / 15
g.	Powered Equipment, Machine and Tools Inspection	0	1	2 / 4	5
h.	Housekeeping and Storage of Materials	0	1 / 4	5 / 10	11 / 15
i.	Personal Protective Safety Equipment	0	1 / 4	5 / 10	11 / 15
j.	Fire Protection Equipment	0	1 / 3	4 / 8	9 / 10
k.	Purchasing Awareness for Safety Control	0	1	2 / 4	5
	Add up numbers circled in each column	+	+	+	+
	Grand Total Point Value of Circled Numbers:	=		x.20 =	

Audit Content

The actual items that will be measured during a formal audit should be developed to represent all of the hazards and safety program elements within an organization. If a consulting firm is developing the audit guidelines, be sure that they visit the site(s) they will be auditing. If the proper guidelines and elements are to be developed, a physical visit is necessary. Management and the safety committee should be consulted when developing guidelines.

Audits should be modeled for the specific building or operation to which they are applied. Many elements of an effective safety and health program are universal and would apply to almost any location. These basic elements should not be excluded from an audit.

The following categories and individual elements could be used in an effective warehouse safety audit.

1) Safety Organization and Administration

   a) Safety policy posting

   b) Responsible safety representation in the facility

   c) Warehouse safety-rules program

d) New employee/transferred employee orientation

e) Monthly review of supervisors' safety activities

f) Investigation of incidents and injuries

g) Use of handbook and manuals

h) Safety committee meetings

i) Emergency programs

j) Audit responses

2) Hazards Control

a) Control of flammables, chemicals

b) Lockout/tagout—machine guarding

c) Material safety-data sheets

d) Condition of building

e) Inspection of power equipment, tools, machines

f) Housekeeping and storage of materials

g) Personal protection equipment

h) Fire protection equipment

i) Safety considerations in purchasing

3) Occupational Health and Hygiene

a) Noise control

b) Facility ventilation

c) Respirator program

d) Protecting the eyes and skin

e) Facility sanitation

f) Ergonomics

g) Exposures to toxic or harmful elements

h) Preemployment/special physicals

i) Medical supplies, emergency oxygen

j) Training conducted by outsiders

4) Safety Training

a) First aid/CPR

b) Forklift training

c) Training of supervisors

d) Job hazard analysis

e) Safety meetings with employees

f) Job safety observation

g) Use of films, slides, visuals

h) Human-relations material for supervisors

i) Fire committee and emergency team

j) Injury-repeaters program

5) Record Keeping, Workers' Compensation

a) OSHA record-keeping

b) Audit-planning corrections

c) Posting of bulletins

d) Monthly forwarding of safety program materials

e) Means of identifying injury costs

f) Responses to inspections by federal agencies, fire department, etc.

g) Fire protection record-keeping

h) Quality of injury investigations

i) Use of safety objectives for supervisors

j) Quality of overall records

6) Communications and Awards

a) Safety posters

b) Use of signs and labels

c) Safety bulletin boards

d) Recognition programs—employees

e) Recognition programs—supervisors

f) Use of safety campaigns

g) Development of safety bulletins

h) Newsletters for employees

i) Safety performance in salary review

j) Off-the-job safety programs.

Most if not all of these items could be included in a formal safety audit. To be effective, the overall safety and health program must be identified item by item and placed in a format that can be easily followed by the individuals conducting the audit.

Purposes of Auditing

Auditing can serve the need of evaluating and verifying safety, health, and environmental compliance. The desire is to measure compliance with specific regulations, standards, or company policies. Some of the benefits of auditing programs include:

■ Increasing the overall level of safety, health, and environmental awareness

■ Establishing annual goals or objectives that require reaching specific levels of achievement

■ Determining and documenting specific audit requirements

■ Improvement of the overall safety program

■ Protection of the organization from liabilities

■ Potential for creating new and improved program concepts based on current compliance with the program

■ Improved involvement in safety at various levels of management. More ideas and feedback can be provided to auditors.

■ A means of measuring progress over a period of time. If numerical ratings are a part of the final audit each year, increases in scores indicate greater compliance. More compliance should equate to fewer injuries.

■ A means of discussing pending legislation on new corporate programs that may be a part of the next audit format.

When Audits Are Conducted

Formal safety audits should be conducted annually, if at all feasible. The timing of the audit should be close to the date of the prior audit. For first-time audits, consider the impact on the location. Will the facility be in the middle of inventory? Is it the busiest season of the year? Is the facility undergoing labor negotiations? All of these questions should be asked in advance.

Should the facility be notified of the audit? Showing up at a warehouse for an unannounced safety audit could pose a problem. There may be conditions present that make it difficult to complete an audit at that time. Many safety professionals prefer to let the management at the facility know that an audit will be conducted on a certain date. The grading of elements such as housekeeping, overall appearance, and audit preparation can be more rigid if the audit is preannounced.

Length of Audits

Depending on the physical size of the building and property, an audit can take from one day to several days. If the facility has been providing evidence of their ongoing safety program, there would be less of a need to scrutinize documents for elements such as employee safety meetings, training, injury investigations, incident reports, safety committee meetings, warehouse inspections, and special-project documents.

A complete physical inspection of the facility is in order. Perhaps additional visits to the facility floor will be needed when specific documents are evaluated and discussed. Preparation in advance can reduce the time spent at the site.

Who Should Conduct the Audit?

Audits are usually lengthy and require evaluation and preparation. To prepare for a formal audit, a preaudit should be conducted by various members of the warehouse staff. If the staff is large enough, components could be assigned to individuals knowledgeable in particular subjects. For those locations that are progressive or involved in the OSHA VPP process, facility workers should also assist in some way. If a warehouse is small and has a limited staff, a designated person should complete a self-audit by spacing it out over several months. The task may be too difficult to accomplish in a short timeframe.

Formal audits should be conducted by an individual trained in safety and health or completed by a certified safety professional (CSP). If an organization has a limited number of sites, one individual should be the designated auditor. The program elements can be evaluated much easier by someone using identical measures for all sites. Where possible, additional audit team members should be used. Also, employees should participate where possible in the audit process.

SUMMARY

The intent of the chapter was not to offer an inspection process for every facet of a warehouse safety and health program. Within this book there are inspection forms for ergonomics, fire, new employee orientation programs, lockout/ tagout, and racking. This chapter focused on three specific inspecting and auditing processes.

Powered industrial trucks require daily inspections before they are put into use. This is one of the most neglected parts of a forklift safety program. The material in this chapter provides a means to properly inspect each forklift. Without inspections, forklifts can cause injuries due to faulty brakes, steering or other mechanical failures. The inspection form should be processed properly so hazards are corrected on a timely basis. Because powered hand trucks are frequently inspected on a regular basis, a form, Figure 12-8, was created.

Figure 12-8. Powered Pallet Truck Inspection Form

Operators, inspect your walkie or rider pallet jacks at the start of each shift. If any problems are discovered, notify your supervisor. *Never operate a vehicle that is not safe!*

Item	Status		
	Yes	No	N/A
Is horn functioning?	☐	☐	☐
Are the gauge and meters functioning?	☐	☐	☐
Are there any cracks in the forks?	☐	☐	☐
Are wheels functioning and not broken?	☐	☐	☐
Are the tires safe?	☐	☐	☐
Do forward and reverse controls work?	☐	☐	☐
Are any leaks detected; battery/hydraulic?	☐	☐	☐
Is there any external damage?	☐	☐	☐
Are labels and signs in place?	☐	☐	☐
Is the load backrest in place?	☐	☐	☐
Does the steering arm move freely?	☐	☐	☐
Does the lift control work?	☐	☐	☐
Does the braking mechanism work?	☐	☐	☐
Is the standing platform on a rider a non-skid surface?	☐	☐	☐
Is the cover for the electrical controls in place?	☐	☐	☐
Does the battery show any signs of corrosion?	☐	☐	☐
Other	☐	☐	☐

Comments:

_____

_____

_____

Operator Name: _____ Date: _____

Vehicle Name or Number: _____

Facility inspections are very important in the workplace. Forms should be designed specifically for a location, department, or facility. A wide variety of items requiring inspection at docks, battery- charging areas, small-parts areas, mezzanines, in the main warehouse, and in the maintenance area have been specified. There may be particular items that were not listed but require inspecting on a regular basis. There was no way that this list could be complete.

Safety auditing is probably one of the most important parts of a safety program. If designed properly, a formal audit can help guide a warehouse staff through self-evaluations and program progress. Many organizations include safety audits as part of annual salary reviews or bonus programs. The model used in this chapter has individual scoring of items for a maximum of 100 points. Each item and section are weighted accordingly for the completed audit score. Many organizations do not use formal audits. This may be a matter of poor judgment because audits are excellent tools to uncover weak links in the program as well as highlight those programs that are successful in the facility.

REFERENCES

Armco Steel Corporation. "Conducting Planned Safety Inspections." *Accident Prevention Fundamentals and Industrial Hygiene*. Middletown, OH, 1976, pp. 7-1–7-16.

Bureau of Business Practice. *Want to Boost Overall Safety? Put Your Supervisors on the Audit Trail*. Number 414, September 1997, pp. 414–15.

National Safety Council. *Accident Prevention Manual, Safety, Health and Environmental Auditing*. Chicago, IL, 11th Edition, 1997, pp. 102–3.

National Safety Council. *Warehouse and Storage Safety*. Chicago, IL, 1990, pp. 1–13.

13

Ergonomics in the Warehouse

The National Institute for Occupational Safety and Health (NIOSH) has predicted that by the next century 50 percent of the workforce will suffer from repetitive strain injuries, (RSIs), which can result in claims ranging from $20,000 to well over $100,000. The demands of the work performed in a warehouse can easily cause RSIs if hazards are not corrected. Every year approximately nineteen million workers suffer disabling injuries from musculoskeletal causes at a cost of $100 billion.

Moving product **safely** through a warehouse or distribution center is very important. In addition, today's business climate demands a quicker turnaround of customer orders. Product handling now requires additional time and attention involving special processing, labeling, packing, and the scanning of bar codes.

In addition to customer satisfaction, there is a need to reduce workers' compensation costs and to meet OSHA requirements. Economic condition of the late 1990s have led to reductions in the workforce as well as increased demands for just-in-time service. Warehouse employees must be protected if a better bottom line is to be achieved.

Ergonomic improvements will help an employer to be competitive. During the 1980s and 90s the subject of ergonomics has given rise to many articles, books, seminars, and trained consultants. OSHA has proposed an ergonomic standard and various states have proposed this legislation as well.

UNDERSTANDING ERGONOMICS AND ITS COSTS

It is important for readers to have a basic understanding of what ergonomics is and how it can be applied to the warehouse environment. The word ergonomics is derived from the Greek words *ergo* (work) and *nomos* (natural laws). Ergonomics encompasses the relationship between a worker's job performance and well-being, as well as the tools, equipment, tasks, and overall environment.

Many new technologies have simplified tasks on the job, but many jobs still require handling product manually and repetitively. These motions can cause injury to the hands, arms, shoulders, back, knees, and ankles. Back injuries are very common throughout the warehousing industry. In one particular study involving injuries at three wholesale grocery warehouses employing 1,500 workers, some 115 back injuries were recorded. This represented 30 percent of the total injuries at these facilities. Individuals who selected

205

and lifted product were injured the most often. Some of the containers being lifted weighed over 70 pounds and two containers were lifted each minute. Lifting a loaded box from the floor over 120 times each hour would be a difficult task for any employee. Back injuries tend to be the most costly of workers' compensation claims and also include the highest numbers of days away from work. The estimated cost of back problems in the United States is $210 billion per year.

The National Safety Council estimates that some 31 percent of all injuries in the workplace are musculoskeletal overexertion injuries; 22 percent of all injuries are overexertion injuries of the lower back. Some of the industries with a greater risk of back injuries are general building, contracting, heavy construction, and warehousing. When back pain is considered, the problem becomes much larger. It is estimated that as much as one-third of the population may be afflicted with back pain at some point in their life.

BLS Statistics

Job-induced repetitive stress injuries is the fastest-growing category of workplace injuries. Specific stress factors include repetitive motion, awkward posture, heavy lifting, or a combination of these factors. According to the Bureau of Labor Statistics (BLS) lost- time injuries and illnesses reported in 1993 included the following:

BLS Lost-Time Injuries—1993

- Repetitive stress injuries   27%
- Contact with objects   27%
- Falls   19%
- Transportation related   3%
- Violence   1%
- All others   22%

In another part of the BLS report, organizations that insure for workers' compensation estimated 2.73 million workers' compensation claims for repetitive stress injuries in 1993. These injuries cost employers more than $20 billion.

BLS Causes of Lost Workdays and Median Days Away from Work

- Carpal tunnel syndrome   30 days
- Amputation   22 days
- Fractures   20 days
- Tendinitis   10 days
- Sprains, strains   6 days
- Bruises, contusions   3 days

There are many individuals in the health care, insurance protection coverage, and safety professions who think that repetitive stress injuries are rising faster than any other workplace health concern. This problem is not confined to the warehouse environment. It is not unusual for a manufacturer of computer keyboards to lose a court case for injuries suffered from the use of their product. A major keyboard manufacturer lost a court case in 1996 in which a worker in New York was awarded $5.3 million. The settlement amount may be unusual, but equipment manufacturers have been the targets of numerous product liability lawsuits.

Surprisingly, workers have been known to file compensation claims for carpal tunnel syndrome injuries in warehouses. Their jobs are out on the warehouse floor, not at a keyboard. There are ways to reduce these injuries to the back, wrist, shoulders, neck, arms, and legs. In most cases a modification to the workplace is necessary. Management must assist in correcting workplace hazards, such as those that produce carpal tunnel syndrome.

The DuPont Corporation believes that every time a company makes an ergonomics improvement in the operating system, they make it easier for the employees to do their jobs. In addition, the company gains in quality and productivity. With improvements in ergonomics there is almost a direct visible improvement in productivity. Management concepts such as value-added manufacturing or just-in-time principles lend themselves to ergonomic improvements. Ergonomics is the one area in which the link between enhancing safety and enhancing the production cycle is most evident. Many times these workplace improvements occur by looking at things a different way and then making the proper corrections.

BASICS OF ERGONOMICS

Ergonomics helps adapt the job to fit the person rather than forcing the person to fit the job. The objective of ergonomics is to adapt the job and workplace to the worker by designing tasks, workstations, tools, and equipment that are within the worker's physical capabilities and limitations.

The focus of ergonomics is on the work environment and includes factors such as design of workstations, controls, displays, safety devices, tools, and lighting to fit the employees' physical requirements and to ensure their health and well-being. Many times a restructuring of the work environment helps to reduce the stressors that cause cumulative trauma disorders (CTDs) and repetitive motion injuries (RMIs).

The vast numbers of injuries in the workplace are linked to technological advances such as more specialized tasks, higher assembly line speeds, increased repetition, and a lack of ergonomically designed technologies. As a result of these exposures, workers frequently experience injuries to the arms, hands, wrists, neck, shoulders, back, and legs. The tasks performed by employees involve thousands of repetitive twisting, lifting, forceful, or flexing motions each workday. This can place undue stress on workers' tendons, muscles, and nerves. Recognizing ergonomic hazards in the workplace is an essential first step toward correcting the hazards, improving worker protection, and reducing workers' compensation costs.

The consequences of this lack of attention to ergonomics in a warehouse will result in higher injury rates, more employee turnover, higher absenteeism, and lower employee morale. The processing of orders could be late, inventories could increase, and picking accuracy could decline as a result of poor ergonomics. Many of these factors could impact future sales, customer service, and the bottom line. Warehouses that apply good ergonomic principles are more productive and efficient.

CUMULATIVE TRAUMA DISORDERS

Cumulative Trauma Disorders (CTDs) occur when stresses build up over time in a part of the body and cause pain or other discomfort. CTDs are often difficult to identify, classify, and manage because employees respond differently to stress, and they can be aggravated by activities outside the warehouse. Causes are sometimes difficult to isolate and control.

Cumulative trauma disorders may include:

- Bicipital tendinitis
- Calcific tendinitis
- Frozen shoulder
- Rotator cuff syndrome
- Thoracic outlet bursitis
- Cubital tunnel syndrome
- Ulnar nerve entrapment
- Bursitis
- Golfer's elbow
- Tennis elbow

- Raynaud's phenomenon
- Tendinitis
- Tenosynovitis
- Carpal tunnel syndrome
- DeQuerians disease
- Trigger finger
- Internal derangement of the knee
- Patellar bursitis
- Tarsal tunnel syndrome
- Plantar fascitis.

ERGONOMIC ISSUES—HANDS AND WRISTS

Carpal tunnel syndrome

Second only to back injuries is a very common CTD, carpal tunnel syndrome. The median nerve that runs through an area of the wrist called the carpal tunnel can be damaged by excessive or repetitive movement, undesirable hand positions, or exertions that impose stress on the affected tissues. The carpal tunnel is susceptible to employee injury because the hand does not weigh much in relation to other parts of the body. The hands are strong and have an average grasping strength of 50–60 pounds. The muscles that generate this grasping force are located primarily on the forearms. The forearm muscles transmit force to the hands just like that of a pulley and rope system.

Early symptoms of carpal tunnel syndrome include numbness or tingling and burning sensations in the fingers. More advanced problems can involve ongoing pain, wasting away of the muscles at the base of the thumb, dry or shiny palms, and clumsiness. The pain is first noticed at night and may be confined to one side of the hand.

The BLS reported that lost workday cases of carpal tunnel syndrome injuries declined for the third year in a row in 1996, from a high of 41,000 cases in 1993 to 29,900 in 1996. The report also showed that female workers suffering from carpal tunnel syndrome accounted for 70 percent of lost workdays for this ailment.

Tendinitis/tenosynovitis

The tendons and sheaths can become inflamed from repetitive use. When the tendons are overstretched or constricted, the chance of pain and injury increases. With further exertion, some of the fibers that make up the tendon can actually fray or tear apart. The tendon becomes thickened, bumpy, or irregular in certain parts of the body, such as the shoulder. The injured area may calcify. Without rest and sufficient time for the tissues to heal, the tendon may be permanently weakened.

Tenosynovitis is an inflammation or injury to the synovial sheath surrounding the tendon. Synovial fluid is secreted from these sheaths and the lubricant reduces friction during movement. When the hands and wrists are subjected to repetitive motion, an excess of synovial fluid is secreted and the sheath becomes swollen and painful.

DeQuervians disease

This ailment is an inflammation of the tendon sheath in the thumb. It is attributed to excessive friction between two thumb tendons and their common sheath. Twisting and forceful gripping motions with the hands, similar to a clothes-wringing movement, can place sufficient stress on the tendons to cause DeQuervians disease.

Reynauds syndrome

Repeated exposure to vibration can damage the blood vessels and sensitive tissues of the hand. This damage to the blood vessels reduces their oxygen-carrying capacities, which deprives the skin and muscles of the hands and fingers the much-needed oxygen. The functions of the skin and muscles become impaired and eventually deteriorate. Symptoms include circulatory impairments in the fingers. The digital arteries become spastic and restrict blood flow to the fingers, and the result is numbness and a tingling sensation. In more advanced cases, the skin becomes blanched, permanent loss of hand control develops, and there is a reduced sensitivity to heat, cold, and pain.

ERGONOMIC ISSUES—ARMS AND SHOULDERS

Poor workplace design can injure the arms and shoulders of warehouse workers. Tasks that require employees to work with their arms outstretched or their elbows up may result in fatigue of the muscles in the arms and shoulders. There may be pain and injury caused by compression and entrapment of the nerves that run through the shoulder, similar to carpal tunnel syndrome of the wrist. The entrapment of the nerves in the shoulder is a condition known as thoracic outlet syndrome.

Stock on warehouse shelving should be arranged so that employees are not required to repeatedly raise their arms or hold them above shoulder height. Tasks should be designed that permit the arms to be kept low and the elbows down. Repetitive handling of warehouse stock is costly because it adds no value to the product. This action also increases the employees' vulnerability to injury. Many times, minor changes in workplace methods or design will reduce injuries associated with repetitive handling.

Risk factors identified with cumulative trauma in upper extremities are:

- Awkward postures by employees

- Static load and work

- Organization of the work

- Force, repetition, and duration of work

- Fit, reach, and vision

- Cold, vibration, and local mechanical stress.

ERGONOMIC ISSUES—THE BACK

Next to the common cold and the flu, back injuries are the most frequent cause of absenteeism. According to the National Safety Council, 22 percent of all injuries are overexertion injuries to the lower back. It is estimated that the total cost of current back problems in the United States is approximately $210 billion per year.

Back problems are among the most common work-related injuries. Many days are lost each year both off and on the job as a result of back problems. The majority of back problems result from movements over a lifetime: Lifting, standing, pushing, pulling, bending, and twisting all place a strain on the back. All of these motions are part of a worker's activity in a warehouse.

Back problems fall into two classifications: muscle strain (sprain related), or long-term disc-related problems in the lower back. Working in awkward positions or lifting load improperly are the most common causes of problems.

The discs can be easily damaged through compression and twisting. Holding a light box or product can easily harm one's back if a twisting motion is involved. A warehouse worker may believe he is handling a load comfortably but may still be experiencing enough compression to damage the back.

Back injuries are difficult to control—even in those warehouses that maintain good safety programs. The most effective long-term approach to minimize back injuries is to utilize correct ergonomic programs that help change the workplace. Some focus has to be on the worker that involves education, training, and enforcement of sound lifting practices. Among the factors to consider for worker safeguards are the following:

- What is the amount of weight being lifted?

- Is the object difficult or awkward to lift?

- Where must the object be moved to?

- Where must the object be moved from?

- How much pulling or pushing is involved?

- How often must the lifting take place?

- How high is the item from the floor?

Some basic considerations for proper lifting include:

- Keep loads situated from knee level to chest level for easier lifting.

- Whenever possible, avoid placing loads on the upper shelf or on the floor.

- Never bend over at the waist to lift a load—regardless of what it weighs.

- Never bend or twist to reach a load.

- Keep the upper body upright, erect, and in line with the hips.

- It is best to push a load instead of pulling it. A person can usually push twice as much as he/she can pull.

- When possible, use lifting devices such as forklifts rather than manually handling loads.

- For work activities that require standing and lifting, never pivot at the waist and never lean forward with the weight in hand.

- Sitting for prolonged periods is not good for the back. It is important to move around, walk, and stand even if one maintains a job that requires seating.

- Keep in good physical condition. Individuals that are large in the waist tend to be more prone to lower-back problems. In addition, keep shoes in good repair; work shoes with worn heels or soles can affect the back.

- Before lifting, always size up the load and plan how it will be lifted. The correct size of gloves may be helpful in protecting the hands as well as obtaining a good grip.

- If possible, place one foot alongside the load and one foot behind it. Center the weight of the body over the load and keep the feet comfortably spread.

- Bend the knees and get a firm grasp on the load while tucking in the chin.

- Keep the load close to the body and lift with the legs and arms.

- Plan your route for carrying the load. Shift the feet, not the torso during movement. Set the load down by using the legs, tuck in the chin, and keep the fingers clear of any pinch points.

- Get help from fellow workers on any lift that is considered too heavy or awkward, or if you feel you are experiencing any back problems. An employee should always minimize lifting.

Risk factors that contribute to lower-back injuries and disorders are:

- Lifting posture

- Lifting technique

- Work environment

- Duration of the task or work

- Characteristics of the load

- Nonuniform loads

- Organization of the work

- Frequency of handling the load

- Space confinements

- Lack of handles or grasping area

- Twisting the torso.

Pulled or strained muscles, ligaments, tendons, and discs are perhaps the most common back problems and may occur to almost one-half of the workforce. These injuries cause problems over the course of a worker's lifetime. (This statistic produces results that can take place over a lifetime.) Back muscles or ligaments are often injured from repetitive lifting, pulling, and straining. The back can be weakened and lose its ability to support the body, making additional injuries more likely.

Many back disorders are caused by the cumulative effects of faulty body mechanics. These include:

- Excessive twisting

- Bending

- Reaching

- Carrying

- Moving loads that are too heavy or too big

- Staying in one position too long

- Poor posture

- Poor physical condition.

Since back problems will affect between 50 and 80 percent of people at one time or another, management must do all it can to minimize injuries. There are many causes of back injuries, thus it is hard to diagnose and quantify. Many back problems result from ordinary movements over a lifetime.

Compression to the disc is the primary cause of back damage. Discs are easily damaged through compression and twisting. Holding even a light weight while twisting can cause tears in a disc. Pain will occur when enough fibers tear or the worker's disc actually herniates and places pressure on the muscles, ligaments, or nerves.

METHODS TO IMPROVE ERGONOMICS

To improve warehouse ergonomics, an effective program should be developed that includes:

- Employee training and education

- Employee participation

- Management support

- Purchasing authority

- Survey and inspection programs.

Training and education. Employees should receive training and education on all ergonomic principles. There are many programs on ergonomics that can be purchased for training purposes. Organizations such as the National Safety Council, the American Society of Safety Engineers (ASSE), NIOSH, and OSHA offer educational programs for this purpose. Consultants can also offer specialized ergonomic programs. Without proper ergonomic education and training of the employees, the purchase of lifting devices, work stations, specialized equipment, modern conveyors, and/or improved powered industrial trucks would be of no value. Employees must be educated if they are to develop safe working habits. Supervisors must also be a part of the training process.

Training should include classroom discussion by those knowledgeable in ergonomics. Visuals are essential to promote an understanding of the subject, including overhead transparencies, slides, videos, and handout materials. Long-term retention of training comes from repetition; a one-time training session is not enough and must be considered just a start.

Employee participation. If management wishes to know how employees feel about safety or any other issue, they should be asked. Who knows more about operating machines such as powered industrial trucks or any other operation than the employees? Employees can help in achieving ergonomic solutions. Some organizations have formed ergonomic teams or committees to encourage employee involvement. For any program to succeed, be it quality, production, or safety, employees must be a part of the overall plan.

Management support. This is essential to any safety program. Once the cost benefits of ergonomics are demonstrated to management—all levels of management— acceptance is more likely. The bottom line is definitely helped by good ergonomic practices. Those organizations that place ergonomics on a higher level find that injuries and all associated costs are reduced. A written policy on ergonomics can be very helpful. By budgeting adequate funding for the program, management can demonstrate its commitment. A senior management review of injury reports involving ergonomic issues should be established.

Purchasing. This must be coordinated to ensure that the proper ergonomic equipment is obtained. In many cases, ergonomic-related equipment must be purchased for workstations or material handling. It is important to select quality equipment. There are many vendors that make quality equipment, and there are others that only presume to do so. A wise investment must be preceded by a search for the best equipment. Thoughtful purchasing can minimize or reduce any risks of poor selection. State-of-the-art devices will definitely make jobs easier.

Figure 13–1. Ergonomic Evaluations of Warehouse Employees

Supervisors are to use this form to assess various jobs in the warehouse to determine if ergonomic improvements are needed.

Job Title of Evaluation: _____

Date: _____ Warehouse: _____

Department: _____

Names of Individuals Involved: _____

	Yes	No	N/A
Lifting Assessment			
Does the job involve lifting?	☐	☐	☐
Is bending involved in this job?	☐	☐	☐
If lifting is involved, what is the weight of the object?	☐	☐	☐
How many times is the object lifted every 30 minutes?	☐	☐	☐
Does the object contain handles?	☐	☐	☐
Does lifting take place below knee height?	☐	☐	☐
Does lifting take place above shoulder level?	☐	☐	☐
Does the employee have to reach out more than 20 inches to lift the object?	☐	☐	☐
Does the employee have to climb a ladder to lift the object?	☐	☐	☐
Work Environment Assessment?			
How would you rate the lighting at the employees' workstation/area (i.e.: poor, fair, good, excellent)?	☐	☐	☐
Is the floor level and free of cracks, debris?	☐	☐	☐
Does the work area generate noise levels above 85 decibels?	☐	☐	☐
Is the work area properly ventilated?	☐	☐	☐
Additional Considerations			
Does the employee have to perform work at a level more than six inches below the waist?	☐	☐	☐
Does the employee have to complete the job with the upper arm in a horizontal position (from the elbow to the shoulder)?	☐	☐	☐
If a chair is used, does it contain a backrest and footrest?	☐	☐	☐
Are arm rests available? If yes are they used?	☐	☐	☐
Is the employee pushing or pulling an object?	☐	☐	☐
Does the employee have to apply force to get the job done?	☐	☐	☐
Does the employee throw (or forcefully place) items into bins, cages, trucks, etc.?	☐	☐	☐
Is the speed of the conveyor adjustable?	☐	☐	☐
Does the employee have to flex the wrists to complete the job?	☐	☐	☐
Does the employee wear gloves?	☐	☐	☐
Does the employee use a tool of any kind?	☐	☐	☐

	Yes	No	N/A
If the employee uses a tool, does it vibrate?	☐	☐	☐
Does the use of the tool require force?	☐	☐	☐
Is the handle of the tool padded in any way?	☐	☐	☐

Job Specifics

How often is the job performed? ☐ Continuous ☐ Hourly ☐ 1/Day ☐ 1/Week ☐ Rarely

Are the fingers: ☐ Straight ☐ Slightly Bent ☐ Fully Bent ☐ Tight Grip ☐ Loose Grip

Are the wrists: ☐ Straight ☐ Slightly Bent ☐ Fully Bent

Are the wrists positioning ☐ Up ☐ Down ☐ Toward Thumb ☐ Away from Thumb

Are the arms: ☐ Overhead ☐ Shoulder Level ☐ Extended ☐ Bent at Elbow ☐ Almost Lowered

Position of the body: ☐ Upright ☐ Back Slightly Bent ☐ Back Bent ☐ Crouch Position ☐ Body Twist

Comments:

Survey and Inspection Programs. It is necessary to evaluate the workplace on a regular basis. Once the ergonomics program has been initiated it is important to survey work areas. Individuals with knowledge in ergonomics must be part of each survey. Observations of warehouse lighting, height of work benches/tables, floor mats, height of conveyors, signage, warning lights, and employee work methods are to be assessed. A formal evaluation sheet, Figure 13-1, a two-page form, has been included with this chapter to help prevent any ergonomic oversight.

Supervisors must include ergonomic issues during their daily trips through the various warehouse departments. Ergonomic programs are ongoing; continuous change and improvements are expected. In addition to department surveys, a thorough analysis of each job is needed. Job hazard analysis includes a step-by-step evaluation of specific tasks completed by an employee. In the process of completing a work task, such as unloading a trailer, each step should be reviewed for not only the safe way of performing the task, but also the ergonomically correct way. Ergonomic programs must be an integral part of an overall safety program in a warehouse.

ERGONOMIC TIPS TO IMPROVE THE WAREHOUSE

Powered Industrial Trucks

Manufacturers of lift trucks continue to improve ergonomic factors through design. When leasing or purchasing a new piece of equipment, ergonomic benefits for the operator are important. Allow operators to utilize a specific piece of equipment for several weeks before purchasing it. During the evaluation process make inquiries as to how the equipment is performing. This effort can prove valuable. Keep the following ergonomic factors in mind regarding powered industrial trucks:

■ Good visibility is essential to operate the lift truck. Operators should not have to lean out to the side; they should be able to see through the masts for safe driving.

■ All functions and displays should be easy to read. This is especially important for a new operator. The newer models of powered equipment have much improved displays and controls.

■ Seats and cab compartments should be designed for comfort and function. Proper cushioning for seats and feet is essential. Whole-body vibration increases the risk of back injury and other musculoskeletal injuries. New equipment should be purchased with vibration damping. Older-model trucks can be modified with damping. Shoe inserts to avoid the impact of foot vibration can also be helpful.

■ Seats should allow for adjustments both vertically and horizontally. On some new models the seat tilts for better viewing by the operator.

■ Controls should be within easy reach of the operator and located to improve visibility, which will help improve posture. The ergonomic positioning of controls helps minimize extended forward and side reaching, and forearm rotation, and it keeps the operator wrists straight, as they should be.

■ A rule of thumb for deciding between a lift truck that requires the operator to stand, or one that requires the operator to be seated, involves the actual time spent operating the truck each day. If an operator must stand for more than four hours each day, then a sit-down model is recommended. If the operator must get off the vehicle every five minutes or so, then a stand-up model is recommended.

■ Quick foot movement between pedals is important. The pedals must be easily reached. For maximum benefit, the operator should be able to change leg positions to avoid fatigue. If metatarsal safety shoes are worn while operating a lift truck, the metatarsal guard should be designed into the shoe to prevent the guard from hanging up on the pedal.

■ Steering should be power-assisted when the vehicle is parked or when it becomes difficult to steer.

■ Electric powered industrial trucks have the benefit of not producing the carbon monoxide emissions created by internal combustion models. Consideration must be given to the propane gas tanks, which can weigh upwards of 40 pounds and are awkward to lift. Back injuries from moving empty or full propane tanks are not uncommon.

Negative Ergonomic Factors

The following ergonomic factors should be eliminated or corrected in the workplace. The warehouse environment should be evaluated to determine if any of these factors exist.

■ Hand tools that have sharp edges or ridges

■ Hand tools that need sharpening

■ Hand tools that allow air to be directly exhausted onto the hand

■ Hand tools that are not balanced or are difficult to hold

■ Vibration from powered hand tools

■ Hand tools that require a flexed wrist

■ Tools that are difficult to reach

■ Twisting, clothes-wringing motions of the wrist

■ Tools with a grip span of more than 4 inches between the thumb and forefinger

■ Working with the neck bent at a 15° angle

- Repetitive arm, shoulder, hand, and back motions

- Working with the body leaning forward

- Standing or sitting for long periods

- Handling product or materials from heights above the shoulder or below the knee

- Handling large bulky objects regardless of weight

- Handling tote boxes without handles

- Working in an immobile position for extended periods

- Static muscular work

- Frequent or extreme lifting requirements

- Excessive carrying, pushing, pulling

- Excessive twisting or stretching

- Working with arms or elbows held high or outstretched

- Poorly designed chairs

- Improper glove sizes for employees

- Tables or work surfaces that are too high or too low for the height of the worker

- Lack of cushioning floor mats

- Lack of casters or poor-quality

- casters on rolling equipment

- Lack of use of powered equipment

- Use of manual pallet-handling equipment versus powered equipment

- Poor lighting

- Slippery, rough, cracked floor surfaces

- Cluttered walkways

- Machinery or equipment that is noisy or does not operate smoothly

- Lack of proper signage to guide workers

- Work space that does not accommodate the shortest or tallest employee for reach or lifting

- Working tasks that require the eyes to focus on a variety of distances

- Screen glare on VDTs

- Controls that require too much actuating force to operate easily

- Poor lighting on controls

- Controls that are difficult to read or understand

- Under-powered or poorly-designed equipment

- Control systems that do not consider reflex actions in an emergency

- Inadequate temperature controls, requiring employees to work in extreme heat or cold without means of personal protection.

ERGONOMICS IN THE OFFICE

Many workplace injuries occur in the offices, and ergonomic problems also exist there. Many workers develop carpal tunnel syndrome and other ailments as a result of the use and design of their workstations.

Management must not overlook the need for improved ergonomics in warehouse office areas. Important considerations for computer workstation safety include:

- The top of the computer screen should be at eye level.

- The operator should be an arm's length away from the screen.

- The work surface should be at elbow level.

- The chair should have adjustable armrests that support the arms at elbow level. If the operator's back arches away from the back of the seat, a cushion or rolled-up towel may be placed there.

- The knees should be raised slightly above the hips.

- The chair must have a seat that can adjust to allow the feet to rest flat on the floor. The knees should protrude a hand's width from the edge of the chair.

- A five-pronged chair base with casters is best.

- If the operator's feet cannot reach the floor, be sure to get a foot rest.

- Lighting should be considered to avoid screen glare.

- The operator should not be looking into the sunlight or an open window when lifting the eyes from the screen.

A comprehensive checklist developed by OSHA has been included in this chapter. Figure 13-2 offers a two-page evaluation form for office ergonomics.

SUMMARY

The subject of ergonomics in the workplace is here to stay. Many ergonomic improvements have taken place in workplace design, powered equipment, training, and worker education. Any investment in ergonomic improvements will also benefit productivity along with safety. Studies have shown that improving the ways in which workers handle product, operate equipment, process product, and generally move throughout a warehouse provides for a better bottom line. Workers work smarter, not harder.

The Bureau of Labor Statistics reported that there were 281,000 musculoskeletal injuries in 1996. Workers suffering from musculoskeletal injuries were out of work an average of seventeen days, more than for any other injury. The average recovery time for a work-related injury is five days.

In order to improve workplace ergonomics, professional assistance is needed to educate both workers and management. Many times the most basic improvements pay big dividends with little or no investment. Workers should be involved in any improvement process so that they can offer their expertise as a result of working for years at a particular job. Management can't do it alone.

Figure 13-2. Working with Computer Terminals and Office Ergonomics

A practical checklist for ergonomics training in the office can help your employees work more comfortably and effectively. Check off when corrected.

ADJUST THE CHAIR

☐ Adjust the height of the chair's seat so that thighs are horizontal, feet rest flat on the floor, and arms and hands are comfortably positioned at the keyboard.

☐ If the chair is too high, use a footrest. This takes pressure of the back of the thighs.

☐ Armrests should be adjustable up/down and inward/outward, and padded.

☐ Adjust the back rest so that it supports the lower back and fits the curvature of the spine. Seat pans should be adjusted for proper slope and comfort.

☐ Seat cushions should be firm, not soft.

☐ Utilize chair mat to decrease carpet resistance and provide more maneuverablilty.

ADJUST THE DISPLAY

☐ Position the screen to minimize glare and reflections from overhead lights, windows, and other light sources. Place the screen so that windows are not directly in front of or behind the employee when seated.

☐ Adjust the display so that the top of the screen is slightly below eye level when sitting at the keyboard. The top of the screen should not be above eye level.

☐ Set the contrast or brightness of the screen at a comfortable level. (This may have to be done more than once a day, as the light in the room changes.)

☐ Where it is impossible to avoid reflections or adjust lighting, an anti-glare filter placed over the screen can be helpful. However, filters may affect the clarity of the image on the screen and should be tried only after other methods of reducing glare have been exhausted. An electrically grounded nylon micromesh glare filter is effective also in removing the static charge from a screen.

ADJUST LIGHTING

☐ Draw the drapes or adjust blinds to reduce glare.

☐ Adjust desk lamp or task light to avoid reflections on the screen. Light sources should come at a 90 degree angel, with low watt lights rather than single high watt.

☐ The task lighting should not be less than light at screen.

☐ Reduce overhead lighting (where possible) by turning off lights or switching to lower wattage bulbs.

☐ Use indirect or shielded lighting where possible.

☐ To limit reflected glare, walls should be painted a medium or dark color and not have reflective finish.

ADJUST DOCUMENT HOLDER

☐ Position document holder close to screen and at the same level and distance from the eye to avoid constant changes of focus.

☐ Rotate position of document holder to opposite side of screen periodically.

WORK SMART

☐ Encourage employees to change position, stand up or stretch whenever they start to feel tire. Encourage a soft touch on the keyboard, keeping hands and fingers relaxed, and wrists and body in neutral positions.

☐ Become aware of other tasks such as manual stapling, sorting through large volumes, and mail sorting where repetition and awkward positions may contribute to repetitive motion injuries. Seek alternate ways to perform the tasks, reduce the load, or rotate jobs.

CONSIDER POSTURE

☐ The head should be straight and balanced over the spine while looking forward at the screen. Eliminate the flexed-neck position.

☐ Elbows should be bent at 90 degrees when hands are at keyboard.

☐ Wrists should be in a neutral position. Utilize wrist rests at the edge of the keyboard for support. Keyboards should be detachable for VDT and slightly sloped at about 10-15 degrees.

☐ Utilize a back rest for support in lumbar area of back.

☐ Feet should rest flat on floor or a foot rest should be utilized.

Source: *United States Department of Labor OSHA Safety Training Newsletter*

REFERENCES

Auguston, Karen. "Ergonomic Aids Ease Manual Palletizing." *Modern Materials Handling*. October 1995, pp. 48–49.

Bettendorf, Robert. "Good Ergonomics Can Mean Good Economics." *The Office*. June 1990, pp. 32–37.

Britt, Russ. "Hands and Wrists Are Thrust Into the Hiring Process." *The New York Times*. September 21, 1997, p. 11.

Gross, Clifford M. Ph.D. "To Prevent Wrist Injuries." *Quarterly Stressors, Assembly*. September 1997, p. 24.

Harps, Leslie Hansen. "What Supervisors Need to Know About Order Picking Ergonomics." *Warehousing Management*. May/June 1997, pp. 48–49.

J.J. Keller & Associates, Inc., *Special Report—Ergonomics*. Volume 7, Number 10, October 1997.

Katzel, Jeanine. "Introduction to Ergonomics." *Plant Engineering*. June 6, 1991, pp. 48–55.

La Bar, Greg. "Lifting: How Much Is Too Much?" *Occupational Hazards*. July 1997, pp. 35–36.

Laurie, Nancy, Robert Andres, and David Wood. "Ergonomic Job Analyses of Picking Tasks in a Wholesale Grocery Warehouse Distribution Center." *Advances in Industrial Ergonomics and Safety*. 1995. pp. 403–8.

Material Handling Engineering. "Ergonomics Disorders at Ford - Calculating the Cost." September 1997, pp. 75–79.

—. "Managing Ergonomics, Tools for Ergonomics." 1997/98. pp. A-5 – A-13.

—. "Workplace Safety—Ergonomic Designer and Lift Trucks." October 1995, p. 17.

Mital, Anil. "Recognizing Musculoskeletal Injury Hazards in the Upper Extremities and Lower Back." *Occupational Health and Safety*. August 1997, pp. 91–99.

Occupational Hazards. "Carpal Tunnel Cases Decline." July 1998, p. 19.

"The Role of Ergonomics in Today's Warehouse." *Modern Materials Handling*. June 1997, pp. E-3 – E-22.

Schwind, Gene. "Ergonomics: Expanding Toward 2000." *Material Handling Engineering*. October 1995, pp.

14

Chemical Exposures in the Workplace

The inherent hazards associated with chemical exposures in a warehouse are often ignored or treated casually. There are chemicals of one kind or another in every warehouse. A particular chemical could be very dangerous or be a minor hazard. Every employee must know the risks of each chemical being stored or handled within or outside the building. Management and employees should be knowledgeable in specific warehouse hazards. This chapter will focus on the following details associated with chemicals in the warehouse:

■ The Hazard Communication Standard (OSHA 1910.1200)

■ Handling and storage of chemicals

■ Chemical spills

■ Carbon monoxide.

THE HAZARD COMMUNICATION STANDARD

It is estimated that some 32 million workers are potentially exposed to approximately 650,000 existing chemicals in the workplace. Chemicals can pose a serious hazard for every employee in a warehouse. Chemical exposure may cause or contribute to many serious health effects such as heart ailments, kidney and lung damage, sterility, cancer, burns, and skin rashes. Some chemicals may also be safety hazards and have the potential to cause fires, explosions, and other serious incidents or injuries.

The federal regulation, OSHA 1910.1200, was issued in May 1986. Surprisingly, some thirteen years after the passage of this chemical hazard law, many employers continue to misunderstand the need for this program. In addition, some employers have no concept of the hazard communication program and the fact that it applies to every workplace.

The purpose of the Hazard Communication Standard (HCS) is to create an awareness of hazardous chemicals in the workplace. Also, the law allows for appropriate precautionary measures that workers may take for their personal protection.

221

OSHA's HCS program requires chemical manufacturers and importers of chemicals to perform hazard determinations on their products. The hazards associated with their products must be made known to the employers who purchase them through the use of product labels and material safety data sheets. Employers must then develop a hazard communication program to educate employees on how to protect themselves from the hazards associated with the chemicals they handle.

The flow of information on hazardous chemicals is achieved by way for four distinct components:

1. A written hazard communication program

2. Material safety data sheets (MSDSs)

3. Product warning labels

4. Employee training.

WRITTEN PROGRAM

Employers must develop, implement, and maintain at the workplace a written, comprehensive, hazard communication program. The program must include the following provisions:

■ A list of all the hazardous chemicals in each work area, and the means the employer will use to inform employees of the hazards of nonroutine tasks

■ Container labeling that will furnish the employee with a brief synopsis of the chemical and other needed information

■ The collection and availability of material safety data sheets on every chemical and hazardous product in the workplace, which provide details on chemical and physical dangers, as well as safety procedures and emergency response techniques

■ Employee information and training that communicates the hazards of the chemicals, protective measures, and specific procedures for handling and identifying chemicals.

MATERIAL SAFETY DATA SHEETS (MSDS)

Chemical manufacturers and importers must develop an MSDS for each hazardous chemical they produce or import. They must provide the MSDS automatically at the time of the initial shipment of a hazardous chemical to a downstream distributor or user. Distributors must also ensure that downstream employers are similarly provided an MSDS.

Each MSDS must be in English and include information regarding the specific chemical identity of the hazardous chemical(s) and their common names. The MSDS must also provide information on the physical and chemical characteristics of each hazardous chemical. This would include known acute and chronic health effects, related health information, exposure limits, and whether the chemical is considered a carcinogen. In addition, the MSDS must contain precautionary measures, emergency and first aid procedures, and the identification of the organization responsible for preparing the MSDS.

Copies of the MSDS for hazardous chemicals found in the warehouse must be readily accessible to employees during each work shift.

From the compilation of MSDSs, the employer must develop a list of all hazardous chemicals in the warehouse. For those chemicals that arrive without an MSDS, a letter requesting it must be sent to the manufacturers. As an added safety program benefit, the sheets should be in a three-ring binder. A numerical tab behind each MSDS should match the chemical list. This storage and filing system allows for ease in locating the required sheet(s). OSHA does not stipulate that a three-ring binder or numerically tabbed sheets be a part of the program.

Employees should always read and understand an MSDS before starting a job with a hazardous chemical. This reading allows the employee to:

- Identify the chemical's hazardous ingredients

- Identify the physical and chemical characteristics

- Identify safety procedures

- Identify any other associated hazards.

An MSDS is arranged in specific parts. A typical MSDS will contain the following:

- Chemical product and company identification

- Ingredients

- Hazards identification

- First aid measures

- Fire-fighting measures

- Accidental release measures

- Handling and storage of the chemical

- Exposure controls and personal protection

- Physical and chemical properties

- Stability and reactivity

- Toxicological information

- Ecological information

- Disposal considerations

- Transport information

- Regulatory information.

PRODUCT WARNING LABELS

Inadequate warning labels are a prime target for OSHA citations. Chemical manufacturers, importers, and distributors must be sure that containers of hazardous chemicals leaving the workplace are labeled, tagged, or marked with the identity, appropriate hazard warnings, and the name and address of the manufacturer or other responsible party.

Within each warehouse, each container must be labeled, tagged, or marked with the identity of hazardous chemicals contained therein. The label must also show hazard warnings relevant for employee protection. Labels must convey the hazards of the product, and the related warning statement must include the effects on target organs, such as "causes irritation of the nose and upper respiratory tract." A label that simply states "harmful if inhaled" is not a sufficient warning.

The hazard warning can be any type of message, words, pictures, or symbols that convey the hazards of the chemical(s). Labels must be legible, in English (plus other languages, if desired), and prominently displayed. Bags, barrels, bottles, boxes, cans, cylinders, drums, and storage tanks must carry labels.

Color-coded systems are used to label hazardous materials. Some labels use colored bars or diamonds that indicate the type of hazard. A red bar or diamond indicates a fire hazard. Yellow bars or diamonds indicate a reactivity hazard. Blue bars or diamonds indicate health hazards. White bars identify the need for personal protective equipment such as glasses, gloves, faceshields, rubber aprons, or respirators. A white diamond contains symbols regarding the health hazards the chemical may cause, warnings such as OX for oxidizer, ACID for acid, ALK for alkali, COR for corrosive, W̶ for "use no water," and a radioactive symbol.

In addition, the horizontal bars or diamonds will display a number that indicates the degree of the hazard. The numbers range from 0 to 4. A "0" indicates no hazard, a "1" indicates a slight hazard, a "2" indicates a moderate hazard, a "3" indicates a serious hazard, and a "4" indicates a severe hazard.

For employee awareness in labeling, The Hazardous Materials Identification System (HMIS) utilizes color-coded bars to identify the hazard focus. The National Fire Protection Association (NFPA) uses a diamond system for the same purpose. Figure 14-1 identifies the two forms of warning labels.

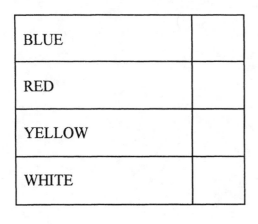
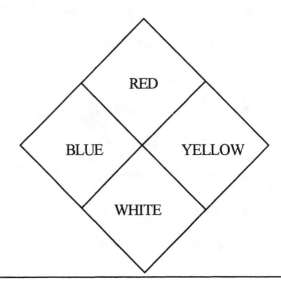

Figure 14–1. HMIS-NFPA 704 labels

EMPLOYEE TRAINING

Employers must establish a training and information program for employees exposed to hazardous materials in their work areas. The training is required at the time of initial assignment and whenever a new hazard is introduced to the work area.

At a minimum, the discussion must include the following items:

- The hazard communication standard and its requirements

- The components of the hazard communication program in the employees' workplaces

- Operations in work areas where hazardous chemicals are present

- Where the employer will keep the written hazard evaluation procedures, communication program, lists of hazardous chemicals, and the required MSDS forms.

The training program must consist of the following elements:

- How the hazard communication program is implemented in the warehouse, how to read and interpret information on labels and the MSDS, and how employees can obtain and use the available hazard information

- The hazards of the chemicals in the work area. The hazards should be discussed by individual chemical or by hazard categories such as flammability.

- Measures employees can take to protect themselves from the hazards.

- Specific procedures put into effect by the employer to provide protection, such as engineering controls, work practices, and the use of personal protective equipment (PPE).

- How methods and observations such as visual appearance or smell can be used by workers to detect the presence of a hazardous chemical to which they may be exposed.

Those working in a warehouse should put some thought into selection of chemicals. Safety and health considerations must be a part of the selection process. Three important categories of hazards must be examined when comparing the relative safety of different chemical products for the same task. The categories are fire and explosion potential, acute health effects, and chronic health effects.

When purchasing a chemical, consideration must be given to flashpoint as well as fire and explosion potential. The flashpoint is the temperature at which a liquid gives off vapor in sufficient concentration to be ignited. As an example, the flashpoint of toluene, a product which could easily be present in a warehouse, is 40° F. Any liquid that is identified as having a flashpoint lower than 100° F. is to be considered a flammable. The lower the flashpoint, the more volatile the liquid. Gasoline, as an example, has a flashpoint of -35° F. If a chemical is listed as having a flashpoint greater than 100° F, it is classed as a combustible. Brake fluid, as an example, has a flashpoint of approximately 275° F.

FLAMMABLE (EXPLOSIVE) LIMITS

The term "lower flammable limit" (LFL) describes the minimum concentration of vapor to air below which propagation of a flame will not occur in the presence of an ignition source. The term "upper flammable limit" (UFL) is the maximum vapor-to-air concentration above which propagation of flame will not occur. If a vapor-to-air mixture is below the lower flammable limit, it is described as being "too lean" to burn, and if it is above the upper flammable limit, it is "too rich" to burn.

When the vapor-to-air ratio is somewhere between the lower flammable limit and the upper flammable limit, fires and explosions can occur. The mixture is then said to be within its explosive or flammable range. When the mixture happens to be in the intermediate range between the LFL and the UFL, the ignition is more intense and violent than if the mixture were closer to either the upper or lower limits.

Workers exposed to certain chemicals may suffer immediate (acute) or long-term (chronic) harm. Injury may result from chemicals that are corrosive, reactive, and/or toxic.

Corrosives are either acids or bases. These are materials that can cause burns and destruction of skin or fatty tissue under the skin. Bases are also referred to as alkaline materials and sometimes as caustic materials. The relevant piece of information needed for evaluation is the pH level. The pH indicates how acidic or basic a material is. A 7.0 pH is neutral, neither an acid nor a base. Zero to 7.0 is the acid range. It is physically possible, but rare, to have an acid with a pH less than 0 or a base with a pH greater than 14. When selecting a chemical, choose one that is closes to a pH of 7.0 for safety reasons.

Reactive chemicals should be avoided, if possible. Included in this class of reactive chemical hazards are cyanide compounds that can release deadly hydrogen cyanide gas. Carefully read the reactivity section and the fire and explosion section of the MSDS for each product being compared.

The toxicity hazard of a chemical is determined by review of the OSHA PEL (permissible exposure limit) of the material on the MSDS. When choosing a chemical, choose the one with the highest PEL. This section, as well as other sections of an MSDS, should be discussed with a trained professional to ensure worker safety.

Some chemicals cause chronic health effects. Always select a noncarcinogen over a carcinogen. Chemicals tend to collect in and act on one or more specific organs of the body, called target organs. Trained professionals should be used to guide selection and use of any chemical.

HANDLING AND STORAGE OF CHEMICALS

Chemicals are handled in warehouses daily, either as product or by direct use in the warehouse. An issue of *Warehousing Management Magazine* featured an article about a serious chemical spill that occurred in a Denver, Colorado warehouse. A 55-gallon drum of lacquer thinner was punctured by the forks of a forklift resulting in a spill that covered between 2,500 and 5,000 square feet of the facility before it was contained. Management should instruct workers to refrain from extracting the forks in situations such as this so the leak would be minimized. Fortunately, this incident did not result in a fire or employee injury. In Figure 14-2, a forklift ran into a box and fluid leaked.

Twenty-three percent of the readers of *Warehousing Management*, in responding to a survey, reported that they experienced chemical spill incidents during the past year. Seventeen percent reported employee injuries as a result of the chemical spills. Most incidents involved eye irritation or skin exposure resulting in hospitalization and lost time.

Figure 14-2. Clean up chemical spills promptly.

During fiscal 1995 OSHA statistics indicated that warehouses and motor freight transportation facilities were cited for spills or other chemical-related issues. According to the National Response Center (NRC), 27,427 spills were reported in 1997. If a facility stores, handles, or transports liquids, it is a prime candidate for a spill. The reporting of a spill can be very confusing. Many of the federal regulations overlap. A spill or leak may require the filing of reports with two, three, or more agencies at the national, regional, and/or local level.

Noncompliance penalties can be severe, resulting in civil or even criminal charges and fines. The penalties levied against an employer can be as much as $25,000 to $75,000 per day, per violation.

OSHA requires specific levels of training for workers engaged in hazardous materials emergency and postemergency response cleanup activities. OSHA rule 1910.120, Hazardous Waste Operations and Emergency Response (HAZWOPER), training requirements are task specific. The amount of training required is primarily dependent on the roles and responsibilities of an individual during an emergency response and/or postemergency response cleanup.

Spill cleanup is essential if there is an incident. Figures 14-3 and 14-4 illustrate the preparations in this warehouse. Several different types of spill cleanup kits are available. Also, special containers are made available for containing leaking 5-gallon buckets.

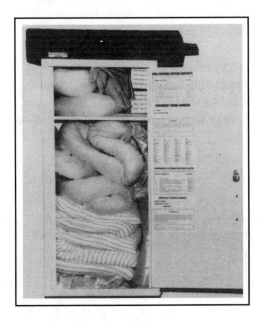

Figures 14-3 & 14-4. This spill clean up equipment is close at hand and ready to use.

CARBON MONOXIDE

Exposures to the chemical carbon monoxide (CO) can be very significant in a warehouse environment. Carbon monoxide is the by-product of the incomplete combustion of any material containing carbon such as gasoline, natural gas, oil, propane, coal, or wood. CO is a colorless, odorless, tasteless gas that can cause harm without warning. Unintended exposure to CO in the United States claims more than 800 lives each year. The Centers for Disease Control identified 11,547 CO deaths from 1979 to 1988. Some 40 percent of all CO poisonings occur at work sites, may of which are warehouses, states the National Safety Council.

Sources of CO in a warehouse can be from:

- Malfunctioning appliances such as furnaces, stoves, ovens, and water heaters

- Vehicle exhaust—specifically powered industrial trucks

- Blocked chimney flues

- Charcoal grills (when used in confined spaces)

- Power washers, compressors, and boilers.

Symptoms of CO poisoning resemble the flu, but without fever. Also, the victim will experience dizziness, fatigue, sleepiness, headache, and nausea. Symptoms resulting from CO inhalation depend primarily on its concentration in the air, as well as the duration of exposure and the exposed person's degree of exertion. Additional physical effects on the employee could include vomiting, chest pain, and fluttering and throbbing of the heart. Unconsciousness and possible death may occur. If a person is exposed to high concentrations, there can be a rapid loss of consciousness or life without first producing any other significant symptoms.

CO enters our the body through the lungs, where it is absorbed into the bloodstream. Once in the blood CO rapidly binds with hemoglobin to form carboxyhemoglobin. CO displaces oxygen in the blood because hemoglobin has as much as 200 times greater affinity for carbon monoxide than oxygen. This lack of oxygen, or hypoxia, will cause the heart and brain to become vulnerable to injury. The blood's hemoglobin, given a choice between oxygen and CO, will snub the oxygen and instead process CO through the circulatory system. The body's cells and tissues thus become deprived of sufficient oxygen and hypoxia results.

Fatal CO poisoning may occur in atmospheres containing less than 0.15 percent— 1,500 parts per million (PPM)—because of the gas's ability to displace oxygen. Health professionals can determine the degree of CO poisoning by measuring the amount of carboxyhemoglobin in the blood. CO poisoning can be reversed if caught in time. Even if the person recovers, acute poisoning may result in permanent damage to parts of the body that require oxygen, such as the heart and brain.

EVIDENCE OF CO EXPOSURE

There are numerous articles and research papers regarding the effects of CO in industrial workers. In many cases, a powered industrial truck using propane, gasoline, or diesel fuel to power it has caused CO poisoning.

- In a suburban Chicago factory two teens working part-time to pay for college expenses were overcome by carbon monoxide and found dead. The youths were using a propane-powered forklift to perform their duties at the plant. The authorities stated that a combination of Saturday morning stagnant air, humidity, and a temperature inversion apparently caused the lethal carbon monoxide concentration.

- In another plant on the south side of Chicago, some fifty employees complained of headaches and nausea that sent twenty-two others to a nearby hospital. The cause of the CO poisoning was from a boiler in the facility.

- A small manufacturing plant in a suburb of Toronto, Canada, had twenty-four employees overcome by carbon monoxide gas. A heating contractor was called in to check the heaters. This evaluation determined they were not the source of the problem. A forklift was discovered to be the source of the CO poisoning. The Canadian Ministry of Labor recommends a limit of only 1 percent CO in forklift truck exhaust; this particular forklift was measured at 11 percent.

- A wholesale beverage distributor in Colorado transported a fifty-three-year-old worker to a local hospital because of chest pain. The employee had been working for approximately 9.5 hours. Within the facility, two propane forklifts were operating. It was discovered through tailpipe measurements that the forklifts were producing CO levels of 95 and 100 PPM throughout the main warehouse and offices. The cause of the employee's chest pain was the high concentrations of CO.

- An oil packaging firm in Illinois was cited by OSHA for the deaths of three employees from CO poisoning. A faulty overhead gas heater was the source of deadly gas. A report from the coroner's office indicated that one of the employees had twice the CO level that would cause death.

- In another case, a twenty-four-year-old man driving a forklift powered by propane gas was treated for CO poisoning in an emergency room in Colorado. He had reported dizziness, headache, and nausea after 8.5 hours of operating the forklift. His condition warranted sending him to a hyperbaric chamber at another hospital. The employee handled pallets of bagged sugar from railroad cars to a warehouse. Since the warehouse had no heaters or ventilation, the propane-powered forklift was the focus of the investigation.

- Three employees in a manufacturing plant sought medical treatment for CO poisoning. Propane forklifts were being used in the plant; airborne concentrations of CO measured 300 PPM. There were no heaters working in the building at the time; the forklift was the target of the investigation.

- At a small warehouse in a Chicago suburb, a gasoline-powered forklift was being used to handle heavy automotive parts. The electric forklifts in the facility, which were normally used, were unable to handle the heavy loads. The gasoline-powered lift truck had not been used for some time and was not properly maintained. Six employees were transported to a local clinic and treated for nausea, headache, upset stomach, and dizziness. CO poisoning was responsible for the clinic visits.

- Workers in a 115,000-square-foot warehouse and assembly area complained of severe headaches. After investigation and the elimination of several possible problem areas, the company found high levels of CO in its fourteen propane-powered forklifts. The fourteen lift trucks were sending over 1 million PPM of CO into the warehouse area through the tailpipes.

Measurements and Guidelines

OSHA has set a permissible exposure limit of 50 PPM of CO as a time-weighted average (TWA) over an 8-hour work shift. OSHA has also established a 40 PPM exposure for a 10-hour work shift and 33 PPM for a 12-hour work shift. The American Congress of Governmental Industrial Hygienists (ACGIH) recommends a 25 PPM TWA limit of CO for an 8-hour work shift. For a 10-hour work shift the recommended limit is 18 PPM, and it's 13 PPM for a 12-hour work shift.

Carboxyhemoglobin averages 1 to 2 percent in the general nonsmoking urban population. For pack-a-day smokers, the mean concentration of carboxyhemoglobin is 5 to 6 percent. For heavy cigarette and cigar smokers the levels can reach as high as 10–15 percent. Symptoms of CO poisoning usually begin at 10–20 percent. At 20–30 percent, (150–300 PPM CO), headache general weakness, and nausea develop. At 30–50 percent (300–650 PPM) severe headache, nausea, vomiting, dizziness, and confusion may be present. Weakness and disorientation at this level may inhibit the victim's ability to escape, and loss of consciousness and collapse may occur.

The propane-powered forklift appears to be frequently implicated in CO poisonings and fatalities. Emissions from propane lift trucks must be monitored and controlled. There are nearly 800,000 internal combustion engine lift trucks in operation in in the United States. Over 80 percent of these are propane powered.

CO emissions taken from a tailpipe of a propane lift truck normally range from 5,000 to 7,500 PPM. When a forklift is operating at full power, these same readings will produce readings of 2,000 to 5,000 PPM. The forklift must be properly maintained and the fuel system must be properly sized and tuned. If the lift truck is poorly maintained, vehicles can yield readings of CO in excess of 10,000 PPM regardless of the type of fuel used. Studies at sites that involved serious CO exposures measured tailpipe emission levels up to 88,000 PPM. Air monitors mounted within the building will help to measure air quality in the warehouse.

To aid in controlling CO emissions, catalytic converters can be added to lift trucks. The lift truck must be at the proper operating temperature for the converter to be fully functional. Catalytic converters are only able to convert forklift emissions such as oxides of nitrogen and carbon monoxide into harmless gases when the converter reaches a temperature of approximately 600° F. It should be noted that the use of catalytic converters is not the final answer to the control of CO emissions. Testing of emissions every six months as well as following manufacturers' guidelines for care and maintenance of the system is important. Exhaust fans are helpful to improve warehouse air quality. A certified industrial hygienist can assist in measuring CO within the building and place personal sampling devices on employees.

Electric-powered industrial trucks offer a very good solution to the carbon monoxide problem. However, even though electric lift trucks do not produce carbon monoxide, they do present other hazards such as exposure to corrosive battery acid and an explosive atmosphere from the hydrogen gases emitted by the electric truck battery. Each type of powered industrial truck poses its own set of potential problems.

Carbon monoxide may also be controlled by using compressed natural gas (CNG) to power forklifts. Manufacturers of these systems state that the use of CNG costs 30 to 50 percent less than propane or gas and as much as 70 to 80 percent less than electricity. CNG is reported to eliminate up to 90 percent of the CO, of the 50 percent hydrocarbons, and of the 30 percent carbon dioxide emissions. Even the potential for back injury is reduced by using CNG, since there is no need to lift a propane cylinder off and onto a lift truck. These portable cylinders can weigh as much as 40 or more pounds.

SUMMARY

Preventive maintenance is the method favored by health professionals in reducing the carbon monoxide emitted by propane fueled internal combustion vehicles. The program must include a tune-up based on exhaust gas measurement. Measurements make it possible for the vehicle maintenance mechanic to balance the substances present in the exhaust gases. This quality control for vehicle maintenance helps maintain company compliance with air quality standards and reduces worker exposure to CO. Manufacturers provide training and documents to assist the mechanic.

Compliance with the Hazard Communication Law is a necessity for each warehouse. Many employers find compliance with this regulation difficult, because of its broad requirements. The continuous juggling of employee training, material safety data sheets, labeling, and a written program can be challenging for any organization.

The potential for employee injury through exposures to chemicals that are corrosive, explosive, toxic, or poisonous is common in warehouses. Workers must be protected from workplace chemicals. Containers should be properly labeled when the chemical arrives at the warehouse. It is not uncommon for containers of chemicals to be dropped from forklifts or be otherwise damaged by a forklift-mishandling incident. Spearing of bags or barrels with the forks of the forklift occurs quite regularly throughout industry. Special precautions are required to clean up and properly dispose of chemical waste. The need for PPE cannot be underestimated; injury and illness from chemical exposure may be serious or deadly for an unprotected, untrained worker.

REFERENCES

Arndt, Michael. "Fatal Plant Accident Ends 2 Youths' Dreams." *Chicago Tribune*. Monday, February 25, 1985, Sect. 1, p. 11.

Brody, June E. "Where Carbon Monoxide May Be Lurking." *The New York Times*. Wednesday, December 13, 1995, p. B9.

Business and Legal Reports, Inc. *Your Right to Know*. Madison, CT, Revised 7/97.

Coastal Video Communications Corp. *Hazard Communication*. Virginia Beach, VA, 1995.

Fegelman, Andrew. "Plant Hit with Citations After Gas Fumes Killed 3." *Chicago Tribune*. February 9, 1985.

Genesove, Leon. "Carbon Monoxide: The Silent Killer." *Accident Prevention*. November/December 1996, pp. 15–19.

Industrial Hygiene News. "Device Controls CO Emissions From Distribution Center Fork Lifts." May 1997, p. 4.

Kartye, Craig. "A Guide to Spill Response Training." *Environmental Protection*. April 1998, pp. 18–21.

Klein, Lawrence R. "Hazard Communication." *Compliance Magazine*. April 1996, pp. 12–15.

Michigan Occupational Health. "Industrial Lift Trucks." Volume 29, No. 1, Spring 1996.

Payne, Mike. "Carbon Monoxide: Silent Suffocation." *Ohio Monitor*. February 1988, pp. 5–9.

Reynolds, Larry. "Preventing CO Exposure from Propane Forklifts." *Occupational Health and Safety*. September 1997, p. 54.

Roberge, Brigitte. "Evaluation and Control of Carbon Monoxide Exposure from Propane-Fueled Forklifts." *Applied Occupational Environmental Hygiene*. March 1998, pp. 183–91.

Salkin, Steven E. "Hazardous to Your Wealth." *Warehousing Management*. March/April 1997, pp. 16–21.

Sankey, Matt. "Reporting a Spill." *Environmental Protection*. April 1998, pp. 22–25.

Schwind, Gene F. "CO Dangers Still Lurking." *Material Handling Engineering*. September 1996.

Sly, Orville M. Jr. "Flammable and Combustible Liquids." *Fire Protection Handbook*. National Fire Protection Association. July 1991, pp. 3–47.

U.S. Department of Labor, OSHA. *Carbon Monoxide Poisoning*. Fact Sheet No. OSHA 92-11.

U.S. Department of Labor, OSHA. *Chemical Hazard Communication, OSHA 3084, 1995 (Revised)*.

15

Personal Protective Equipment

Despite the many safeguards that should be provided in the workplace to ensure employee safety, injuries can still occur. There are situations in which the hazard cannot be completely guarded or controlled; thus the need for personal protective equipment (PPE) for workers. This chapter will focus on the typical safety equipment that employees would wear in a warehouse. Some organizations may have sites where other types of personal protective equipment are used. There are many manufacturers of safety gear that can assist in the proper selection for employee protection.

TYPES OF EQUIPMENT

It is important to identify the various pieces/types of personal protective equipment and provide specific information on the individual items. In a typical warehouse or distribution center, the following PPE may be required.

- Hard hats
- Steel toe shoes or boots
- Safety glasses
- Safety goggles
- Face shields
- Cutting goggles
- Welding helmets

- Gloves for various jobs
- Dust masks
- Respirators
- Ear plugs/muffs
- Body harnesses/fall arrest systems
- Rubber aprons.

HARD HATS

Employees are to wear protective helmets when working in areas where there is a potential for head injuries from falling objects. Hard hats in warehouses provide for greater employee protection because of the risk involved in the storage of product throughout the building. Most of the product and materials in a warehouse are stored on racking and shelving; employees must work and walk beneath these storage areas.

There are other reasons to wear a hard hat. Many times workers must reach under racking to retrieve product. Any time a worker is under shelving or racking there is the potential for a struck-against injury. Workers can also strike their heads against fixed objects, product protruding into aisles, while walking or working under stairs, and exiting or gaining access to a forklift seat.

Protective helmets must comply with American National Standards Institute (ANSI), Z89.1. There are three types of hard hats:

- Class A hats protect against falling objects and 2,200 volts of electricity for one minute.

- Class B hats protect against falling objects and 20,000 volts for three minutes.

- Class C hats protect against falling objects but offer no electrical protection.

Bump caps are not listed as a means of protection for employees in warehouses. There are no federal standards, regulations, or guidance for the use of bump caps. Since hard hats are intended to protect one's head from a falling object, a bump cap would not provide this protection. It is not recommended that bump caps be available or worn in a warehouse or distribution center.

During hearings on the proposed OSHA Personal Protective Equipment rule, it was pointed out that most blows to the head come from the front, back, or sides. The ANSI Z89.1—1986 standard addresses only protection for the top of the head; the hard hat is designed essentially for falling-impact protection. It is important to point out that there are limitations to any piece of PPE.

Hard hats/helmets used in industry today are lightweight, durable, more comfortable, and safer than those hard hats used thirty or so years ago. The shells of hard hats are made of molded plastics such as polycarbonate or polyethylene. The suspension within the hard hat is made of nylon and vinyl.

Currently, some equipment manufacturers are experimenting with new helmets; a few manufacturers have already developed new models. The ANSI standard has identified guidelines for a "level 1" helmet that provides protection from objects striking from above, and a "level 2" helmet that provides for protection against impact from the sides, front, and back. These new lateral-impact helmets contain a foam liner under the shell along with a chin strap. The manufacturers recommended that this new type of hard hat be worn for rescue work, logging, mining, or other exposures where workers could be struck by swinging or flying objects.

One manufacturer pointed out that the cost of new helmets is about four times that of a standard hard hat. The hats are hotter and heavier and place more strain on the neck. Also, it is unknown how many employees would be saved through the use of a lateral-impact hard hat. Those employers that wish to choose this type of helmet now have that option, and the ANSI standard will formalize manufacturing guidelines.

Here is some important information to know about protective helmets.

■ The shell and suspension absorb the force of a striking object and reduce its impact on the head and spinal cord.

■ Safety helmets must pass three tests conducted on a random sample of each lot of that is manufactured. The first test requires an 8-pound missile be dropped from a 5-foot height onto the top of the safety cap, which is mounted on a metal headform.

■ The second test requires that a 1-pound plumb bob be dropped 10 feet onto the mounted helmet. Penetration by the plumb bob cannot exceed three-eighths of an inch into the material of the helmet.

■ The third test uses an electric charge to test electrical resistance.

■ Helmets are tested at 0° and 120° F.

■ Helmets should be cleaned on a regular basis by immersing them into warm water, and a mild detergent should be used to scrub the shell inside and out. Suspensions should also be cleaned regularly and replaced when inspections reveal defects. Suspensions should be changed annually.

■ Never use an adhesive to repair a cracked hard hat—the hat must be discarded. Never allow a defective hard hat to be passed on to any employee or to be taken home.

■ Never drill holes in a helmet unless the manufacturer authorizes this procedure. Approved attachments can be placed on a hard hat per manufacturer's specifications.

■ Chemicals and ultraviolet light can damage a hard hat.

■ Aluminum hard hats must never be worn in a warehouse. This type of hard hat offers little impact protection compared to the current thermoplastic models.

■ Suspensions in a hard hat allow for adjustment so that the wearer can work in comfort.

■ Manufacturers suggest inspecting hats before each use. It's time to replace a hard hat when:

  • Cracks appear in the shell or the internal suspension.

  • The shell becomes brittle. To test for brittleness, slightly flex the brim of the helmet.

  • Any deep gouges are cut into the shell.

  • Concentric rings appear on the shell.

  • The shiny surface of the shell turns chalky or appears dull.

  • Tears or cuts appear in the nylon straps or webbing of the internal suspension.

■ Never paint on a hard hat. Models come in various colors and can easily be used to identify units, departments, or individuals, i.e.; green = safety committee, red = fire committee or maintenance, yellow = visitors, etc.

■ Never etch or carve anything on the hard hat. Only approved decals can be used.

■ Winter liners can be added inside the hard hat to provide protection from inclement weather.

FOOT PROTECTION

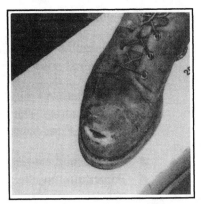

Figure 15-1. This steel toe boot was struck by a pallet truck. The protective cap saved the employee from injury.

Whenever there is a chance of foot injuries due to impact, falling, or rolling hazards, objects piercing the sole, or electrical hazards, approved safety footwear is required. This broad requirement was a part of the 1994 OSHA PPE standard 1910.136. Management is required to make a hazard assessment of the workplace to make a determination as to what PPE is required. The forms needed to make these assessments are at the end of this chapter. All protective footwear must comply with ANSI Z41.1 1991 "American Standard for Personal Protection – Protective Footwear. The standard steel toe shoe or boot must be chosen to fit the tasks, hazards, and environment in which they will be worn. Some 180,000 disabling foot and toe injuries occur each year. The number of injuries requiring first aid treatment is unknown. In addition, the number of times that a foot is saved because a box, roll, pipe, spike, steel bar, or other heavy object bounces off the steel toe is not known. Most workers continue working and do not give the incident much thought. Figure 15-1 illustrates a steel toe boot that was struck by a pallet truck. The worker was not injured.

The typical steel toe boot or shoe offers protection for the toe area with the exception of the little toe, which cannot be covered. The reason for this unprotected area is that the required flexing of the foot and shoe rules out a steel toe (or fiberglass toe) that extends further back onto the shoe. If the steel toe were larger, employees could not bend the shoe properly to walk, bend, or climb. Metatarsal guards offer more protection to the instep of the foot from falling objects. The metatarsal bones can be easily injured. When the metatarsal bones are injured the victim has difficulty in standing or walking.

Electricians or anyone else facing electrical hazards should be equipped with a specially manufactured shoe that has safeguards from high-voltage exposures.

EYE AND FACE PROTECTION

The Bureau of Labor Statistics (BLS) reports that there are more than 85,000 eye injuries in the workplace each year. Of all the individuals that experience eye injuries at work, the BLS reports that only 10 percent were wearing eye protection. Studies also show that if employees are not accustomed to and trained to wear eye protection at work, it is more likely that off-the-job injuries to the eyes will continue to be a societal problem. A breakdown of injuries reveals this national problem. The United States Eye Injury Registry (USEIR) from December 1992 revealed the following data:

- 42 percent of those injured stated "home incidents" as the cause.

- 17 percent stated "industrial premises" were the cause.

- 16 percent identified recreation or "sport-related" incidents.

- 10 percent were listed as "other."

- 7 percent were listed as "unknown."

Experts state that 90 percent of all eye injuries are preventable. There are many jobs within a warehouse that require eye protection. If possible, employees should wear eye protection at all times for maximum protection. At the very least it is needed when:

- Placing banding/strapping on a pallet or load, or removing banding or strapping

- Sweeping or emptying debris into a trash container manually or from a floor sweeper

- Working on or handling batteries

- Using a cutting torch or welding machine for maintenance purposes

- Handling chemicals or cleaning up a chemical spill

- Any other eye injury exposure.

The types of eye and face protection required on the job can be found in ANSI Z87.1 "American National Standards Practice for Occupational and Educational Eye and Face Protection." Management and employees must be made aware of the proper eyewear selection process to ensure a safer workplace. The Food and Drug Administration (FDA) has established standards for eyewear for the public. The impact quality of this eyewear offers less protection than the industrial eyewear that ANSI requires. See Figure 15-2 for the ANSI standard.

Studies have shown that polycarbonate plastic lenses are significantly more shatter-resistant than other types. Glass and plastic lenses that were tested met federal standards for shatter resistance, but only polycarbonate did not break when struck with the kind of force generated during common incidents and injuries. Research showed that shattered lenses were possibly to blame for many eye injuries.

There are pros and cons regarding the various advantages and disadvantages of eyeglass lenses. Note the chart in Figure 15-3 that highlights these differences.

SAFETY GOGGLES

Safety goggles can be classified as having many of the same protective properties as safety glasses with side shields. Goggles can easily fit over prescription eyewear to further protect the eyes as well as offer protection for the eyewear itself. Goggles can be bulky and would be difficult to wear for an entire day if the job required walking, riding, or operating equipment. Most times goggles are used when the hazards of chemicals, sharp wires, banding, strapping, or heavy dusts are present. The wearing of goggles requires that the worker don them prior to the start of a project or when the hazard is present, and then remove them when the danger has passed.

Pointers to keep in mind regarding the use of protective goggles include the following:

- Keep them clean by storing in a container of some kind. Many times goggles are hanging by a machine or operation and they tend to get very dirty.

- If goggles aren't cleaned, dirt or dust from them may easily get into the eyes while they're being worn.

Figure 15-2. ANSI Standard Goggles.

A. Spectacle, No Sideshield

B. Spectacle, Half Sideshield

C. Spectacle, Full Sideshield

D. Spectacle, Detachable Sideshield

E. Spectacle, Non-Removable Lens

F. Spectacle, Lift Front

G. Cover Goggle, No Ventilation

H. Cover Goggle, Indirect Ventilation

I. Cover Goggle, Direct Ventilation

J. Cup Goggle, Direct Ventilation

K. Cup Goggle, Indirect Ventilation

L. Spectacle, Headband Temple

M. Cover Welding Goggle, Indirect Ventilation

N. Faceshield

O. Welding Helmet, Hand Held

P. Welding Helmet, Stationary Window

Q. Welding Helmet, Lift Front

*The illustrations shown are only representative of protective devices commonly available at the time of the writing of this standard. Protective devices do not need to take the forms shown, but must meet the requirements of the standard.

Notes:

(1) Care shall be taken to recognize the possibility of multiple and simultaneous exposure to a variety of hazards. Adequate protection against the highest level of each hazard must be provided.

(2) Operations involving heat may also involve optical radiation. Protection from both hazards shall also be provided.

(3) Faceshields shall only be worn over primary eye protection.

(4) Filter lenses shall meet the requirements for shade designations.

(5) Persons whose vision requires the use of prescription (Rx) lenses shall wear either protective devices fitted with prescription lenses or protective devices designed to be worn over regular prescription eyewear.

(6) Wearers of contact lenses shall also be required to wear appropriate eye and face protection devices in a hazardous environment. It should be recognized that dusty and/or chemical environments may represent an additional hazard to contact lens wearers.

(7) Caution should be exercised in the use of metal frame protective devices in electrical hazard areas.

(8) Welding helmets or handshields shall only be used over primary eye protection.

(9) Non-sideshield spectacles are available for frontal protection only.

Eye and face protection is necessary for operators where the job requires it. (Reprinted from American National Standards Practice for Occupational and Educational Eye and Face Protection, ANSI Z87.1-1989, approved by the American NAtional Standards Institute on February 2, 1989 and published by the American Society of Safety Engineers as the Secretariat of the standards project).

Figure 15-2. (continued) ASSE/ANSI Eye and Face Protection Guidelines.

AMERICAN NATIONAL STANDARD Z87.1-1989

	SELECTION CHART			PROTECTORS		
		ASSESSMENT SEE NOTE (1)	PROTECTOR TYPE	PROTECTORS	LIMITATIONS	NOT RECOMMENDED
I M P A C T	Chipping, grinding, machining, masonry work, riveting, and sanding.	Flying fragments, objects, large chips, particles, sand, dirt, etc.	B,C,D, E,F,G, H,I,J, K,L,N	Spectacles, goggles faceshields SEE NOTES (1) (3) (5) (6) (10) For severe exposure add N	Protective devices do not provide unlimited protection. SEE NOTE (7)	Protectors that do not provide protection from side exposure. SEE NOTE (10) Filter or tinted lenses that restrict light transmittance, unless it is determined that a glare hazard exists. Refer to OPTICAL RADIATION.
H E A T	Furnace operations, pouring, casting, hot dipping, gas cutting, and welding.	Hot sparks	B,C,D, E,F,G, H,I,J, K,L,*N	Faceshields, goggles, spectacles *For severe exposure add N SEE NOTE (2) (3)	Spectacles, cup and cover type goggles do not provide unlimited facial protection. SEE NOTE (2)	Protectors that do not provide protection from side exposure.
		Splash from molten metals	*N	*Faceshields worn over goggles H,K SEE NOTE (2) (3)		
		High temperature exposure	N	Screen faceshields, Reflective faceshields. SEE NOTE (2) (3)	SEE NOTE (3)	
C H E M I C A L	Acid and chemicals handling, degreasing, plating	Splash	G,H,K *N	Goggles, eyecup and cover types *For severe exposure, add N	Ventilation should be adequate but well protected from splash entry	Spectacles, welding helmets, handshields
		Irritating mists	G	Special purpose goggles	SEE NOTE (3)	
D U S T	Woodworking, buffing, general dusty conditions.	Nuisance dust	G,H,K	Goggles, eyecup and cover types	Atmospheric conditions and the restricted ventilation of the protector can cause lenses to fog. Frequent cleaning may be required.	
O P T I C A L R A D I A T I O N				TYPICAL FILTER LENS PRO- SHADE TECTORS SEE NOTE (9)		
	WELDING:					
	Electric Arc		O,P,Q	10-14 Welding Helmets or Welding Shields	Protection from optical radiation is directly related to filter lens density. SEE NOTE (4). Select the darkest shade that allows adequate task performance.	Protectors that do not provide protection from optical radiation. SEE NOTE (4)
	WELDING:			SEE NOTE (9)		
	Gas		J,K,L, M,N,O, P,Q	4-8 Welding Goggles or Welding Faceshield		
	CUTTING			3-6		
	TORCH BRAZING			3-4	SEE NOTE (3)	
	TORCH SOLDERING		B,C,D, E,F,N	1.5-3 Spectacles or Welding Faceshield		
	GLARE		A,B	Spectacle SEE NOTE (9) (10)	Shaded or Special Purpose lenses, as suitable. SEE NOTE (8)	

16

Figure 15-3. Eyeglass Lenses: Advantages and Problems

MATERIAL	PROS	CONS
Allyl resin plastic	Relatively light (half the weight of glass)	Thickest of all lenses; not as scratch-resistant and abrasion-resistant as glass; doesn't block all ultraviolet light.
High-index plastic	Thinnest and lightest; most attractive and comfortable for strong prescriptions; blocks 100% of ultraviolet light.	Less shatter-resistant than allyl resin plastic; may cause distortion of peripheral vision, especially in strong prescriptions; highly susceptible to scratches and abrasions unless specially coated; most expensive.
Polycarbonate plastic	Most impact-resistant; thin and lightweight; blocks 100% of ultraviolet light; manufactured with coating that makes it more scratch-resistant than other plastic lenses.	Can blur and cause color fringes on peripheral vision images, especially in strong prescriptions; not available in some styles, including some progressive bifocals; can be damaged by solvents like nail polish remover or dry-cleaning fluid.
Glass	The most scratch-resistant; causes the least distortion of vision.	The heaviest lens; blocks the least ultraviolet light.

■ Use warm water to wash dust from goggles to keep the lens clear and free of scratches. A soft cloth should be used to wipe the lens after washing.

■ A fog-free type of goggles can be purchased. Employees are more likely to wear this piece of equipment if they can properly see through it.

■ As with any PPE, goggles must be maintained properly and their use enforced by management. Comfort and style of eyewear will go a long way in promoting its use.

Face Shields

Face shields offer full face protection from chemical splashes and other eye and face hazards. If a hard hat is required on the job, a means of properly attaching the face shield to the hard hat is needed. The manufacturer can accommodate this need in the use of equipment to make the attachment.

If eye or face protection is needed for a specific job, a clean face shield can offer the same protection as safety glasses or goggles. Face shields are not intended to take the impact like that of polycarbonate lenses but can offer protection from dust, chemical splashes, wires, and banding. As with any exposure, seek out professional advice to ensure the proper protection is being offered.

Use a mild detergent and warm water to clean a dirty face shield. Scratching of the surface can easily occur if improper cleaning procedures are used. As with eyeglasses and goggles, workers are more likely to use clean equipment that they can see through.

Cutting Goggles/Welding Helmets

Though not typical in a warehouse operation, maintenance or repair work may require the need for welding various objects or using a cutting torch to modify something. In both cases, sparks, heat, radiation, and molten metal can damage the eyes and skin. The ANSI Z87.1 1989 standard provides specific guidelines for worker protection. The proper equipment must be chosen for the task. A check with the ANSI selection guide included with this chapter will not only assure compliance with OSHA requirements, but will provide maximum protection for workers.

There is also a need to provide the proper lenses for protection against radiant energy. Manufacturers of this type of PPE can be very helpful in recommending the appropriate equipment.

It should be noted that the use of open-flame torches and welding machines is not a part of normal warehouse operations. This type of work must be left to those that have the skills and training. The use of torches and welding can easily start a fire. Every precaution must be taken to ensure that the work area is free of combustibles, flammables, and any other ignition source. Even when the job has been completed, a fire watch should be in place to ensure the safety of the building and employees. More information on the use of welding and cutting operations can be found in Chapter 20.

This summary of the eye and face protection PPE—safety glasses, goggles, face shields, welding helmets, and cutting goggles—provides additional information. Important points to keep in mind are:

- Wear the proper eye and face protections to prevent eye injuries. Employees working on a special project as well as those in the immediate area need this protection.

- Bureau of Labor Statistics studies have shown that many employees suffer eye injuries even while not working at a task that could subject them to injury. These numbers demonstrate that all employees should be required to protect their vision.

- Regular, standard street-wear safety glasses do not provide the same protection as industrial eyewear, especially the full benefits gained from polycarbonate lenses.

- Contact lenses are not a substitute for protective eyewear. Proper eyewear must be worn over contact lenses to provide full protection. If prescription lenses are not necessary, discourage employees from wearing them on the job.

- Visitors are to be provided the proper safety equipment for full protection.

- When handling chemicals, safety glasses or goggles may not be sufficient. A full face shield over protective eye wear must be worn.

- Ensure that eye and face protection meets the ANSI standard and that it is comfortable for workers. Offering different styles and models allows employees to make a choice. The equipment will more likely be worn if employees have a hand in the selection process.

- Maintain the PPE per manufacturer's guidelines, including proper inspection, cleaning, and replacement of defective parts.

- Proper lighting allows workers to see their workplace better, leading to improved quality or work as well as compliance in wearing PPE.

■ Eye wash units as well as proper procedures and plans to deal with injuries, incidents, and emergencies help to assure proper care when something occurs to endanger the eyes of a worker. At least 15 minutes of eye washing is required.

■ Eye examinations conducted during preemployment screenings will go far to ensure that vision requirements for the task at hand are satisfied. Those individuals that are assigned to operate powered industrial equipment should have eye examinations similar to those required for drivers' licenses.

■ The sure way to prevent eye and face injuries, in addition to the above-mentioned items, is to enforce a company policy of wearing protective equipment.

GLOVES

This form of PPE has not received significant attention in the past, as shown by a high incidence of hand injuries together with evidence that hand protection is either not being worn by employees or is being worn for the wrong type of hazards. OSHA decided to add hand protection (1910.138) to the 1994 PPE standard as a result of these studies.

The National Safety Council reports that over 500,000 disabling hand injuries occur to workers each year. Many of these injuries can be reduced or eliminated through the wearing of the proper protective gloves. OSHA's PPE standard requires that an employer's hand protection program result in the protection of employees' hands from recognized hazards.

The hands and fingers are very vulnerable to injury throughout the workplace. Employees in warehouses can experience cuts, bruises, fractures, burns and chemical injury in the performance of their jobs. There is also concern about blood-borne pathogens and the effect of blood on the hands and skin.

An assessment of the workplace and processes can help to identify potential health hazards. The survey, or assessment, is a requirement of OSHA and the program will be detailed in the latter part of this chapter. In the development of the PPE standard, OSHA stated that it is unaware of any gloves that provide protection against all potential hand hazards. Many commonly available gloves provide only limited protection against many chemicals.

Hand protection for particular hazards must be properly selected. For chemical exposures from handling hazardous chemicals or spill cleanup situations, knowing more about a glove's resistance factor can provide greater protection.

Chemical protective gloves are made of the following materials:

■ *Polyvinyl alcohol (PVA)* These gloves are resistant to petroleum solvents, chlorinated solvents, and aromatics.

■ *Polyvinyl chloride (PVC)* Protection is provided when handling mineral acids, caustics, organic acids, and alcohols.

■ *Natural rubber* These gloves offer resistance to ketones, alcohols, caustics, and organic acids.

■ *Neoprene* Worker protection is provided when handling mineral acids, organic acids, alcohols, and petroleum solvents.

■ *Nitrile* Resistance is offered to mineral acids, caustics, and petroleum solvents.

It is incumbent upon management to know which chemicals are in a facility and maintain the proper gloves for employee protection. The reaction time to an incident can be immediate, but if improper equipment allows for employee injury, the planning process is flawed.

A few key points to remember regarding chemical hazards and protective gloves:

■ When choosing gloves, keep in mind that the glove can have a limited life based on the chemical it is exposed to. Estimate the time an employee will be in contact with a particular chemical and choose a glove that provides appropriate breakthrough time. Breakthrough indicates when permeation of the glove first occurs.

■ Some employees may have a serious allergic reaction to latex gloves.

■ Reuse of gloves, if not decontaminated, can cause harm to other workers. Ensure that the decontamination process does not cause the glove to degrade.

■ There is no glove that offers resistance to all chemicals.

■ Thickness of gloves can vary with the manufacturer. If a particular brand of glove is providing the proper service, continue to order that model to ensure quality of the product.

■ Contact the glove manufacturer with questions regarding the potential mixing of chemicals and the appropriate gloves required, resistance factors of gloves, employee sensitivity to the glove, and to get a recheck of the glove being used versus the chemical being handled.

■ As with any safety program, ensure that additional PPE such as goggles, glasses, face shields, rubber boots, etc., are being worn in addition to the gloves.

■ Evaluate gloves for tears, cracks, holes, deformation, stiffness, and color changes.

■ Gloves should be purchased to fit the hand sizes of employees who will use them. If a glove doesn't fit properly, the worker will be less likely to wear it.

Consider the following items when selecting any clothing for protection against chemicals:

■ All chemicals pass or permeate through protective barriers sooner or later. This change may go unnoticed.

■ Always inspect before using. Workers must be trained to recognize problems with the protective clothing.

■ A barrier may protect a worker against one chemical but may perform poorly against other chemicals.

■ When protective clothing is exposed to high temperatures, breakdown of the materials occurs. Check with the manufacturer for guidance on this subject.

■ More layers, or a greater thickness of material, provide more protection to the worker.

■ Choose protective materials to match the task.

■ Always decontaminate the protective clothing before it is reused The best time for decontamination is immediately after use if at all possible.

■ All protective clothing has a shelf life as well as a length of time for use. Check with the manufacturer.

Additional types of gloves include the following:

■ Leather gloves offer protection against abrasives, rough surfaces, heat, welding operations, and sharp objects. A cut-resistant glove under the leather glove will offer more protection in high-hazard areas.

■ Fabric gloves such as cotton, the least expensive type of glove used, offers minimal protection against heat and sharp objects. This glove would not protect a worker from chemical hazards. Most cotton gloves have a short working life.

■ High-performance fiber gloves are used for special work projects. These gloves are very durable.

■ Disposable gloves can offer protection from minor irritants and can be used in the prevention of blood borne pathogens. Some employees are allergic to latex gloves. Use caution and check with the manufacturer and their doctor.

RESPIRATORY PROTECTION

The need for respirators in a warehouse setting may be minimal. Job processes in warehousing usually do not involve those same respiratory hazards that exist in manufacturing or construction. However, there may be occasions where respirators will be needed to fully protect the health of the worker. These situations could include:

■ The spraying or use of insecticides

■ Spray painting

■ Floor sweeping

■ Emptying the debris from a sweeper

■ Hazardous spill cleanup

■ Handling chemicals

■ Exposure to various contaminants.

Most likely a warehouse worker would not wear a respirator on a daily basis. If a contaminant is in the air, then management must provide a means for substituting to a less toxic substance, reducing the amount of contaminant, completely stopping the use of the contaminant, or providing respiratory protection. Respirators should only be worn where a hazard exists. To determine the potential exposure to a hazard, air monitoring equipment is needed. Properly selected and correctly used instruments can measure the air for any workplace contaminants. OSHA has established limits on various chemicals, and the purpose of measuring and controlling is to ensure the worker is not exposed to harmful chemicals, gases, sprays, dusts, fumes, mists, or vapors.

Written Program Requirements

Employers are required to develop and implement a written respirator program if respirators are being worn or if the permissible exposure limits (PELs) exceed those required by OSHA. . OSHA's 1910.134 respiratory protection standards require the following components.

- The work site procedures must be specific to that operation.

- The program must be updated and revised to reflect workplace changes that could affect the use of a respirator.

- Procedures must exist for the proper selection of respirators.

- Medical evaluations are required for those employees required to use respirators.

- Fit-testing procedures must be established for tight-fitting respirators.

- Procedures must be established for the proper use of respirators in routine and reasonably foreseeable emergency situations.

- Procedures must be established for:

  - Proper cleaning

  - Disinfecting

  - Storing

  - Inspecting

  - Repairing

  - Discarding

  - Other maintenance procedures.

- For atmosphere-supplying respirators, procedures are needed to ensure adequate air quality and flow of breathing air.

- Employees must be trained to recognize and protect themselves from the respiratory hazards during routine work and emergency situations.

- Additional employee training is required for:

  - Instructing employees in the proper use of respirators

  - Putting on and removing respirators

- Limitations of the equipment

- Ongoing equipment maintenance.

■ Procedures must be established to regularly evaluate the effectiveness of the program.

■ Respirators shall be selected from those jointly approved by the Mine Safety and Health Administration (MSHA) and the National Institute for Occupational Safety and Health (NIOSH).

New OSHA Rule

On January 8, 1998, OSHA issued a final rule for respiratory protection. This final rule replaces the previous 29CFR1910.134 that was adopted by OSHA in 1971. Major changes to the respiratory standard include:

■ Definitions important to the standard

■ Requirement for a program administrator

■ Requirements when respirator use is not required, but permitted

■ Establishment of a cartridge change schedule when gas and/or vapor respirators that do not have end-of-service-life indicators are used

■ Restrictions for nonhigh-efficiency particulate air filters approved under 30CFR11 to particle-size distributions of contaminants with a mass median aerodynamic diameter (MMAD) of less than 2 microns

■ Mandatory medical evaluation questionnaire

■ Requirements for fit-testing all tight-fitting respirators with a repeat frequency of at least every 12 months.

■ Specific qualitative and quantitative fit-testing protocols.

Respirator Selection

There are two basic types of respirators:

■ Air purifying, which use filters to remove particulate from the air and cartridges or canisters to remove vapors and gases

■ Air supplying, which include air-line supplied and self-contained type units, used in oxygen-deficient environments or when concentrations of airborne contaminants are immediately dangerous to life or health.

In both the air purifying and air supplied respirators, fresh air is provided from an uncontaminated external source.

Once the appropriate respirator classifications have been identified, the next step in respiratory selection is to gather information concerning workplace conditions and characteristics of the environmental hazard. A certified industrial hygienist (CIH) should be called upon to conduct air sampling evaluations and to advise management on the program.

OSHA has established the following eleven areas to consider in regard to respiratory selection:

1. The nature of the hazard

2. Physical and chemical properties of the air contaminant

3. Adverse health effects of the respiratory hazard

4. The relevant permissible exposure limit (PEL)

5. The results of workplace sampling of airborne concentrations of contaminants

6. The nature of the work operation or process

7. The time period the respirator is worn

8. Work activities and stress

9. Fit-testing

10. Warning properties

11. Physical characteristics, functional capabilities, and limitations of respirators.

If respirators must be worn, management must ensure that the equipment is being worn properly. Abuses of respirators are many. Workers wear them improperly, fail to properly clean and store them, cartridges don't get changed regularly, and many times the incorrect respirator is used for the task at hand.

Dust Masks

Dust in the workplace is very common. Where employees desire to wear a dust mask, OSHA has allowed a provision that covers the voluntary use of dust masks (filtering face pieces). Employers are not required to include a written respiratory program for those employees who choose to wear a dust mask.

New Filter Choices

NIOSH's 42CFR Part 84 regulation introduces a new vocabulary for respiratory protection. Previously, employers chose respirators labeled as dust/mist, dust/mist/fume, paint spray, pesticide, etc. The new approach uses a letter and number system to differentiate products. There are three types of filters.

■ N series provides protection against solid and water-based particulates such as nuisance dust.

■ R series provides protection against any particulates, including oil-based materials. The use of the R series filters are generally limited to one 8-hour shift if oil aerosols are present.

■ P series provides protection against any particulates, including oil-based materials, with no specific time limit.

Each of the three filter types is available in three levels of efficiency: 95 percent, 99 percent, and 99.97 percent. The higher the number for the filter's efficiency, the less filter leakage there is. Readers can contact NIOSH by calling (800)35-NIOSH and ask for NIOSH publication 96-101, a 22-page selection guide.

To fully cover the respiratory standard and to develop a comprehensive written program, readers are urged to contact their local OSHA office, loss-control representative, or certified industrial hygienist for compliance assistance. The subject of respiratory protection is very broad and cannot be properly covered in the course of this book. This section was intended to provide basic highlights regarding respirators.

HEARING PROTECTION

Hearing protection may be needed where job exposures result in decibel readings of 85 or higher. As an example, a handheld power saw or drill can easily exceed 85 decibels. These pieces of power equipment might be used for cutting wood to place in racking as support shelves or to tap holes into a concrete floor to anchor protective posts. Manually handling or moving individual metal pipes or hollow product inside a trailer can easily produce readings of 90 decibels.

Many workers aren't aware of the potential harm that can be associated with hearing loss at work. A warehouse is not a manufacturing plant and as a result the workplace environment is expected to be quieter. Regardless, the need for awareness and employee training is great.

More than 25 million people in the United States have a hearing impairment. It is important to warehouse workers to understand how the human ear works and how it can be harmed. This information, once known by the workers, will most likely be heeded by many or all of the staff in an effort to protect their hearing. As with any program or piece of PPE, once the reasons for the need are provided to everyone, compliance becomes less difficult.

How does the human ear work?

- First sound is gathered by the outer ear and funneled down the middle ear to the eardrum.

- Next sound waves striking the eardrum cause it to vibrate. The vibrations are passed to the inner ear by three small bones: the hammer, anvil, and stirrup.

- Next the sound waves are transferred from the stirrup to the cochlea where they are transplanted into electrical nerve impulses. The cochlea is a snail-shaped organ that contains thousands of hair cells or nerve endings in a liquid chamber.

- Lastly the cochlea sends the impulses to the brain by way of the auditory nerve.

These are the three types of hearing loss and frequency of occurrence:

1. Sensori-neural (nerve loss)   90%

2. Conductive   10%

3. Genetic   less than 1%

Sensori-neural loss is caused by problems with the inner ear or the auditory nerve. Loud noises damage the hair cells in the cochlea, which results in hearing loss. People who are affected by this problem have trouble understanding language: They hear speech but cannot understand the words. Distinguishing such words as "thin" and "fin" is a common problem. This problem will become worse if background noise is present. The most common causes are aging and the exposure to harmful noise. High fevers, birth defects, and high doses of certain antibiotics can also cause damage. Correction is generally through the wearing of hearing aids rather than surgery or medicine.

Conductive hearing loss is a form that usually involves an outer or middle ear obstruction that reduces transmission of sound vibrations through air space, bone, or tissue into the middle ear. The treatment for this problem is with medicine or surgery. Hearing aids may also be used.

TYPES OF EQUIPMENT

OSHA's PPE Program is a necessity in any warehouse. The need for workers to wear the proper protective equipment is one way in which injuries can be reduced. This OSHA program went into effect on July 5, 1994. The rules are intended to be more comprehensive regarding protective equipment and are more consistent with today's industry practices. The original OSHA standards for head, eye, face, and foot protection were adopted form ANSI standards more than twenty-seven years ago. The new PPE rule reflects the latest ANSI standards and now includes a section on hand protection, as noted in this chapter. Figures 15-4 and 15-5 provide a PPE training form and PPE hazards survey assessment to use in a warehouse to comply with the OSHA PPE rule.

Organizations are now required to:

■ Provide employees with training in the use of personal protective equipment. Employers must train employees to know when equipment is necessary; what equipment is necessary; how to put on, remove, adjust, and wear the equipment; the limitations of PPE; and its proper care, maintenance, useful life, and disposal.

■ Provide a hazard assessment (comprehensive survey) of the workplace to determine if any hazards are present that would necessitate PPE. The employer then will have to select appropriate equipment for the hazards that were found.

Forms to document the training of warehouse workers have been included in this chapter.

The hazard assessment can confuse some employers. What is needed is to evaluate prior OSHA #200 logs and injury reports, minutes of safety meetings, and any air or noise surveys. This should be followed by a thorough walk-through of the warehouse to look for:

■ Sources of rolling or pinching objects that could crush the feet

■ Sources of sharp objects that could pierce the feet or cut the hands

■ Layout of the workplace and location of coworkers

■ Sources of falling objects or potential for dropping objects that could pose a compression or projectile hazard to employees' head, face, hands, or feet.

Figure 15-4. PPE Hazards Survey

	Yes	No
Are there any sources of motion - machinery or processes where an injury could result from movement of tools, machine elements or particles, or movement of personnel that could result in collisions, blows or tripping around stationary objects?	☐	☐
Are there any sources of high temperature that could result in burns, eye injury or ignition of protective equipment?	☐	☐
Are there any types of chemical exposures such as splash, vapor, spray or immersion that could cause chronic illness or physical injury?	☐	☐
Are there any sources of harmless dust that can accumulate or become airborne and cause a physical hazard to employees' eyes? If a material safety data sheet indicates that accumulated or airborne dusts of material used in the facility can be a pulmonary hazard, the employer is obligated to confirm the hazard through sampling under other regulation.	☐	☐
Are there any sources of light radiation, such as welding, brazing, cutting, furnaces, heat treating, high intensity lights?	☐	☐
Are there any sources of falling objects or potential for dropping objects that could pose a compression or projectile hazard to employees' head, face, hands or feet?	☐	☐
Are there any sources of sharp objects that might pierce the feet or cut the hands?	☐	☐
Are there any sources of rolling or pinching objects that could crush the feet?	☐	☐
Have you evaluated the layout of the workplace and location of co-workers?	☐	☐
Are there any electrical hazards?	☐	☐

P.P.E. LOCATION SURVEY

On _____, _____

       (date)   (print name)

Conducted a facility survey to ensure

	YES	NO
P.P.E. is being worn properly	☐	☐
P.P.E. use is being enforced	☐	☐
P.P.E. is clean/not damaged	☐	☐
P.P.E. in use has been approved	☐	☐

Figure 15-5. PPE Training Form

The following employees have been properly trained on the proper use of PPE requirement of care of PPE and disciplinary procedures for the PPE program.

Check training received:

☐ Eye	☐ Hand	☐ Respiratory
☐ Face	☐ Ear (Hearing)	☐ Other _____
☐ Foot	☐ Head	☐ Other _____

Employee Names/Signatures

Name (Print)	Signature
1.	
2.	
3.	
4.	
5.	
6.	
7.	
8.	
9.	
10.	
11.	
12.	
13.	
14.	
15.	

Training Provided By: _____   Date: _____

- Any electrical hazards

- Sources of harmful dust that can accumulate or become airborne and cause a physical hazard to employees' eyes. If a material safety data sheet indicates that accumulated or airborne dusts of a material used in the warehouse can be a pulmonary hazard, the employer is required to confirm the hazard through air sampling

- Types of chemical exposures such as splash, vapor, spray, or immersion that could cause physical injury or chronic illness

- Sources of high temperatures that could result in burns, eye injury, or ignition of PPE

- Sources of motion-machinery or processes where an injury could result from movement of tools, machine elements or particles, or movement of personnel that could result in collisions, blows, or tripping around stationary objects.

It is evident that many hazards are present in a warehouse. A checklist for a hazard assessment in warehouse operations has been included in this chapter.

There are some types of PPE that have been included here but are not a part of OSHA's PPE program. Not included in the standard is respiratory protection, electrical protective devices, chemical protective clothing, and fall protection equipment. Back belts are also not a part of the standard. Information on this subject has been included in Chapter 11, Materials Handling.

FALL ARREST SYSTEMS/FALL PROTECTION

Some twenty-three years ago, European regulatory agencies decided to replace body belts with safety harnesses. The U. S. regulators were not as quick to investigate the technology and require this improved fall protection and fall arrest safety gear. On January 1, 1998, a final rule was passed by OSHA that affects the construction industry.

The passage of this standard, 1926.500-503, is intended to curb the rise in workplace fatalities due to falls. While workplace fatalities continue to decline, fatalities from falls continue to increase. There were 684 deaths throughout industry in 1996 as a result of falls. Falls represent 11 percent of the total for all workplace fatalities.

Even though the January 1, 1998, passage of 1926.500-503 applies to the construction industry, there is a definite need for fall protection in general industry. Within warehouses, body harnesses and lanyards are to be worn while working off ladders, on or near elevations not protected by handrails, on roofs, on crane runways, on forklift platforms, or in any other workplace situation where the worker is not protected from falls by railing or netting. Twelve to fourteen workers die each year as a result of falling from the forks of a lift truck.

What convinced the European regulatory agencies to adopt the safety harness rather than the continued use of the body belt (a safety belt that fastens around the waist) was through the analysis and use of lifelike dummies during drop tests. Additional research has shown that a motionless worker knocked unconscious in a fall could survive only briefly before being rescued if suspended only by the body belt. The belt itself could cause internal injuries and asphyxiation. In a safety harness, a worker could survive the same fall for a much longer period and would be spared most of the injuries caused by a body belt.

If someone were to fall while wearing a safety harness, it would allow for a rescue. If only a body belt was worn, rescue efforts might not be able to be implemented in time to save the person. Body belts can do much harm during a fall when the body folds into the "nose-to-toes" position. Workers have stated that they would rather have taken their chances of an actual fall because the pain of hanging in a body belt was so intense.

Harnesses have straps around the thighs, waist, chest and shoulders to more evenly distribute the force of a fall and cradle the worker. Harnesses are the safer choice; a harness can be used in a variety of situations and a harness can do everything a belt can do. A personal fall-arrest system should consist of an anchorage, connectors and body harness, lanyard, deceleration device, lifeline, or suitable combination of these items, according to OSHA.

Harnesses are a bit more complicated than body belts. All of the straps that wrap around the legs and shoulders must be properly adjusted to fit the wearer. Harnesses should fit snugly but not be uncomfortably tight All harnesses are to be fitted to the employee. Proper fit and adjustment of the harness makes it more effective if one were to fall.

Manufacturers provide several fall protection systems.

Fall Arrest. A system designed to stop a user's free fall of up to 6 feet and limit the maximum arresting forces imposed on the user to 1,800 pounds or less

Work Positioning. A system designed to hold and sustain the user at a work location and limit the fall to 2 feet or less

Restraint. A system designed to prevent the user from reaching an area in which a free fall could occur

Suspension. A system designed to suspend and support the user while being raised up or down (transported), not allowing a free fall

Rescue. A system designed to raise or lower a user to safety in the event of an emergency. Confined Spaces, also covered in Chapter 20, discusses some of the details associated with rescue.

The location of the back D-ring is important. The ring should be located between the shoulder blades, not at the waist or up in the neck area. In addition to hardware requirements on the harness, all nonlocking snap hooks must be replaced with locking snap hooks.

Snap hooks connect the harness to one end of lanyards or lifelines. Effective January 1, 1998, only double-locking snap hooks can be used. Traditional single locking snap hooks cannot be connected to each other because of the possibility of an employee roll-out. A lanyard is a flexible line of rope, wire rope, or strap that has a connector at each end. Lifelines use a flexible line that connects to an anchorage point in the fall arrest system.

Lanyards are connected from the person to an anchor point that can withstand 5,000 pounds of force. All of the hardware and locations where a lanyard is to be connected must be capable of withstanding the force of someone falling, thus the 5,000- pound requirement. As an example of a poor choice of anchorage, in a warehouse a worker was observed working out of a lift cage being supported by a forklift. A lightweight chain and snap hook served as the handrail to the front of the lift cage. The worker had snapped his lanyard around the chain, erroneously believing that if he fell, the chain would support his fall.

Only qualified and competent individuals are allowed to design and evaluate systems to prevent fall hazards. The design includes all of the equipment being worn, anchorage points, hardware, employee training, and compliance with standards. In any warehouse there are situations where workers are periodically exposed to falls. Management should not attempt to resolve the issues of fall arrest systems without the help of trained professionals.

In many warehouses a very common practice, and one with the potential for falls, is the worker on a narrow-aisle platform truck. The platform is raised up and down while the lift truck travels through an aisle. Many organizations continue to allow workers to wear a body belt and not an approved harness. In addition, the lanyard being used may be too long. A lanyard must have only enough play in it to allow the employee to comfortably perform the job. Lanyards can be equipped with a deceleration device or a "shock absorber," which reduces the arresting forces from 1,800 pounds to 900. When a worker falls with a lanyard that is too long, he/she experiences a longer fall before the system aides the worker. Falls are limited to 6 feet but, if the distance of a fall can be reduced, an employer should do so by requesting specific equipment that provides additional worker protection.

This section is intended to provide some basic information on fall protection and is not fully descriptive of all possible product and technical guidelines. OSHA has a specific fall protection program for general industry (1910.23). However, OSHA's 1910.66 fall protection standard *does* apply to anyone working on a powered platform, which would operate inside or outside of a building to provide maintenance. There is no specific reference to a standard that applies to a worker on a lift truck platform. In this case, the technology and engineering used in the 1926 construction standards are used for worker protection. OSHA would use the 5(a)(1) general duty clause to cite employers if they were not in compliance.

Contact the manufacturers of fall arrest systems or their representatives to ensure compliance and worker safety. Information on anchorage connectors, self-retracting lifelines, suspension supports, rope grabs, and deceleration devices are also available. In addition to providing quality products and training, they can assist in conducting a survey of any other applications where fall protection is needed.

RUBBER APRONS

When acid splashes on clothing, not only can the clothing be damaged, but the acid could possibly penetrate the clothing and harm the skin. An acid-resistant apron should be worn in addition to acid-resistant boots, gloves, goggles, and face shields while performing battery maintenance and servicing.

With all PPE, follow the manufacturers' guidelines for care and use of the equipment. PPE is of no value unless it is being worn properly by the employee and management is enforcing its use.

SUMMARY

Personal protective equipment provides safeguarding when workplace exposures cannot be fully guarded. Many parts of the body are vulnerable to a variety of injuries from objects and substances. Head protection in a warehouse should be commonplace throughout the industry, but isn't. Despite the danger of being struck by falling or moving objects or striking against objects, many employers and employees resist the need for head protection.

The eyes, face, hands, and feet are also vulnerable to flying objects, chemical splashes, falling object, and a variety of other warehouse hazards. One only need look at the on-going incidents or injury reports in a warehouse and the need for more specific PPE becomes evident.

Hearing and respiratory exposures may not pose health risks in most locations. Illnesses from excessive noise and lung impairment are possible if employers fail to monitor the workplace and insist on the correct PPE. Noise can be deceptive because workers feel that they "get used to it" after a while. Respirators may be needed during special operations within the building, when the risk may be great; this form of protective equipment must receive special consideration.

Fall protection is many times overlooked in warehouses. Workers may feel that because they are not on a construction site, the rule does not apply to them. The use of body belts is no longer an acceptable means of fall protection.

REFERENCES

Arrotti, Gerard. "Fit the Gloves to the Hazard." *Occupational Health and Safety*. May 1995, pp. 50–54.

Bailey, Melissa A. "OSHA's Amended Respiratory Standard." *Occupational Hazards*. May 1998, pp. 21–23.

Bidwell, Jeanne. "Choosing the Right Respirator." *Plant Engineering*. February 1997, pp.104–108.

Blais, Edward. "Eye and Face Personal Protective Equipment." *Occupational Health and Safety*. March 1997, pp. 30–36.

Burke, Adrianne. "Banning Body Belts." *Industrial Safety and Hygiene News*. January 1998, p. 41.

—. "Complying with OSHA's PPE Standard." *Industrial Safety and Hygiene News*. July 1995, pp.17–18.

—. "Handle with Care." *Industrial Safety and Hygiene News*. September 1997, pp. 21–22.

Calmbacher, Charles W. "Breathe Easy." *Environmental Protection* May 1998, pp. 17–20.

Camplin, Jeffrey C. "Understanding OSHA's New Respiratory Standard." *Compliance Magazine* May 1998, pp. 34–35.

DBI/SALA. "Pocket Brochure on Fall Arrest, Restraint and Rescue Equipment." Red Wing, MN. 1994, Revised 1/96, 52 pp.

Desoff, Alan L. "Get a Grip on Hand PPE. Personal Protective Equipment" *Safety and Health*. July 1995. pp. 62–65.

Gagnet, Grace. "New Rule Mandates Hazard Assessment to Specify Protective Equipment Needs." *Occupational Health and Safety*. August 1994, pp. 50–58.

Gilbert, Susan. "Polycarbonate Eyeglass Lenses Found Significantly Safer in Study." *The New York Times*. Wednesday, January 8, 1997, p. B10.

Goforth, Candace. "Mind Your Hard Hat." *Occupational Hazards*. July 1996, pp. 43–44.

Hans, Mick. "Don't Ask OSHA What to Wear in Your Warehouse." *Safety and Health*. February 1993, pp. 44–47.

Herring, Ronald N. "42CFR part 84: It's Time to Change Respirators...but how?" *Engineers Digest*. March 1997, pp.14–22.

Hough, Jeanette. "Eye Emergencies." *Industrial Safety and Health News*. February 1997, pp. 33–34.

Johnston, Alan. "NIOSH Respiratory Standard: Are You Ready for the Transition?" *Plant Engineering*. April 1998, pp. 70–74.

Kababer, Thomas H. "Save Your Skin: Use Gloves Correctly." *Safety and Health*. September 1997, pp. 56–60.

KW Powersource. *Battery Service Manual, Protective Clothing*. March 1997, p. 13.

LaBar, Gregg. "Are You Picking the Right Foot Protection?" *Occupational Hazards*. August 1997, pp.43–44.

—. "Harnessing the Full Power of Fall Protection." *Occupational Hazards*. February 1998, pp. 29–32.

Magid Glove. *Safety Matters—Fall Protection Programs Spring into Action*. Volume Four, Issue One, 1998, pp. 1–2.

McQueen, Gregg. "Shhhh! Listen to the Benefits of Noise Control." *IMPO*. May, 1997, p. 54.

Meade, Vicki. "Heads Up—What's New in Protective Gear." *Occupational Health and Safety*. July 1995, pp.33–35.

National Safety Council. "Fall Arrest Systems." *Accident Prevention Manual*. Itasca, IL, 1997, pp. 173–80.

—. "Respiratory Protection." *Accident Prevention Manual*. Itasca, IL, 1997, pp. 180–194.

Occupational Hazards. "The Safety Managers Guide to PPE—Fall Protection." January 1998, pp. 56–57.

—. "The Safety Managers Guide to Personal Protective Equipment." Respiratory Protection. January 1998, pp. 68–70.

Occupational Safety and Health Standards, Subpart I—Personal protective Equipment, 29 CFR 132, 133, 134, 135, 136, 138. U. S. Department of Labor, OSHA. July 1, 1994.

OSHA 1910.134, Respiratory Protection.

Rook, Martin. "Heads Up—Hard Hats Reduce the Effects of Shocks and Knocks." *Ohio Monitor*. February 1987, pp.7–8.

Rose Manufacturing Company. *1997 Catalog: Safety at Heights and in Confined Spaces*. Pittsburgh, PA, 26 pp.

Roughton, James E. "Understanding OSHA's Fall Protection Standard." *Plant Engineering*. October 1996, pp. 74–78.

"Safety helmets and Head Protection." *Plant Engineering*. April 11, 1985, pp. 52–54.

Spotts, Steve. "Planning and Selecting Anchorages: Do's and Don'ts." *Professional Safety*. May 1997, pp. 18–19.

Strack, Bob. "New OSHA P.P.E. Rule." *Chemical Processing*. June 1994, p. 11.

3M Regulations Update. "Respiratory Protection." Number 21, March 1998, 13 pp.

Threlkeld, Diane M. "Workplace Safety—Personal Protective Equipment." *Manufacturers Alliance*. LAR - 302, April 14, 1994.

U.S. Dept. of Labor. "OSHA Publishes Final Rule to Enhance Personal Protective Safety Equipment for 11.7 Million Workers." USDL 94-164, April 6, 1994.

16

Injuries, Incidents, and Investigations

THE NATURE, CAUSES, AND RESULTS OF INJURIES

Injuries that occur to warehouse employees share common elements with all injuries. They interrupt work, they usually involve a contact of some kind, and they are an unexpected occurrence to the employee.

A broader definition of the first two points is needed.

Work Interruption

All injuries involve some amount of work stoppage or interruption. When the injury occurs at work, stoppage takes place. The more serious the injury, the greater the work stoppage.

As an example, a warehouse employee slips and falls on hydraulic fluid that has dripped onto the floor. The worker slowly gets to his feet, wipes the hydraulic fluid off of his pants, and walks to the first aid station for evaluation. He was slightly injured but did not require more medical attention.

In a similar situation a supervisor slips and falls on a hydraulic spill. In this case the supervisor fractures his wrist and requires extensive medical care.

Both of these examples represent an injury to the employees. In the first example a minimum amount of time was lost by the employee seeking medical care. In the second example the result was a very serious injury with significant lost time.

If an organization were to analyze the many thousands of minor incidents and injuries, the realization of significant dollar losses would be evident. Some of the key points to consider regarding work interruption are:

- Key employees may be lost for extended periods of time.

- Employees may leave their workstations to see what happened or to help the injured person.

- Machines or processes may be stopped to assist the injured person.

- Machines or processes may be damaged as a result of the incident.

- Time that could be spent on production is consumed investigating and reporting the injury.

- OSHA or other government agencies could occupy management's time investigating the injuries.

There are supervisors and plant managers who believe injury prevention is not a part of their jobs. Many believe that their main function is to produce and earn a profit. Safety professionals have reminded managers and supervisors for years that production and safety go hand in hand. One is very difficult to separate from the other. When safety improves, injuries are reduced and productivity increases. When supervisors conduct discussions and meetings with employees, it is as important to discuss the need for injury and incident prevention as productivity.

Contact

When analyzing injuries and incidents other than exertion and strain type injuries, employees usually make contact with something in their environment. This contact produces the injuries. Preventive measures can be devised to educate employees in injury avoidance.

Classification of these injury types are as follows:

- struck by

- contacted by

- caught between

- contact with

- fall—same level

- fall—lower level

- caught on

- caught in

- struck against

- overexertion

- exposure.

When an injury occurs, it is important to identify the type of injury. Armed with that knowledge, the supervisor can make a more educated investigation of the incident or injury. Once these eleven injury types are learned, supervisors, safety committee members, and medical aid personnel can use this information in preventing injuries.

The following are definitions of these injury types:

- A **struck by** injury is one in which an employee has been contacted abruptly and forcefully by some object. The person that is struck can be moving or standing still. Struck by incidents or injuries could include an employee struck by a falling carton, or an employee struck by a steel band being cut on a pallet.

- A **contacted by** incident or injury is one in which the employee has been contacted by some substance that has an injury-upon contact characteristic. This injury type could include an employee being contacted by battery acid while performing battery maintenance. Another example, and a very real one, involved a fork lift operator who dropped a pallet load of paint cans on the top of his overhead guard. He was covered with paint and had to undergo extensive cleanup. His contact was with spilled paint, not the 1-gallon metal cans.

- The **caught between** injury is one of the most common. The term "pinch point" comes into play for this type of injury. Pinch points are very common in warehouses. This type of injury is one in which the employee has a part of his body pinched, crushed, or otherwise caught between a moving object and a stationary object, or between two moving objects.

Examples of this injury type are many. An employee, while operating a powered hand truck, traps his hand between the operating handle and a section of racking. While walking between a backing forklift and a steel beam, the employee can be trapped and crushed by the forklift. In such cases, the operator did not see the pedestrian. An office secretary closes a file drawer on her right hand resulting in a fractured finger.

- A **contact with** incident or injury is one in which the employee has made contact with some substance or object. The employee can make contact with a hot steam pipe, corrosion on a battery, or any other harmful chemical in the warehouse.

- The **same level fall** is very common both at work and off the job. The injury occurs when the employee falls and makes contact with the floor or other object, which can cause serious injury. Fractures to the arm, wrist, hand, ankle, shoulder, and skull could result. Tripping or slipping on slippery floors, objects, holes, or chemicals are very common.

- **Falls to below** are very hazardous and can be deadly or crippling. The employee can be walking, climbing, or standing. Falls from ladders, mezzanines, pallets, forks of a lift truck, stairs, roofs, and open holes take many lives each year. Also, the distance one falls isn't always a means of judging the severity of a fall. A fall from a short stepladder or down a few stairs can be very dangerous.

- A **caught on** incident or injury is one in which a part of a person's clothing, or the person, is caught on some protruding object. Sharp pipes or palletized product can cause a pant leg to be caught, which could trip the employee. An employee could be caught on a moving object and injured while being moved, lifted, or dragged.

- The **caught in** injury does not occur very often. This is one in which part of a person's body or the person is trapped in some type of opening. For example, an employee steps into a hole or pit, the foot becomes caught, and the employee falls and injuries the leg or foot. A more serious example is the employee who becomes trapped in a vat, chamber, or tank and can't get out.

- A **struck against** incident or injury is one in which an employee makes contact with something in his work environment. At times this can happen abruptly and with force. When the employee is in motion and walks into a beam, doorway, forks on a forklift, or product storage, a struck-against injury can occur. Most times the employee is stunned by the impact because it is not expected.

- The **overexertion** incident or injury is one in which an employee feels pain as a result of excessive strain on a part of the body. Lifting a load from the warehouse floor without bending the knees and keeping the load close to the body can cause a back injury. Lifting product and placing it on upper shelves can injure the shoulder as a result of overreaching. This type of injury is difficult at times to connect to the workplace or job. The ergonomics standard pursued by OSHA includes overexertion injuries.

- An **exposure** incident or injury can have a broad base. Employees may be exposed to noise, carbon monoxide, toxic gases, toxic fumes, oxygen deficiency, temperature extremes, and harmful vapors from chemicals. Management should use professionals, such as certified industrial hygienists, to evaluate the warehouse in the process of attaining safe levels of exposure. Also, some of the exposure elements can be eliminated rather than reduced. A good example of this is to eliminate carbon monoxide exposures by using electric lift trucks rather than internal combustion engines types.

CAUSES OF INJURIES

Eliminate the causes and injuries are prevented. Management must have a firm understanding of what causes injuries. Without this knowledge, the investigative process will not be successful in preventing future injuries.

The cause of an injury can be anything and everything that has contributed to the occurrence of the injury. It could be the employee, actions of a coworker, defects in tools, unsafe equipment, machines, materials, atmospheres, or the physical or mental condition of the employee.

When supervisors are investigating injuries, a common remark on the investigation report is that the employee was careless. Instead of seriously considering the broad range of potential elements that can cause injuries, management finds a quick solution in the word "careless." When this happens nothing is resolved; the real causes go unidentified.

Most discussions centering around employee injuries focus on the unsafe actions of employees and unsafe conditions in the workplace. Too much emphasis is placed on the unsafe actions of employees. Some studies focus on an 85-15 ratio. That is, the unsafe act is responsible for 85 percent of all injuries and unsafe conditions make up the balance.

What is needed to reduce injuries is to correct the unsafe conditions and properly train employees and supervisors to recognize workplace hazards. Injuries will decline when employees are trained and hazards are corrected. A very good slogan to use is: Condition Corrected—Injury Prevented.

Studies show that if injuries are going to be reduced, the errors that produce the injuries have to be reduced or eliminated. This effort must be practiced by everyone at all levels of an organization. Most safety standards that require the elimination of unsafe conditions may not be as effective as behavioral controls.

Unfortunately, if one is conducting research of injury reports, the investigation form that is filled out may not identify unsafe conditions. Thus, the percentages given to unsafe acts and unsafe conditions may need revision.

Unsafe Acts

Management must rely on supervisors to enforce work rules, which include safety rules. If safety rules have been established for the warehouse, it is important that everyone know what the rules represent. However, some supervisors make the mistake of thinking that the only unsafe acts committed by employees are safety-rule violations. Unsafe acts are not always violations of established safety rules. Many supervisors may not recognize or take action against employees committing unsafe acts if a safety rule has not been violated. Management must be concerned with all unsafe acts, not just those safety rules that have been established as work rules.

When training new employees or supervisors regarding workplace safety, the following list of unsafe acts must be identified. This listing would apply to any warehouse operation.

1. *Taking an unsafe position or posture.* Many employees are injured when they place themselves in hazardous positions relative to the surrounding workplace. Climbing over a conveyor or working in a department where a hard hat is required, without the benefits of safety equipment, are two common examples.

   Since back injuries are very common and very costly throughout industry, incorrect postures are often the cause. A very common cause of lower back injury involves an employee who twists his back rather than shifting the feet when moving a load.

2. *Using defective equipment or tools.* In an effort to complete their daily work, employees may fail to alert management of defective tools, power equipment, or ladders. Daily inspections of powered equipment are required. If faulty brakes are detected at the beginning or during the work shift, the employee may not alert supervisors. A second shift or another employee attempting to operate the equipment may harm a fellow worker or collide with racking, product, or the building.

3. *Failure to wear personal protective equipment.* Safety gear such as hard hats, gloves, steel toe shoes, hearing protection, or eye/face protection are a must for warehouse employees. Recently a warehouse worker suffered a serious eye injury because he failed to wear safety glasses while cutting metal banding on a pallet. The wearing of glasses was a job requirement because of past incidents as well as the obvious danger with the banding. Safety glasses were kept on his forklift only a few feet from the pallet. The employee stated that he felt it was only a quick job, just two bands; that's why he didn't wear his glasses.

4. *Operating or using equipment without authority.* If you can drive a car, you can operate a forklift—so the saying goes. This is not true and when anyone steps onto a piece of powered equipment they must be trained. OSHA requires operator training, which makes good sense. (However, this particular rule regarding the training of operators, many times involves them exhibiting unsafe behavior.) Unsafe behavior causes injuries in many warehouses because of the presence and easy availability of powered equipment.

Another piece of equipment that is often operated without authority is the powered hand truck or pallet jack. Managers or visitors simply grasp the operating handle and attempt to operate the equipment. The result is usually damage to the product or the building. At times injuries occur, especially to the hands and feet. In some cases the load being moved or the hand jack strikes someone. The process looks easy to the onlooker, but it takes skill to operate these units.

5. *Failure to secure against unexpected movement.* If a piece of equipment can start up or move unexpectedly, injuries may occur. Materials can roll, slip, drift, or fall if they aren't secured properly. Materials can fall from racking because pallets were not secured properly. Shrink wrapping helps to secure material on pallets that are stored on racking. Metal or plastic strapping can secure loose product from shifting when the load is being stored. Wheel chocks or trailer restraints help to secure trailers at the dock to prevent trailer drift or pull-away.

6. *Operating or working at unsafe speeds.* It is not unusual for employees to rush to get the job done. In their haste, pieces of power equipment may be operated too fast. This haste can easily lead to injuries, and pedestrians being struck is the second leading cause of death from powered equipment. Visitors are also frequently injured as a result of being struck by powered equipment being driven too fast.

In addition, employees injure themselves and others by rushing to complete a task. Throwing of product, running in the warehouse, or taking shortcuts can cause injury. Many times fellow employees are injured as a result of someone else's haste.

7. *Removing or making safety devices inoperative.* When guards, interlocks, and other safety devices are bypassed, removed, or made inoperative, injuries can easily occur. Any activity such as this must be regarded as a serious safety infraction.

Guards can be removed in order to perform repairs or to lubricate machines. Interlocks on trash compactors and other machines are intended to stop a machine when a guard or door has been opened. Speed governors and back up alarms on lift trucks are provided for the protection of employees and pedestrians. An example that must always be a high priority to prevent is removing a lockout and tagout device from an electrical box or machine, which can result in serious injury or death.

8. *Failure to warn or signal as required.* Pedestrians and fellow employees can easily be struck by powered equipment. More than twenty fatalities occur each year in the workplace as a result of pedestrians being struck by forklifts. Using a horn to signal others of equipment movement is essential. Signaling, however, must not be overdone or employees will ignore the signals. Placement of barriers, barricades, lights, and other visual and audible warnings are important where holes, drop-offs, overhead work, maintenance, or construction work can pose a hazard.

9. *Riding hazardous moving equipment.* Moving equipment poses a hazard by its very nature. Trucks, trailers, powered equipment, equipment elevators, and conveyors can cause injury to someone who decides to ride on them. The rule of no riders is essential in any list of warehouse safety rules. Employees can easily fall off of the moving equipment or become trapped between machines, rollers or moving parts.

10. *Using tools or other equipment in an unsafe manner.* Many times an employee will find unique uses for tools or equipment that have nothing to do with the intention of the manufacturers. Using a

hammer and chisel to break metal banding on pallets or other loads can be dangerous. A properly designed band cutter is highly recommended for this purpose. Portable ladders require safety feet as well as placement following the 4-in-1 rule. That is, for every 4 feet of height, the ladder should be 1 foot from a wall or surface. In addition, rubber feet on the ladder help keep it sturdy for climbing and essentially free of slipping.

However, it is not uncommon to find employees placing a ladder too far from a wall and, as a result, increasing the ladder angle. There are cases where the safety feet of the ladder are against the wall and not on the floor as required.

In addition, ladders are placed in front of doors that could easily be opened, striking the ladder. Lift trucks have been known to round a blind corner only to have another employee knocked off a ladder that has been placed in a roadway.

11. *Performing service on energized, moving, or otherwise hazardous equipment.* Lockout/tagout regulations require a zero-energy state. Serious injury can occur when employees fail to deenergize, shut down, depressurize or secure equipment prior to cleaning, adjustment, inspection, lubrication, or repair of a machine or device. Each warehouse employee should be familiar with the lockout/tagout program. Only trained and authorized employees can perform maintenance on equipment, machinery, or devices. No employee should ever risk his/her life or that of anyone else simply because he/she felt that it was too much bother to use safe procedures. In many cases, injured employees will comment that the repair was only going to take a minute or so and it seemed unnecessary to use lockout/tagout.

12. *Indulging in horseplay, startling others, practical joking or distracting fellow workers.* There is no place in any safety program for this type of behavior. Serious injuries can occur from joking or employees disregarding correct procedures. There was a situation in a large warehouse where a practical joke backfired and seriously injured an employee. The practical joker placed grease on the steering wheel of a forklift of a friend. When the operator climbed onto the lift truck, he activated the controls and pulled forward only to discover that he couldn't hold on to the steering wheel. He ran the forklift off a dock and suffered serious injuries as a result.

The occurrence of unsafe behavior does not necessarily mean that it will result in injury. Many unsafe acts can be repeated many times and not produce any consequences to the employee. In the long run, however, this dangerous behavior will catch up with the employee. This is one of the main reasons why management must correct unsafe or dangerous behavior when it is observed. These twelve types of unsafe behavior are worthy of serious discussions with employees.

Any unsafe act increases the probability of injury. Friendly persuasion on behalf of a supervisor is more effective before an unsafe practice becomes a habit.

UNSAFE CONDITIONS

Many safety professionals and human resource managers are of the belief that more than eight injuries out of ten are the result of unsafe behavior. While there is merit to part of this theory, the focus of employee injury cannot be on unsafe acts without serious consideration for the work environment. The real meaning of injury investigation will be lost if this is the case. An evaluation of both unsafe conditions and behavior must be a part of each investigation.

It must also be pointed out that unsafe conditions can be created as a result of unsafe behavior. To cite a common situation containing both of these elements, a focus on forklift inspections is needed.

Daily forklift inspections are required both as a regulatory practice and as a "best" practice. A forklift was leaking hydraulic fluid from a hose. The operator failed to inspect his lift truck for several weeks. Hydraulic fluid collected under the lift truck wherever it was parked. The slippery hydraulic fluid caused a fellow worker to slip and fall. He suffered a serious back injury as a result.

The unsafe behavior involved the failure to properly inspect the forklift and record the results. Management was never notified of the defective hydraulic hose. The unsafe conditions were the leaking hose and assorted puddles of hydraulic fluid.

Management also plays a role in this example. First management failed to require routine documented inspections of powered equipment. They also failed to ensure the defects were being reported to maintenance. They failed to train the operator to inspect, document, and report hazards. Management also failed to react to the obvious trail of hydraulic fluid on the warehouse floor.

The message is an obvious one: Both employee behavior and conditions must be a part of each injury investigation.

Unsafe conditions are conditions in the workplace involving equipment, tools, materials, workplace design, machinery, air pollutants or the building structure that create an atmosphere making it more likely an injury will occur. Unsafe conditions may also include poor product arrangement, layout defect in design, equipment corrosion or misuse, or improper storage or deterioration of product. It is obvious that unsafe conditions are ever-present and can easily be responsible for injuries.

Warehouse management and employees should be aware of the more common examples of unsafe conditions.

1. *Hazards created by poor housekeeping.* Housekeeping practices that safeguard employees and demonstrate order and cleanliness are important to any business. Tripping hazards on floors and stairs must be avoided. Extension cords left across aisleways, metal or plastic banding dropped on the floor, and grease, oil, or water spots can all cause trip-and-fall type injuries. Proper sweepings either manually or through the use of a power sweeper will contribute greatly to the image in the warehouse as well as a safer environment.

2. *Hazardous storage or product arrangement.* Warehouse storage of materials is the prime function of the building. Product storage that is neat, organized, and safely stacked is less likely to fall onto employees. Proper storage takes up less space, and space is at a premium in warehouses. Likelihood of damaged or ruined product is less when storage of product is secure and protected from damage by powered equipment.

    Materials that are stored at knee to chest levels are easier to lift and handle. Employees should not have to reach above their heads to lift product. Lifting loads from the floor can easily result in lower-back injuries. Product that is bulkier or heavier should be handled by two employees or powered equipment.

    When materials are stored where employees must walk under, around, over, or through, injuries can easily occur. If left unchanged, conditions such as these will result in costly injuries. Poor housekeeping practices could also create walking and working areas that create close clearances and congestion. Where movement of personnel is restricted, the working area can create potentially serious storage and housekeeping conditions.

3. *Hazardous personal attire.* All of the personal clothing and personal protective equipment worn by employees must be in good condition. Shoes that need new soles, shoes that have the steel toe protruding through the leather cap, incorrect fall protection such as a safety belt versus an effective safety harness, oil-soaked clothing, and finger rings all contribute to hazards. The wearing of hazardous personal attire is not necessarily unsafe behavior as much as is the employee who becomes a walking unsafe condition.

As an example of a very serious "hazardous attire" injury, a warehouse employee climbed a rack to retrieve a box of automotive parts. He should have used a nearby ladder instead. He then jumped off the rack because he couldn't use his hands to hold on—his hands were occupied with the box. His wedding ring caught on the racking, and in the process the ring and his falling body weight pulled his finger off his hand.

Not only was this injury tragic to the employee and his family, it was very costly. The serious nature of this injury disrupted work in the warehouse for the entire day, and many days later employees were still discussing the incident. The employee's ring was a definite unsafe condition.

4. *Lack of or inadequate warning systems.* Warning systems such as alarms, horns, bells, whistles, signs, tags, lights, and barricades are intended to alert employees to a hazard. Back up alarms on counterbalanced forklifts have been known to provide an added measure of protection to pedestrians. Barricades, signs, and lights added to the work area can warn of excavations or overhead work. No-smoking areas such as those in battery charging or storage of flammables require safeguarding through signage and internal safeguards. Even something as simple as yellow lines painted on the floor can designate a safer walkway for pedestrians or employees. Without these distinct guidelines, the control of people-traffic could pose a serious problem.

5. *Hazardous environmental elements.* There are potential unseen problem areas within a warehouse that can cause serious harm or even death, including toxic or hazardous elements such as vapors from chemicals being handled or stored, carbon monoxide, dust, noise, and ergonomic factors. In some cases the danger goes unnoticed because the human senses cannot always detect the risk.

A forklift could easily drop a container of toxic chemicals at a dock or from a rack. The fork of the lift truck could easily spear and puncture a 55-gallon drum of solvent in a paint storage warehouse. Potentially deadly carbon monoxide could easily permeate an entire building. Poorly designed work areas could cause injuries to the arms, wrists, shoulders, and back because of material handling.

Environmental hazards are many times insidious in a warehouse. These harmful conditions can be reduced or eliminated by first detecting them and then taking appropriate corrective steps. Trained professionals such as industrial hygienists can be very helpful to management in addressing these hazards.

6. *Hazards of fire and explosion.* Many employees do not understand the difference between flammables and combustibles. Terms such as "flash point" and "explosive limits" are not always taught to those who handle dangerous chemicals. Many warehouses handle and store containers of liquids that contain chemicals with flash points below 100° F. The lower the flash point the more dangerous the chemical is

for fire. The evaporation rate of the liquid would allow vapors from a punctured or damaged container to mix with the atmosphere. If the proper conditions are present any sparks or flames could easily ignite this flammable mixture.

Ordinary fire hazards also pose an unsafe condition in a warehouse. A serious fire occurred in a warehouse office after an employee used linseed oil to wipe off paneling. The rags soaked with linseed oil were left in a corner of the room and later ignited from spontaneous combustion; the fire was a serious one.

7. *Inadequate illumination.* Walking and working areas must be properly illuminated for safety as well as a means of meeting production quotas. Aisles, ramps, passageways, docks, building exteriors, mezzanines, product, electrical power panels, utility services, and offices must be properly lighted. There must be serious consideration given to the safe handling of products and processes as well as quality of job performance, customer satisfaction, and security. Housekeeping practices also improve when there is proper lighting.

8. *Lack of safety devices and improper or inadequate guarding.* Unsafe conditions exist when guards are missing or defective. Guarding includes the physical barrier that a guard provides as well as any electrical devices or interlocks and controls. Open gears and pulleys on machines, conveyors, roll-up doors, and compressors pose serious hazards. The lack of mirrors, back up alarms, limit switches, horns, lights, barriers and signals are also a part of this unsafe condition. Ongoing inspections and an aggressive maintenance program will help to correct these obvious hazards.

9. *Unexpected movement hazards.* Powered equipment, materials, and product are often left in a precarious position and could easily drift, roll, slide, or go into unexpected movement. When equipment moves unexpectedly, it creates a hazardous condition. A forklift parked on an incline without having the wheels chocked could easily roll down the ramp. Bulky product left on a stopped conveyor could easily fall on employees if the conveyor starts unexpectedly.

10. *Protruding object hazards.* Injuries could occur to employees and visitors alike from objects that protrude in the walking, working, or break areas. A serious injury occurred to an office timekeeper who ventured into the warehouse to collect time cards. A broken fluorescent bulb was placed in a trash can. The sharp glass edges were protruding into the walkway. Her arm made contact with the sharp edge and she severely lacerated her arm.

Additional hazards could include ends of lumber, pipes, or stored product Employees could easily be struck by parts or product protruding out of a load being transported by a powered industrial truck.

Protruding nails in pallet boards are very common and cause hundreds of foot injuries each year from employees stepping on them when stepped on. In one case, a warehouse employee was using a nail with a large head on it to secure heavy-duty cardboard to pallets. This process created a storage container. When nails fell onto the floor, they usually landed point up. In one year sixteen foot injuries occurred from employees stepping on nails. Supervisors finally saw the need to use a staple gun to secure the cardboard to the pallet.

11. *Defective tools, machines, and equipment.* Day-to-day use of ladders, ropes, hand tools, power tools, and powered equipment could cause them to become unsafe. Ladder rungs could crack or splinter, powered equipment could require mechanical repair, tools could require new handles or electric cords. During the course of daily activity in a warehouse, management and workers should look for defective items so they can be tagged and taken out of service for repair.

Unsafe conditions are ever present in the workplace and, if left uncorrected, will eventually injure someone. A defective wooden ladder could easily be left leaning against a wall for many months. When needed, the ladder will be used to gain access to an elevated area. The ladder may not break at that point but could easily result in a serious fall for the employee. Each injury has contributing factors and, when investigating, all of these factors must be considered.

INJURY INVESTIGATION

With the understanding of how injuries occur and what causes injuries in warehouses, it is important to review what is needed for proper injury investigation. Minor injuries that require only first aid treatment and do not contribute to disability are as important to investigate as those that are more serious. Lessons must be learned from minor injuries so that the occurrence of serious injuries is minimized. If any injury goes unreported, nothing is learned from the injury to prevent the next one.

When injuries are not reported, the conditions or employee actions that contributed to the injury are left uncorrected. In addition, employees could form poor reporting habits, meaning future incidents could continue to go unreported.

A few tips for supervisors to encourage the reporting of injuries are:

- Emphasize the reporting of all incidents and injuries.

- Emphasize that the cause of a minor injury can be full of potential for a serious injury.

- Instruct new employees to report all injuries because it is a warehouse rule.

- Never embarrass, belittle, or become angry when injuries or incidents are reported.

- Firmly point out to the employee failing to report a personal injury that neglected injuries may result in infections or other serious consequences.

When an injury does occur, management is responsible for determining all of the relevant facts so a determination can be made about why and how it occurred. The employee's supervisor is the most likely person to conduct the investigation. Properly evaluate the statements made by the employee and witnesses, if any, to arrive at the correct conclusion. Just recording the account of the injury offered by the injured employee provides only one version of the event. Asking the right questions is important. This investigation process is more than just completing a form. It is definitely not a time to look for fault or to lay blame on anyone

The sole purpose of an injury investigation is to establish all of the relevant and important facts, details, and opinions of everyone involved. Conclusions are to be formed so that the prevention of future injuries is achieved. It has been said that the search for facts about an injury is really the search for a solution to prevent recurrence.

Injuries should be investigated as soon as practical after they have occurred. Injuries that are minor in nature should be investigated by the supervisor. In some warehouses, employees from the safety committee or safety steering committee may assist in the process. Where serious injuries or incidents occur, a management and employee team approach should be used. This process may help uncover more facts, and a variety of appropriate solutions can be achieved by the group.

The injured person's version of the injury is important and obtaining this information should take place as soon as possible. In the event the injured employee needs medical care, or is uneasy, upset, or emotional, a delay in discussing the injury may be necessary. Proper care and treatment of the injured employee is most important.

The quality of the completed report is essential to problem solving. It is obvious that anyone conducting an investigation should be properly trained for the task. A standard form should be used and the entire staff should be familiar with the procedure for promptly providing the required details. Someone should be designated to oversee the completion and quality of the reports. If a supervisor is submitting poorly written or late reports, additional training may be needed. A complete rewrite may be necessary. An injury investigation form is shown in Figure 16-1. Use of this form will provide enough information regarding any warehouse injury.

Quality injury investigation results in corrective action so a similar injury cannot occur.

- If the corrective action on the report recommended a physical change such as a guard, a new ladder, new brakes, etc., follow-up must take place. Management is responsible for checking to ensure that the unsafe condition or behavior has been corrected.

- By personally observing others performing the same job that injured the employee, further recommendations are possible. Studying a job being performed is an excellent method to improve the workplace. New layout, better lighting, or ergonomic improvements may be needed.

- Ask others to assist in observation and follow-up. Supervisors, safety committee members, and fellow employees can help monitor the work area or task being performed and offer their own thoughts on improvement.

- Include discussions of the injury at safety meetings in the various departments so similar injuries are prevented elsewhere in the warehouse.

- Videotape the scene of the injury and study the facts as they present themselves and then study the scene during the day-to-day operations. Much can be learned from this approach.

When interviewing the injured employee, it is important to get the employee to fully cooperate and give the true and complete facts as to what occurred. Minimize any fears the employee may have. The interview process should:

- Serve as a reminder to the employee as to why you are asking the questions.

- Enable the employee to give a complete version of what happened.

- Allow the employee to give a full description without being interrupted.

- Never allow the employee to repeat or demonstrate an unsafe action.

- Include any additional questions to fill in gaps.

- Include restating the version back to the employee, as he/she stated it.

Figure 16-1. Injury Investigation Form

REPORT OF INJURY INVESTIGATION TO BE COMPLETED WITHIN 24 HOURS AFTER AN ACCIDENT			
Date of Report:		Employee Name:	Employee Title:
Date of Injury:	Time Shift Started:	Warehouse Location:	Time of Injury: Length of Employment:
Body part injured:		Was first aid administered? Yes ☐ No ☐	Social Security Number: - -
Description of injury:			
Description of how injury occurred:			

Shop Managers Estimation of Accident: ☐ Work Related ☐ Non-Occupational ☐ Undetermined ☐ Disabling	Employee able to return to work? ☐ Yes ☐ No	Doctor or hospital treating employee:	How long will employee be disabled?
Was Employee performing regularly assigned job? ☐ Yes ☐ No Was Employee instructed in this particular job? ☐ Yes ☐ No	Machine, tool or device involved:		How much production time was lost?

Injury was caused by:

☐ Inattention to Duty Being Performed

☐ Inadequate Instruction

☐ Failure to Follow Procedures

☐ Lack of Knowledge & Skill

☐ Inadequate Enforcement of Rules

☐ Unsafe Act or Behavior

☐ Improper Job Instruction

☐ Unsafe Mechanical Condition

☐ Other - Describe:

_____

Protective Equipment:	Required	Being Worn
Hard Hat		☐
Glasses	☐	☐
Goggles	☐	☐
Safety Shoes	☐	☐
Gloves	☐	☐
Long Sleeves	☐	☐
Face Shield	☐	☐
Ear Plugs/Muffs	☐	☐
Other?	☐	☐
	☐	

Give details on who, what, where, why and how, of accident:

What will you do to keep this type of accident from reoccurring?

Figure 16-1. Injury Investigation Form (continued)

What do you feel were the main causes of the accident?	
List any additional details or comments here:	
Shop Manager Signature: _____ Date.	List any costs associated with the accident; medical, workers comp payouts, damaged equipment, etc.:

- Solicit ideas from the employee about what he would do or recommend to prevent recurrence.

- Conclude with thanking the employee and asking if there is anything that can be done to assist him.

- Have the employee's version of the details of the injury in writing, completed by the interviewer after the employee leaves.

If it becomes necessary to interview witnesses to the injury, several key points should be considered

- The interview process should not be delayed. Conduct the interview in a private or separate area rather than asking questions in front of coworkers.

- Ask that they be frank and honest about the details, and assure them that the purpose of the interview is not to find fault or to find the injured person guilty of any wrongdoing.

- Use the same interview method for a witness as was used with the injured person. Let them speak, do not interrupt, do not record the details at that time. Refrain from becoming upset or judgmental toward the injured person.

- When asking questions, be specific. As an example, an employee fell while using a portable wooden ladder. When filling in the missing information for the injury, a supervisor should ask the witness, "What rung was he standing on when you saw him?" rather than, "He wasn't standing on the top rung, was he?"

- Summarize your findings with the witnesses and thank them for their assistance.

If a reenactment of the injury is necessary, ensure that the injured employee or witnesses do not repeat any unsafe acts. Stop them from taking any risk. Reenactments should be slow and deliberate so that the exact details can be studied. Treat the injured person with respect.

Use Figure 16-2 to measure the effects of the investigation process.

Figure 16–2. Productive Injury Investigation Rating Sheet

PRODUCTIVE INJURY INVESTIGATIONS — SELF RATING SHEET			
NAME:		RATING	
DATE:	LOCATION:	GOOD	POOR
Do I hear about all injuries in my department?			
Do I investigate each one as promptly as possible?			
Do I get a detailed story from the injured employee?			
Do I actually investigate all minor cases thoroughly to find causes?			
Do I check all witnesses, so as to get a complete story?			
How completely do I fill out injury report forms?			
Do I seek help from the safety department or insurance company representatives to assist in developing suitable corrective action?			
Do I use as many tools as possible in order to make a factual injury investigation (such as camera, warehouse inspection report, incident reports)?			
Do I use injury investigations to provide safety education in my department?			
Do I have repetitive types of injuries which indicate I have not really eliminated or controlled certain hazards?			
Do I periodically review all injury reports and first aid logs so as to spot trends, injury repeaters, problem areas and operations?			
Do I follow through to see that corrective action is taken?			
Do I check JHA's to determine which jobs or steps in jobs are responsible for the injuries?			
Do I use day-to-day incident reports to take corrective action before an injury occurs?			
Do I permit safety committee members the opportunity to assist in the investigation process?			

INCIDENT REPORTING

Incidents, for purposes of this discussion, could include:

- close calls (near misses)

- fires of any size

- product damage

- building damage

- first aid type injuries

- discovery of an unsafe condition

- observing unsafe behavior.

If an organization is truly interested in preventing injuries, eliminating damage to property or product, and reducing costs, a focus must be placed on the prevention of day- to-day incidents. Incidents are precursors to injuries. Many hundreds of incidents will occur before an injury takes place. Today's close call could be tomorrow's fatality. Unfortunately, many safety programs do not include an element that places a focus on incident investigation.

Figure 16-3. A lift truck lost this load of steel tubing. No one was injured.

Figure 16-3 illustrates a close call in a small-parts department. A forklift was passing by and lost a load of steel tubing. The load fell into an area where a worker was previously standing.

Incidents are ever-present in a warehouse. With the heavy use of power equipment, the frequency of product movement, dock activity, and movement of people, incidents are commonplace. Incidents are taking place in every department during every hour of every day. Some of them cause minor damage or minor injuries. Some of them will go unnoticed because they are daily events. Some will cause minor fires, damage the building, or even cause slight injuries. It is difficult to imagine any workplace without incidents.

Since most of the industrial safety programs primarily focus on injury investigation, the most serious part of loss prevention, incident investigation, goes unused. Does management heed the warning signs? Are injuries blamed on careless employees because management fails to correct defective equipment, or unsafe conditions, and ignores unsafe behavior? To be effective, a safety program must be complete and comprehensive.

When an injury occurs, it is not unusual for someone to comment, " I knew he was going to get hurt one day by doing that." Another comment is, " But we've always done it that way." If the primary purpose in injury investigation is to prevent the recurrence of injuries, day-to-day incidents must be corrected.

Chance is one determining factor of whether employees or visitors escape injury. Safety professionals agree that many incidents, or opportunities for injury, will occur before an injury takes place. If supervisors believe that they are too busy to investigate incidents, they are missing a golden opportunity to improve the efficiency of their departments, in addition to preventing injuries.

Many incidents seem so commonplace, that everyone forgets that correction is needed. At times, combinations of incidents eventually result in something serious. As an example, a lift truck has a problem with a brake fluid leak. The leak goes unreported. Warehouse employees walk through the fluid, and powered equipment drives through it. Everyone is too busy to take the defective lift truck out of service. The warehouse manager is escorting a visitor through the building when the visitor slips on the brake fluid and fractures his elbow. Prior to this unfortunate injury, the brakes on the defective lift truck failed and it crashed into several pallet loads of canned goods. This rather serious event should have been followed up by management; the product damage was unnecessary and expensive.

Had the warehouse personnel conducted daily lift truck inspections and management enforced the inspection process, the injury and expensive incident would have been prevented. Management should have intervened many weeks earlier. Correct maintenance procedures were ignored. Housekeeping was compromised. Everyone was too busy to correct the problem when it was small. Once a serious problem occurred, everyone became concerned.

Studies demonstrate that the correction of incidents helps injuries decline. Product damage and waste is reduced. Damage to racking and buildings is reduced, thereby requiring less maintenance. OSHA violations are minimized. Complaints and grievances are also reduced.

The warehouse supervisor is the person in the best position to investigate and correct incidents. In addition, it is not unusual for warehouse employees to generate incident reports. The process is rather simple. When walking through the warehouse or when alerted by employees, the supervisor should evaluate the incident and complete a report. The report should be handwritten. Corrective action is an important part of the form. Drawings can be produced on the back of the page to illustrate what took place. Photos of the problem and then another photo of the correction makes for good documentation. Incident reports can also be used during safety meetings.

Figure 16-4 provides an excellent form for investigating and recording incidents.

Why wait for an injury to occur? If a defect in the system or a machine is obvious, why should management delay corrective action if injury or other economic losses may happen?

SUMMARY

Injuries in the workplace are inevitable. Effective safety programming should provide preventive steps to keep injuries from occurring in the first place, but when injuries do occur, the proper investigation must take place.

Injuries and incidents have a negative impact on the bottom line. Injuries are costly both on a direct and indirect basis. Daily incidents do much to damage property and product, and incidents are precursors to injuries. That is why it is so important to spend time investigating incidents.

Figure 16-4. Non-Injury Incident Report

+---+
| NON-INJURY INCIDENT REPORT |
| PROPERTY DAMAGE REPORT |
| AND/OR |
| DISCOVERY OF POTENTIAL HAZARD |
+---+

(CHECK ALL THOSE THAT APPLY)

☐ Near Hit ☐ Non-Injury ☐ Property Damage ☐ Incident/Event ☐ Fire Loss ☐ Unsafe Condition

Facility/Location: _____ Department: _____ Date Occurred: _____

1) Describe the incident or what occurred:

_____

_____

_____

_____

2) Machine or equipment involved (number/name):

_____

3) Extent of damage/cost of repair, replacement, etc (describe):

_____

_____

4) How much lost time or down time was involved (describe):

_____

_____

5) How many employees were involved in the incident:

_____

6) Was anyone injured?	☐ Yes	☐ No
7) Was first aid administered?	☐ Yes	☐ No
8) Was there a fire?	☐ Yes	☐ No
9) Was employee wearing required personal protective equipment?	☐ Yes	☐ No

10) What steps were taken by you to prevent recurrence:

_____

_____

11) What steps were taken by others (maintenance, management, outside sources, etc.) to prevent recurrence?

_____

_____

12) Was a health hazard or exposure involved:	☐ Yes	☐ No
13) Can this incident or event take place again:	☐ Yes	☐ No

14) Identify additional factors or comments on back of this report.

15) Have you drawn a sketch of the details on the back of this report or attached a photo: ☐ Yes ☐ No

Signature: _____ Date: _____

Workers can be injured as a result of unsafe conditions or unsafe behavior. Most injuries occur when both conditions and employee actions violate safety principles. Employees can be injured in one or more ways: by being struck by, contacted by, caught between, contacted with, caught on, caught in, or striking against something, or from overexertion, exposure, and falls.

Once an injury or incident occurs, asking the injured worker the correct questions and documenting the details are important. Investigations can be done correctly by using the forms provided in the chapter. Once recorded, corrective action is needed to prevent the same injury from occurring again. The only good thing to come out of an investigation is the prevention of another similar injury.

REFERENCES

Armco Steel Corporation. Accident Prevention Fundamentals and Industrial Hygiene. Middletown, Ohio. 1976.

Petersen, Dan, and Jerry Goodale. Readings in Industrial Accident Prevention. NY, NY: McGraw Hill 1980. pp. 18–25.

Swartz, George. "Incident Reporting: A Vital part of Quality Safety Programs." Professional Safety. October 1993, pp. 32–34.

17

Job Hazard Analysis

Employers can help reduce warehouse injuries, whether minor or severe, and the associated financial losses through proper employee training. When employees lack the proper safety training, errors can easily be made that ultimately end in injury or illness. Training employees in safe job procedures can be accomplished through job hazard analysis (JHA). There are other names given to this process, but the end result of the program is usually the same as JHA. Other titles include job safety analysis, safe work procedures, and detailed safety analysis.

This chapter will focus on the JHA process and includes several useful forms to assist in a JHA program. The following components of JHA are covered:

- Definition of Job Hazard Analysis

- Definition of the word "job"

- Developing a master JHA list

- Selection of jobs to be analyzed

- Starting the JHA process

- Identifying the potential hazards or injuries

- Completing the JHA

- Definition of forms

- Taking the program further

- Economic benefits to consider for JHA.

DEFINITION OF JOB HAZARD ANALYSIS

What is JHA? JHA is a method of studying a job in order to:

- Identify the hazards or potential injuries associated with each step of the job.

- Develop solutions that will eliminate, nullify, or prevent such hazards.

Two of the very basic methods of injury prevention are spotting potential injury causes, and correcting or eliminating these potential causes. JHA is designed to implement both of these two methods. If the causes of injuries are known before the injury occurs, then it is more likely that injuries can be prevented by eliminating the causes.

Job hazard analysis is a special injury prevention and incident investigation tool that has long been used by many organizations with a great deal of concern for safety. The correct use of JHA can bring about significant reductions in injuries, the severity of injuries, and daily incidents.

Basic Steps of a JHA

There are four important components in completing a JHA.

1. Select the job to be analyzed from a master list.

2. Break the job down into basic steps.

3. Identify the hazards or potential injuries.

4. Develop methods to eliminate potential injuries, and describe how to properly complete each job step.

DEFINING THE WORD "JOB"

The standard definition of the word "job" refers to the position or occupational title that an employee holds. These titles can include: fork lift operator, material handler, warehouseman, UPS packer, pallet walkie operator, maintenance worker, or electrician. The term "job," as used in this chapter, applies to specific job assignments such as unloading a trailer, painting a wall, using a pallet truck, or unloading a conveyor. When using JHA to analyze a job, the employee's occupation is not being studied; the task that that the employee is completing is being evaluated.

This definition of a job identifies a sequence of definite steps or separate activities that together accomplish a work goal. The jobs have in common the fact that they involve a sequence of steps of work. When the last step is completed, a work goal has been completed (e.g., the truck is loaded, the pallets are stacked, the conveyor is loaded, the forklift inspection is completed, and so on). Again, JHA applies to jobs or tasks, not occupations.

The end goal of JHA is to make a job safer to work. If supervisors or workers do not know the hazards and injury potential associated with a job, they cannot do anything about the hazards to make the job safe. Therefore, the first thing that must be done to make a job safe is to identify and understand the hazards and potential injuries associated with each job step.

Solutions must also take the form of a prescribed safe way to avoid the hazard. For every known hazard associated with a job step, there must be a solution that nullifies the hazard.

DEVELOPING A JHA LIST

Prior to starting the JHA process, it is necessary to develop a complete list of jobs in the warehouse. Figure 17-1 can be used for this process. This listing of jobs could be started in a classroom setting or each supervisor could develop a list and give it to management in the preparation of a master list. Supervisors could pool their thoughts to be sure all jobs in the warehouse are considered for the list.

Instructions: In the chart, record the jobs performed by each position that require special emphasis on safety due to their hazardous nature. The idea is to develop a list of the most hazardous jobs performed by each position.

Reminder: When compiling a list of jobs, it should be remembered that all jobs are to be listed. However, all jobs do not have the same risks or hazards. Even though the master list requires a listing of all known jobs, those jobs that are the most hazardous will be given a JHA early in the program. Not all jobs involve the same risk, therefore, selection on a priority basis associated with risk is recommended.

To aid the reader, a sample list of thirty typical warehouse jobs follows. This list is, by no means, a complete one, but is intended to represent typical jobs that may appear on a master list. The jobs are not listed by any specific priority.

Typical Warehouse JHA Titles

- Unloading palletized product from a trailer
- Loading a conveyor
- Unloading a conveyor
- Charging a battery
- Cleaning a battery
- Assembling racking
- Cutting bin dividers
- Using the mobile sweeper
- Inspecting a forklift
- Emptying the floor sweeper
- Sweeping the floor
- Disassembling racking
- Inspecting pallets
- Placing wheel chocks
- Operating a pallet walkie truck

- Taking inventory
- Using a scissors lift
- Changing light bulbs
- Manually lifting boxes
- Using the mechanical elevator
- Operating a narrow-aisle truck
- Loading empty pallets on a trailer
- Cleaning dock wells
- Using an extension ladder
- Using a portable nail gun
- Using the spill cleanup kit
- Picking small parts
- Replacing defective sections of racking
- Sprinkler testing
- Cleaning under dock plates.

Figure 17-1. JHA Form #1 – Jobs Requiring Special Emphasis upon Safety

Instructions: Record the titles and code numbers of positions (occupations) under your supervision at the head of each section. In the chart, record the jobs performed by each position that require special emphasis on safety due to their hazardous nature. The idea is to develop a list of the most hazardous jobs performed by each position.

1.	31.
2.	32.
3.	33.
4.	34.
5.	35.
6.	36.
7.	37.
8.	38.
9.	39.
10.	40.

11.	41.
12.	42.
13.	43.
14.	44.
15.	45.
16.	46.
17.	47.
18.	48.
19.	49.
20.	50.

21.	51.
22.	52.
23.	53.
24.	54.
25.	55.
26.	56.
27.	57.
28.	58.
29.	59.
30.	60.

Note that the listing of jobs is quite varied. Warehouses may have special operations and situations that will require a listing of a broad spectrum of jobs. The sample list of jobs is merely a means of providing assistance in the development process. Be sure to consider jobs that may take place inside and outside the building. Perhaps jobs take place on the roof, in a confined space, or on the building property; be sure to list all of these jobs. Include such items as maintenance tasks, snow removal, and any jobs that are completed involving risks. The JHA list becomes the road map in going forward with the program.

Completed JHAs are living documents; information recorded on the forms at present may not be applicable in the future. Processes could change, machines may no longer exist, technology could change, and worker involvement in the job could change. The point is that jobs can be added or deleted from the list. In addition, being able to develop a complete list at the very start of the JHA program is unlikely. There are always seasonal or unusual jobs that are not remembered until the job is ready to be completed. It is expected that the JHA master list will take different forms as time passes.

SELECTING THE JOB TO BE ANALYZED

The first component requires that a job be selected for analysis. Each supervisor in each department will require a complete listing of jobs. It is important to prepare a listing of position titles, hazardous jobs, jobs that have resulted in close calls, jobs that are nonroutine and jobs that have resulted in disabling or severe injuries. A typical warehouse may compile of list of between 75 and 150 jobs.

In selecting the job to be analyzed, consideration must be given to the following.

- All jobs that have a history of producing many injuries are excellent choices for a JHA. It is a safe assumption that a job that has produced a large share of injuries in the past will continue to produce injuries unless changes are made to the job. The greater the number of injuries associated with a job, the greater the need to be a part of JHA.

- Jobs that have produced disabling injuries are also excellent candidates for JHA. Obviously, these jobs should take priority over those that have produced less serious or first aid injuries. Disabling injuries are very costly as well as devastating to the injured worker and his/her family.

- Some jobs have a history of producing few injuries but have the potential of being severe when they do occur. The injury could be crippling or fatal. These jobs cannot be excluded from JHA because they seldom produce injury.

- Newly established jobs must also be included in the JHA list. Any changes in tools, equipment, or processes will require JHA. These jobs may not have a history of producing injures. However, it is important to create safe working procedures *before* anyone can be injured. The JHA can also provide excellent training for every new employee or transferred employee that may work at these jobs.

- Ergonomic job evaluations can easily be included in the JHA process. Supervisors must be trained in how to properly evaluate the workstation and the various body positions that the worker utilizes. In the past, the opportunity existed for ergonomic evaluations while completing JHA. Very few organizations took advantage of this opportunity to not only prepare a safe procedure for a task, but to include a proper ergonomic assessment. JHA provides a perfect opportunity to provide both studies for worker protection.

STARTING THE JHA PROCESS

Training supervisors to complete JHAs requires detailed instruction. The proper method of evaluating a job from start to finish must be thoroughly discussed. The proper placement of job steps, hazards, and safe procedures on the forms needs special emphasis. The completed forms must be systematically discussed and evaluated in formal training sessions with supervisors. Simply reading this information as a guide on how to complete JHAs will not ensure a quality program; hands-on workshops are necessary to assure quality work.

There are three main methods to use when completing JHA's; each method may have a plus or minus associated with it.

Supervisor-employee. This process allows the supervisor to observe and discuss the job being performed at the work site with the employee. The employee should be skilled at the job so that he/she can give insight to all of its details. Much can be gained by asking the employee questions about actual job details and hazards. After all, who knows more about how the job gets done! Of the three methods listed, this one is the most effective for information gathering, employee involvement, and efficiency.

Select the right person to observe. The person selected should be experienced at the job and cooperative. If more than one employee is doing the job, select the employee who will get the most out of the JHA. Be sure to explain what JHA is all about and what you intend to do before starting. Let him/her know that you are relying on his/her experience to complete a quality JHA. When complete, discuss the findings with the employee.

Once the JHA rough draft has been completed by the supervisor and employee, someone skilled in JHA should critique the form and provide feedback. It would also be beneficial to allow other supervisors and employees to read the rough draft and provide feedback. All of the comments should be incorporated into the final draft so that an accurate document is developed. Figure 17-2 illustrates the form, JSA Form #2, to utilize for developing the rough draft.

Supervisor-group. This process includes employees of a department in a formal classroom setting. The discussion leader, usually the supervisor, leads the group toward completion of a JHA for a task with which they are all familiar. This method provides opportunity for a wide cross-sampling of opinion and experience. Somewhere in this multithought and discussion process, the real details of JHA are hidden. It is up to the discussion leader to extract the correct information. At times, group discussions may become heated because of disagreement with the details. Some employees may argue against a specific procedure because they have been performing the job a different way. In addition to the potential disagreements, this process can be time-consuming.

Any JHA completed by a group or committee should be given to an individual who is skilled in JHA so that a comprehensive document can be developed. If the discussion leader is skilled in JHA, the process can be completed at the group meeting.

Supervisor (alone). Supervisors frequently create JHAs at their desks or at home. They have a lot of workplace experience and can sometimes use this knowledge to draft JHAs. This is probably the least desirable method because the employee is not involved; it should be discouraged by management.

Many safety professionals refer to this system as the "recall and check" method. Working from memory, the supervisor breaks the job down into basic steps, identifies the potential injuries associated with each

Figure 17-2. JHA Form #2 - Job Hazard Analysis

JHA #	Title of Job
Location	
Supervisor	
Employee(s) Involved in JHA	
Date Completed	Date Revised
PPE Required	

Basic Job Steps	Job Hazards	Safe Job Procedures

Key for Job Hazards:	CB = Caught between	CBY = Contact by
CI = Caught in	CO = Caught on	CW - Contact with
E = Exposure	FB = Fall to below	FS = Fall same level
SAG = Struck against	SB = Struck by	SO = Overexertion

step, and develops safety solutions as well as the procedures for performing the job. This individualized development of JHA is intended to create a preliminary document that should be reviewed by others, including employees.

SELECTING THE JOB

Now that the methods to use in completing a JHA have been identified, it is time to actually interface with an employee on the warehouse floor. As in any program, there are basic rules and guidelines that must be followed to properly complete the JHA.

Select the job to be analyzed. It bears repeating that job selection should be chosen on a priority basis and should be based on:

- Jobs that have produced serious injury in the past

- Jobs that produce ongoing injuries to workers

- Jobs that are inherently hazardous that may not have produced an injury

- Jobs that have involved ergonomic issues (cumulative trauma)

- Jobs that are infrequently performed (semiannually/annually) that may have a high risk

- Jobs that have resulted in minor injuries or first aid cases.

The above guidelines are prepared in a priority listing. It makes sense to select a high-risk job for evaluation rather than one that has a history of producing few injuries. A supervisor should consider, "What's the worst thing that can occur in my department; what operation could produce the most serious injury?" The selection of these high-risk jobs is the correct place to start. Eventually, all of the jobs in the warehouse will be analyzed and those of lowpriority/low risk will be completed.

Once the job is selected, approach the employee and explain what you are about to do. The supervisor will need the employee's help in completing the JHA. Without employees involvement there is no learning. Use the blank form as identified in Figure 17-2. Ask the employee to start the job from the beginning and explain what he/she is doing.

Write down the basic step with just a few words in the left column. As the employee to comment on hazards or risks in each step of accomplishing the task.

FORMS USED FOR JHA

To properly plan for and complete JHAs, the use of specific forms is necessary. Each of the following forms has a place in the JHA process.

Figure 17-1 is Form #1, the place to list all of the jobs that are a part of the warehouse operations. Note the sample listing of thirty jobs that may be typical for a warehouse, offered earlier in the chapter. A completed list may have between 50 and 100 or more. Supervisors and employees should "brainstorm" and develop as complete a listing of jobs as possible. New jobs or jobs that were omitted from the original list can be added later. Even though there may be a group of employees working on the development of separate lists, all of the lists should be consolidated into one master list and each job appropriately numbered.

Figure 17-2 identifies Form #2, the two-page JHA form the warehouse supervisor uses to complete the job evaluation with the employee. Form #2 is intended to act as a rough-draft copy of the job hazard evaluation.

Figure 17-3 identifies JHA Form #3, which is to be used after the rough details have been smoothed out from form #2 and the final details of the JHA have been reviewed and corrected. A completed final copy of Form #3 should be appropriately filed and a laminated copy should be posted near the job. It is useful to neatly post completed JHAs near jobs such as battery charging areas, product elevators, conveyors, sprinklers, dock doors, and trash compactors.

These posted JHA copies would have been reviewed and revised to the point that the document is correct. Any employee preparing to complete a specific task can easily review the posted JHA to review the safest method of working the job. New employees can easily be briefed by a supervisor or fellow employee before starting a job. Posted JHAs serve as great training tools.

Figure 17-4 identifies a JHA review form. Periodically, JHAs must be reviewed for accuracy, quality, and changes in the job, and evaluated in the event of an injury. If the JHA is in need of revision, affected employees are to be a part of the review and revision process that is documented on this review form. Once reviewed, the original JHA on Form #3 (Figure 17-3) should be corrected.

Figure 17-3. JHA Form #3 - Final Evaluation Steps

JHA NUMBER: 56	JOB OPERATION TITLE: Raising and Lowering Manual Dock Plate	DEPARTMENT: Shipping POSITION TITLE: Forklift Operator
NAMES OF EMPLOYEES ASSISTING: Sam Spitale, Pierre Belanger, Jon Reis		
PPE REQUIRED: Hard Hat, Steel Toe Boots, Gloves		
BASIC JOB STEPS	POTENTIAL HAZARDS	RECOMMENDED SAFE JOB PROCEDURE
1. Lift Dock Plate	1. SO Strain lower back when pulling chain	1. Ensure trailer is chocked. Stand behind the dock plate, bend knees, keep the back flat. Place fingers on pull ring, lift upward to activate dock plate.
2. Lower Plate Onto Trailer	2. F Could fall if dock plate is slippery	2. Walk forward on raised dock plate, plate will lower onto trailer bed. Keep feet clear of lip of dockplate. Be alert to the walking surface on the dock plate.
3. Lift Plate Up	3. SO Strain to lower back when pulling chain FS Could fall on slippery Surface	3. When completed with loading of the trailer, stand behind dock plate, bend knees, keep the back straight, grasp chain ring and pull upward to retract dock plate. Be aware of walking surface
4. Put Plate in Place	4. FS Could fall on slippery surface SB Could be struck by plate as it closes	4. After pulling chain, plate will rise up and the lip of the plate will fold down. Walk forward on the plate to place it into its original position. Be alert for the walking surface and the potential of being struck by the plate (Other employees).

Figure 17-4. JHA Form #4 - Review Sheet

Date of JSA Review: _____

Warehouse: _____

JSA Number: _____

JSA Title: _____

Employees Involved in JSA Review: _____

_____

_____

_____

_____

Are changes needed in this JSA?	☐ Yes	☐ No
Was the JSA actually changed/improved?	☐ Yes	☐ No
Has the modified JSA been processed for typing?	☐ Yes	☐ No

Comments on Review / Recommendations for Change

_____

_____

_____

_____

(Always attach the revised JSA form to the original copy.)

IDENTIFYING POTENTIAL HAZARDS OR INJURIES

Supervisors and employees must be aware that there are eleven main categories of potential injury-causing situations. One or more of the following eleven ways an injury could take place is to be added to the middle column of the JHA. It is possible for a particular step to be free of hazards. If this is discovered during the review process, simply place dashes or the word "none" on the form.

1. *Struck by (SB)*. An employee or someone else may be struck by a part, vehicle, falling object, or moving object. Struck by usually implies that something is in motion and the worker(s) can be struck by the object. As an example, an employee can be struck by a forklift.

2. *Struck against (SAG)*. A struck against injury implies that the worker is somehow in motion and strikes against an object. For example, an employee struck his head against racking while reaching in for a part.

3. *Caught between (CB)*. A caught between injury usually involves a pinch point. The worker is somehow in motion and can be caught between two objects. This situation can be illustrated by a powered walkie truck operator who got his hand caught between the operating handle and racking. A very serious caught between example is the employee or visitor who is pinned between a forklift and a fixed object.

4. *Contacted by (CBy)*. A contacted by injury occurs when something in motion, such as a chemical splash, makes contact with the worker. This could occur at the battery recharge station when a worker is contacted by a sulfuric acid splash.

5. *Contact with (CW)*. In this case the worker has made contact with a hot surface, sharp edge, an exposed electrical wire, or a chemical. The hazard may or may not be visible. This could happen when a worker makes contact with an exposed razor blade while reaching for a pencil in the desk drawer.

6. *Caught in (CI)*. A caught in injury is an entrapment injury of some kind and does not occur very often. The most serious caught in incident would be that of an employee being trapped in a room, walk-in safe, or vessel. An example of this type of injury would be a worker walking through the warehouse who steps into a small drain hole, getting his foot caught.

7. *Caught on (CO)*. A caught on injury implies that something is in motion. An object moving past a worker can catch a piece of clothing and drag the employee. Or the employee in motion may become caught onto a fixed object. Employees have been known to get the hook of a crane caught in their gloves as the crane hook goes up. Another example would be an employee who climbed racking to retrieve product rather than using a ladder. Jumping down off the racking, the ring on his finger got caught.

8. *Fall to below (FB)*. When an employee is working at a height, such as on a mezzanine or scissors lift, there is a danger of falling. Walking down the steps can result in a fall. This always involve falls to a lower level.

9. Fall—same level (FS). An employee can trip on a shoe lace, or slip on ice, hydraulic fluid, oil, brake fluid, or any other chemical. All examples involve falls at the same level that the employee is working.

10. *Strain/overexertion (SO)*. This is a common type of injury producer in a warehouse. The continuous lifting of parts places a wear and tear on workers. Lifting improperly from the floor can produce a strain or overexertion injury. When studying JHAs for ergonomic improvements, this injury-producing cause should be seriously evaluated. For example, an employee's complaint of sore wrists while working in the small-parts department was diagnosed as carpal-tunnel syndrome—a strain/overexertion injury.

11. *Exposure/Environmental (E)*. Many workers are harmed each year by chemicals in the workplace. A chemical such as carbon monoxide causes many visits to clinics and hospitals each year. There may be other jobs in the warehouse where the risk of exposure to chemicals exists. Even if the chemical is in a sealed container, it may be released by puncturing or dropping the container, the chemical is now free to do its damage. The purpose of the JHA would be to alert the employee to this risk and ensure the proper precautions are taken. A sample case would be an employee who complained of headache and an upset stomach after working in a trailer with his propane-powered fork lift running. He was diagnosed with carbon monoxide poisoning.

Once the supervisor understands how workers can be harmed by the above-mentioned eleven factors, he/she can properly evaluate a job. The worker assisting with the JHA may not recognize the hazards or may not consider the steps as hazardous. This is an opportune time for education. Both the supervisor and worker will come away from the JHA preparation much smarter than when they started. Knowing and understanding the eleven injury types is a real plus for injury prevention.

As the worker identifies the basic step in the left-hand column, the supervisor asks, "Can you hurt yourself doing that?" or "Do you think that is dangerous?" or "Have you ever been injured doing this job?" or "What can go wrong here?" Potential causes of injury are identified in the middle column of the JHA form.

The supervisor may wish to just walk the employee through the basic steps of the job and the injury hazards that are evident and then stop. This would satisfy the search for the eleven injury types. If he/she does not have the time to complete the JHA, the task can be completed at a later date. If possible, the entire JHA should be completed during the first meeting.

COMPLETING THE JHA

The column on the far right of the JHA will have more verbiage than the first two columns. Only three to five words should be used to describe the basic step in the far left column. The purpose of abbreviating this comment is to set the stage for the step itself. The basic step does not identify who, when, where, how, why. All of these questions are answered in the right-hand column. This is the place on the form where the specific details of how to do the job safely are explained.

Figure 17-5 shows the first line of a typical warehouse JHA. Note the short wording in the basic step, the identification of the hazards associated with the step, and the exact method to use to safely complete the step.

Figure 17-5. Job Hazard Analysis - Operating a Scissors Lift

BASIC STEPS	POTENTIAL INJURIES	RECOMMENDED SAFE JOB PROCEDURES
1. Inspect scissors lift	1. FB Worker could fall off unit while inspecting	1. Inspect all four tires and the lower portion of the lift. Climb ladder with both hands and inspect working area of the scissors lift. Fasten handrails in place; ensure the flashing lights and alarms are functional.

As Figure 17-5 demonstrates:

■ The job being analyzed is a typical one for a warehouse. In this case it is operating a scissors lift.

■ Step 1 instructs inspection prior to use. The basic step has only three works (be sure to always keep the basic step short on words).

■ The middle column describes the only hazard present while inspecting the scissors lift: The worker could fall off the unit if precautions are not taken to secure the handrailing.

Continuing with the JHA would further develop the complete analysis. Each step must be numbered and the same format followed as in the example. Refer again to the completed sample in Figure 17-3. To process more JHAs simply follow the illustrations.

TAKING THE PROGRAM FURTHER

Once the JHA program and process has begun there are program elements that must be carried through for further development.

■ A quota for completions should be established for each supervisor. Most programs request one completed JHA per quarter per supervisor.

■ Someone that is skilled in JHA development should review each completed JHA before making it a final and approved document. If a completed form needs significant corrective action, it should be sent back to the supervisor with written comments so future mistakes are not made.

■ Once reviewed and approved, completed JHAs should be posted, enclosed in plastic, near the work site if possible. Also, there should be a completed JHA binder for each department.

■ A numbering system should accompany each completed JHA as well as those copies on a master list. The master list serves as a ready reference to use when looking for specific JHAs.

■ New employees should be shown completed JHAs and someone from management or the safety committee can walk them through the correct procedures. Many injuries occur to new employees. JHA is an excellent preventive training tool.

- JHA photobooks or a JHA video can be developed by using an approved JHA and allowing the employees involved to be a part of the job instructions. Double training takes place when workers go through the JHA step-by-step to demonstrate correct procedures for the camera.

- After several years each JHA should be reviewed for accuracy. Processes and procedures change along the way and the forms must be updated to reflect the changes, which often are minor. While reviewing any JHA, Figure 17-4 can be used to identify the need for changes in the document.

- If an injury occurs and a JHA has been completed for that particular job, it is important to review the JHA for potential error. If the JHA is free of error, it should be reviewed with the employee when appropriate. The separate injury investigation document should have sections showing the specific job and pertinent JHA information.

ECONOMIC CONSIDERATIONS FOR JHA

While a supervisor is observing an employee and completing a JHA he/she should be focusing on the entire job process. In addition to the potential injuries that could occur, this process can be used to improve the job in other ways—materials, tools and equipment used, methods, and personnel all may be considered. Can the job be improved?

Each supervisor should ask the following key questions regarding each job.

For Materials:

- Can a less costly material or process be substituted and still satisfy the job?

- Are there processes or materials that can be purchased at a better cost?

- Can material waste or time spent completing the job be reduced?

- Are materials or product being damaged in transit within the warehouse or to the warehouse?

- Are there excess parts or product at the work site?

- Is there a more efficient method to transfer product?

For Tools and Equipment:

- Can other tools or equipment be used that will do the job more safely and efficiently?

- Are hand tools and equipment ergonomically designed?

- Can a power tool be used in place of a manually operated tool?

- Are the tools or pieces of equipment in need of any repair?

For Personnel:

- Are there too few or too many workers completing the job?

- Are the most qualified workers assigned to do the job?

- Are employees spending idle time waiting for product to arrive or be removed from the workstation?

For Job Methods:

- Can a job step be eliminated by a change in job method?

- Can a particularly slow or difficult job step be modified?

- Should more preplanning go into the job prior to start?

- Can ergonomically designed equipment be used to substitute worker labor with machine labor?

- Are there any environmental conditions present at the work site? Can these hazards be reduced or eliminated?

SUMMARY

Job Hazard Analysis can be one of the most effective programs an organization implements. JHA can be used to address ergonomic issues that may be a part of a future ergonomics standard being developed by OSHA. JHA provides the opportunity to evaluate a task from beginning to end. JHA can provide a needed boost to a safety program when management believes that the "basics" aren't working.

Utilization of the proper JHA forms is very important. Once the supervisors' training has taken place and they are beginning to complete JHAs, someone with skills in this program must step in to make corrections. The learning curve will increase with the number of jobs being evaluated. Management must not settle for half-hearted attempts to complete JHA. After all, the document provides details on exactly how to safely complete a task. Taking the time to refine the details involving exactly how to do a job and how to be free of associated hazards is worth the effort.

The involvement of workers is essential; the JHA program will suffer if they are not involved. Once evaluated and approved, JHAs can be posted near specific workstations where new or experienced employees can be briefed on how to safely do the job. Despite the work involved in training, evaluation, interviewing, corrective action, and final copy, JHA is worth the investment of time and effort.

REFERENCES

Armco Steel Corporation. "Accident Prevention Fundamentals." *Job Safety Analysis*. Chapter 5. Middletown, OH, 1975.

Business & Legal Reports, Inc. "Job Hazard Analysis." Madison, CT. 1996, pp. 145-1:145-15.

DeReamer, R. "Job Hazard Analysis." Modern Safety and Health Technology. New York: John Wiley & Sons, 1980. pp. 160–73.

National Safety Council. *Job Safety Analysis, Instructor Manual*. Itasca, IL,1995.

—. "Safeguarding - Job Safety Analysis." *Accident Prevention Manual*. Itasca, IL, 1992, pp. 377–82.

—. *Job Safety Analysis - Identifying and Controlling Hazards*. Itasca, IL, 1994.

Swartz, George. "Using Job Hazard Analysis for Powered Equipment." *Forklift Safety*. Rockville, MD: Government Institutes. 1997. pp. 159–74

U.S. Department of Labor, OSHA. *Job Hazard Analysis, OSHA 3071*. 1988.

18

Warehouse Emergencies

An integral part of a safety program for any warehouse and adjacent community is a facility emergency plan. Most of the efforts that go into making the workplace safer enhance the emergency program. Focus and attention on housekeeping, fire prevention, medical care, control of flammables, signage, sprinkler testing, spill cleanup and the PPE program contain elements that do much to prevent emergency situations from occurring.

Despite these efforts toward a zero-risk environment, contingency plans must be formulated and communicated to all employees. Typical warehouse emergency programs include:

- Weather emergencies
- Fire emergencies

- Chemical spill emergencies
- Medical-related emergencies.

As the programs are being planned, a documented safety procedure must be developed. This is not a job for one person but for a committee or a group of individuals with special skills in emergency controls. When developed, the system must be tested, corrected, and tested again. The wrong time to consider emergency planning is during an emergency.

Among the key points to include in the planning process are the following.

- Request that the local fire department come into the warehouse for a safety tour. They will point out safeguards to include in the programs as well as offer reminders of observed weaknesses in the system. Many fire departments can offer professional advice that is invaluable. It's possible that a few employees in the warehouse may serve on the volunteer fire department and will bring this expertise to the planning process.

- The overall emergency plan should include alerting adjacent businesses and the possible sharing of resources. A serious fire could easily damage or destroy another structure nearby.

- Prepare a comprehensive program that is well documented, yet easy to read and understand. Allow for simple directions and guidelines. Each employee must be familiar with the program, and somehow be a participant in the planning and execution.

WRITTEN PROGRAM

The written program should include provisions for the following elements.

■ Emergency phone numbers for fire, police, ambulance, and hazardous waste spills are essential. They should also be posted by telephones, on the warehouse emergency maps, in facility phone books, and possibly on stickers placed inside hard hats.

■ If the telephone system should fail, plan for the use of cellular phones. Preprogrammed phone numbers of police, fire, etc., can easily be used. A periodic testing of the numbers is beneficial. Alerting responders in advance of the testing of calls will prevent any misunderstandings.

■ Install a tornado alert system if the facility is in a tornado-prone area. Receivers can be purchased and installed that will sound an alarm before local sirens in the community are sounded. Install the system in an area where it will be heard.

■ Be sure all evacuation doors and passageways are properly identified. Glow-in-the-dark signs can aid employees in darkened areas. Warehouse emergency lighting must be functional and periodically tested. In addition, doors must open outward so the area can be properly evacuated. Inward-opening doors can be a hindrance in an evacuation.

■ Have evacuation routes clearly marked on emergency maps. Employees must follow these routes during practice drills. Also, the program must provide alternative routes to be taken if the primary routes are not accessible. Assign to specific employees the responsibility of taking a head count once everyone has assembled at a preplanned area away from the building.

■ Kits for cleaning up spills should be installed throughout the facility for use in the event of a chemical spill. The absorbents should be selected for the chemicals being used or stored in that particular area. The kits must be readily available in all areas; access must not be blocked by product, debris, machinery, etc. Employees must be trained in the proper use of cleanup materials, the protective equipment they will wear, and the proper disposal techniques. Programmed inspections in the warehouse should include an evaluation of the cleanup kits.

■ Reduce the amount of potentially hazardous chemicals that are stored in the warehouse, if possible. If the quantity of chemicals cannot be reduced, move the chemical storage area to a location in which the exciting of the warehouse will not be impeded if there were a spill or fire.

• If an organization can replace a hazardous chemical with a less dangerous one, employees will be exposed to less danger during a workday or during any emergency situations.

• Be sure that the proper material safety data sheets (MSDSs) are readily available for information gathering if there is a chemical spill or incident. Having a detailed listing of all warehouse chemicals is required by OSHA. These chemical information sheets can be kept in files, binders, near the chemicals they represent, or in a computerized file. Employees must know where the sheets are kept and be allowed accessibility to them. If kept in a 3-ring binder, the sheets should be numerically tabbed to match the chemical listing.

■ A checklist should be developed identifying those elements in the program that must be reviewed on a regular basis.

■ The written plan must be shared with everyone involved in the facility. If a security force is on site, they must also know the plan and how to react in an emergency. If emergency vehicles are summoned, the security staff should know where to direct the vehicles. All of the doors should be identified to match the details on the facility emergency map. The maps should be large, color-coded if possible, posted throughout the facility, and updated as changes occur in the warehouse. Figure 18-1 illustrates a form that can be used for conducting an emergency meeting with employees.

■ If inhouse emergency medical care is provided, first aid and CPR training should be completed on an ongoing basis. Individuals should be provided with those skills needed to assist in limited medical care. Trained professionals should be summoned to assist if serious injuries occur. First aid kits, blankets, stretchers, and emergency oxygen should be readily available, in proper working order, in sufficient quantity, and of the proper quality. Periodic practice by members of the team administering first aid care is essential. Trained professionals should demonstrate proper health and emergency care techniques.

The use of emergency oxygen is an example of the need for specific training. A warehouse in Indiana developed a comprehensive emergency plan that included the use of emergency oxygen. There was a serious health-related incident involving one of the employees and the local emergency services were summoned. While waiting for the ambulance, emergency oxygen was properly administered to the employee. The ambulance was delayed by a train while en route to the warehouse. When the emergency team arrived, they praised the manager for his emergency care. In administering the oxygen, the life of the employee was saved.

■ If self-contained breathing respiratory equipment (SCBA) is required, extensive employee training and inspection of these devices must be a part of the program. The use of these devices is limited to individuals who have been trained in the proper use, care, and maintenance of the respirators. Medical evaluations must be provided for these workers to make sure they are capable of wearing the respirators. Training must be ongoing. The storage area of the respirators must be sanitary and properly identified.

■ Safe storage of potentially hazardous debris and work-related scrap should be a part of the provisions of the emergency plan, since the prevention of fire or other incidents is the first step in a safety program. To prevent spontaneous ignition, oily rags, especially those used with linseed oil, must be placed in containers with a tight-fitting lid. Paper that has been in contact with certain chemicals and metal shavings must also be stored in metal containers as a fire precaution.

■ Ready access to phone numbers for local clinics and hospitals is essential. In the written plan maps are needed that indicate primary and alternate routes to take to the local clinic or hospital.

■ Personal protective equipment such as safety glasses, goggles, gloves of all types, face shields, rubber aprons, boots, respirators, hard hats, steel toe boots, and hearing protection may be needed in emergency situations. Specific equipment must be readily available to complement the written emergency program.

Figure 18-1. Emergency Training for Employees

All employees should be instructed on how to handle and respond to various warehouse emergencies. This form is intended to assist you in this effort.

The following topics should be discussed:

☐   Emergency evacuation procedures for the entire warehouse.

☐   Specific job/duty assignments

☐   How to handle medical emergencies

☐   Use of fire extinguishers, identification of types of fires

☐   Weather emergencies

☐   How to handle chemical spills or chemical emergencies

☐   Other?

_____

Warehouse: _____   Meeting Date: _____

Employees Attending Meeting	Employee Signature
1.	
2.	
3.	
4.	
5.	
6.	
7.	
8.	
9.	
10.	

Name of Person Conducting Meeting: _____   Date: _____

■ Areas adjacent to the facility should receive proper housekeeping. Roadways should be in good repair; well marked and lighted. The potential for fire exists in dry grass or weeds, so the control and clearing of these hazards should be a part of the plan. In addition, the existence of snakes is possible in tall weeds. A plan to eliminae snakes or other harmful animals or insects should be developed.

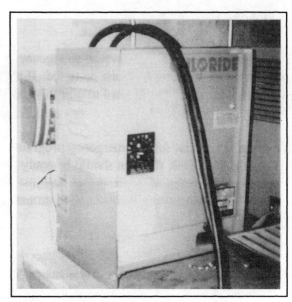

Figure 18-2. This fire alarm is inaccessible.

■ Fire prevention is addressed in Chapter 5 and this material should be helpful in developing the fire section of an emergency plan. Among the emergency program elements that must be in place are: How to call the fire department, directing emergency vehicles, actions of the fire control team, sprinkler valve control, sprinkler head replacement, and post-fire cleanup responsibilities. Figure 18-2 shows a warehouse fire alarm box blocked by a battery charger.

■ Contingency planning must include the potential loss of electrical power to the facility so that emergency power is available if needed for the operation of sprinkler pumps, fire doors, or any other needed emergency device.

■ The insurance carrier, often through the loss control representative, can provide assistance in the development of the emergency program. Also, professional fire organizations such as Factory Mutual or the National Fire Protection Association are very helpful.

■ For weather emergencies, the program should include plans for shutting down machines to facilitate early dismissal, if necessary. In the event of snow and ice storms, the facility must be prepared for the clearing of snow and ice from exits, sidewalks, doors, and driveways. For those employees working outdoors, consideration must be given to wind chill factors and the need for protective clothing. Provisions for the possibility of flooding must also be considered if the warehouse is located in a flood-vulnerable area.

■ Warehouses located in earthquake zones must have plans in place for an earthquake emergency. Local authorities and loss control representatives from insurance companies may have programs available to assist in this project. For internal hazards generated during an earthquake, corrections should be made as soon as details are known. Anchoring racking properly, securing storage of product, and any additional safeguards will be needed to protect workers. Engineers should be consulted in the design of racking as well as in the anchoring of racking to the building. Loss control representatives may have additional programs to add to the emergency plan.

SUMMARY

Each facility is required to have an emergency plan, which must be developed with input from many sources. Once on paper, it must be tested. If problems arise, correct them and test the program again. The program must be communicated to all of the employees. Employees should be an integral part of the program's development.

Preplanning is vital for an emergency program. All facets of the program must be considered, and when an emergency arises, the plan should be ready to be put into action. If a plan is developed, not communicated to employees, and not tested, it may just sit in a binder on a shelf. There must be a constant evaluation of the plan to ensure it will function properly.

REFERENCES

Davis, Larry, and Jeffrey Moore. "Warehouse Pre-Fire Planning and Fire Fighting Operations." *Fire Protection Handbook.* Seventeenth Edition. Quincy, MA: National Fire Protection Association. 1991. pp. 8-26 to 8-31.

Katzel, Jeanine. "Planning for Plant Emergencies." *Plant Engineering.* January 6, 1983, pp. 34–41.

National Safety Council. "Emergency Preparedness." *Accident Prevention Manual.* Itasca, IL., 1997, pp. 350–71.

OSHA 1910.38, Employee Emergency Plans and Fire Prevention Plans

U.S. Department of Labor, OSHA. "How to Prepare for Workplace Emergencies." *OSHA 3088, 1995 (Revised).* 16 pp.

19

Batteries and Fuels for Powered Equipment

Moving product through a warehouse cannot take place without some form of powered equipment. This chapter will address the various means that provide power for forklifts. There are several specific forms of vehicle power:

- Electric truck batteries

- LPG (liquified petroleum gas)

- Compressed natural gas

- Gasoline

- Diesel fuel.

The information provided here is not a substitute for the training and information that can be provided by the various manufacturers and suppliers of this equipment but should be used as a basic guide.

ELECTRIC TRUCK BATTERIES

The lead-acid battery is very basic to material movement and handling. A lead-acid motive power battery is a portable source of energy supplying direct electrical current (DC) to electric powered vehicles. A battery is a device that stores energy in a chemical form and releases that energy on demand, from the operator, in an electrical form to an external load—such as a motor. The battery releases power by the reaction of the electrolyte (sulfuric acid and water) with the active material of positive and negative plates (electrodes) within the battery.

There are basic guidelines intended to protect the operator and equipment when charging or handling batteries.

- Sulfuric acid within the battery can burn the skin and eyes and dissolve clothing. The following personal protective equipment must be worn to prevent injury.

- Rubber gloves
- Rubber apron
- Rubber boots with steel toes
- Safety glasses and face shield
- A nonconductive hard hat if falling hazards or overhead cranes/hoists are being used.

■ Emergency equipment such as an ABC or CO_2 class of extinguisher must be available at charging sites. In the event of a chemical spill, neutralizing agent and water must be available, and cleanup kits are necessary to handle the spilled neutralized electrolyte. Follow EPA guidelines for disposal. Bicarbonate of soda is one type of neutralizer. Contact the organization supplying batteries to ensure this method can be used.

Figure 19-1. Protective equipment is in place at this battery charging area.

■ Eye wash units should be permanently plumbed into the building to furnish at least 15 minutes of eye flushing with the water. Full-body deluge showers may also be necessary. Install and use per manufacturers' guidelines and provide the appropriate signage. Figure 19-1 illustrates the eye wash unit and other safety apparel at the charger area.

■ Battery-charging areas must be designated as no smoking. Hydrogen gas is produced by the batteries and is explosive. Avoiding any situation that creates sparking or an open flame is essential to safety. Use nonsparking tools, no open lights, and follow manufacturers' recommendations.

■ Ventilation must conform to safety codes. Ensure all charging is done in approved areas. All electrical installations must conform to National Fire Protection Association (NFPA) - 70, National Electric Code.

■ Each charger should be labeled to correspond with the matching electrical disconnect. In the event of fire or malfunction, electrical power can be quickly removed.

■ Only trained and authorized employees are permitted to handle batteries and other potential power sources for industrial powered trucks.

■ To avoid shock, do not touch both line leads together from the battery and lead terminals. Avoid wearing jewelry and always disconnect the battery from the lift truck before providing any service.

■ Before charging a battery:

- Be sure to wear all required personal protective equipment.

- Inspect the overall condition of the battery, the connectors, battery cables, and caps. The connector wire from this battery has a frayed cord. Figure 19-2 illustrates the exposed wires; a potential hazard.

- Remove vent caps (where provided) to check water levels. Low electrolyte level in a cell can cause the plates to oxidize and shorten the life of the cell and battery. Water levels should be above the separator protectors between the battery plates. Since batteries should only be filled at the end of the charging cycle, securely replace vent caps during the inspection cycle.

Figure 19-2. The electrical connection is frayed and should be replaced.

- Check the charger to be sure that it is in the "off" cycle. Contact maintenance if there is a problem.

- The racks that support the batteries must be made of materials that will not generate sparks. Placing chargers on racking is acceptable providing the legs of the chargers are on wood or rubber surfaces.

- Check that all walking and working surfaces, including wooden slats, mats, rubber mats, and floorboards, are clean, intact, and undamaged.

- Check ventilation to be sure that fans and other air circulation systems are functional and will not be an ignition source.

- The capacity of the charger must match that of the battery. If they do not match, permanent damage will occur to one or both of the devices.

■ Connecting the charger to the battery:

- Keyed connectors eliminate the possibility of hooking up a battery to the wrong vehicle or charger. Different plugs and connectors along with color keys can help to assure correct connections.

- Ensure the charger is in the "off" position before plugging it into the battery. At this time, plug the charger into the battery connector.

- There is a 5–10-second delay before the charger comes on. Be sure the charger has started.

- The battery charger will operate for at least 8 hours. Allow for an 8- hour cool down for the battery.

- Avoid over discharge of a battery.

- Avoid intermittent charging, which is using the battery for three hours or so followed by one or two hours of charging, etc.

- It is recommended that batteries be charged for 12 hours once a week to extend battery life.

■ After charging the battery:

- Confirm that the charger is turned off.

- With each hand, grasp the charger plug and battery plug and disconnect them; do not pull on the wires.

- Add water to cells; fill to the proper level. Use only distilled water or tap water that does not contain harmful chemicals. Overfilling is the most common error made when watering, because it can cause loss of capacity and corrosion of the battery tray. Corrosion, in turn, can cause extensive damage to the battery. Figure 19-3 illustrates spilled electrolyte caused by an overfill.

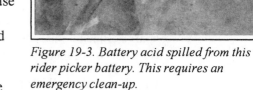

Figure 19-3. Battery acid spilled from this rider picker battery. This requires an emergency clean-up.

- Low electrolyte level in a cell can cause the plates to oxidize and shorten the life of the cell and battery.

- Always clean up spilled electrolyte or water from the top of the battery. Be sure to wear protective equipment. Be sure vent caps are tight before cleaning.

- Allow the battery to cool for 8 hours.

- Never place metal objects on top of the battery.

- Someone experienced in battery care should periodically check the battery for cell voltages, specific gravities, damage to the case, unseen corrosion, and battery tray damage.

- Keep charger leads off the floor. The leads should be attached to a recoil spring or small take-up reel to prevent damage. Figure 19-4 illustrates battery-charger wires that are attached to coil springs to keep them off the floor.

- Avoid charging the battery if water levels are below the visual point on the plate levels. Use a flashlight to check water levels if needed. Never use a match or open flame.

- A rag dipped in a mild solution of baking soda can be used to wipe off the top of the battery. Wear personal protective equipment as required and properly dispose of rags.

- There must be a periodic cleaning of the battery by removing it from the truck. All corrosion and dirt must be cleaned off the battery, truck walls, and battery tray. Check battery cables and connectors, and tighten or replace parts where necessary. Use a vacuum cleaner to clean out the interior of the charger after unplugging it. This cleaning procedure is recommended every six months. Only trained and authorized personnel can perform this job.

Figure 19-4. Springs keep these battery charging cables off of the floor.

- Only trained and authorized personnel are permitted to add acid to the battery.

- Additional information is available in the *National Fire Protection Association (NFPA) #505, Powered Industrial Trucks*; and *NFPA 70. National Electric Code.*

- Batteries are very heavy and can easily weigh over 1,000 pounds. It is necessary to use a rack with rollers to prevent injury while pulling batteries out and putting new batteries into the forklift. Be sure to add the battery retainer clip where required to prevent battery shifting. Figure 19-5 illustrates the replacement of a battery retainer clip.

- For batteries that are placed and removed from forklifts by a hoist or crane, special care must be exercised by all employees. Ensure that nonconductive parts are used on the spreader block that is attached to the battery. When working below cranes or hoists, employees should be wearing hard hats. Figure 19-6 illustrates the use of a crane to handle batteries.

- A battery should not be discharged below 80 percent of a complete depth of discharge. When more than 80 percent discharge occurs, the life of the battery is shortened as well as the life of the truck's components.

Changing the battery

Employers are concerned with the amount of time it takes to remove a battery from a lift truck and exchange it with one that is fully charged. For multishift operations, changing batteries is a necessity. An automated system can change a battery in about two minutes. Manual changing may take two operators ten minutes to manhandle the battery. Over a period of time, the automated systems can easily pay for themselves.

Workers are frequently injured while changing batteries, since some models can weigh up to 4,000 pounds. Injuries occur to the hands, feet, and back as a result of manual handling.

Figure 19-5. Secure batteries properly before operating the machinery.

Some manufacturers have improved on the battery handling operation by designing machines to mechanically change batteries. Changers use typical vacuum, electromagnet, or manual chain and hook systems to pull batteries. The changers may be designed to allow lift truck dealers the opportunity to perform preventive maintenance on both lift trucks and changers at the same time.

It is advisable to allow the battery changer manufacturer the opportunity to be included in the design of a warehouse. Consideration must be given to the slope of the floor, plumbing, drains, and electrical supply. It's also important to consider the future growth of the battery room, and there is a need to design the system to state codes, city codes, and OSHA regulations. The efficiencies of costs and labor must be considered when planning improvements in the battery changing process. The employees must also be a part of the plan so that the operations are safely and ergonomically designed.

Figure 19-6. Safe battery handling with a hoist. (Courtesy of Clark Material Handling Company)

LIQUIFIED PETROLEUM GAS

Propane, also referred to as liquified petroleum gas (LPG), is a manmade, high- octane, colorless, odorless, tasteless, nontoxic, noncorrosive compound. It is produced from natural gas, light crude oil, butane, and oil refinery gases. During the chemical processing of LPG, the manufacturers add a chemical, ethyl mercaptan, which produces an odor.

There are approximately 800,000 internal combustion engines being used throughout industry. Approximately 80 percent of these engines are fueled by LPG.

As a fuel, propane is better than gasoline in several respects:

- LPG produces much lower exhaust emissions.

- LPG helps to reduce engine maintenance and repair costs.

- LPG offers faster coldstarting.

- LPG is nonpolluting if spilled.

- LPG provides lower cost of operation.

LPG must be stored, handled, and used properly, and specific safety precautions are needed.

- LPG is heavier than air and will seek low-lying areas. A cigarette thrown on the floor can ignite an LP gas pocket that might not have been detected by odor.

- LPG is easily ignitable with any flame, spark, or hot surface. The vapors are very dangerous. This fuel acts like a liquid and can soak into clothing and ignite.

- LPG is compressed under high pressure in the tank and can cause injuries if a leak occurs. It also has a temperature of -44°F in a liquid state. The low temperature will cause frostbite if skin comes into contact with the fuel or a frosted surface.

- Propane can be hazardous if not handled properly. In a newspaper article titled, "Propane Explosions Rock Business Park," fire officials in Aurora, Illinois reported on a series of explosions and fires from LPG cylinders. A worker was sorting propane cylinders when a leaking cylinder ignited while being removed from a lift truck. The worker escaped serious injury, but the explosion caused 10–20 other thirty-three pound cylinders to explode. The industrial park was partially evacuated and the fire was brought under control in 30 minutes.

GENERAL SAFETY GUIDELINES

- Workers must not be smoking or be near any open flames when handling tanks. Any area near the use or storage of LPG must be designated as a nonsmoking area. Post appropriate signs and properly instruct all employees.

- Wear protective clothing when handling propane tanks or parts. Gloves, preferably rubberized, and protection for the eyes and face are necessary.

- Propane tanks come in 20, 33½, and 43½-pound pressure tanks. Tanks are made of aluminum or steel; aluminum tanks are lighter to handle. A full tank can contain up to 200 pounds per square inch of pressure. The liquid changes to a vapor when used as a fuel.

- Injuries to the back or hands can occur when lifting and handling empty or full tanks. Use proper lifting techniques, and seek assistance if needed. Tanks should not be dragged or rolled; a two-wheel dolly is a good means of transporting them.

- It is recommended that *NFPA No. 58-95, Storage and Handling of Liquified Petroleum Gases*, be utilized to comply with OSHA regulations.

- A specific area must be designated for the storage and changing of LPG tanks. When storing the tanks, always store them in an upright position with all gauges on top whether empty or full. This area should be away from the flow of traffic and away from heat, sparks, and flames. Proper ventilation of the storage area is essential.

- Inspect tanks for damage or dents before use. To ensure safe tank design, they are manufactured to meet U.S. Department of Transportation (DOT) standards. Under these standards cylinders are certified for twelve years. After twelve years they must be recertified or retired. The date of manufacture and recertification requirements are stamped on each portable cylinder. The cylinders must be periodically inspected and the results recorded and kept on file for the life of the tank.

- When parking a truck at the end of a shift or overnight, turn the service valve to the "off" position. Do not park a truck near any areas that may generate sparks, open flames, or heat.

- When handling LPG always wear personal protective equipment; never touch ungloved hands or other bare skin on a fitting or a frosted area.

- Only trained and authorized employees are permitted to fill LPG tanks. Employees should be familiar with fire control techniques, and be trained in the safe handling of the containers being used as well as the filling equipment involved and the safe fuel-filling technique.

- Never fill a tank while it is on a lift truck.

- Any storage of tanks must comply with NFPA and OSHA codes.

- When a tank is ready for changing, and while wearing gloves, close the service valve and allow the engine to idle until all of the fuel is used. Then turn off the ignition/key.

- The flat "O"-ring seal at the end of the coupler between the tank hose and the truck hose must be in place and free of damage. The hose will leak if this ring is not in place.

- Lift tanks off the lift truck by first unclamping two holding clamps. To prevent back injury, operators must use proper lifting techniques, employing leg strength as well as the arms to lift off the old tank. Set it out of the way in an upright position. Lift the new tank with the arms and legs and set it on the tank holder. Keep the relief valve at the top; the hydrostatic relief valve must be pointing toward the rear of the truck and away from the operator. Place the tank in the pin provided at the base of the tank holder, which keep the tank in place. Lock the clamps in place. Figure 19-7 illustrates the unlocked holding straps on the forklift tank.

- While still wearing PPE, inspect hoses and place hoses together, ensuring that the "O" ring is in place. Hand-tighten the connection.

- Slowly turn on shut-off valve and check for leaks. If no leaks are present, slowly turn valve fully in counter-clockwise motion.

COMPRESSED NATURAL GAS (CNG)

CNG is supplied by an underground pipeline at low pressure but is compressed and transferred to the tank under high pressure. The manufacturer adds a foul-smelling odorant to this odorless gas so that leaks in the tanks or piping can be detected.

Figure 19-7. This gas tank is not properly secured.

The contents of a CNG tank require extreme caution. The gas is flammable and under extreme pressure. A no-smoking rule must be enforced for the protection of life and property.

Both CNG and LPG are excellent fork truck fuels. There is a difference between these two fuels. CNG remains at high pressure in the tank while LPG is at moderate pressure. CNG is lighter than air and will more readily dissipate. LPG, being heavier than air, will seek out lower levels and dissipate more slowly.

CNG costs 30 to 50 percent less than propane and up to 70 percent less than electricity. CNG burns cleaner, has a higher octane rating, and helps to reduce maintenance costs.

CNG is also credited with reductions in carbon monoxide emissions by 90 percent, as well as reductions in hydrocarbons and carbon dioxide by 50 and 30 percent respectively.

CNG does not require the employee to lift off an empty tank and replace it with a full tank. All of the refueling is provided from a fueling port that has been properly designed to codes for this purpose.

No-smoking restrictions, proper ventilation, and protection from heat, sparks, and flame must be a part of the system.

CNG tanks are made of steel plate ¼-inch thick with reinforced fiberglass. Approximately 670 cubic feet of fuel, or the equivalent of 6 gallons of gasoline, are in each tank. CNG tanks are mounted permanently in the lift truck.

CNG tanks have a manual shut-off valve to control the fuel flow from the tank. A relief valve is also on the tank that is both heat and pressure activated. The manual shut-off valve must be fully closed by hand at the end of each work shift. Never over-tighten this valve.

The fuel pressure gauge on the tank reads from 0 to 6,000 pounds per square inch (PSI). A full tank should register at 3,000 PSI on the gauge, the maximum working pressure. When the pressure drops below 500 PSI, the truck should be refueled. In the event the filling station malfunctions, a safety relief valve built into the line is designed to activate at 5,000 PSI.

An emergency shut-off valve is located on the lift truck near the tank to be used in the event of a fuel leak. The valve only requires a quarter turn to shut off the fuel in an emergency. If any worker smells natural gas in or around the engine area, there may be a leak in the CNG system. The quarter-turn valve should be turned to the "off" position and a trained and authorized mechanic should evaluate the truck.

When refueling a CNG lift truck, specific safety rules must be followed.

- Ensure that the refueling station is designed specifically for this purpose and all safeguards are in place.

- Properly park the lift truck with forks flat on the ground, parking brake set, key off, and controls in neutral.

- There must be a no-smoking rule as well as adherence to guidelines for no sparks, open flames, or heat when refueling. In the event of a fire, a dry-chemical fire extinguisher should be used. Figure 19-8 illustrates the need to know where the extinguisher is and how to use it.

- Any fuel leak must be corrected before putting the lift truck in service.

- Only trained and authorized employees are to refuel CNG. **Proper filling and emergency procedures must be adhered to.**

- Contact a supervisor for any questions or concerns with the filling process.

- Wear the required PPE such as gloves, glasses, hard hat, apron, or face shield.

- Only refuel in ventilated and approved areas.

- Before putting the lift truck back into service, check for leaks.

To start a CNG fueled fork lift, a few basic procedures are necessary.

- Ensure the parking brake is on and the gears are in neutral.

- Turn the tank valve slowly in a counter-clockwise motion to the full and open position. The tank gauge should read between 500 and 3,000 PSI, which is the system operating pressure.

Figure 19-8. Always know where the nearest fire extinguisher is. (Courtesy of the National Safety Council)

- Do not depress the accelerator pedal. Turn the ignition key to *start position* and when the engine starts, release the key to the *run position.*

At the end of the work shift, shutdown procedures are necessary for CNG:

- Park the truck in an approved location with forks flat on the floor, parking brake on, and controls in neutral.

- Check the fuel pressure gauge for capacity. Refueling may be necessary.

- While allowing the engine to run at a low-speed idle, turn the control valve to the "off" position. The engine will burn off the remaining fuel in the system. Turn the ignition key off.

There are some notable benefits when using a CNG fuel system:

- CNG may cost approximately 50 percent less than LPG or gasoline.

- CNG is less polluting than LPG or gasoline.

- CNG gives off less carbon monoxide in the workplace, up to 95 percent less carbon monoxide pollution than LPG.

- Refueling tends to be faster, and employees do not have to lift or carry heavy tanks.

- CNG is looked upon as a safer fuel during the refueling process because natural gas, unlike propane, is lighter than air and will dissipate into the air.

- Natural gas is more readily available than other fuels.

- CNG burns cleaner, thus creating lower maintenance costs.

GASOLINE AND DIESEL FUELS

Gasoline is a highly flammable fuel having a flash point of approximately -35°F. Handling, storage, and fueling of gasoline must be performed in accordance with NFPA and OSHA guidelines.

Guidelines for gasoline or diesel lift truck fuels include the following:

- Refueling stations must be located out-of-doors and designed specifically for the purpose of refueling. Distances from structures must be adhered to per OSHA guidelines.

- Employees should not be wearing jewelry and must not smoke near any operation involving flammable liquids or gases.

- Any lift truck with a fuel leak must not be started. The leak must first be repaired.

- Use a tagout procedure to alert others as to the problems with the lift truck.

- The wearing of approved personal protective equipment may be necessary when handling fuels.

Check with a supervisor for assistance.

- When parking the truck, lower forks flat on the floor, put on the parking brake, turn off the key, and put the gear in neutral.

- Know and understand the fire-fighting requirements should a fire occur. Dry- chemical extinguishers are best for a flammable-liquid fire. Carbon dioxide extinguishers can also be used. Do not use a water extinguisher on a flammable liquid fire.

- If it becomes necessary to fill a gasoline or diesel fuel lift truck with a portable container, only UL/FM (Underwriters Laboratory/Factory Mutual) cans may be used. The can must have the proper pouring spout to avoid fuel spillage.

- The cap on the lift truck's gas tank must be a cap approved by the manufacturer.

- When replacing parts on the lift truck, only those parts recommended by the manufacturer may be used.

- Never overfill a tank. Always wipe off spilled fuel. Do not get any fuel on clothing, as this can easily be ignited long after the wet fuel has dried.

- Diesel fuel has a flash point of approximately 160° F. and is classified as a combustible gas. However, the fuel is placed under pressure, which lowers the flash point to the flammable range, thus allowing the fuel to burn. Even though diesel fuel is much less flammable than gasoline, it does have the possibility of ignition.

- Be sure fuel containers are well marked and labeled.

- Both gasoline and diesel fuel produce carbon monoxide gas and can easily exceed OSHA guidelines for exposure. Gasoline and diesel lift trucks should only be operated out-of-doors. If the engine needs tuning, CO levels could be much higher.

A warehouse in Chicago had several battery powered lift trucks break down and a gasoline-powered lift truck from another warehouse was brought in on the back of the flatbed truck. By noon, nine employees became ill as a result of CO poisoning even though it was summer and the bay doors were open. Two of the nine employees missed several days of work because of their illnesses.

SUMMARY

Despite the type of fuel or power used on lift trucks, safety precautions must be in place. Each source of power has both positive and negative points. Battery-powered vehicles do not produce carbon monoxide but can expose employees to sulfuric acid, the danger of explosion, electricity from chargers, and back injuries from pulling or pushing batteries into place.

Gasoline, propane, and diesel fuel all produce carbon monoxide gases; gasoline is the most dangerous for CO problems. All of these internal combustion fuels can burn; gasoline and propane are also explosive.

Compressed natural gas produces less carbon monoxide, does not involve lifting portable tanks, and appears to be cost-efficient. Natural gas can burn and under certain conditions explode.

Employers must ensure that proper safety precautions are in place for all of the fuel and powered sources that would be used to power a lift truck. Manufacturers or their representatives must be consulted for safety guidelines in the design, construction, and everyday use of any fuel or battery. Consult the NFPA, FM, or OSHA codes for guidance. Personal protective equipment, fire-protection methods, and emergency plans must be in place to protect workers and property.

REFERENCES

Batteries Inc. *Battery Safety Information*. W. Sacramento, CA.

Clark Material Handling Company. *Operator Training Manual—Instructors Guide*. Lexington, KY. January 1997.

—. Video: *Safe Handling of IC Fuels*. 96-003. Lexington, KY, 1996.

Fernald, Donald. "Propane Gas: Handle With Care." *Plant Engineering*. April 1996, pp. 79–82.

KW Powersource, Inc. *Battery Service Manual*. Ooltewah, TN, March 1997, 52 pp.

Modern Materials Handling. "Improve Battery Handling Safety." February 1997, p. 42.

National LP Gas Association. *Safe Use of LP-Gas in Industrial Trucks*. 1980, 7 pp.

National Safety Council. "Inspection and Maintenance." *Accident Prevention Manual*. Itasca, IL, 1997, pp. 519–23.

Natural Gas Applications In Industry. "Natural Gas Forklifts Clear the Air." Fall 1994, pp. A–10, A11.

—. "Smart Company Makes Smart Move to CNG." Fall 1995, pp. A–11, A12.

Reynolds, Larry. "Preventing CO Exposure from Propane Forklifts." *Occupational Health and Safety*. September 1997, pp. 52–53.

Schneider, David. "Evaluating Propane-Powered Lift Trucks." *Plant Engineering*. July 10, 1995, pp. 66–68.

Schwind, Gene F. "Batteries and Chargers—Key to Lift Truck Maintenance." *Material Handling Engineering*. July 1996, pp. 57–58.

—. "LP-Gas Requires Common-Sense Training." *Material Handling Engineering*. June 1996, p. 18.

Simpson, Robert. "Plant-Built Battery-Changing System Simplifies Lift Truck Battery Maintenance." October 9, 1986, pp. 63–65.

Trunk, Christopher. "Changing Your Thinking About Battery Changers." *Material Handling Engineering*. July 1998, pp. 51–56.

20

Miscellaneous

There are many other safety and health issues that demand attention in warehouse operations. The intent of this chapter is to give a brief overview of six separate program elements that could require employee training, planned inspections, and OSHA compliance. Many of the program elements would require more details and information than is being presented here. To learn more about them individually, check with equipment distributors, safety consultants, or OSHA.

This chapter's programs are:

- Ladder safety

- Safety incentives and recognition

- Confined space safety

- Electrical safety

- Welding and cutting issues

- Job safety observation (JSO).

LADDER SAFETY

The use of ladders in warehouse operations is very common. Each year 238,000 injuries occur at work and at home as a result of falls from ladders. Fatalities also occur as a result of falls and electrocutions involving ladders. Employees must be trained in how to inspect and safely use the several types of ladders typically found in warehouses. Ladder safety should be incorporated into the overall safety programs.

Types of ladders

Fixed ladders have specific requirements based on OSHA regulation 1910.27. Among the basic recommendations in this standard are the following:

- If designing or erecting a fixed ladder, ensure that a competent person such as an engineer is involved.

- The distance between rungs shall be a uniform 12 inches throughout the ladder, the width of the ladder cleats must be 16 inches, and the distance between fixed objects behind the ladder to the rungs must be 7 inches.

- For fixed ladders greater than 20 feet, a cage must be installed to protect the climber. The length of the ladder cannot exceed 30 feet. The distance from the floor to the bottom of the cages must be between 7 and 8 feet. Cages may be needed on shorter ladders depending on the location and hazards.

- Where the fixed ladder provides access to an upper level, guardrails or handholds must extend 3 feet above the landing.

- Ladder climbing devices may be necessary for special applications. It is strongly recommended that a manufacturer of these safeguards be contacted for assistance.

Portable ladder injuries usually result from faulty care or improper use of ladders and not from manufacturers' deficiencies. Some of the most frequent causes of ladder incidents include: using a broken ladder, improper climbing procedure, improperly securing the ladder, and selecting the wrong ladder for the task at hand.

Figure 20-1. Check ladders for defects or damage before use. (Courtesy of the National Safety Council)

- All wood parts must be free of splinters and sharp edges. Portable wood ladders are identified in OSHA 1910.25.

- Only heavy-duty industrial ladders should be used.

- Read the manufacturer's labels and guidelines before use. Figure 20-1 identifies the need to check ladders before use.

- Always place the ladder in such a way that reaching or extending the body is not required.

- Always set ladders on secure, nonskid bases.

- Always look overhead and keep clear of electrical wires before moving a ladder.

- Always place ladders properly to avoid being struck by powered equipment or doors. Follow the 1 in 4 rule; that is, the base of the ladder should be one-fourth the ladder length from the vertical plane.

- Always secure the top of the ladder to prevent sliding or movement of any kind.

- Never splice ladders together to obtain a longer ladder.

- Only one person is to be on a ladder at a time.

- Do not remove the manufacturer's labels and warnings.

- Keep away from any electrical wires, open holes, and elevations.

- Defective ladders must be removed from service, tagged, and then repaired or discarded. Do not discard a defective ladder unless it has been rendered unusable.

- Use both hands when climbing up or down the ladder.

- Always lock spreader and latch devices.

- Seek assistance in handling or setting up a ladder.

- Keep both feet on the rungs and one hand on the side rail when climbing or working.

- Always face the ladder when climbing or descending.

Rolling metal ladders are common in warehouses and are used mostly for placing and retrieving product. Some basic guidelines on these ladders include the following.

- Read manufacturers' instructions for the care and use of ladders. Follow prescribed safety guidelines.

- When using a ladder, always be alert for the movement of powered equipment.

- Keep ladders stored in areas protected from lifttruck traffic. One of the most frequently damaged pieces of equipment in a warehouse is a rolling metal ladder.

- Inspect ladders before use; follow manufacturers' guidelines.

- Replace rubber stoppers as they wear to ensure a nonskid grip.

- Ladders must be tall enough to allow for completion of the job.

- Where ladders are equipped with handrailings, the rails are intended to provide security while climbing. Figure 20-2 illustrates a properly maintained rolling ladder with no damage or defects.

- Always place a ladder near the product to be picked; do not overextend or overreach. Always hold onto the ladder.

- Always face the ladder when climbing or descending.

- Keep away from electrical wires.

Figure 20-2. This rolling ladder is free of the usual damage caused by forklifts.

Falls from ladders are very common. Every worker should strive to secure a ladder or place it in such a way that it cannot be struck by powered equipment. Where possible, ladders should be secured at the top to prevent movement.

Additional safety rules:

- Always include ladders on departmental safety inspection forms.

- Never place a ladder on a movable object.

- Ensure that the soles of shoes are free of grease, mud, oil, or any other slippery substance prior to climbing.

- Keep manufacturer's tags and labels intact.

- Never climb a ladder beyond the third rung from the top of extension ladders or the second step on a stepladder.

- Never slide down a ladder.

- Only one person is to be on a ladder at a time.

- Do not climb the ladder from the back side.

- Never use a defective ladder.

- Never use a ladder as a scaffold or runway.

- Store ladders in a dry location, away from snow, rain, and ice.

- If materials must be handled while on a ladder, raise or lower tools, building materials, or maintenance-related items by using a rope.

- Carry tools in a proper holder or container.

- Always place the top of the ladder against a solid object.

- Use care in painting ladders; the paint could easily hide defects.

- Always ensure locking devices are engaged before climbing.

INCENTIVE AND RECOGNITION PROGRAMS

Many organizations include some form of an incentive program in their overall safety management system. Incentive programs can be effective if used properly, or the program could be detrimental to the goal of reducing injuries. Many safety professionals feel strongly about the following issues regarding incentive programs.

- Reward activities and conditions that promote a safer workplace.

- Design programs so that the reporting of all injuries is achieved.

- The workplace must be free of hazards if incentive programs are to succeed. The use of incentives must be a small item within the larger framework of a comprehensive safety and health program.

- A key objective to any safety and health program is to ensure that all injuries, property damage incidents, close calls, and product damage incidents are identified, reported, and corrected. Failure to report and correct any incident does not promote a safer workplace.

- Merchandise alone is not an effective or reliable way to motivate employees to work safely.

Some say that the key to reducing injuries in the workplace is not only to reward but to remind. A successful safety and health program includes constant reinforcement by all members of the management team. Employees must be a part of the program development if it is to succeed.

To achieve the objective of safety programs, the focus must be on the elimination of injuries. It is not practical to issue safety prizes because individuals have not had an injury. The development and utilization of a safety recognition or incentive program should reward employees for such things as:

- Constantly wearing their personal protective equipment

- Contributing to the reduction of incidents by completing incident reports

- Submitting safety suggestions

- Achieving 100 percent on forklift quizzes or other training quizzes

- Attending first aid, CPR, or fire training in the evenings or on weekends

- Enrolling in a safety class at a local college or university and successfully completing the course

- Serving on a safety committee

- Constantly checking and utilizing all safeguards on their machine

- Offering awards for the wearing of seat belts during a seat belt check. Those not wearing seat belts receive literature on the need for wearing them.

The items listed above are only suggestions of ways in which employees can be recognized for safe performance. When it comes to what to provide employees as recognition for their diligence in safety, the list is endless. Some of the safety incentive items include: key chains, mugs, garden tools, gift certificates, apparel, belt buckles, smoke alarms, fire extinguishers, safety shoes, cameras, gift certificates, carbon monoxide alarms, tickets to sporting events, theater tickets, and travel awards. It must be kept in mind that employees may look forward to a particular award in one facility and in another facility be turned off by the same award. Be sure to target the audience so that the safety program fits the culture of the facility.

Allow employees to participate in the program development. Create a budget and collectively structure the program. What are the goals of the program, and what will be the awards? Be sure to properly promote the program. Track its results on a regular basis and evaluate the progress against the goals that have been established.

Within the framework of any recognition or incentive program, positive feedback must be provided for safe behavior. The program must not manipulate the reporting of injuries so that injuries are hidden or covered up. The thrust of the program must be to reduce injuries. The reduction of injuries is not accomplished by games, gimmicks, or prizes but by eliminating those things that cause injuries to workers. The correct program must also include training in safety for both workers and management.

CONFINED SPACES

Each year, sees an average of 54 deaths and 10,949 injuries occurring in confined spaces. This section cannot be a substitute for the OSHA standard 1910.146 but will provide an overview of confined spaces.

A confined space program contained ten key elements.

1. Hazard identification

2. Hazard control

3. A permit system

4. Specialized equipment

5. Employee designation

6. Testing and monitoring

7. Outside contractors

8. Emergency response

9. Information and training

10. Program review.

Confined Space Hazards

A confined space is any area that is not designated for continuous human occupancy. It is large enough for an employee to bodily enter and perform work. It has limited means of access and egress and ventilation. A confined space can present the following hazards:

- Oxygen deficiency

- Electrical shock

- Falling from an elevation

- Radiation

- Fire or explosion

- Toxic gas or vapor

- Inundation from water

- Inundation from solid particles

- Sloped sides.

Experts agree that one must assume the worst when entering a confined space because it may contain an unseen or unexpected hazard. To determine if confined spaces exist at a facility, they must first be identified. OSHA requires the use of permits to gain access to identified spaces that could be hazardous. Permit-required confined spaces are those that:

- Contain, or have the potential to contain, a hazardous atmosphere

- Have an internal configuration such that an entrant could be trapped or asphyxiated by inwardly converging walls or by a floor that slopes downward and tapers to a smaller cross-section.

- Contain a material that has the potential to engulf an entrant

- Contain any other recognized serious safety or health hazard.

Types of Hazards in Confined Spaces

The following hazards may be associated with, or present in, a confined space that could be a part of the warehouse environment:

- Oxygen deficiency

- Combustible atmospheres

- Flammable atmospheres

- Explosive atmospheres

- Toxic gases or vapors

- Steam

- Falling or tripping hazards

- Moving parts

- Highway traffic

- Corrosive chemicals

- Biological hazards

- Electrical hazards

- Rodents, snakes, spiders

- Poor lighting

- Weather

- Wind

- Insecure footing.

Oxygen deficiency is one of the primary causes of approximately 50 percent of all confined-space fatalities. OSHA has established a safe oxygen range for confined spaces without the use of auxiliary air supplies. These levels are 19.5 to 23.5 percent. Special equipment, supported by training, is necessary to test the atmosphere of a confined space prior to entry.

Nitrogen, methane, or carbon dioxide can displace oxygen. The impact of oxygen deficiency in a confined space can be gradual or sudden, depending on the overall oxygen concentration, concentration of other gases in the space, or the activity levels of the workers. When the oxygen level rises above 23.5 percent, by volume, the atmosphere is considered to be oxygen enriched and prone to being unstable. An increase in the likelihood and severity of a flash fire or explosion could be the result of a higher oxygen level.

Note the physiological effects of oxygen:

Percent of Oxygen	Physiological Effect
19.5 – 16	Possible disorientation
16 – 12	Increased breathing rate; accelerated heartbeat; impaired attention, thinking, and coordination
14 – 10	Faulty judgment and poor muscular coordination; rapid fatigue caused by muscular exertion; intermittent respiration
10 – 6	Nausea, vomiting, inability to perform vigorous movement, or loss of the ability to move; unconsciousness followed by death
Below 6	Difficulty breathing; convulsive movements; death in minutes

Flammability Testing for Confined Spaces

There is also a need to test for combustible gases or vapors, which combined with oxygen and an ignition source can create a fire or explosion. Each combustible has its own lower explosive limit (LEL) and upper explosive limit (UEL). It is more likely that an explosion or fire will take place when the conditions are midway between the UEL and LEL.

Ignition sources can be static electricity, welding, sparking tools, or lighting. A trouble light could easily fall and the bulb could break; this condition could ignite flammable vapors or gases.

When using instruments, the oxygen levels can affect the accuracy of readings for flammability. Any reduction in the oxygen levels can result in lower flammability readings. LEL readings must be taken in the presence of acceptable oxygen readings to ensure the accuracy of the LEL readout. Typically, sensor readings are set at 10 percent oxygen, or higher.

Flammable gases can also be poisonous. A safety factor to keep in mind is that the LEL of flammable gases is much higher than the level at which the gas is toxic.

Procedures must be established that provide for sampling protocol along with the correct use and calibration of instruments. Each employee and supervisor involved in the confined-space program should be trained by a professional in all facets of instrumentation.

Employee Training

OSHA's 1910.146 requires that all employees who enter confined spaces received training and information on the following topics.

- Expected duties of the attendant, authorized attendant, and entry supervisor

- Contents, location, and availability of the organization's confined-space entry plan

- Contents, location, and availability of the department plan

- Atmospheric conditions

- Entry/exit access

- Engulfment conditions

- Specific-confined space entry procedures

- Operating and rescue procedures

- Confined spaces entry permit forms and authorization

- Test equipment procedure and calibration/maintenance schedule.

Training of employees provides them with the skills and knowledge they need regarding confined spaces and associated hazards. NIOSH produced a study involving the deaths of thirty-seven workers in seventeen states; the study identifies the lack of confined-space training and planning.

- 95 percent of confined-space entries were authorized by supervisors.

- 85 percent of confined-space events took place in the presence of the supervisor.

- 43 percent of confined-space victims were would-be rescuers.

- 31 percent of companies with fatalities had written confined-space entry procedures.

- 29 percent of the fatalities were supervisors.

- 15 percent of the fatalities had completed confined-space training.

- None of the fatalities followed written procedures.

- None of the confined spaces was evaluated or tested prior to entry.

- None of the confined spaces was ventilated.

- None of the companies experiencing fatalities had a rescue plan.

Key Points to Consider

Again, the information being presented here is very brief and will not bring an organization into compliance with the OSHA standard. To learn how to achieve compliance, contact OSHA, an insurance carrier, or a reputable consultant and/or distributor of instruments. There are many points to consider in developing a comprehensive plan. Ensure that trained professionals include all of the above-mentioned items in the plan.

ELECTRICAL SAFETY

Electrical safety violations are frequently a part of OSHA inspections. Violations of the electrical standard can be grouped into three key areas:

- General electrical requirements

- Ground fault circuit interrupters (GFCIs)

- Lighting for confined spaces and hazardous areas

A few typical electrical hazards and incorrect safety practices that may be present in a warehouse are:

- Lack of a comprehensive lockout/tagout program

- Lack of training for employees on the use of lockout/tagout

- Failure to unplug appliances or machines before working on them

- Failure to unplug a power tool when changing saw blades or drill bits

- Allowing untrained and unauthorized employees to work on equipment

- Failure to require the removal of jewelry or other conductive material while performing electrical work

- Failure to match the correct fuse or breaker to the correct circuit

- Failure to inspect the entire length of an extension cord before using it

- Failure to correct cord plugs that have had the ground prong removed

- Allowing frayed cords or open wires on machines, appliances, or tools

- Allowing powered equipment to run over unprotected electrical cords

- Failure to remove defective equipment from service

- Failure to install explosion-proof wiring and devices in flammable liquid storage areas

- Allowing circuit breaker boxes and electrical disconnects to be blocked by equipment or product

- Failure to use ground fault circuit interrupters where needed

- Failure to properly train employees in the correct use of fire extinguishers in electrical fires and the hazards associated with electricity

- Improperly identifying individual switches in a circuit breaker box

- Failure to enforce housekeeping practices

- Failure to supply or inspect double insulated tools

- Failure to utilize the National Electric Code.

Electrical Failures

A major insurance company conducted a series of electrical inspections and found that 75 percent of all electrical failures are caused by a lack of preventive maintenance. Connections could be dirty or loose, moisture could be a problem, defective or inadequate insulation or short circuiting could be an issue. These conditions could easily cause a buildup of heat, which could melt equipment and potentially cause arcing that could ultimately result in a breakdown or fire.

Electrical systems failures are second only to heating and cooling failures as the most common equipment breakdown. More than 90 percent of failures occur in standard commercial business. Poorly maintained equipment could cause a major business interruption. The cost of prevention is small as compared to the costs of electrical failure.

Electrical Injuries

Electrical shock is blamed for approximately 1,200 deaths each year. Contact with electrical current killed 347 workers in 1995, the most recent statistics available. Electrical current can damage the heart, digestive organs, bones, cartilage, muscles, and eyes.

Electrical trauma injuries are compared to slowly ticking time bombs. When a worker receives an electrical shock, damage to the nerves and muscles continues to progress long after the initial contact with the electrical source. According to the Electrical Power Research Institute (EPRI), approximately 85 percent of workers hospitalized following contact with high voltage become permanently disabled. Even though the initial injuries appear to be relatively minor, they continue to progress.

Sometimes the electrical shock impact on the body is known immediately. As an example, heart attacks are a relatively common occurrence following electrical shock. However, some injuries related to the trauma, such as cataracts, do not show up for weeks, months, or even years later.

Amputation of limbs; fingers, hands, and arms is not uncommon for the victims of high-voltage injuries. Estimates for amputation of at least one limb resulting from high- voltage injuries range from 32 to 72 percent. In recent years these numbers have come down as a result of improved reconstructive surgery.

Electrical injuries are divided into low voltage—less than 1,000 volts, and high voltage—above 1,000 volts. Most occupational injuries occur at 7,200 volts, the last high-voltage line before the current is stepped down for household use.

Low-voltage shocks must be of concern even though they do not cause thermal burns and progressive deep-tissue injuries. Low-voltage shocks can be killers. The heart can easily be injured by low voltage in the 110–220 volt range with currents alternating at 60 cycles per second. Low–voltage shock can cause ventricular fibrillation, depending on the amount of current, the length of contact, and the cycle of the heart.

Employee Training

Without proper training, an employee might not be able to recognize a hazardous condition, or might create a hazardous condition that could lead to injury. Proper maintenance of all electrical equipment is an important part of the injury and incident prevention process. Routine maintenance programs are a must for any industrial operation. Anyone associated with electrical service and/or maintenance must be knowledgeable and authorized to perform the duties.

WELDING AND CUTTING

A warehouse may have a maintenance staff on hand to provide care and repair of the building and its equipment, which would include welding and cutting. If the warehouse has no provisions for this service, a local welding or cutting provider would be contacted to do the work. There are inherent hazards in both welding and cutting processes, including fires. Additional hazards could affect the workers and property. This section will highlight some of the program elements to consider when performing welding or cutting or having this service provided by an outside contractor.

Toxic Gases and Fumes

Both welding and cutting involve hot temperatures and molten metals. In the welding process metals are melted and are bonded together as they cool. During the cutting process, a torch fueled by oxygen and acetylene is used to cut away metals to provide separation of components. Key elements to consider in both of these processes are:

- Personal protective equipment for workers

- Evacuation and ventilation of any fumes or gases

- Precautions to prevent fire and explosion

- Employees authorized and trained to perform this work

- Coordination between workers and contractors

- Compliance with OSHA standards 1910.252-255.

Toxic gases can easily be generated by welding or cutting on galvanized, painted, chromed, or coated surfaces. OSHA maintains permissible exposure limits (PELs) for a variety of gases, fumes, dusts, vapors, and mists.

Toxic gases create inhalation exposures as they are generated during welding and could produce one or more of the following effects:

- Inflammation of the lungs (chemical pneumonitis)

- Pulmonary edema (swelling and accumulation of fluids)

- Emphysema (loss of elasticity of the lungs; only a small percentage of emphysema cases are caused by occupational exposure)

- Chronic bronchitis

- Asphyxiation.

Primary pulmonary gases that can impair or injure the lungs and pulmonary system of workers when inhaled in hazardous amounts are:

- Ozone, created by electrical arcs

- Oxides of nitrogen, very irritating to the eyes and mucous membranes

- Phosgene, produced when metals have been cleaned with chlorinated hydrocarbons or the welding is taking place near chlorinated solvents

- Phosphine, created from metals that have been coated with a phosphate rust-proofing.

Nonpulmonary gases are also generated during welding; they are carbon monoxide and carbon dioxide.

Particulate matter can be generated from welding and deposited in the lungs of the worker. Proper ventilation is necessary to keep exposure levels as low as possible. A few of the metals that generate particulate matter are aluminum, iron oxide, and tin.

Other metals that can be classified as pulmonary irritants or toxic inhalants are: beryllium, cadmium, chromium, copper, fluoride, lead, manganese, magnesium, mercury, molybdenum, nickel, titanium, vanadium, and zinc.

Precautions must be taken to prevent inhalation of any harmful by-products of welding. If possible, substitute the metal being welded with a less harmful metal. If welding on painted surfaces, first remove the paint. Provide material safety data sheets for each metal so action can be taken to keep exposures below OSHA PELs. Workers must be protected with proper welding masks/hoods, hard hats, safety glasses, leather gloves, sleeves or jackets, and the proper shade of lens in their welding masks. The use of a respirator may be considered, but the correct local ventilation along with any substitution of metals or welding wire/rods being used, will help to reduce exposures.

General Safety Guidelines

There are additional safety guidelines to follow if welding takes place in the warehouse or somewhere on the property.

- Welding can create fire hazards. The proper fire-protection equipment must be available for use. Anyone working on a roof should have several fire extinguishers nearby for use.

- Remove combustibles, flammable liquids, and compressed gas cylinders to a distance at least 35 feet away from any welding processes.

- Place welding curtains or screens around the welding area to protect the sight of workers in that area.

- A fire watch should be kept in place for at least 30 minutes after welding has stopped.

- Never weld on a container that may have held any flammable or combustible liquids, powders, paints, or other chemicals.

- Never weld on a pressure vessel unless authorized and trained to do so.

- Utilize material safety data sheets (MSDS's) for the welding rods, wire and metals on all of the welding projects.

- Provide the proper amount of ventilation. Take advantage of wind currents, doors, windows, and fans to aid in removing gases and particulates. Local ventilation, however, is the best method of capture for fumes and gases.

- Substitute a less hazardous material for one that is classified as harmful.

- Utilize lockout/tagout procedures on equipment if necessary.

- Only authorized and trained personnel are to be used for welding operations. Authorization to weld should be provided by management to the worker or contractor.

- A member of management should oversee any welding operations to ensure proper safeguards are being taken to protect workers and property.

- Ensure that any welding operations do not cause activation or impairment of sprinkler systems.

- Do not weld in any atmosphere that contains gases, flammables, vapors, liquids, or dusts.

- OSHA guidelines must be followed if any welding takes place in a confined space.

- Welding cables, wires, and cords must be kept clear of walkways and other traffic areas.

- If electrodes are used in the welding process, the electrode is to be removed from the handle grip during lunch and at the end of the work shift.

- Keep all of the equipment in good repair and follow manufacturers' guidelines. Ensure there are no bare wires and that the welding cabinet is properly closed.

- Never weld on any item or structure if it has not been properly secured from movement.

- Properly ground the piece of material used in the welding process. Do not weld on a crane hook or on any materials suspended from the crane.

- Do not weld on any pipeline, vessel, or container without the proper authorization. All safeguards must be taken to ensure no harmful elements are in the pipes or containers.

- Employees must be protected from falling to a lower level, if welding in an area that is not protected by barriers, handrailing or other safeguards.

- Follow correct lifting procedure to prevent back injuries.

- Follow safe housekeeping rules.

- Never remove covers and guards from welding equipment without first bringing the machine to a zero-energy state.

Torch-Cutting Operations

Using a cutting torch in a warehouse can also generate sparks, heat, fire, fumes, gases, and exposures harmful to the lungs, eyes, skin, and body. There are specific guidelines for the use of cutting torches that could be applied directly to warehouse operations.

- Wear all prescribed PPE, i.e., cutting goggles, leather gloves, longsleeve cotton shirt or leather sleeves on jacket. There may be additional PPE required in the warehouse such as hard hats and steel toe boots.

- Follow manufacturers' recommendations for use of the torches and supporting equipment.

- Heed fire safety when torches are being used. Move combustibles and flammables at least 35 feet from the torch activity.

- Keep CO_2 or ABC multipurpose fire extinguishers available for use in an emergency. Keep a fire watch in place for at least 30 minutes after torch work is completed.

- Never use a cutting torch on any drum, cylinder, pipe, keg, vessel, or container that has held or is holding chemicals, gas, flammable liquids, powders, dusts, or any other chemical.

- Provide proper ventilation while using a cutting torch. Avoid breathing in gases or fumes from the cutting process.

- All compressed-gas cylinders must be properly marked. A material safety data sheet is necessary for each chemical and gas.

- Keep cylinders in a secured upright position away from heat, sparks, and flames. The storage area within the building must be well ventilated.

- Keep oxygen and acetylene cylinders separated by at least 20 feet or use a noncombustible barrier at least 5 feet high with a fire-resistance rating of at least one-half hour while in storage.

- Cylinder caps, gauges, fittings, hoses, connections, and valves must be kept free from oily or greasy substances. Never use oily hands or gloves to handle parts or cylinders.

- Never lift a cylinder by using the valve protector cap. Never roll or drag cylinders. A wheeled cart with a cylinder-supporting chain must be used to transport the cylinders.

- Valves must be closed on cylinders before moving them—after work is completed or when the cylinder is empty.

- Cylinders must be kept far enough away from sparks and heat to prevent fire or explosion.

- Cylinders must not be used as rollers.

- Cylinders must not be placed where they cannot make contact with an electrical circuit.

- Never tamper with cylinders or attempt to mix gases.

- Always store and use cylinders while they are in an upright position.

Since a fire created by any welding and cutting operation could be devastating to a warehouse, strict adherence to safety practices is essential. Only trained and authorized individuals shall be allowed to weld or cut with a torch. Because the risk of fire is so great, management must be a part of the planning and execution of welding and cutting projects.

This section on welding and cutting is intended to serve as a reminder of the dangers posed by various sources of fire. The section is not a substitute for the OSHA regulations or those guidelines offered by the manufacturers and suppliers of welding and cutting equipment. The regulations guiding these activities are very broad and require special training, equipment, and preparation to properly comply.

Hot Work Permits

To fully protect a warehouse from any fire generated from welding or cutting, a hot work permit system is needed. Hot work permits require that authorization be secured before equipment capable of igniting combustible materials is used outside of their normal areas. Since warehouses can contain a variety of combustible and flammable products, extreme care must be exercised when allowing welding or cutting to take place. A factory that utilizes welding and cutting as part of the normal course of work has established a work environment that includes fire safety provisions. Warehouses are another matter; one of the last things that anyone wants to see in a warehouse is an open flame from a cutting torch or the sparks and molten metals from welding. Because of this potential high-risk situation, special precautions must be taken for property protection as well as employee safety.

Welding and cutting operations may be performed by internal maintenance personnel or by outside contractors. Full cooperation and coordination with those performing welding and cutting must be achieved. The following phases of a hot work permit program are necessary.

1. Notify the insurance carrier prior to hot work processes and ask them for assistance and guidance to protect lives and property.

2. Perform an inspection of the area where the work will take place. Determine what hazards will be encountered during the work.

3. If available, use a job hazard analysis to determine the various steps and safeguards involved in the work.

4. Properly mark off all working areas. Remove all fire hazards from the working area and an additional 35 feet beyond if possible.

5. No work is to begin until all safeguards are in place. For outside contractors, this point will have to be stressed during the bid process. If a contractor does not wish to take the proper safeguards and does not have a strong concern for safety, he/she should not be hired. VPP sites are required to inquire about contractors' safety programs and to evaluate them for quality and thoroughness. Just because a job bid is the lowest and a firm is hired to do the job, this does not ensure that they will do the job correctly. An entire warehouse can burn down as a result of poor contractor safety practices.

6. Work permit tags must be signed by both the company representative and the employee or the contractor. All employees are to be notified of this work and the need to be more observant of nonemployees working in the area and the hazards associated with hot work.

7. A trained observer should oversee the work to ensure it is being done correctly and safely.

8. Fire-fighting equipment must be readily available.

9. Prepare for the unexpected. Someone could easily set off a sprinkler head or damage one. Quick response would be needed to prevent water damage.

10. Signed permit cards are to be kept with the worker performing the work.

11. If an extinguisher is used, a standby unit must be readily available for use. Empties must be returned for recharging.

12. Completed tags are to be returned at the end of the day or shift. Cards are to be properly filed. New cards are to be issued following the correct procedures at the start of the next workday or work shift.

13. An observer should stand watch for 30–60 minutes after work is completed to ensure a smoldering fire isn't present.

14. Ensure that the sprinkler system is fully intact and operational during all phases of the work.

Hot work permits require that authorization be secured before equipment capable of igniting combustible or flammable materials is used outside their normal work areas. Using a cutting torch or welding machine is not a normal warehouse operation. Placing the requirements for the hot work permit system in writing is a first step in the development of the program. Ensure that someone knowledgeable in this work evaluates and approves the written procedure.

JOB SAFETY OBSERVATION

One of the best ways to learn more about job process is through deliberate observation. Rather than just casually looking at a machine operating or a worker performing a task, the job should have a specific focus for management. In order to reduce workplace injuries, workers must abide by safe work rules. One good way of ensuring that safe work rules are being followed is to observe workers performing tasks.

Job safety observation (JSO) is a program that asks a supervisor to spend several minutes during the course of the day observing workers in his/her department. The time to openly observe the worker is when a specific task or function is being performed. As an example, many workers are killed or injured at docks each year. If a lift truck operator was unloading a trailer, the supervisor should not only observe the movement of the lift truck, but also whether the wheels of the trailer are chocked, the dockplate is properly in place, and the operator is wearing a seat belt if on a counterbalanced lift truck.

There is more to JSO than just watching someone work. Forklift operators have to know many safety rules and guidelines. In the example cited above, observation of the worker includes a focus on the adherence to forklift safety rules. If the worker is performing the job in an unsafe manner, the supervisor must advise the worker on the safe way to do the job. If conditions in the work area need correcting, the supervisor must also work toward the elimination of any unsafe conditions. Driving into an unchocked trailer is an unsafe condition as well as unsafe behavior. It is the duty of the lift truck operator to ensure that trailers are chocked.

JSO Benefits

Benefits of the JSO program are many.

- Observations, which are planned, allow the supervisor to interface with the worker on a safety issue.

- Workers will come to recognize the observation process and will safely perform their jobs while being observed. This is a plus, since they can demonstrate that they know how to work safely. In repetition there is learning; as a result of repeated observations, job safety performance should improve.

- Jobs that have produced injuries in the past will be observed, to ensure the conditions that produced the injuries have been corrected.

- Workplace conditions are improved because the workers' total environment is being evaluated. JSO provides corrective action as a part of its process. Monthly safety inspections are intended to identify unsafe conditions; JSO is an added program to improve conditions.

- The supervisors' interface with the employees each month while they are performing various jobs helps to educate management about the job process, especially if the supervisor is new to the company or department.

- JSO is a way for minor workplace issues to be resolved before they become bigger issues. As an example, if a supervisor is observing a lift truck operator perform different tasks of moving product, the condition of the forklift is as important as the safe work practices that are expected from the operator. Is the forklift leaking hydraulic fluid? Is there a problem with the brakes? JSO is intended to focus on the entire job, not just the operator. If the brakes are not functioning properly and the operator has repeatedly asked that they be checked, lack of management action could result in a grievance being filed or OSHA being contacted.

- If product is being damaged or the building is showing signs of forklift abuse, JSO can help correct these problems. Observing how product is handled and stored will determine if safe work procedures are being followed.

- Management's quick response to correcting unsafe conditions and improving the workers' environment will benefit morale as well as communications with workers.

- JSO can help to uncover problems in the work processes. Perhaps an aisle needs enlarging, barriers may need to be placed in front of walkways, improved techniques for stacking of product may be realized; many of these changes are made because someone has taken time to observe the work process for efficiencies as well as safety.

If the unsafe conditions and the unsafe worker behaviors are not corrected, injuries will continue. If the work was performed in an unsafe manner, the employee must be reinstructed. This can include friendly persuasion, a firm warning, or possibly disciplinary action. When reinstructing employees, the Golden Rule should be followed: Do unto others as you would have them do unto you. Note the difference between these two statements made during JSOs.

1. John, I saw you lift that carton wrong; you should know better than that.

2. John, I noticed that when you lifted that carton you kept your legs straight and you bent over at the waist. When you lift that way, John, you're putting a strain on your lower back and almost none on your legs.

How JSO Works

JSO is a method of selecting a particular employee in a department who is performing a particular phase of a task and observing him/her work. What is the employee doing and what are the conditions he/she is working in? The supervisor alerts the employee that a job safety observation is taking place and that the employee should report any questionable condition in the work area. The employee is expected to perform the job safely.

The supervisor records the observation on a specific form. Observations are expected to take 5 to 10 minutes. The form in Figure 20-3 is designed for simplicity. The far right column asks that the employee initial the form to verify that an observation took place. Observations are not intended to be hidden in any manner. The supervisor is expected to alert the employee of this activity. The initialing of the form is also enables the worker to be sure that the reported unsafe conditions are placed on the form.

Figure 20–3. Job Safety Observation Monthly Activity Report

Supervisor: _____ **Location:** _____ **Month of** _____, 19 ____.

Employee Name	Job Being Performed	Was Job Performed Safely?	Identify Unsafe Conditions	Was Employee Reinstructed?	Was A Verbal Warning Issued?	Were Unsafe Conditions Corrected?	Date of Observation	Comments	Employee Initials*

*If employee does not wish to initial form, write D.N.I. (Did Not Initial)

Make Additional Comments on The Back of This Form

Depending on the size of a department or warehouse, a single form may serve for a month of JSOs. Conditions that were highlighted on the form during the monthly JSO process are to be corrected. Employees who performed jobs in an unsafe manner must be told how to perform the jobs safely, without being criticized. Never allow an employee to commit an unsafe act if it is anticipated. Offer words of caution, and warnings that performing a job in a certain way can cause injury.

Follow-up JSOs may be needed for new employees or for those employees that have a history of taking shortcuts. On the whole, one planned observation per employee each month should be sufficient. JSOs are not to be considered safety meetings; this program is an addition to the overall safety program.

Key Points of JSO

- JSO focuses on a phase of a job. A job can be defined as a task or phase of a worker's overall job description. The observation is intended to evaluate a short segment of time in the job's process—not the entire job.

- If a phase of the job is potentially more dangerous than other segments of the job, focus on the dangerous segments to assure safe performance.

- Properly complete the form during each JSO. JSOs are intended to be spread out over the course of a month, not all of them completed in one day. Supervisors often fall behind on their safety-related duties and play catch-up by rushing through fifteen or twenty JSOs in a single day. This program is not intended to function this way—spread out the observations.

- Keep completed forms on file so that reference can be made to them when needed. If an injury has occurred in a particular department and a JSO was recently completed there, were any violations noted on the JSO form?

- Over a period of time, employees will come to recognize the moment a supervisor is about to complete a JSO. Employees must always be alerted to programmed JSOs. An employee who is not observing safe practices should receive either a follow-up programmed JSO or an informal JSO by the supervisor. Informal JSOs just require observation of a specific task, without using a form to document the results.

- Be sure the following JSO elements are discussed with the employee:

  - Explain what was observed.

  - Use show and tell techniques if possible.

  - Be sensitive to employee comments regarding the job and the conditions of the work area or equipment.

  - Explain a safer alternative.

  - Attempt to convince the employee to follow safe work procedures.

SUMMARY

The 1980s and 90s has been the era of behavioral safety. Many articles, books, training programs, and seminars have used the theme of behavioral change to improve safety performance. Many of the programs discuss the need for incentives or awards. There is an enormous amount of information on this subject. This chapter just touches on some of the key issues involved in employee recognition and incentive programs.

Additional program elements such as ladders, confined spaces, electrical safety, and welding and cutting are also given basic overviews. The technical information needed for full compliance could be much broader than what is presented here. If anything, readers are reminded that these issues must be factored into the safety program for the entire warehouse. There are many additional sources of information to learn more about these subjects. OSHA has very specific guidelines on confined spaces and a full program must be instituted if a warehouse has even a single confined space. The NFPA can provide additional information on electrical safety with its National Electrical Code, and the guidelines for fire safety in welding and cutting. OSHA also has information on fire safety, welding and cutting, ladders, and electrical safety.

REFERENCES

Bailey, Nancy Coe. "Tight Spaces." *Utility Fleet Management*. September 1997, pp. 12–16.

Barr, Jim. "Awards? Incentives? Defining the Difference." *Occupational Health and Safety*. July 1998, pp. 35–37.

—. "Cultivating Culture." *Occupational Health and Safety*. May 1998, p. 32.

Barry, Thomas, *et al.* "Fire Loss Prevention and Control Management - Hot Work Permit Program." *NFPA Fire Protection Handbook*. Quincy, MA, 1991, pp. 9–21/22.

Bayer, Stephen, and Alfred W. Keiss. "What You Can't See Can Hurt You: How to Reduce Risk in Confined Spaces." Plant Engineering. February 1998, pp. 64–68.

Bell, Dave. "Safety Practices for Oxy-Fuel Cutting and Welding." *Industrial Hygiene News*. September 1997, pp. 30–31.

Benefield, Jimmy. "Work Team CPR." *Occupational Health and Safety*. May 1998, p. 34.

Bureau of Business Practice Newsletter. Compliance Advice on Confined Spaces to the Rescue." Number 2289, September 10, 1997.

Campbell, Chris. "All About Confined Spaces." *Professional Safety*. February 1990, pp. 33–35.

Finnegan, Lisa. "Will OSHA Regulate Incentive Programs?" *Occupational Hazards*. June 1998, pp. 63–64.

Genesore, Dr. Leon. "Health Hazards of Welding." *Accident Prevention*. July/August 1997, pp. 28–30.

Goldberg, Allan T. "Taming the Cost of Accidents. *Occupational Health and Safety*. June 1998, pp. 66–70.

Hazard Information Newsletter. "Ladders." Vol. Three, Issue Three, June 1998.

Johnson, Linda F. "Zapping Electrical Hazards." *Occupational Health and Safety*. June 1998, p. 35.

Keck, Larry K. "Cutting and Welding—Putting Safety First." *Engineers Digest*. September 1992, pp. 10–11.

Kemnebeck, M.E. "Eight Points to Ponder for Safe Welding and Cutting." *Welding Journal*. September 1988, pp. 67–69.

Krause, Thomas R., and Stanley J. Hodson. "A Close Look at Safety Incentives." *Occupational Health and Safety*. May 1998, pp. 28–36.

Lemke, Peter T. "Compressed Gas Cylinders: Safe Transport, Storage and Handling." *Occupational Hazards*. February 1998, pp. 43–45.

Ligos, Melinda. "Incentives for the Ages."*Successful Meetings*. May 1998, pp. 49–54.

Madland, John. "Effective Confined Space Training." Occupational Health and Safety. February 1998, pp.32–37.

Manz, A. F. "Welding and Cutting." *Fire Protection Handbook*. Quincy, MA: National Fire Protection Association, 1991. pp. 2-159 to 2-165.

National Safety Council. "Confined Spaces." Accident Prevention Manual. Itasca, IL, 1997, pp. 21–22.

—. "Fire Prevention Activities: Hot-Work Permits." *Accident Prevention Manual*. Itasca, IL, 1997, p. 267.

—. "Ladders." *Accident Prevention Manual*. Itasca, IL., 1997, pp. 63–67.

—. "Welding and Cutting." *Accident Prevention Manual*. Itasca, IL, 1997, pp. 604–27.

The Orange County Register. "Heed the Advice Printed on Ladders Sides and Be Safe." Saturday, June 13, 1998, p. 4.

OSHA 1910.25 Portable Wood Ladders.

OSHA 1910.26 Portable Metal Ladders.

OSHA 1910.27 Fixed Ladders.

OSHA Subpart Q Welding, Cutting and Brazing 1910.252, 253, 254.

Peavey, Buck. "Building a Complete Incentive Program." *Occupational Health and Safety*. October 1997, pp. 72, 77–78.

Rekus, John F. "Many Confined Space Programs Are Not Effective: Is Yours?" *Occupational Hazards*. June 1998, pp. 47–52.

Smith, S. L. "Electrical Trauma: Unlocking the Secrets." *Occupational Hazards*. March 1998, pp. 41–42.

—. "The Pros and Cons of Safety Incentives." *Occupational Hazards*. November 1997, pp. 37–40.

—. "Using Recognition to Rev Up Safety." *Occupational Hazards*. June 1998, pp. 55–62.

Stearns, Patrick. "Electrical Safety Shouldn't Be An Accident." *Occupational Hazards*. January 1998, pp. 73–74.

Steinauer, Joan M. "Motivation 101." *Incentive*. June 1998, pp. 20–26.

Weinstein, Mindy. "Electric Slide." *Risk and Insurance*. February 1998, pp. 19–20.

Appendix A

OSHA's New Forklift Operator Training Standard

OSHA has revised its existing requirements for powered industrial truck operator training, 1910.178 (1), and has issued new requirements on December 1, 1998 to improve the training of those operators. The new requirements are intended to reduce the average of 101 annual fatalities caused by lift trucks by 10 percent. Injuries total 94,570 each year and are expected to decline by 9,422 as a result of the new requirements. The annualized cost of the program is approximately $16.9 million for all affected industries.

The new provisions will apply to the following industries:

- general industry
- construction
- shipyards
- marine terminals
- longshoring operations.

Agricultural operations will not be regulated by this program.

The effective date of the program is March 1, 1999. The table below identifies the timetables for operator training.

If the employee was hired:	The initial training and evaluation of that employee must be completed:
Before December 1, 1999	By December 1, 1999
After December 1, 1999	Before the employee is assigned to operate a powered industrial truck.

Within the standard, a powered industrial truck is defined as a mobile, power-driven vehicle used to carry, push, pull, lift, stack, and tier material.

The vehicles are commonly referred to as:

- high lift trucks
- counter balanced trucks
- cantilever trucks
- rider trucks
- forklift trucks
- high lift platform trucks
- low lift trucks

- low lift platform trucks
- straddle trucks
- reach rider trucks
- single side loader rider trucks
- high lift order picker rider trucks
- motorized hand/rider trucks
- counter balanced front/side loader lift trucks.

Vehicles used for earth moving or over road haulage are excluded from the scope of this consensus standard, and consequently from coverage by the OSHA standard. The use of a single characteristic to describe truck, such as "highlift" truck does not fully describe a single type of truck but rather defines a group of different trucks that have the same characteristic. A given powered industrial truck can only be accurately described by referring to all of its characteristics. For example, the common type truck used in a warehouse is a highlift counterbalanced, sit-down rider truck.

There are seven classes of powered industrial trucks:

- Class 1 — Electric motor, sit-down rider, counterbalanced trucks (solid and pneumatic tires)
- Class 2 — Electric motor narrow aisle trucks (solid tires)
- Class 3 — Electric motor hand trucks or hand/rider trucks (solid tires)
- Class 4 — Internal combustion engine trucks (solid tires)
- Class 5 — Internal combustion engine trucks (pneumatic tires)
- Class 6 — Electric and internal combustion engine tractors (solid and pneumatic tires)
- Class 7 — Rough terrain forklift trucks (pneumatic tires)

Each of the different types of powered industrial trucks has it own unique characteristics and some inherent hazards. To be most effective, operator training must address these unique characteristics of the type of vehicles the employee is being trained to operate.

It is not possible to identify all the hazards that are encountered in all industrial truck operations. Accordingly one cannot develop a single "general" operator training program that covers in detail all hazards for all powered industrial trucks and all workplaces.

Four major areas of concern need to be addressed in an effective powered industrial truck training program:

- The general hazards that apply to the question of all or most powered industrial trucks
- The hazards associated with the operation of particular types of trucks
- The hazards of workplaces generally
- The hazards of the particular workplace where the vehicle operates. The requirements that OSHA is promulgating are performance-oriented to permit employers to tailor a training program to the characteristics of their workplace and the particular types of powered industrial trucks being operated.

The training requirement in the revised standard reflects three approaches to training:

- Training is required in a specific topic unless it is not relevant to the types of vehicles or the employer's workplace
- The training requires that topics specific to the employers workplace are covered
- Information or lessons learned from injuries and accidents that have occurred in the employer's workplace must be addressed.

Training can be administered in many forms, such as a supervisor:

- discussing the correct way to operate a vehicle
- correcting an error in the way an employee is doing a job, or
- showing the employee how to perform a particular task properly. Alternatively, training may consist of detailed structural instruction using formal training methods such as:

- lectures
- formal demonstrations
- practical exercises
- examinations.

The revised training provisions require employees to develop a training program based on:

- the general principles of safe truck operation
- the type of vehicles used in the workplace
- the hazards of the workplace created by the use of the vehicles
- the general safety requirements of the OSHA standard

Refresher training will be necessary when

- an operator is involved in an accident or near-miss accident
- an operator has been observed operating the vehicle in an unsafe manner
- an operator has been determined to need additional training as a result of an evaluation
- there are changes in the workplace that could affect the safe operation of the truck.

OSHA is not specifying the time that must be spent on the training, or the exact methods that must be used to train operators. OSHA is, however, requiring that trained operators know how to do the job properly and safely, as demonstrated by workplace evaluations at the time of initial and refresher training, and at periodic intervals (at least once every three years). This approach gives employers the flexibility to develop training programs appropriate to their workplace and avoid unnecessary specifications.

All training must be conducted by a designated person with the requisite knowledge, training, and experience to train powered industrial truck operators and judge their competency. OSHA does not require that the training be conducted by the employer, a supervisor, or any other particular person, only that the training be conducted by a person who is qualified to do so.

OSHA proposes that operators must successfully complete their training and be evaluated. The evaluation is an essential element of any training program. The evaluation of the classroom part of the training should be left to the trainer. This performance-oriented approach allows the employer to determine that the employee has successfully completed the training, including the classroom and practical training and demonstration elements. A successfully completed written or oral test by the employee is a part of the classroom element and the trainer or employer must evaluate the results. Successful completion of the practical training requires the trainee to perform all operations safely.

Only powered industrial truck operators and trainees are covered by this final rule. Not all "potential" operators are covered. Operators that have other duties, but sometimes operate a powered industrial truck, are covered by this rule.

Trainees are to receive practical training in powered industrial truck operation only in areas where it is safe to do so. This training must be under the direct supervision of a person with requisite knowledge, training, and experience. Employees in the surrounding area are to be alerted to the training activities that are occurring in their areas.

1910.178(l) Operator Training

(l)(1) Safe operation.

(l)(1)(i) The employer shall ensure that each powered industrial truck operator is competent to operate a powered industrial truck safely, as demonstrated by the successful completion of the training and evaluation specified in this paragraph (l).

(l)(1)(ii) Prior to permitting an employee to operate a powered industrial truck (except for training purposes), the employer shall ensure that each operator has successfully completed the training required by this paragraph (l), except as permitted by paragraph (l)(5).

(l)(2) Training program implementation.

(l)(2)(i) Trainees may operate a powered industrial truck only:

(l)(2)(i)(A) Under the direct supervision of persons who have the knowledge, training, and experience to train operators and evaluate their competence; and

(l)(2)(i)(B) Where such operation does not endanger the trainee or other employees.

(l)(2)(ii) Training shall consist of a combination of formal instruction (e.g., lecture, discussion, interactive computer learning, video tape, written material), practical training (demonstrations performed by the trainer and practical exercises performed by the trainee), and evaluation of the operator's performance in the workplace.

(l)(2)(iii) All operator training and evaluation shall be conducted by persons who have the knowledge, training, and experience to train powered industrial truck operators and evaluate their competence.

(l)(3) Training program content. Powered industrial truck operators shall receive initial training in the following topics, except in topics which the employer can demonstrate are not applicable to safe operation of the truck in the employer's workplace.

(l)(3)(i) Truck-related topics:

(l)(3)(i)(A) Operating instructions, warnings, and precautions for the types of truck the operator will be authorized to operate;

(l)(3)(i)(B) Differences between the truck and the automobile;

(l)(3)(i)(C) Truck controls and instrumentation: where they are located, what they do, and how they work;

(l)(3)(i)(D) Engine or motor operation;

(l)(3)(i)(E) Steering and maneuvering;

(l)(3)(i)(F) Visibility (including restrictions due to loading);

(l)(3)(i)(G) Fork and attachment adaptation, operation, and use limitations;

(l)(3)(i)(H) Vehicle capacity;

(l)(3)(i)(I) Vehicle stability;

(l)(3)(i)(J) Any vehicle inspection and maintenance that the operator will be required to perform;

(l)(3)(i)(K) Refueling and/or charging and recharging of batteries;

(l)(3)(i)(L) Operating limitations;

(l)(3)(i)(M) Any other operating instructions, warnings, or precautions listed in the operator's manual for the types of vehicle that the employee is being trained to operate.

(l)(3)(ii) Workplace-related topics:

(l)(3)(ii)(A) Surface conditions where the vehicle will be operated;

(l)(3)(ii)(B) Composition of loads to be carried and load stability;

(l)(3)(ii)(C) Load manipulation, stacking, and unstacking;

(l)(3)(ii)(D) Pedestrian traffic in areas where the vehicle will be operated;

(l)(3)(ii)(E) Narrow aisles and other restricted places where the vehicle will be operated;

(l)(3)(ii)(F) Hazardous (classified) locations where the vehicle will be operated;

(l)(3)(ii)(G) Ramps and other sloped surfaces that could affect the vehicle's stability;

(l)(3)(ii)(H) Closed environments and other areas where insufficient ventilation or poor vehicle maintenance could cause a buildup of carbon monoxide or diesel exhaust;

(l)(3)(ii)(I) Other unique or potentially hazardous environmental conditions in the workplace that could affect safe operation.

(l)(3)(iii) The requirements of this section.

(l)(4) Refresher training and evaluation.

(l)(4)(i) Refresher training, including an evaluation of the effectiveness of that training, shall be conducted as required by paragraph (l)(4)(ii) to ensure that the operator has the knowledge and skills needed to operate the powered industrial truck safely.

(l)(4)(ii) Refresher training in relevant topics shall be provided to the operator when:

(l)(4)(ii)(A) The operator has been observed to operate the vehicle in an unsafe manner;

(l)(4)(ii)(B) The operator has been involved in an accident or near-miss incident;

(l)(4)(ii)(C) The operator has received an evaluation that reveals that the operator is not operating the truck safely;

(l)(4)(ii)(D) The operator is assigned to drive a different type of truck; or

(l)(4)(ii)(E) A condition in the workplace changes in a manner that could affect safe operation of the truck.(l)(4)(iii) An evaluation of each powered industrial truck operator's performance shall be conducted at least once every three years.

(l)(5) Avoidance of duplicative training. If an operator has previously received training in a topic specified in paragraph (l)(3) of this section, and such training is appropriate to the truck and working conditions encountered, additional training in that topic is not required if the operator has been evaluated and found competent to operate the truck safely.

(l)(6) Certification. The employer shall certify that each operator has been trained and evaluated as required by this paragraph (l). The certification shall include the name of the operator, the date of the training, the date of the evaluation, and the identity of the person(s) performing the training or evaluation.

(l)(7) Dates. The employer shall ensure that operators of powered industrial trucks are trained, as appropriate, by the dates shown in the following table.

If the employee was hired:	The initial training and evaluation of that employee must be completed:
Before December 1, 1999	By December 1, 1999
After December 1, 1999	Before the employee is assigned to operate a powered industrial truck.

Appendix B

Sources of Help

American Industrial Hygiene Association
2700 Prosperity Avenue
Fairfax, VA 22031

American National Standards Institute
11 W. 42nd Street - 13th Floor
New York, NY 10036
(202) 642-4900
www.ansi.org

American Society of Safety Engineers
Professional Safety Magazine
1800 E. Oakton Street
Des Plaines, IL 60018-2187
(847) 699-2929

Canadian Standards Institute
178 Rexdale Blvd.
Rexdale, Ontario
Canada M9W 1R3

Conveyor Equipment Manufacturers Association
(941) 514-3441
www.cemanet.org

Department of Transportation (DOT)
Hotline (800) 467-4922

Environmental Health Center
c/o National Safety Council
1050 17th Street NW, Suite 770
Washington, D.C. 20036
(202) 293-2270

Environmental Protection Agency
401 M Street SW
Washington, D.C. 20460
(202) 260-2090
www.epa.gov

Industrial Accident Prevention Association
250 Yonge Street, 28th Floor
Toronto, Ontario
Canada M5E 2N4
(416) 506-8888

Industrial Safety & Hygiene News
237 Lancaster Avenue, Suite 201
Devon, PA 19333
phone: 610-254-0766
www.ishn.com

Industrial Truck Association
(800) 447-3221
www.indtrk.org

International Association of Refrigerated Warehouses
(301) 652-5674

International Warehouse Logistics Association
(847) 292-1891

Material Handling Engineering (Magazine)
Penton Publishing Company
1100 Superior Avenue
Cleveland, OH 44114-2543

Material Handling Industry of America
(704) 676-1190
www.mhia.org

Material Handling Product News
A Cahners Publication
301 Gibraltar Drive, Box 650
Morris Park, NJ 07950-0650
(973) 292-5100

Modern Materials Handling Magazine
A Cahners Publication
P.O. Box 7564
Highlands Ranch, CO 80126-7500

National Fire Protection Association
1 Batterymarch Park
Quincy, MA 02269-9101
(800) 34403555

National Safety Council
1121 Spring Lake Drive
Itasca, IL 60143-3201
(630) 285-1121
www.nsc.org

National Wooden Pallet and Container Association
(703) 527-7667

Occupational Hazards Magazine
Penton Media
1100 Superior Avenue
Cleveland, OH 44114-2543
(216) 696-7000

Occupational Health and Safety (Magazine)
5151 Beltline Road, Suite 1010
Dallas, TX 75240
(972) 687-6700

Occupational Safety and Health Administration
(202) 219-8148
www.osha.gov

ASHA On-Site Consultation Program
Room N-3476
200 Constitution Avenue, NW
Washington, D.C. 20210

Warehousing Education and Research
1100 Jorie Blvd, Suite 170
Oak Brook, IL 60523-2243
(630) 990-0001

Warehousing Management (Magazine)
A Cahners Publication
8773 South Ridgeline Blvd.
Highlands Ranch, CO 80126-2329

Voluntary Protection Programs Participants Association
 (VPPPA)
7600 E. Leesburg Pike, Suite 440
Falls Church, VA 22043
(703) 761-1146

Glossary

Accident: An unplanned and sometimes injurious or damaging event that interrupts the normal progress of an activity and is invariably preceded by an unsafe act, unsafe condition, or some combination thereof. An accident may be seen as resulting from a failure to identify a hazard or from some inadequacy in an existing system of hazard controls. Based on how it is used in casualty insurance, an accident is an event that is definite in point of time and place but unexpected as to either its occurrence or its results.

Acute toxicity: The acute adverse effects resulting from a single dose of or exposure to a substance.

Administrative controls: Methods of controlling employee exposures by job rotation, varying tasks, work assignment, operational procedures, or time periods away from the hazard(s).

Aerosol: A fine aerial suspension of liquid or solid particles small enough in size to confer some degree of stability from sedimentation.

Air contamination: The result of introducing foreign substances into the air so as to make the air impure.

ANSI: The American National Standards Institute is a nonprofit, voluntary, membership organization that coordinates the U.S. Voluntary Consensus Standards System and approves American National Standards.

Anthropometric evaluation: A study of human body sizes and modes of action to better design tools and machines to meet human capabilities.

Approved: Tested and/or listed as satisfactory; meeting predetermined requirements of some qualifying organization.

Arc welding: One form of electrical resistance welding using either uncoated or coated rods.

Arc-welding electrode: A component of the welding circuit through which current is conducted between the electrode holder and the arc.

Asphyxiant: A vapor or gas that can cause unconsciousness or death by suffocation (lack of oxygen).

Backup alarm: A device used on some trucks and buses and required on some off-road vehicles that automatically sounds a continuous or intermittent signal whenever the vehicle is backing up.

Barrier guard: Physical protection for operators and other individuals from hazard points on machinery and equipment.

Fixed barrier guard A nonmovable physical enclosure attached to the machine or equipment.

Interlocked barrier guard An enclosure attached to the machinery or equipment frame and interlocked with the power switch so that the operating cycle cannot be started unless the guard is in its proper position.

Adjustable barrier guard An enclosure attached to the frame of the machinery or equipment with front and side sections that can be adjusted.

Gate or movable barrier guard A device designed to enclose the point of operation to exclude entry prior to equipment operation.

Bonding: The interconnecting of two objects by means of an electrical conductor. Its purpose is to equalize the electrical potential between objects. (*See* Grounding)

Bump cap: A hard-shell cap, without an interior suspension system, designed to protect the wearer's head in situations where the employee might bump into something.

Carbon monoxide: A colorless, odorless, toxic gas produced by any process that involves the incomplete combustion of carbon-containing substances.

Carcinogen: A substance or agent that can cause a growth of abnormal tissue or tumors in humans or animals.

Carpal tunnel syndrome: An affliction caused by compression of the median nerve in the carpal tunnel, where it passes through the wrist into the hand.

Chemical cartridge respirator: A respirator that uses changeable cartridges containing various chemical substances to purify inhaled air of certain gases, vapors, mists, and fumes.

Chock: A wedge-shaped device made of wood or metal, used to block drums, barrels, or the wheels of parked vehicles to ensure that they do not move, especially on inclined surfaces.

Circuit breaker: A device that automatically interrupts the flow of an electrical current when the current exceeds a specific level.

Citation: A written change issued by regulatory representatives alleging specific conditions or actions that violate maritime, construction, environmental, mining, or general industry laws and standards.

Combustible liquids: Those having a flash point at or above 37.8° C, and below 93.3° C (100 - 200° F).

Compressed gas cylinder: A cylinder containing vapor or gas under higher than atmospheric pressure, sometimes to the point where it is liquified.

Confined space: Any area that has limited openings for entry and exit that would make escape difficult in an emergency, has a lack of ventilation, contains known and potential hazards, and is not intended nor designated for continuous human occupancy.

Contact dermatitis: Dermatitis caused by skin contact with a substance—gaseous, liquid, or solid. May be due to primary irritation or an allergy.

CPR: Cardiopulmonary resuscitation.

CSP: Certified Safety Professional, a designation from the Board of Certified Safety Professionals.

Cumulative trauma disorder (CTD): A disorder caused by one or more of the following: repetitive excessive motion of a body part, excessive force, or awkward body posture.

Current: Flow of electrons in an electrical circuit measured in amperes (amps).

Decibel (dB): A unit used to express sound power level (L_w). Sound power is the total acoustic output of a sound source in watts (W). By definition, sound power level, in decibels, is: $L_w = 10 \log W/W_o$ where W is the sound power of the source and W_o is the reference sound power.

Dock: The area where an over-the-road truck trailer can be driven onto by a lift truck for loading and unloading cargo. The dock height above the truck and trailer road level is commonly about 54 inches.

Double insulated: A method of encasing electric components of tools so that the operator cannot touch parts that could become energized during normal operation or in the event of tool failure.

Dynamic lateral tipover: A lift truck falling onto its side when in motion either forward or reverse. The term refers to a forward-traveling lift truck that falls to one side in a turn.

Ear: the entire human hearing apparatus, consisting of three parts: middle ear or tympanic cavity, membrane and eustachian tube, and the inner ear or labyrinth.

Emergency plan: A plan of action for an anticipated, unwanted occurrence/disaster.

Shower A water shower for an employee when the employee has had chemical contamination that needs to be washed off quickly.

STOP (switch) A switch or other device that, when activated, disengages the power source of and quickly stops the controlled mechanisms.

Energy-isolating device: A mechanical device that physically prevents the release or transmission of energy. Some examples include a manually operated circuit breaker, a disconnect switch, a line valve, or a block. The following are *not* energy-isolating devices: push buttons, selector switches, and other circuit-control devices.

Engineering controls: Methods of controlling employee exposures by modifying the source, or the means of exposure, or by reducing the quantity of hazards.

Ergonomics: The study of human characteristics for the appropriate design of living and work environments.

Eye protection: "Safety" glasses, goggles, face shields, etc., used to protect against physical, chemical, and nonionizing radiation hazards.

Fall arresting system: A system consisting of a belt (sometimes with a torso or subpelvic harness), a lanyard or lifeline, and an arresting mechanism with built-in shock absorber designed for use by a worker performing tasks in a location from which a fall would be injurious or fatal, or where other kinds of protection (e.g., enclosure, handrail, net) are not practical. Also called fall protection system, free-fall restraint system, or personnel lowering device and lifeline.

Fire doors: Doors tested and rated for resistance to various degrees of fire exposure and utilized to prevent the spread of fire through horizontal and vertical openings.

First aid: The immediate care given to the injured or suddenly ill person.

Flammable: Any substance that is easily ignited, burns intensely, or has a rapid rate of flame spread. Flammable and inflammable are identical in meaning; however, the prefix "in" indicates negative in many words and can cause confusion. Flammable, therefore, is the preferred term.

Flammable liquid: Any liquid having a flash point below 37.8° C. (100° F.).

Flammable range: The difference between the lower and upper flammable limits, expressed in terms of percentage of vapor or gas in air by volume; also often referred to as the "explosive range." *See* Lower explosive limit and Upper explosive limit.

Flash point: The lowest temperature at which a liquid gives off enough vapor to form an ignitable mixture with air and produces a flame when a source of ignition is present.

Floor load: 1. The weight that may be safely placed on a floor without danger of structural collapse. 2. The actual load (weight) placed on a floor.

Fume: Airborne particulate formed by the evaporation of solid materials, e.g., metal fume emitted during welding. Usually less than one micron in diameter.

Gas: A state of matter in which the material has very low density and viscosity; can expand and contract greatly in response to changes in temperature and pressure; easily diffuses; and is neither a solid nor a liquid.

General exhaust: A system for exhausting air from a general work area, accomplished mechanically by air-handling units that drain air from the space.

General ventilation: System of exchanging air in a general work area by either natural means or by mechanically inducing fresh air movements to mix with the existing room air.

Ground: A contact with the ground that becomes part of the electrical circuit.

Grounding: The procedure used to carry an electrical charge to ground through a conductive path.

Hand protection: Coverings worn over the hands to protect against physical, chemical, biological, thermal, and electrical hazards.

Hard hat: A helmet so constructed as to help prevent head injuries from falling objects of limited size.

Hazard: An unsafe condition or activity that, if left uncontrolled, can contribute to an accident.

Hazard analysis: An analysis performed to identify and evaluate hazards for the purpose of their elimination or control.

Hazard control: A program to recognize, evaluate, eliminate, or control the existence of and exposure to hazards.

Hazard material: Any substance or compound that has the capability of producing adverse effects on the health and safety of humans.

Health hazard: A chemical, biological, or radiological material for which there is statistically significant scientific evidence that acute or chronic health effects may occur in exposed employees.

Hearing conservation: The prevention or minimizing of noise-induced hearing loss through the use of hearing protection devices; the control of noise through engineering and administrative methods, audiometric tests, and employee training.

Helmet: A device that shields the eyes, face, neck, and other parts of the head.

Hip restraint: The bracket attached to the sides of a lift truck seat to limit lateral movement of the operator's hips.

Housekeeping: Cleanliness, neatness, and orderliness of an area, with the designation of a proper place for everything and everything in its proper place.

Incidence rate (as defined by U.S. OSHA): The number of injuries and/or illnesses or lost workdays per 100 full-time employees per year, or per 200,000 hours of exposure.

Incident: An undesired event that may cause personal harm or other damage. In the United States, OSHA specifies that incidents of a certain severity be recorded.

Indirect costs: Losses, other than those costs that are insurable ultimately measurable in a monetary sense that result from an accident.

Industrial hygiene: The science (or art) devoted to the recognition, evaluation, and control of those environmental factors or stresses (i.e., chemical, physical, biological, and ergonomic) that may cause sickness, impaired health, or significant discomfort to employees or residents of the community.

Inert gas: A gas that does not normally combine chemically with other substances.

Inhalation: The breathing in of a substance in the form of a gas, vapor, fume, mist, or dust.

Injury: Physical harm or damage to the body resulting from an exchange of mechanical, chemical, thermal, or other environmental energy that exceeds the body's tolerance.

Inrunning nip (point): A rotating mechanism that can seize loose clothing, belts, hair, body parts, etc. It exists when two or more shafts or rolls rotate parallel to one another in opposite directions. *See also* Nip point and Pinch point.

Inspection: Monitoring function conducted in an organization to locate and report existing and potential hazards having the capacity to cause accidents in the workplace.

Interlock: A device that interacts with another device or mechanism to govern succeeding operations. For example, an interlocked machine guard will prevent the machine from operating unless the guard is in its proper place. An interlock on an elevator door will prevent the car from moving unless the door is properly closed.

Job safety analysis: A method for studying a job in order to (1) identify hazards or potential accidents associated with each step or task and (2) develop solutions that will eliminate, nullify, or prevent such hazards or accidents. Sometimes called Job Hazard Analysis.

LEL: Lower explosive limit. *See* Lower explosive limit and Upper explosive limit

LFL: Lower flammable limit. *See* Lower explosive limit.

Limit switch: A switch fitted to electric lifts, traveling cranes, etc., in order to cut off the power supply if the lift-car or moving carriage travels beyond a specified point.

Liquified petroleum gas: A compressed or liquefied gas usually composed of propane, some butane, and lesser quantities of other light hydrocarbons and impurities, obtained as a byproduct in petroleum refining. Used chiefly as a fuel and in chemical synthesis.

Lockout/tagout: A program or procedure that prevents injury by eliminating unintentional operation or release of energy within machinery or processes during setup, start-up, or maintenance.

Loss control: A program designed to minimize accident-based financial losses. The concept of total loss control is based on detailed analysis of both indirect and direct accident costs. Property damage as well as injurious and potentially injurious accidents are included in the analysis.

Loss prevention: A before-the-loss program designed to identify and correct hazards before they result in incidents that produce actual financial loss or injury.

Lost workday: The number of workdays (consecutive or not), beyond the day of injury or onset of illness, that an employee was away from work or limited to restricted work activity because of an occupational injury or illness.

Lower explosive limit (LEL): the lower limit of flammability of a gas or vapor at ordinary ambient temperatures expressed as a percentage of the gas or vapor in air by volume. *See* Upper explosive limit and Flammable range.

Materials handling: *Manual* - Lifting, transporting, and depositing material by human means. In the manual handling of materials, a variety of hand or hand-operated accessories may be used, such as hooks, bars, jacks, handtrucks, dollies, and wheelbarrows. *Mechanical* - Transporting of material with mechanized devices or equipment, such as hoisting apparatus, conveyors, elevators, railways, powered industrial trucks, and ropes, slings, and chains.

MSDS: Material Safety Data Sheet. A document prepared by a chemical manufacturer, describing the composition, properties, and hazards of a chemical along with recommended safeguards to handling, storage, and use.

MSHA: The Mine Safety and Health Administration of the U.S. Department of Labor; federal agency with safety and health regulatory and enforcement authority for the mining industry established by the Mine Safety and Health Act.

NFPA: The National Fire Protection Association is a voluntary organization whose aim is to promote and improve fire protection and prevention.

NIOSH: The National Institute for Occupational Safety and Health is a branch of the U.S. Department of Labor. It conducts research on health and safety concerns, tests and certifies respirators, and trains occupational health and safety professionals.

Nip point: The point of intersection or contact between two or more surfaces when one or more are moving.

Noise-induced hearing loss: The slowly progressive inner ear hearing loss that results from exposure to continuous noise over a long period of time, as contrasted to acoustic trauma or physical injury to the ear.

Nonflammable: Not easily ignited, or if ignited, not burning with a flame (smolders).

Nuisance dust: Has a long history of little adverse effect on the lungs and does not produce significant organic disease or toxic effect when exposures are kept under reasonable control.

Off-the-dock: When a lift truck drives off or tips over at a loading dock. *See also* Trailer pull-away.

Operator restraint system: The term used for the components on lift trucks that restrain the operator of the lift truck, primarily consisting of the seat belt and hip restraint. It also includes seat mounting, hood, and hood hardware where applicable; and instructional material such as warning decals and the operator's manual.

OSHA: The U.S. Occupational Safety and Health Administration of the Department of Labor; federal agency with safety and health regulatory and enforcement authorities for general United States industry and business.

Permanent disability or permanent impairment: The partial or complete loss or impairment of any part or function of the body.

Permissible exposure limit (PEL): The legally enforced exposure limit for a substance established by OSHA. The PEL indicates the permissible concentration of air contaminants to which nearly all workers may be repeatedly exposed eight (8) hours a day, forty (40) hours a week, over a working lifetime (30 years) without adverse health effects.

Personal protective equipment (PPE): Devices worn by the worker to protect against hazards in the environment.

Pinch point: Any point at which it is possible to be caught between the moving parts, stationary parts, or the material being processed. *See also* Nip point and Inrunning nip point.

Pollution: Contamination of soil, water, or atmosphere beyond that which is natural.

ppm: Parts per million of air by volume of vapor or gas or other contaminant.

Preventive maintenance: The systematic actions performed to maintain equipment in normal working condition and prevent failure.

Respiratory protection: Devices that will protect the wearer's respiratory system from overexposure by inhalation to airborne contaminants.

Right-to-know law: Popular name for the hazard communication standard issued in 1983 by OSHA. Also any law under which the residents of a community are entitled to know what hazardous substances are transported to or from, stored at, and used by any organization within the community.

Safeguarding: The term used to cover all methods of protection against injury or illness.

Safety: The control of recognized hazards to attain an acceptable level of risk.

Safety belt: A life belt worn by linesmen, window washers, etc., attached to a secure object (such as a window sill) to prevent falling. A seat or torso belt securing a passenger in an automobile or airplane to provide body protection during a collision, sudden stop, air turbulence, etc.

Safety can: An approved container of not more than 19 liters (5 gallons) capacity, having a spring-closing lid and spout cover, and so designed that it will safely relieve internal pressure when subjected to fire exposure.

Safety program: Activities designed to assist employees in the recognition, understanding, and control of hazards in the workplace.

Sampling: A process consisting of the withdrawal or isolation of a fractional part of a whole.

Seat belt: The belt, retractor, and buckle components attached to the seat to restrain the operator at the waist and hips. It can also be referred to as a lap belt.

Serious violation: As defined by OSHA, any violation in which there is a substantial probability that death or serious physical harm could result from the violative condition.

Solvent: A substance that dissolves another substance.

Spontaneously combustible: A material that ignites as a result of retained heat from processing, or that will oxidize to generate heat and ignite, or that absorbs moisture to generate heat and ignite.

Standard: A written guide that may or may not be a legal requirement.

Tenosynovitis: Inflammation of the connective tissue sheath of a tendon.

Tip over: A lift truck rotating laterally or longitudinally approximately 90 degrees; most commonly a lift truck falling onto its side.

Torso: The portion of the human body from the hips to the shoulders; the human trunk.

Trailer: Refers to the cargo-carrying trailer of a large highway truck.

Trailer pull-away: The motion of a highway truck or trailer away from a loading dock. Refers to the type of tip-over that occurs when a lift truck falls from a loading dock when the trailer moves away.

Truck restraining hook: A hook designed to secure a truck trailer to the dock at which it is parked, until loading/unloading operations are completed. When the hook, which automatically adjusts to the correct height, is engaged on the trailer's rear impact guard protection device (sometimes called ICC bar), it holds the trailer, prevents it from creeping, limits forward sway, and reduces the possibility of the trailer's landing gear collapsing. The restraining hook incorporates lights that warn the driver it is in locked position. Sometimes called vehicle restraining system.

Upper explosive limit: The highest concentration (expressed in percent of vapor or gas in the air by volume) of a substance that will burn or explode when an ignition source is present. *See also* Lower explosive limit and Flammable range.

Volatile (Percent volatile by volume): The percentage of a liquid or solid (by volume) that will evaporate at an ambient temperature of 70° F. (unless some other temperature is stated). Examples: butane, gasoline, and paint thinner (mineral spirits) are 100 percent volatile; their individual evaporation rates vary, but over a period of time each will evaporate completely.

Welding: The several types of welding are electric arc-welding, oxyacetylene welding, spot welding, and inert or shielded gas welding utilizing helium or argon. The hazards involved in welding stem from (1) the fumes from the weld metal such as lead or cadmium metal, or (2) the gases created by the process, or (3) the fumes or gases arising from the flux.

Welding and cutting permit: Authorization for the use of open flame and spark-producing devices in areas near combustible and/or hazardous materials, where their use is normally prohibited. Frequently extended to the use of open-flame devices and/or high heat-producing devices.

Winged seat: A seat with wing-like protrusions near the operator's upper torso; usually refers to the Clark winged seat (Clark PN 1831394).

Workers' Compensation: An insurance system under law, financed by employers, that provides payment to injured and diseased employees or relatives for job-related injuries and illnesses.

Work hours: The total number of hours worked by all employees.

Work injuries: Injuries (including occupational illnesses) that arise out of, or in the course of, gainful employment regardless of where the accident occurs. Excluded are work injuries to private household workers and injuries occurring in connection with farm chores, which are classified as home injuries.

Zero mechanical energy (ZME): An old term, now called energy isolation, that indicates a piece of equipment without any source of power that could harm someone.

SOURCES

American Society of Safety Engineers, *Dictionary of Terms Used in the Safety Profession,* Des Plaines, Illinois, 1982.

National Safety Council, *Accident Prevention Manual - Glossary*, Itasca, Illinois, 1997.

Index